Beiträge zur
Dialogforschung   Band 31

Herausgegeben von Franz Hundsnurscher und Edda Weigand

Dialogue Analysis IX: Dialogue in Literature and the Media

Selected Papers from the 9th IADA Conference, Salzburg 2003

Part 2: Media

Edited by
Anne Betten and Monika Dannerer

Max Niemeyer Verlag
Tübingen 2005

Bibliografische Information der Deutschen Bibliothek

Die Deutsche Bibliothek verzeichnet diese Publikation in der Deutschen Nationalbibliografie;
detaillierte bibliografische Daten sind im Internet über *http://dnb.ddb.de* abrufbar.

ISBN 3-484-75031-6   ISSN 0940-5992

© Max Niemeyer Verlag GmbH, Tübingen 2005
http://www.niemeyer.de
Das Werk einschließlich aller seiner Teile ist urheberrechtlich geschützt. Jede Verwertung außerhalb
der engen Grenzen des Urheberrechtsgesetzes ist ohne Zustimmung des Verlages unzulässig und
strafbar. Das gilt insbesondere für Vervielfältigungen, Übersetzungen, Mikroverfilmungen und die
Einspeicherung und Verarbeitung in elektronischen Systemen.
Printed in Germany.
Gedruckt auf alterungsbeständigem Papier.
Druck: Laupp & Göbel GmbH, Nehren
Einband: Nädele Verlags- und Industriebuchbinderei, Nehren

Inhalt / Table of contents

Vorwort / Preface IX

I. Plenarvorträge / Plenary papers

Kerbrat-Orecchioni, Catherine
    Le fonctionnement du dialogue dans un ‹genre› particulier:
    La confidence dans le roman-photo 1
Schmitt, Christian
    «Dire l'interdit» 17

II. Workshop

    Interkulturelle Medienanalyse / Intercultural media analysis
    (Gerda Lauerbach /Anita Fetzer)

Schieß, Raimund
    Lights, camera, action: visualizing TV election nights across cultures 31
Lauerbach, Gerda
    Election nights: a cross-cultural analysis of presenting practices 43
Hampel, Martin
    Intersubjective positioning in election night discourse. A cross cultural analysis 55
Becker, Annette
    Interviews in TV election night broadcasts:
    a framework for cross-cultural analysis 65
Johansson, Marjut
    Represented discourse as a form of mediation from a contrastive point of view 77
Fetzer, Anita
    Non-acceptances in political interviews:
    British styles and German styles in conflict? 87
Desmarchelier, Dominique
    Argumentative strategies: the French debate about immigration 97
Simon-Vandenbergen, Anne-Marie / Ajimer, Karin
    The discourse marker *of course* in British political interviews
    and its Dutch and Swedish counterparts: a comparison of persuasive tactics 105

Janney, Richard W. / Yakovlyev, Andriy
    Cyberwar perception management in the Middle East: a view from pragmatics 113

Sauer, Christoph
    Christmas Messages 1998 by heads of state on radio and TV:
    pragmatic functions, semiotic forms, media adequacy 127

III. Sektionsreferate / Session papers

1. Dialog und Dialogizität in Printmedien / Dialogue and dialogicity in print media

Livnat, Zohar
    "Like in the movies": Dialogue between different voices
    in the public discourse in Israel 139

Hoffmannová, Jana
    Interviews in Zeitungen und Zeitschriften: Frage- und Antwortbeziehungen 149

Sergo, Laura
    Die Wiedergabe von bewertenden und metasprachlichen Elementen
    in der Übersetzung von Zeitungsinterviews 161

Berlin, Lawrence N.
    Media manipulation 173

Schnöring, Stefanie
    Personnel advertisements as a form of mediated dialogic interaction 183

2. Dialog und Dialogizität in Radio, Film und Fernsehen / Dialogue and dialogicity in radio, film and television

Harvey, Anamaria / Granato, Luisa
    Discussions in the media 193

Karhanová, Kamila
    Rhetorical questions in polemical media dialogue 203

Bolívar, Adriana
    The president and the media in Venezuelan political dialogue 215

Magda, Margareta
    Zur argumentativen Funktion der Gesprächsformeln im öffentlichen Dialog
    (am Beispiel der rumänischen Massenmedien) 227

Ghido, Diana
    Fragmentation in talk shows 239

Dascălu Jinga, Laurenția
  Other-correction in TV talk shows 249
Bubel, Claudia
  "I'm on total ovary overload": The linguistic representation
  of women in *Sex and the City* 259
Pisek, Gerhard
  The translation of comic dialogue for film and television 269

3.   Dialog und Dialogizität in den neuen Medien / Dialogue and dialogicity in new media

Labbe, Hélène / Marcoccia, Michel
  Tradition épistolaire et médias numériques: du billet au courrier électronique 281
Atifi, Hassan
  Les usages conversationnels dans les dialogues électroniques entre Marocains 293
Stame, Stefania
  Marques pragmatiques et marques de l'oral dans le dialogue
  par courrier électronique 305
Manuti, Amelia / Cortini, Michela / Mininni, Giuseppe
  Job on line: The diatextual rhetoric of e-recruitment 315

Allgemeine Aspekte von Dialog und Dialogizität / General aspects of dialogue and dialogicity

Moreno Fernández, Ana I.
  Perceiving coherence and text structure: Which cohesive ties are really textual? 327
Pop, Liana
  De l'*acte* aux *activités*: *les séquences* 339
Zhang, Shuxue
  Accented argumentum ad hominem in mediated dialogues 353

Vorwort

Dialogue Analysis IX. Dialogue in Literature and the Media präsentiert in zwei Bänden eine Auswahl der 118 Referate auf der 9. Konferenz der *International Association for Dialogue Analysis* (IADA) vom 24. bis 27. April 2003 in Salzburg, zu der Teilnehmer/innen aus 21 Ländern gekommen waren. Der erste Band mit 38 Beiträgen ist ausschließlich dem Thema »Dialog in der Literatur« gewidmet; von den 32 Beiträgen des zweiten Bandes behandeln 29 das Thema »Dialog in den Medien«, drei weitere hingegen beschäftigen sich mit allgemeineren dialoganalytischen Themen, da die IADA traditionellerweise bei ihren alle zwei Jahre stattfindenden großen Tagungen neben den jeweiligen Schwerpunktsetzungen für alle Gebiete der Dialogforschung offen ist. So galt auch der (hier nicht veröffentlichte) Eröffnungsvortrag des Präsidenten der IADA, Sorin Stati, über »Old and new problems of method in dialogue analysis. The case of argumentative synonymity« vornehmlich übergreifenden Fragen.

Die weiteren Plenarvorträge – zwei zur Literatur (SCHMITZ-EMANS, BETTEN), zwei zu den Medien (KERBRAT-ORECCHIONI, SCHMITT) – sind in beiden Bänden vorangestellt; darauf folgen Beiträge aus den Workshops, die (wie die Plenarvorträge) trotz gelegentlich engen thematischen Bezügen zu anderen Beiträgen im ursprünglichen Zusammenhang belassen wurden, um das Gesamtkonzept der Workshops zu erhalten. Die Abfolge der Sektionsreferate, die ursprünglich z.T. nach sprachlichen Aspekten vorgenommen war (Englisch, Deutsch, Französisch, vereinzelt auch Italienisch), wurde hingegen nach thematischen Kriterien neu geordnet. Auch die beim Vortrag zeitlich großzügiger bemessenen Eröffnungsreferate der Sektionen wurden hier mit eingereiht.

Alle editorischen Arbeiten und Entscheidungen wurden von den Herausgeberinnen gemeinsam getragen; nur die Schlussredaktion, nach Eingang der Autorenkorrekturen, wurde so aufgeteilt, dass Anne Betten den Literaturband und Monika Dannerer den Medienband zum Druck vorbereiteten.

Das Hauptthema dieses zweiten Bandes, Dialog bzw. Dialogizität in den Medien, ist zwar nicht völlig neu, aber nach wie vor in der Dialog- bzw. Gesprächsforschung eines der zentralen Forschungsfelder. Das große inhaltliche und methodische Spektrum der hier versammelten Beiträge spiegelt die Vielfalt der Forschungsfragen auf diesem Gebiet.

Dies betrifft zum einen die *Bandbreite der Medien*. Sie reicht von den Printmedien (u.a. SCHMITT, BERLIN, KERBRAT-ORECCHIONI, LIVNAT), über das Radio (HARVEY/GRANATO), Film und Fernsehen (u.a. BOLÍVAR, GHIDO, DASCĂLU-JINGA, BUBEL, PISEK) bis zu den »neuen Medien« (LABBE/MARCOCCIA, ATIFI, STAME, MANUTI/CORTINI/MININNI).

Quer zum medialen Aspekt werden im vorliegenden Band einzelne *Textsorten* untersucht, die teilweise mit bestimmten Medien verknüpft sind, teilweise aber auch in unterschiedlichen Medien auftreten. Sie weisen Dialoge bzw. Dialogizität in verschiedenen Ausprägungen auf. Überwiegend handelt es sich dabei um massenmedial vermittelte Textsorten, in denen den Rezipienten – d.h. den Lesern oder Zusehern/Zuhörern – Dialoge präsentiert werden. Einige der Textsorten bestehen aus einem einzigen Dialog, wie z.B. Interview (u.a. BECKER, FETZER, HOFFMANNOVÁ, SERGO) oder Debatte (DESMARCHELIER, HARVEY/GRANATO), andere wiederum verbinden eine Folge von Dialogen, so z.B. Fotoroman (KERBRAT-ORECCHIONI) oder Sitcom (BUBEL).

Daneben werden komplexere Textsorten analysiert, in denen Dialoge neben Monologen eine mehr oder weniger zentrale Rolle spielen, wie z.B. Wahlberichterstattungssendungen (u.a. SCHIEß, LAUERBACH, HAMPEL, BECKER), Talkshows (GHIDO, DASCĂLU-JINGA) oder auch Weihnachtsansprachen (SAUER).

In scheinbar monologischen Textsorten werden schließlich Dialoge thematisiert, die mit den Rezipienten »geführt« werden, z.B. in Stellenanzeigen (SCHNÖRING, MANUTI/CORTINI/MININNI).

Im Bereich der neuen Medien handelt es sich darüber hinaus auch um Dialoge, die medial vermittelt werden, z.B. auf Internetseiten, in Internetforen (MANUTI/CORTINI/MININNI) oder via E-Mail (LABBE/MARCOCCIA, STAME, ATIFI), wobei die computervermittelte Kommunikation vielfach eine Asynchronizität aufweist, die den gewohnten Dialogbegriff stark modifiziert.

Allen Beiträgen ist gemeinsam, dass sie auf *empirisches Material* zurückgreifen. Dabei ist die Zahl der *Sprachen*, die im Rahmen dieser Analysen Berücksichtigung findet, beachtlich: neben Deutsch, Englisch und Französisch sind es Arabisch, Hebräisch, Italienisch, Niederländisch, Rumänisch, Schwedisch, Spanisch und Tschechisch. Die analysierten Texte sind oftmals politisch oder sozial brisant – sei es aufgrund ihres manipulativen Charakters (JANNEY/YAKOVLYEV, BERLIN, BOLÍVAR), sei es aufgrund ihrer spezifischen Themen, z.B. Rassismus (SCHMITT, DESMARCHELIER).

Die eigentlichen *Schwerpunkte* der Analysen bilden ganz unterschiedliche Aspekte, die z.T. miteinander verknüpft werden: der Vergleich verschiedener kultureller Stile (z.B. LAUERBACH, FETZER, JOHANSSON, SAUER), Übersetzungsfragen (SERGO, PISEK), historische Textsortenvergleiche (LABBE/MARCOCCIA), Merkmale von Mündlichkeit in schriftlichen Texten (STAME), einzelne Diskursmarker bzw. »Gesprächsformeln« (SIMON-VANDENBERGEN/AIJMER, MAGDA), die Verwendung von Metaphern im öffentlichen Diskurs (LIVNAT, SCHMITT), der Einsatz von rhetorischen Fragen (KARHANOVÁ, SCHMITT), die Herstellung bzw. Signalisierung von »Vertraulichkeit« (KERBRAT-ORECCHIONI), die Wiedergabe weiblichen Gesprächsverhaltens (BUBEL), semiotische bzw. multimodale Fragestellungen (SAUER, SCHNÖRING, BOLÍVAR, KERBRAT-ORECCHIONI) etc.

Vorwort XI

Wie bereits eingangs erwähnt wird der Band durch drei Beiträge zu allgemeinen dialoganalytischen Themen ergänzt. Sie setzen sich mit Kohärenz (MORENO), Sequenzierung (POP) und spezifischen argumentativen Formen (ZHANG) auseinander.

Sowohl für die Durchführung der Tagung wie auch für die Drucklegung der Akten ist vielen Stellen und Personen Dank zu sagen:

Das österreichische Bundesministerium für Bildung, Wissenschaft und Kultur ermöglichte durch großzügige Reisestipendien einer größeren Anzahl von Referent/inn/en aus sogenannten devisenschwachen Ländern die Teilnahme und finanzierte unser Tagungsbüro sowie die Kaffeepausen.

Die Universität Salzburg unterstützte uns in vielfältiger Weise: Rektor Heinrich Schmidinger übernahm die Kosten für eine studentische Hilfskraft zur Vor- und Nachbereitung der Tagung und für die Layout-Arbeiten der Tagungsakten, des weiteren einen Empfang nach einem Konzert in der Salzburger Residenz auf Mozarts Spuren, zu dem Stadt und Land Salzburg eingeladen hatten.

Vizerektor Peter Eckl und sein Team sowie Dekan Wilfried Wieden standen uns bei der Vorbereitung der Tagung beratend zur Seite. Das Germanistische Institut unter der Leitung von Eduard Beutner übernahm Porto-, Telefon- und Kopierkosten und mannigfache Organisationsaufgaben, die in der Anfangsphase vor allem von Klaus Schiller ausgeführt wurden. Unser Kollege Andreas Weiss widmete sich entgegenkommenderweise der Betreuung der Website und allen technischen Wünschen der Referent/inn/en. Im Tagungsbüro machten sich durch Freundlichkeit und Kompetenz Claudia Heugenhauser als Leiterin sowie Ria Deisl, Michael Gurschler, Irmtraud Kaiser, Justina Nutautaite und Beate Westermayer um die Teilnehmer/innen verdient. Ihnen allen sei herzlichst gedankt, da sie nicht nur einen reibungslosen, sondern einen äußerst angenehmen Ablauf der Tagung ermöglicht haben!

Unsere ebenfalls sehr arbeitsaufwändigen Vorbereitungen für den Druck der Tagungsakten wurden von den IADA-Board-Mitgliedern Catherine Kerbrat-Orecchioni, Bernd Naumann und Edda Weigand durch Kommentare und Korrekturen zu einigen der eingereichten Manuskripte unterstützt; Ben Stephens hat zu zahlreichen englischsprachigen Beiträgen Verbesserungsvorschläge gemacht und uns bei Übersetzungen geholfen. Ria Deisl war ebenso unermüdlich an der Übertragung der Korrekturen in die Manuskripte tätig wie schließlich Dorit Wolf-Schwarz am Herstellen eines perfekten Layouts. Nicht nur unser Dank, sondern sicher auch der der Leser/inn/en dieser Bände ist ihnen sicher!

Salzburg im Mai 2005   Monika Dannerer und Anne Betten

Nachtrag

Da ich als langjähriges IADA-Mitglied die Tagungseinladung nach Salzburg initiiert habe, ist es mir ein besonderes Bedürfnis, last not least Monika Dannerer, die sich – ohne wohl den Umfang dieser Zusage zu ahnen – entschlossen hatte, die Lasten dieser mehrere Jahre umfassenden Arbeit mit mir zu teilen und oft den Löwenanteil getragen hat (was vor allem unsere Autor/inn/en bestätigen werden, mit denen sie umfangreichste Korrespondenzen geführt hat), für ihre außergewöhnliche Einsatzbereitschaft und die hervorragende Zusammenarbeit in allen Etappen persönlich und gewiss auch im Namen der IADA meinen/unseren großen Dank auszusprechen!

Anne Betten

Preface

Dialogue Analysis IX. Dialogue in Literature and the Media, in two volumes, contains a selection from the 118 presentations at the 9th Conference of the *International Association for Dialogue Analysis* (IADA), from April 24 to 27, 2003 in Salzburg, which was attended by participants from 21 countries. The first volume, containing 38 articles, is devoted to dialogue in literature; of the 32 articles of the second volume, 29 deal with dialogue in the media. Three further articles discuss general aspects of dialogue analysis, because the biannual IADA conferences – while having particular focuses – are traditionally open for all questions regarding dialogue research. IADA president Sorin Stati's opening speech on "Old and new problems of method in dialogue analysis. The case of argumentative synonymity" (not published here) also referred to wider dialogue analysis questions.

The further plenary speeches – two on literature (SCHMITZ-EMANS, BETTEN), two on media (KERBRAT-ORECCHIONI, SCHMITT) – precede the two volumes. They are followed by the workshop-articles, which, in order to maintain the concept of the workshops, remain in their original contexts, despite occasional close thematic relationship to other articles. The session papers, which were originally arranged by language aspects (English, German, French; a few held in Italian), were reordered according to thematic criteria, as were the opening speeches of the sessions.

The responsibility for all editorial tasks and decisions was usually shared by both editors; only the final editing, after the authors had sent in their corrections, was allocated in such a way that Anne Betten prepared the Literature volume and Monika Dannerer the Media volume.

The main subject of this second volume, dialogue in the media, may not be entirely new, but it continues to be one of the important areas in dialogue and discourse analysis. The wide thematic range of contributions presented here mirrors the diversity of research questions in this field.

On the one hand a broad scope of media is taken into account here. It stretches from print media (e.g. SCHMITT, BERLIN, KERBRAT-ORECCHIONI, LIVNAT), to radio (HARVEY/GRANATO), cinema and television (e.g. BOLÍVAR, GHIDO, DASCĂLU-JINGA, BUBEL, PISEK) and the "new media" (LABBE/MARCOCCIA, ATIFI, STAME, MANUTI/CORTINI/MININNI).

On the other hand, there is a large variety of text types analyzed in this volume, some of them connected to particular media, some occuring in different forms of media. They display various characteristic types of dialogues and dialogicity: Most of the text types treated are transmitted via mass media and consist of dialogues that are presented to the recipients – i.e. the readers, viewers or listeners. Some of the text types comprise a single dialogue, such as interviews (e.g. BECKER, FETZER, HOFFMANNOVÁ, SERGO), or debates (DESMARCHELIER, HARVEY/GRANATO), others combine a series of dialogues, such as photo romances (KERBRAT-ORECCHIONI), or sitcoms (BUBEL).

In addition to this, more complex text types are analyzed, in which dialogues are combined with monologues, such as election night broadcasts (e.g. SCHIEß, LAUERBACH, HAMPEL, BECKER), talk shows (GHIDO, DASCĂLU-JINGA), or Christmas messages (SAUER).

In some articles apparently monologic text types are treated, where it is not a dialogue between two or more interlocutors that is presented to the recipient, but the dialogue is conducted with the recipient himself, e.g. in job advertisements (SCHNÖRING, MANUTI/CORTINI/MININNI).

In the new media domain there are additionally dialogues that are communicated via media, e.g. on websites, internet forums (MANUTI/CORTINI/MININNI), or via email (LABBE/MARCOCCIA, STAME, ATIFI). These dialogues considerably broaden the traditional concept of dialogue, as computer mediated communication is often asynchronous.

All of the articles are based on empirical data. The number of languages, which are taken into account in these analyses, is considerable: in addition to German, English and French, there is Arabic, Czech, Dutch, Hebrew, Italian, Romanian, Spanish and Swedish.

The texts analyzed and their subjects are often politically or socially explosive – whether this is due to their manipulative nature (JANNEY/YAKOVLYEV, BERLIN, BOLÍVAR), or their controversial content, e.g. racism (SCHMITT, DESMARCHELIER).

The main focuses of the analyses lie on various different aspects, some of which are interconnected: the comparison of different cultural styles (e.g. LAUERBACH, FETZER, JOHANSSON, SAUER), translation problems (SERGO, PISEK), historic text type comparisons (LABBE/MARCOCCIA), characteristics of orality in written texts (STAME), specific discourse markers (SIMON-VANDENBERGEN/AIJMER, MAGDA), the use of metaphors in public discourse (LIVNAT, SCHMITT), the use of rhetorical questions KARHANOVÁ, SCHMITT), ways of establishing and signaling confidentiality (KERBRAT-ORECCHIONI), the reproduction of interfemale discourse behaviour (BUBEL), semiotic and multimodal questions (SAUER, SCHNÖRING, BOLÍVAR, KERBRAT-ORECCHIONI), etc.

As already mentioned three articles on general aspects of dialogue analysis supplement the volume. They deal with coherence (MORENO), sequencing (POP) and specific forms of argumentation (ZHANG).

Finally we would like to thank the many individuals and organizations who supported the conference as well as the publishing of these volumes:

The Austrian Federal Ministry for Education, Science and Culture provided us with generous travel grants, enabling a number of speakers to participate, who otherwise could not have come. The ministry also sponsored our conference office and coffee breaks.

Preface XV

Salzburg University contributed in many ways: Rector Heinrich Schmidinger met the costs of a student assistant for preparations before and work after the conference as well as for the layout of the conference volumes, and for the reception after the concert in the Salzburg Residence, to which we were invited by Salzburg city and province.

Vice rector Peter Eckl and his team as well as dean Wilfried Wieden provided us with valuable guidance when preparing the conference. The German Department and its head Eduard Beutner took care of postage, telephone and copy costs and a multitude of organizational tasks, which were mainly carried out by Klaus Schiller at the beginning. Our colleague, Andreas Weiss, generously devoted himself to maintaining the website and dealing with all of the speakers' technical requests and queries. Claudia Heugenhauser, managing the conference office, as well as Ria Deisl, Michael Gurschler, Irmtraud Kaiser, Justina Nutautaite and Beate Westermayer assisted the participants in a friendly and competent way. Many thanks to all of them for running the conference smoothly and making it very enjoyable!

Our very labor-intensive preparations for the printing of the conference papers were, in part, assisted by the IADA board members Catherine Kerbrat-Orecchioni, Bernd Naumann and Edda Weigand with comments and corrections of some of the manuscripts received. Ben Stephens contributed recommendations regarding the correction of the English articles and helped with the translations. Ria Deisl was equally tireless, emending the manuscripts, as was Dorit Wolf-Schwarz, producing a perfect layout. They are guaranteed not only our gratitude, but also that of the readers of these volumes!

Salzburg, May 2005 Monika Dannerer and Anne Betten

Addendum

Having, as a long-time member of IADA, initiated the conference invitation to Salzburg, it is of particular importance to me to express my immense gratitude towards Monika Dannerer, who – probably not fully aware of what she was letting herself in for – decided to share the load of this work of several years, often doing the lion's share (which especially our authors, with whom she communicated exhaustively, will acknowledge). Her exceptional efforts and her excellent cooperation at every stage cannot be praised enough: I am sure I speak not only for myself, but also for all of IADA!

Anne Betten

Catherine Kerbrat-Orecchioni

Le fonctionnement du dialogue dans un ‹genre› particulier: La confidence dans le roman-photo

1. Introduction

1.1 Genres et types de discours

Si j'ai choisi d'orienter cet exposé vers la question tant débattue des genres, c'est parce que le thème général du symposium de Salzburg, «Dialogue in the litterature and the media», y invitait: la littérature comme les médias sont des ‹macro-genres›, qui se définissent, la première par son caractère fictionnel (les dialogues en particulier y sont ‹fabriqués›), et les seconds par la nature du canal et le type de diffusion («massive»).

En effet, toutes les productions discursives se répartissent en ‹genres›, c'est-à-dire en catégories abstraites qui regroupent, sur la base d'un certain nombre de critères, des unités empiriques se présentant sous forme de ‹textes› ou de ‹discours›. Le nombre de ces catégories génériques, telles qu'elles sont étiquetées par la langue ordinaire et telles qu'elles ont été distinguées depuis l'antiquité par les théoriciens, est considérable (la liste en est même potentiellement ouverte à l'infini), ainsi que le remarque Maingueneau (1998, 45):

> Les locuteurs disposent d'une foule de termes pour catégoriser l'immense variété des textes qui sont produits dans une société: ‹conversation›, ‹manuel›, ‹journal›, ‹tragédie›, *reality-show*, ‹roman sentimental›, ‹description›, ‹polémique›, ‹sonnet›, ‹récit›, ‹maxime›, ‹hebdo›, ‹tract›, ‹rapport de stage›, ‹mythe›, ‹carte de vœux›... On notera que la dénomination de ces genres s'appuie sur des critères très hétérogènes.

Le champ lexical de la dénomination des genres se caractérise donc à la fois par sa richesse, et par l'extrême confusion qui y règne. Pour tenter de clarifier un peu les choses, il convient d'abord d'établir une distinction entre trois types d'objets qui peuvent prétendre au label de ‹genres›, et qui relèvent de trois niveaux différents:
1) Différents *systèmes sémiotiques*: la littérature, comme les interactions orales, relève fondamentalement du système linguistique (exploitation du langage verbal), à la différence par exemple de la bande dessinée, du théâtre représenté, du cinéma et des médias audiovisuels, qui engagent aussi d'autres systèmes de signes (langages iconiques).

2) Les *genres* à proprement parler, comme le roman, la nouvelle, le drame, l'épopée, le pamphlet, etc.: la notion relève du niveau macrotextuel, et renvoie à des catégories de textes plus ou moins institutionnalisées dans une société donnée. A l'oral, les équivalents de ces genres sont par exemple l'entretien, l'interview, la conférence, le débat, la consultation, etc., et l'on parle à ce niveau dans la littérature interactionniste de *types d'interactions* ou d'*événements communicatifs*. Ces grandes unités sont définies d'abord en termes de caractéristiques ‹externes›, c'est-à-dire situationnelles (nature du site et du format participatif, but de l'interaction, degré de formalité, etc.).

3) Mais pour Adam (1992), le véritable niveau pertinent pour une typologie textuelle c'est celui de certaines séquences ou ‹prototypes séquentiels›, qui sont à la base de toute composition textuelle et qu'il appelle *types*, les principaux types (supposés universels) étant le récit, la description, l'argumentation et l'explication (mais on peut aussi en envisager d'autres). Ces types relèvent d'un niveau ‹meso› (intermédiaire entre le macro et le micro); ils se caractérisent d'abord par certains traits de nature rhétorico-pragmatique, ou relevant de leur organisation discursive (connecteurs et deictiques, organisation temporelle, types d'actes de langage, etc.). Nous les appellerons *types de discours* ou *types d'activités discursives*.

Ce qui va m'intéresser ici c'est le fait qu'une même activité discursive (par exemple un récit) peut se réaliser dans différents ‹genres› et même dans différents systèmes sémiotiques, et que tout en conservant par définition certaines propriétés communes, il va voir ses réalisations varier selon l'ensemble plus large dans lequel il s'insère. Idée que je vais illustrer à partir de l'exemple d'une activité discursive particulière: la ‹confidence›.

1.2 La confidence

Définie de façon grossière, la confidence est la «communication d'un secret qui concerne soi-même» (*Le Petit Robert* 1974), définition dont on peut extraire les traits distinctifs suivants:

1) C'est un discours *égocentré*, qui porte sur un état, un fait, un événement qui concerne directement ou indirectement le locuteur (*confidence* vs *potin*, *commérage*, etc.).

2) C'est un discours qui porte sur quelque chose qui est plus ou moins destiné à rester *secret*; il opère une mise à nu du sujet, un dévoilement de l'intime, ce sera donc une activité ‹difficile› et à haut risque. Cela dit, cette information secrète ne correspond pas nécessairement à un fait stigmatisé (*confidence* vs *aveu* ou *confession*): c'est plus la ‹face négative› de l'individu (son ‹territoire›, ou ses ‹réserves› au sens de Goffman) que sa ‹face positive› (autrement dit ‹narcissique›) qui est mise en jeu dans l'activité de confidence.

Voilà en gros ce que l'on appelle *confidence*, terme qui en français se distingue de son doublet *confiance* (tout comme l'on oppose en espagnol *confidencia* et *confianza*, ou en italien *confidenza* et *fiducia*), alors qu'en anglais le terme est polysémique, *confidence* désignant à la fois le sentiment de ‹confiance› que l'on éprouve envers quelqu'un, et l'activité discursive qui nous intéresse ici ; activité de *confiding* que les interactionnistes désignent aussi par l'expression, un peu plus générale toutefois, de *self-disclosure* (Derlega et al. 1993).

Quoi qu'il en soit, la confidence peut se réaliser dans toute sortes de ‹genres›, écrits ou oraux, fictionnels ou non fictionnels : on en rencontre dans les romans ou au théâtre, mais aussi dans les conversations, les entretiens en tous genres, les échanges se déroulant dans les petits commerces ou chez le coiffeur, à la radio ou à la télévision ; ou bien encore dans les films, les spots publicitaires, la chanson, la bande dessinée... Nous nous sommes donc engagés à Lyon dans une recherche collective ayant pour objectif de voir comment cette activité discursive se module de façon diverse selon les contextes dans lesquels elle s'inscrit, et selon les ressources et contraintes propres au type de système sémiotique et d'événement communicatif que la confidence vient investir.

Je me suis personnellement intéressée, entre autres, au cas très particulier du roman-photo ; genre à vrai dire moribond,[1] du fait de la concurrence fatale de la télévision (et des très populaires *telenovelas*), mais qui n'en est pas moins intéressant, en particulier du fait de l'extrême stylisation que ce genre opère sur les structures discursives : les ‹scènes de confidence› y sont présentées de façon ‹chimiquement pure›, et leurs caractères prototypiques s'offrent au regard comme dans un miroir grossissant.

C'est donc à partir de l'exemple du roman-photo que je vais envisager les principales composantes de ce type particulier d'activité discursive qu'est la confidence, en mentionnant au passage certaines variations auxquelles elle se prête lorsqu'elle apparaît dans d'autres genres et contextes.

NB : Le corpus sur lequel est fondée cette analyse est constitué d'extraits, dont certains sont présentés en annexe, de romans-photos publiés dans le magazine spécialisé *Nous deux* (notons que l'un de ses principaux rivaux s'appelle justement... *Confidences*!). Bien que rien ne soit précisé à cet égard, il semble qu'il s'agisse pour la plupart de traductions (l'éditeur de *Nous deux*, Cino Del Duca, est italien).

---

[1] On ne le rencontre plus guère aujourd'hui que sous forme parodique, dans la publicité en particulier.

2. La confidence dans le roman-photo

2.1 Les caractéristiques sémiotiques du genre

Le roman-photo s'apparente au roman en ce qu'il met en scène des personnages fictifs, et que son dispositif énonciatif présente un *emboîtement des circuits communicatifs*: le dialogue (et en particulier la confidence) circule d'abord entre ces personnages, dont les comportements sont censés mimer ceux des locuteurs ‹authentiques›. Mais en amont, ce dialogue est fabriqué par un ou plusieurs ‹auteurs› (qui s'expriment uniquement par personnages interposés), cependant qu'en aval, le dialogue se destine à ces intrus, ces ‹épieurs› (les *eavesdroppers* de Goffman) que sont les lecteurs (selon un dispositif que j'ai proposé de traiter en termes de *trope communicationnel*, voir Kerbrat-Orecchioni 1990, 92-98).

Mais à la différence du roman, le roman-photo associe des éléments relevant de deux systèmes sémiotiques hétérogènes, le langage verbal écrit et la représentation iconique, ce qui lui permet en particulier de *représenter* le comportement mimo-gestuel des personnages, que le roman ne peut restituer qu'approximativement en le *décrivant*. À cet égard, on peut dire que le roman-photo est plus fortement ‹mimétique› que le roman (cela d'autant plus que les images sont de type photographique) – moins toutefois que le cinéma puisque l'on a affaire à des images fixes (à des ‹instantanés›), qui ont d'ailleurs d'autant plus besoin d'être claires et immédiatement compréhensibles: ce sont des *condensés de signification* que nous offrent les vignettes des romans-photos.

Ces deux composantes que sont le texte et l'image, je vais les envisager d'abord par rapport à la question suivante: comment le lecteur sait-il qu'en tel moment du roman, il a affaire à une scène de confidence? quels sont les principaux marqueurs de cette activité discursive?

Signalons d'abord que de façon très systématique, la confidence est présentée sur une seule et unique page: ce découpage spatial est le premier élément démarcatif de la scène.

2.1.1 Le texte

Il comprend d'une part des ‹répliques› imputables aux personnages, et d'autre part des commentaires narratifs (en majuscules) dont le fonctionnement s'apparente fort aux didascalies du texte théâtral, à cette différence près que l'on n'y trouve pas, et pour cause, d'indications sur le comportement non verbal des personnages.
1) Les *répliques* figurent dans des rectangles blancs rattachés à l'émetteur par une sorte de flèche; variante: les trois bulles discontinues, qui indiquent qu'il s'agit d'un monologue intérieur. Selon une convention commune aussi dans la bande dessinée, la lecture se

fait de gauche à droite et de haut en bas, l'ordre haut-bas l'emportant sur l'ordre gauche-droite [exemples: planche 1, vignette 3; planche 2, vignette 2]. La teneur de ces répliques joue évidemment un rôle primordial dans l'identification de la confidence.

2) Les *commentaires narratifs* peuvent eux aussi assurer le marquage du genre, soit de façon *explicite* par la présence dans la didascalie du mot ‹confidence› lui-même [ex. planche 1, vignette 3; ou encore: «Peu à peu, Loïc se confie»; «Avec le temps, Letizia est devenue la confidente de Claudio») ou de quelque variante («Letizia est la seule personne à qui il peut ouvrir son cœur»), soit de façon *implicite* [ex. planche 2, «une semaine plus tard, lors d'une promenade avec sa meilleurs amie»: la mention de la meilleure amie, candidate privilégiée au rôle de confidente, nous met la puce à l'oreille].

C'est donc essentiellement grâce au texte que l'on sait que l'on a affaire à une scène de confidence. Mais l'image joue également un rôle non négligeable à cet égard.

2.1.2 L'image

Dans la scène de confidence, le comportement mimo-gestuel des personnages est si stéréotypé qu'il est difficile de s'y tromper. Au début de la scène, se peint sur le visage du futur ‹confieur› une expression soucieuse et tourmentée [voir planche 1]: front plissé, posture abattue, regard détourné. Le confident de son côté tourne son regard vers le malheureux, qu'il ne va plus quitter des yeux jusqu'à la fin de la scène (alors que le confieur ne regarde son interlocuteur que par intermittence), accompagnant ce regard attentif d'autres manifestations de sollicitude: tête penchée, geste de réconfort…

Les jeux de cadrage sont tout aussi systématiques: la scène débute sur un plan éloigné qui met en place le cadre et le format participatif; puis grâce à un efficace zoom avant nous avons droit, nous les ‹intrus› devenus voyeurs, à un gros plan sur le visage du confieur, ce qui produit un effet de dramatisation tout en permettant au lecteur, dans ce moment précis où la parole se fait plus privée, de la capter au plus près, et de pénétrer dans l'intimité du personnage qui n'est censé se dévoiler qu'à son seul confident.

Tel est le premier aspect de cette ‹stylisation› qu'opère le roman-photo: les scènes de confidence y sont très clairement et immédiatement identifiables, à la différence de ce qui se passe dans les conversations authentiques où il est beaucoup plus difficile de savoir à quel moment exactement on ‹entre dans la confidence›.

2.2 Les composantes de la scène de confidence

Elles seront envisagées sous la forme de réponses aux questions suivantes: *Que* confie-t-on? *À qui? Où* et *quand? Comment?* Et *à quelle(s) fin(s)?*

2.2.1 L'objet confié

Que confie-t-on à autrui? Par définition, une information ‹intime› (fait ou état d'âme, qui peuvent être à caractère plutôt euphorique [planche 2] ou dysphorique [planche 1]). Dans le roman-photo, où l'intrigue tourne toujours autour d'un affaire de cœur, la confidence a nécessairement quelque chose à voir avec le sentiment amoureux (sa naissance ou sa disparition, l'inquiétude concernant les sentiments de l'autre, etc.).

2.2.2 Le/la confidente

L'activité de confidence engage deux rôles dissymétriques. À la suite de S. Durrer j'appellerai *confieur* le locuteur dominant, et pour reprendre un terme mieux installé dans la langue, *confident* celui qui «reçoit les plus secrètes pensées de quelqu'un» (*Petit Robert*), et assiste le confieur dans son activité de confidence.

Le cadre participatif privilégié de cette activité est donc celui du *dilogue* (échange en tête à tête), même si l'on peut avoir des confidences en présence de témoins, des confidences à plusieurs, et même des confidences publiques (c'est le cas par exemple dans les thérapies de groupe, ou dans certaines émissions télévisuelles, du genre *intimity shows*). Mais la confidence prototypique implique que l'on soit deux et seulement deux: si ce n'est pas le cas il faut donc commencer par éliminer l'intrus [voir planche 3].

Quant au confident/à la confidente prototypique, c'est quelqu'un en qui l'on a *confiance* et avec qui l'on a une complicité de longue date (on n'a pas de secret pour lui/elle): le/la candidat(e) idéal(e) pour jouer ce rôle c'est *le/la meilleur(e) ami(e)*, à tel point, comme on l'a vu, que sa seule apparition peut créer chez le lecteur l'attente d'une scène de confidence. Mais là encore, on voit que le roman-photo opère une simplification radicale des possibilités attestées dans la réalité, comme d'ailleurs dans d'autres genres fictionnels plus subtils – voir cet exemple extrait de *La marche de Radetzki* de Joseph Roth (Points 1982, 85), dans lequel la confidence repose non sur une ancienne complicité mais sur une connivence soudaine:

> Chez tante Rési! on allait chez tante Rési! [le lupanar de la garnison] […]
> Le docteur Max Demant, médecin du régiment, fit une timide tentative pour s'esquiver.
> – Êtes-vous obligé d'y aller? demanda-t-il tout bas au lieutenant Trotta.
> – Il va bien falloir! chuchota Charles-Joseph.

> Alors il l'accompagna sans mot dire. Ils étaient les derniers de la bande désordonnée des officiers qui parcouraient les rues tranquilles de la petite ville, à grand bruit de ferraille. Ils ne se parlaient pas. Ils se sentaient liés tous deux par la question discrète et la réponse murmurée. C'était chose faite. Et ils se connaissaient à peine depuis une demi-heure.
> Soudain, sans savoir pourquoi, Charles-Joseph déclara:
> – J'ai aimé une femme. Elle s'appelait Cathy. Elle est morte.
> Le major s'arrêta et se tourna vers le lieutenant.
> – Vous aimerez encore d'autres femmes, fit-il.
> Et ils reprirent leur marche.

Je n'ai trouvé dans mon corpus aucun exemple de ce type, d'abord parce que le stock de personnages que comporte chaque histoire se réduit au strict minimum, ensuite parce que la ‹confidence à un inconnu› constitue un comportement atypique, qui peut même apparaître comme pathologique s'il se reproduit trop souvent (il n'y a guère que chez Marguerite Duras que l'on peut aisément raconter sa vie au premier venu). Dans les romans-photos en revanche, on se confie volontiers à un(e) collègue de travail, comme dans l'exemple de la planche 1 («Sylviane est celle à qui les pensionnaires se confient»: c'est quasiment une ‹confidente professionnelle›), les qualités requises pour faire une bonne confidente étant: une grande capacité d'écoute et d'empathie, une bonne intuition [cf. planche 4: «Si mon intuition est bonne, je crois que vous avez des soucis»], et le don d'arriver au bon moment [*ibid.*: «Merci, Letizia. Vous arrivez toujours au bon moment»].

Pour en finir avec la question du/de la confident(e) idéal(e), ajoutons qu'il est préférable qu'il/elle soit du même sexe que celui/celle qui se confie: notre corpus présente des confidences entre femmes et (quoique moins fréquemment) entre hommes, mais aussi entre homme et femme, ce qui ne va pas sans poser quelque problème car la relation amicale que présuppose la confidence risque alors de ‹dégénérer› en relation amoureuse, ce qui fait basculer le récit dans un autre type de scénario [voir planche 4: «Avec le temps, Letizia est devenue la confidente de Claudio. Cependant, ce rôle commence à lui peser, car elle est tombée amoureuse de lui»][2] – chose qui ne risque pas de se produire dans la tragédie classique, qui a d'emblée écarté ce risque en imposant (d'après Pavis 1980) que confident et confieur soient de même sexe.[3]

---

[2] Il en est évidemment de même dans la situation inverse, plus rare mais attestée, où la confidence se déroule entre une femme et un homme, comme l'illustre un des récits du corpus: le confident se métamorphose soudain en ‹dragueur›, ce qui n'est pas du goût de la confieuse, qui se rebelle vertueusement (et provisoirement).

[3] Cela dit, on ne peut pas affirmer que la confidence exclue toujours une relation de type érotique, étant donné l'existence d'un ‹sous-genre› particulier (non représenté dans notre corpus): la ‹confidence sur l'oreiller›.

2.2.3 Le cadre de la confidence

En ce qui concerne les contextes spatio-temporels favorables à l'émergence d'une confidence, mentionnons rapidement:
1) Lieux privilégiés: la table (salon, restaurant ou terrasse de café, bar), où l'on est confortablement installé, où l'on peut se constituer un espace privé, où l'on peut boire aussi, de préférence quelque boisson alcoolisée, qui favorise les épanchements et libère la parole (on sait que Liber est l'un des surnoms de Bacchus: *in vino confidentia*...); mais d'autres lieux sont également propices à la confidence, comme les lieux de plein air où l'on déambule loin des oreilles indiscrètes, ou les lieux transitoires (couloir, vestiaire, etc.), appropriés aux confidences furtives.
2) Moments opportuns: la confidence exige en principe une certaine prédisposition de la part du confieur (qui doit être ‹en veine de confidence›), ainsi qu'une certaine disponibilité de la part du confident: tous deux doivent être ‹ouverts à la confidence›, laquelle consiste à transférer une information confidentielle d'une intériorité à l'autre, et implique donc un double ‹déverrouillage› du territoire personnel.

Si ces conditions ne sont pas réunies, la confidence va devoir être *négociée* entre les deux parties en présence.

2.2.4 Le déroulement de la scène de confidence

La confidence peut être spontanée ou sollicitée. Dans le premier cas, le confident peut rechigner à endosser ce rôle qui lui est imposé, parfois contre son gré; dans le deuxième, c'est le confieur qui peut résister à la demande de confidence. Or l'activité de confidence doit être menée conjointement par les deux partenaires, qui doivent donc d'abord être d'accord pour s'engager dans cette activité, et si cet accord n'est pas immédiat il doit être ‹négocié› entre eux. Contrairement à ce qui se passe dans les conversations naturelles, où d'après Traverso (1996, 199-200) la confidence est le plus souvent ‹auto-initiée›, elle est dans le roman-photo généralement sollicitée, par des formules telles que:

> Qu'est-ce qui t'arrive, Nicolas? [planche 1]
> Je te sens préoccupée. Que se passe-t-il? [planche 2]
> Que se passe-t-il? [planche 3]
> Si mon intuition est bonne, je crois que vous avez des soucis. [planche 4]

On voit que le démarrage de la scène de confidence est toujours le même:
1) A, le confieur potentiel, produit des signes manifestes de préoccupation: c'est en situation de crise que se produit la confidence;
2) B, le confident potentiel, demande des explications à A;
3) explications que A fournit, parfois en se faisant un peu tirer l'oreille [voir planche 1],

mais tout de même toujours assez rapidement: on l'a dit, la scène doit tenir sur une seule page, l'affaire doit donc être menée tambour battant.

Cela dit, le déroulement de la scène se passe conformément au *script* de ce type d'activité, tel que l'a dégagé Traverso (1999, 114-115), c'est-à-dire en quatre phases:

1) Phase d'*ouverture*, ou ‹entrée en confidence›, laquelle se fait généralement, dans les interactions authentiques comme dans le roman, en douceur, chacun devant progressivement se mettre dans la peau de son rôle;
2) Phase d'*exposition*, prise en charge par le confieur;
3) Phase de *partage*, dans laquelle «le confident manifeste son soutien et souvent propose solutions et conseils»;
4) *Clôture*, généralement prise en charge par le confieur.

On retrouve bien dans le corpus de romans-photos ces quatre phases successives, mais en quelque sorte réduites à leur plus simple expression: la clôture est souvent plus rapide encore que l'ouverture, et même écourtée soit du fait de A [planche 2], soit du fait de B [planche 1], soit du fait d'un tiers [planche 3: «Attention, la voilà!»], qui survient de façon inopportune pour les personnages, mais très opportune pour le tempo du récit.

Tempo qui explique aussi que la principale caractéristique stylistico-rhétorique du dialogue confidentiel ne s'y rencontre qu'à dose infinitésimale, à savoir la présence de traces d'un certain «difficile à dire» (cf. Gardin 1988): balbutiements, hésitations, précautions, et autres ‹figures du silence› telles que la ‹réticence›. Or notre corpus (dont sont plus généralement absents tous les marqueurs d'oralité) est à cet égard indigent par rapport à ce que l'on trouve dans les dialogues authentiques, romanesques ou cinématographiques: ces traces se réduisent à quelques points de suspension [voir par exemple planche 2, vignette 2].

Pourtant, l'activité de confidence est une activité *difficile*, aussi bien pour le confieur (qui ‹s'expose› en se confiant) que pour le confident (qui doit être à la hauteur de ce que le confieur attend de lui). Situation doublement délicate donc, que l'on peut décrire de la façon suivante, en empruntant la perspective et la terminologie de la ‹théorie des faces›:

1) *Pour A* (le confieur), la confidence est un *FTA* (*Face Threatening Act*: acte menaçant) *pour son territoire* (et parfois en outre, si la confidence risque de mettre à mal son ‹image›, pour sa face positive – d'où le sentiment de honte que l'on éprouve parfois rétrospectivement à l'idée que l'on s'est ‹livré› à la confidence).

Vis à vis de cet acte de langage, tout locuteur se trouve pris dans une sorte de *double contrainte*, entre le désir de protéger son territoire et le souci de partager avec autrui (les informations, les émotions…); deux exigences entre lesquelles on doit en permanence ‹composer› (voir Derlega et al. 1993, chap. 4, sur la «privacy regulation», la «tension between disclosure and privacy», problématisée par la psychologie sociale).

2) *Pour B* (le confident), la confidence est à la fois:

un FTA pour son territoire (A envahit son espace mental en même temps qu'il lui fait perdre du temps: «mais je t'embête avec toutes mes histoires!»);

un FFA (*Face Flattering Act*: acte valorisant) *pour sa face positive* (recevoir une confidence, c'est gratifiant en tant que un témoignage de confiance).

Le confident se trouve donc lui aussi pris dans une sorte de double contrainte, entre le souci de protéger son propre territoire (ce qui va l'inciter à s'investir le moins possible dans l'échange confidentiel, ou à chercher à se dépêtrer de la «nasse de la confidence», cf. Traverso 1999, 118), et la tentation d'en ‹faire trop› (risquant alors de sembler «s'approprier l'histoire et l'émotion dont on lui parle»).

Corrélativement, ce sont des séquences conversationnelles particulièrement chargées émotionnellement; voir Thimm/Kruse (1993, 94-96), et surtout Traverso (2000, 208), montrant qu'à ce niveau aussi la tâche du confident n'est pas aisée, qui doit trouver le juste équilibre entre les excès empathiques et l'impassibilité polie:

> On n'attend pas du confident, à qui l'on raconte la tristesse d'un événement tragique qui nous a touché, qu'il éclate en sanglots, encore moins de celui à qui l'on confie qu'on est amoureux qu'il le devienne aussi. [...] Pourtant, un confident impassible est sans doute un piètre confident.

2.2.5 Fonctions et effets de la confidence sur les interactants et l'interaction

Les fonctions et effets de la confidence sont extrêmement divers, qu'on les envisage par rapport à l'actant principal, en l'occurrence le confieur (‹voir clair dans son cœur›, fonction cathartique de la verbalisation, rôle de la mise en discours pour doter de sens les événements subis, etc.), ou sous l'angle de la relation interpersonnelle (rapprochement mutuel par le partage d'informations, d'expériences et d'émotions[4]). Dans le cas du roman-photo, la question doit être envisagée non seulement dans la perspective des personnages, mais aussi par rapport à cette autre instance réceptrice qu'est le lecteur, à qui le discours confidentiel se destine aussi, lui permettant d'avoir accès aux pensées et sentiments cachés de ses héro(ïne)s – aussi et même surtout (il arrive parfois que le confident disparaisse discrètement une fois qu'il a rempli son office): dans de telles scènes, le ‹trope communicationnel› fonctionne à plein régime. Il en est d'ailleurs de même dans le roman, et plus encore au

---

[4] «C'est alors même qu'ils ne savaient toujours rien de la paix, au cours de cette dernière nuit d'ignorance, que *Samad décida de cimenter son amitié avec Archie*. Le plus souvent, *il suffit pour ce faire de communiquer un petit secret*: peccadille sexuelle, confidence amoureuse, passion cachée que les réticences propres à une relation fraîchement nouée ont jusque là empêché de divulguer. Mais pour Samad, rien n'était plus vrai, plus intime, plus authentique que le sang qui coulait dans ses veines.» (Zadie Smith, *Sourires de loup*, Folio 2001, 146-147; italique ajouté)

théâtre, car en l'absence de tout narrateur l'accès à l'intériorité des personnages n'est possible que par le biais de ces épanchements confidentiels; on comprend donc que le théâtre classique ait institué un rôle particulier, celui de ‹confident›, que le *Petit Robert* (1974) définit ainsi:

> Personne qui reçoit les plus secrètes pensées de quelqu'un.
> *Théât*. Personnage secondaire qui reçoit les confidences des principaux personnages pour que le public soit instruit des desseins et des événements.

Telle est la raison d'être des confidents: favoriser les confidences des héros, pour le plus grand bénéfice des spectateurs.

On peut donc conclure, avec Derlega et al. (1993, VIII): «Self-disclosure is a fundamental ingredient of human communication» – la confidence est un ingrédient fondamental de la communication authentique, mais aussi de la communication que mettent en scène les œuvres de fiction: cette activité discursive y est bien représentée, donnant lieu à de véritables *scènes de genre*, et cela tout particulièrement dans les romans d'amour,[5] comme dans ces romans-photos où la codification du genre est poussée jusqu'à la caricature, mettant en quelque sorte à nu le squelette de l'échange confidentiel. Reste à voir comment cet échange peut donner lieu à des élaborations plus sophistiquées, et tout en conservant ses caractéristiques propres, se moduler d'une part en fonction du contexte communicatif dans lequel il trouve place, et d'autre part en fonction du système sémiotique qui lui donne forme.

---

5   Dans lesquels les ‹scènes de confidence› constituent une étape obligée du scénario prototypique, ainsi que l'a bien montré Durrer (1998). Voir aussi Bettinotti (1986) sur les romans de la collection ‹Harlequin›.

Références

Adam, Jean-Michel (1992): Les textes: types et prototypes. Paris: Nathan.
Bettinotti, Julia (1986): La corrida d'amour. Le roman Harlequin. Montréal: Cahiers du Département d'études littéraires 6, UQUAM.
Derlega, Valerian J. et al. (1993): Self-disclosure. Newbury Park: Sage.
Durrer, Sylvie (1998): «Parlez: je vous écoute». La confidence dans le script amoureux. In: Les faiseurs d'amour. Le tiers dans nos relations. Berne: Cahiers du Musée de la communication (éditions Payot, Lausanne), 21-36.
Gardin, Bernard (1988): Le dire difficile et le devoir dire. In: DRLAV 39, 1-20.
Goffman, Erving (1981): Forms of talk. Philadelphia: University of Pennsylvania Press.
Kerbrat-Orecchioni, Catherine (1990): Les interactions verbales t. I. Paris: A. Colin.
Maingueneau, Dominique (1998): Analyser les textes de communication. Paris: Dunod.
Pavis, Patrice (1980): Dictionnaire du théâtre. Paris: Éditions sociales.
Thimm, Caja/Kruse, Lenelis (1993): The power-emotion relationship in discourse spontaneous expression of emotions in asymmetric dialogue. In: Journal of Language and Social Psychology 12, 81-102.
Traverso, Véronique (1994): Les récits de la confidence. In: Brès, J. (éd.): Le récit oral, Université de Montpellier III : Praxiling, 227-239.
– (1996): La conversation familière. Lyon: PUL.
– (1999): L'analyse des conversations. Paris: Nathan (Coll. 128) [113ff., «Confidences romanesques et confidences conversationnelles»].
– (2000): Les émotions dans la confidence. In: Plantin, C./Doury, M./Traverso, V. (éds.): Les émotions dans les interactions, Lyon: PUL, 205-221.

Planche 1: «Difficile d'oublier», *Nous deux* 2741

Planche 2: «Le feu sous la glace», *Nous deux* 2751

Le fonctionnement du dialogue dans un ‹genre› particulier

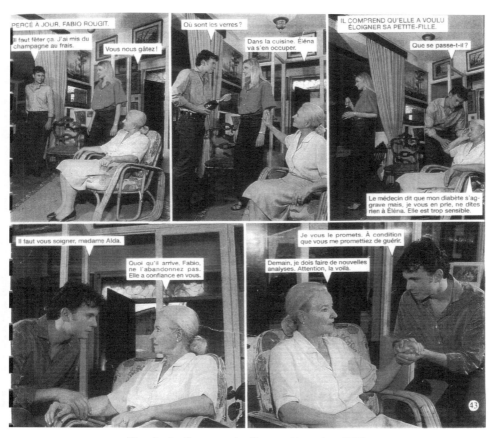

Planche 3: «Les yeux du silence», *Nous deux* 2752

Planche 4: «Contre vents et marées», *Nous deux* 2751 et 2752

Christian Schmitt

«Dire l'interdit»

1. Remarques préliminaires

«Traduire du mensonge en vérité», tel est le devoir moral d'un littéraire engagé, pour Bertolt Brecht expliquant au monde libre l'interprétation qu'il fallait donner aux textes publiés dans les journaux contrôlés par les Nazis; son comportement était donc conditionné par l'emprise d'une société où tout ce qui ne correspondait pas à l'opinion des autorités était *eo ipso* interdit.

Dans la France contemporaine, la situation est diamétralement opposée: tout individu est censé pouvoir s'exprimer librement dans des discours individuels ou publics à condition qu'il respecte les lois de la République et qu'il n'incite pas à la discrimination, à la haine ou à la violence à l'égard d'une personne ou d'un groupe de personnes en raison de leur origine ou de leur appartenance ou non-appartenance à une ethnie, une nation, une race ou une religion déterminée (voir Art. 32, alinéa 2,3 de la Loi du 29.7.1881, modifié par la Loi du 1.7.1972, complété par la Loi du 13.7.1990); cette restriction est faite pour régler la lutte politique et pour façonner les discours portant sur les «sujets sensibles» de l'actualité.

Nombreux sont ceux qui, néanmoins, essaient de *dire l'interdit* en contournant, par le biais des astuces linguistiques les plus diverses, les règles discursives valables pour les *mass media* afin d'exprimer des idées incompatibles avec la législation française et les droits de l'homme. La gauche, comme la droite, ont développé des moyens discursifs: la première en se servant de sa langue de bois, la seconde en développant certaines techniques que les tribunaux, instances peu versées en matière linguistique, n'ont pas encore reconnues dans une mesure souhaitable et nécessaire: on sait que, faute de critères valables, les juristes n'arrivent toujours pas à frapper des «dire» implicites.

A partir de deux textes authentiques ma contribution doit faire comprendre les moyens utilisés par ceux qui ne sont pas prêts à reconnaître les lois fondamentales de la communication politique pour justifier la nécessité d'intervenir dans le cas d'une infraction contre les règles impératives de la communication, ou du moins contre certaines règles essentielles, voire catégoriques. Ce sont avant tout des usages de règles tournant autour du genre de textes ou de discours qui sont enfreints, les auteurs de textes se servant du fait qu'il existe ce que Foucault a appelé *l'Archéologie du savoir* qui forme la base d'une «formation discursive» (1969, 52s.). Nous savons que tout discours suit, peu ou prou, des régularités conventionnalisées et que l'analyse herméneutique est le plus souvent basée sur ces lois intérieures à tout texte. C'est dans cette conception que se rejoignent les notions de Michel Foucault et de Michel Pêcheux, ce dernier (1981) partant d'une représentation mentale générale comme déterminant *ce qui peut et doit être dit* (articulée sous la forme d'une harangue, d'un sermon, d'un pamphlet, d'un programme, etc.) à partir d'une position donnée dans une conjoncture donnée (cf. De Nuchèze/Colletta 2002, 170ss.). Ceci veut dire que tout locuteur ou auteur de textes présentant un sermon, un exposé ou un récit à base d'imagination (populaire ou artistique) peut se fier à une lecture adaptée au titre ou à la rubrique sous laquelle le texte a paru. On dira que l'énoncé a été publié sous forme de «sermon» ou «fable», articulé à travers un genre bien connu, et qu'il existe une relation préétablie entre l'interprétation du texte et le fonctionnement d'un genre défini et que, par conséquent, une certaine lecture s'impose, au moins pour le lecteur habituel qui ne connaît pas le positionnement du locuteur idéologique et doit, par conséquent, accorder sa confiance aux règles élémentaires du genre.

Se servir de cette appréhension préétablie signifie qu'il existe une analyse du discours que je qualifierai de générale ou même préscientifique. L'individu émetteur est bien conscient de l'interprétation la plus vraisemblable de son message auprès du lecteur que représente soit le lecteur partisan, Monsieur Tout-le-monde, soit un magistrat chargé d'appliquer les lois, et peut donc profiter de ses connaissances méta-herméneutiques: sachant qu'une fable est pour la plupart des lecteurs une sorte d'anecdote, nouvelle ou allégation mensongère, il pourra se servir de ce genre pour transmettre, sous forme de récit, de fiction ou d'imagination, des idées cachées, voire une moralité particulière ou des vérités dites générales sans être rendu responsable du contenu de son texte; pour les fables aucune interprétation ne s'impose et les interprétations restent, en général, à la disposition herméneutique usuelle du lecteur. Nous savons bien que les Nazis comme certains membres de partis extrémistes ont pris et continuent à prendre le racisme ou la phobie de tout ce qui est étranger pour des vérités et la «préférence nationale» (Klein 1994) pour la moralité suprême.

Il est donc possible, voire nécessaire, que l'analyse du discours travaille au moins sur deux niveaux, sur deux unités du dit ou de l'écrit: les genres du discours dont se servent les auteurs de textes, entendus comme dispositifs socio-historiques des actes communicatifs humains; et les éléments constitutifs et tailles variables des textes servant de moyen de cryptage pour l'émetteur et de reconnaissance ou d'identification pour le lecteur, étant donné que ce type de textes engagés doit correspondre à deux fonctions élémentaires. En effet, ces unités langagières constituent le moyen par lequel un message est rendu inintelligible en l'absence d'un décodeur approprié et fonctionne en même temps comme instrument servant à l'ancrage des initiés et partisans qui retrouvent ainsi leur positionnement dans le message à l'aide de critères thématiques spéciaux dans les usages langagiers basant sur des messages codés ou, mieux encore, enveloppés dans un entourage langagier cryptique.

2. Comment dire l'interdit

Le procédé correspond dans une certaine mesure à une utilisation intentionnelle de l'implicite si magistralement décrit par O. Ducrot et C. Kerbrat-Orecchioni, mais il se sert d'une perversion de la catégorie logico-sémantique en ce sens qu'il évite l'axiome bien connu *il a dit X, or X implique Y, donc il a dit Y* et établit le présupposé *dire X* (ou se servir du mot X) *est interdit*, son utilisation sera punie, mais *dire Y* (ou se servir du mot Y) *reste ambigu* bien que cette version puisse exprimer la même chose sans risques de poursuite par les magistrats et sans danger de devoir comparaître devant la juridiction pénale. Le locuteur qui se sert de cette technique discursive sait qu'il existe des degrés d'implicite variables et que certains degrés sont automatiquement sujets à l'interprétation bien qu'à force d'être répétés sans cesse ils soient clairs pour le «groupe intérieur» familiarisé avec ce type de discours. Mais puisque cette exégèse dépend à la fois des inférences de l'interprétant à partir de sa compétence linguistique et de celle qu'il attribue à l'interlocuteur, du cadre cognitif de lui-même et de la personne avec laquelle il dialogue, et du contexte donné, on ne pourra imputer de stratégie certaine ni au responsable d'un texte ou d'un énoncé ni à un interlocuteur présent: celui-ci pourra toujours prendre la fuite devant ses responsabilités et se retrancher derrière le sens usuel ou le sens littéral, laissant ainsi à son partenaire l'obligation et la nécessité morale de donner une signification sans équivoque, le chargeant ainsi de l'action d'expliquer ou d'interpréter. En changeant un peu la définition de Ducrot (1977, 40), je dirai donc que dans le cas du «dire l'interdit» nous sommes confrontés au présupposé d'un énoncé, aux indications qu'il apporte, mais sur lesquelles l'énonciateur ne veut pas faire porter l'enchaînement par peur d'infraction contre la législation linguistique. L'énonciateur choisira donc une stratégie qui consiste à utiliser à côté du non-dit peu efficace tous les types d'implicites et d'ambiguïtés utilisées, plutôt, pour éviter toutes sortes de rétorsions et mesures coercitives que d'éventuelles manipulations, car ce qu'il tente avant tout, ce n'est pas la manipulation de sa clientèle qui se trouve sur la même longueur d'onde, mais plutôt le jeu de déguisement et de masquage devant la justice. Du point de vue interactionniste, il rend utile une stratégie hautement consciente de cryptage des contenus, anticipant un calcul interprétatif et certaines négociations chez les protecteurs de la loi forcés de se servir d'un accès aux textes marqué par la neutralité et l'absence d'inférences et de position préjudiciaire.

Les énonciateurs, eux, appartiennent toujours à une idéologie bien définie et à une «famille d'esprit» (Honoré 1986, 153), mais ils n'admettent pas, en général, que leurs actes de persuasion soient soumis à un examen démocratique, au contraire: ils refusent, par principe, ce que Wodak (Wodak et al. 1998, 3) a appelé l'«analyse discursive critique» consistant à rendre perceptible «die ideologisch durchwirkte, oft opake Formen der Machtausübung, der politischen Kontrolle und Manipulation sowie der diskriminierenden [...] Unterdrückungs- und Exklusionsstrategien im [politischen] Sprachgebrauch», car celle-ci ferait découvrir une stratégie double, selon qu'il s'agit des adeptes ou des non-initiés. Pour les adeptes il est important qu'ils puissent retrouver leurs idées propres dans l'implicite alors qu'il est essentiel envers les pouvoirs publics que le locuteur puisse toujours prétendre, même à l'aide d'un juriste, n'avoir voulu exprimer les idées qu'une herméneutique du sens pourrait lui reprocher en interprétant les «signes sublimaux» (Kerbrat-Orecchioni 1986, 24) ou en analysant «une sorte de second code» (Ducrot 1984, 16).

Nous connaissons tous la définition des présupposés selon laquelle ce phénomène textuel comprend toutes les informations qui sans être ouvertement posées, sont cependant automatiquement impliquées et entraînées par la formulation de l'énoncé, dans lequel elles se trouvent intrinsèquement inscrites, quelle que soit la spécificité du cadre énonciatif (Kerbrat-Orecchioni 1986, 25); cette définition reste pertinente dans la plupart des cas, mais elle ne suffit pas, comme le sait tout locuteur ou lecteur, qu'il soit linguiste ou non. Notre expérience textuelle et notre compétence linguistique nous conseillent d'être prudents dans l'interprétation de notions-clés telles que *démocratique*, *social*, *juste*, *droits des citoyens*, selon qu'elles sont proférées par un despote, un homme politique communiste ou un individu foncièrement démocratique. Nous savons donc que les présupposés et l'acte herméneutique dépendent de tout ce que le lecteur ou l'entendeur sait sur l'énonciateur, ses actes, sa position politique et sociale, ses textes antérieurs, les stratégies de son groupe et qu'il ne suffit pas de se fier aux seuls énoncés. Dans ce contexte, on admettra l'existence d'un sens textuel dépassant le cadre littéraire, d'un sens complémentaire comparable à la «suprasummativité» des phrases par rapport aux signes linguistiques constitutifs. Tout énoncé ou tout fragment d'énoncé, outre son sens littéral, peut apparaître comme la reprise non seulement d'une phrase connue ou censée connue (Bachem 1999, 111; Angenot 1982, 279), mais aussi et avant tout comme la réactivation et le réajustement d'idées reçues et attendues du côté de l'énonciateur ou du groupe auquel il appartient ou bien comme résultat de ses actes, voire de son comportement social.

3. Deux études de textes

Ces remarques introductives me paraissent indispensables pour bien comprendre le texte relatif à un phénomène biologique, «La mortelle migration des abeilles tueuses», publié dans *Présent* (30.1.1999, 4), l'un des journaux les plus connus et les plus provocateurs de l'extrême droite française:

3.1 «La mortelle migration des abeilles tueuses»

(1) Los Angeles est atteinte. Plus tôt que ce que l'on prévoyait. Les abeilles tueuses d'origine africaine, introduites au Brésil en 1956, poursuivent leur lente mais inexorable conquête du continent nord-américain ...

(2) A l'origine, le gouvernement brésilien importe de Namibie des abeilles africaines réputées mieux adaptées au climat tropical que les abeilles sud-américaines de souche européenne. Les abeilles africaines prennent donc la route de l'ancienne traite humaine.

(3) Ces abeilles sont surnommés «tueuses». Pour des raisons bien précises: elles ne connaissent pas le repos, se reproduisent beaucoup plus et essaiment fréquemment. Tout cela pourrait être positif, sauf que les africaines sont belliqueuses, deviennent agressives à la moindre vibration constituant pour elles une menace, même virtuelle, pour leur nid: l'alerte est répercutée par phéromone et transforme le nid en base militaire, toutes les abeilles sortent et attaquent tout ce qui se trouve à la portée de leur dard. Surnatalité et agressivité poussent les essaims africains à pénétrer dans les nids d'abeilles européennes et à s'en emparer en tuant la reine de la ruche.

(4) Le problème, c'est que ces insectes sont dangereux pour les autres espèces qui les côtoient. Dont l'espèce humaine. Cette immigration voulue tourne très vite au désastre pour avoir été mal contrôlée. Peu après leur implantation au Brésil, 26 reines s'échappent d'un centre expérimental. Avant leur éducation et acclimatation au terrain et au milieu.

(5) Depuis, elles mènent une guerre de conquête à leur échelle: la grande invasion, qui est de fait une migration, parcourt 500 km par an! Les humains vont alors contre-attaquer en tentant de les stopper avec des insecticides. En vain.

(6) Aujourd'hui, on s'adapte à l'agressivité des intruses pour s'en servir malgré tout en prenant des risques pour la sécurité des apiculteurs. A la longue, on peut redouter une disparition des abeilles européennes ...

(7) On n'en est pas là. Et l'on met des espoirs dans un relatif ralentissement de la progression des tueuses gênées, semble-t-il, par la topographie nord-américaine.

(8) Los Angeles 2000. Le film de science-fiction est déjà d'actualité. Les abeilles tueuses sont sur place au milieu de la grande ville californienne.

(9) Cette petite fable si réelle mérite sans doute une morale. Faut-il vraiment un La Fontaine pour la trouver?

(Présent 30.1.1999, 4)

Tout lecteur familier avec les textes de ce quotidien sera surpris de trouver un texte portant sur le croisement artificiel entre deux variétés d'abeilles, donc entre deux races d'une même espèce. Mais averti par certaines activités du journal et sachant qu'il s'agit d'un métissage en sciences naturelles et que le terme de *métissage* constitue une des notions-clés des disciples et prosélytes de M. Le Pen et du Front national (FN), il ne pourra s'empêcher de sentir un danger imminent, d'être mis en état d'alerte et de pressentir une sorte de menace. L'apiculteur ou le lecteur apiphile ne devraient guère s'intéresser à cet article: ils ne s'attendent pas à lire des informations relatives à leur domaine d'intérêt dans un journal idéologique. Mais quelles peuvent donc être les raisons qui amènent un lecteur politiquement engagé à lire des articles pareils? Et s'agit-il vraiment d'un texte qui pourra nous informer sur l'hybridation et le métissage animal qui auraient provoqué des centaines de morts (d'où le terme anglais des *killer bees*, comme l'explicite l'Internet où l'on parle d'un accident provoqué par l'hybridation)?

De prime abord, il s'agit là d'un récit simple sous forme de rapport dans lequel un auteur inconnu nous informe – apparemment sans arrière-pensée – sur un accident provoqué par l'échappement de 21 reines hybridées qui se sont évadées d'un centre expérimental. Il est indubitable pour le lecteur M. Tout-le-monde que ce récit sous forme de rapport contient quelques informations curieuses qui restent cependant dans le cadre de la vraisemblance et de la crédibilité:

(1) une ville est atteinte par les abeilles tueuses;
(2) celles-ci suivent l'ancienne traite humaine («traite des nègres, des noirs», NPRob, s.v.);
(3) les *killer bees* ne connaissent pas de repos, se reproduisent beaucoup: ceci pourrait être positif, mais – comme l'exige l'implicite vaguement explicité («tout cela pourrait être positif») – ne l'est pas: ces abeilles hybridées pénètrent dans les nids d'abeilles européennes et s'emparent de la ruche;
(4) l'échappement se transforme en immigration voulue dangereuse pour toute espèce, parmi elles l'espèce humaine;
(5) la grande invasion irrésistible sous forme de migration a démarré;
(6) a la longue, l'adaptation à l'agressivité des migrantes peut mener à la disparition des abeilles européennes;
(7) cependant, il existe des obstacles naturels contre l'expansion des abeilles africaines;
(8) force est de constater que les abeilles tueuses se sont emparées des ruches européennes importantes.

Jusqu'ici, le lecteur peut avoir l'impression d'être confronté à une relation écrite de faits vrais, à une sorte de chronique véridique et fidèle d'un accident tel qu'il arrive dans les sciences naturelles; sa compréhension textuelle du récit est basée sur sa connaissance globale des essais expérimentaux: il sait trop bien que dans les laboratoires tout n'est pas contrôlable et qu'il faut s'attendre à d'éventuels accidents.

Cette lecture est brusquement arrêtée, voire détruite et anéantie par l'interprétation implicite donnée dans la dernière phrase qualifiant le texte de fable, donc de récit à base d'imagination et de récit de fiction dont l'intention est, en principe, d'exprimer une vérité générale avec ou sans morale, comme le fait comprendre l'allusion à La Fontaine, déguisée en question rhétorique (Schmitt 2000):

(9) Faut-il vraiment un La Fontaine pour trouver la morale de cette fable si réelle?

Cette question représente donc à la fois un acte illocutoire à valeur pragmatique (Searle 1982) en ce sens qu'elle demande une lecture bien définie, et un acte perlocutoire à force pragmatique par le fait que l'énoncé forme une demande d'information, c'est-à-dire qu'elle demande que l'interlocuteur réponde par «bien sûr, oui, en effet, il y a une morale comme dans les fables de La Fontaine», si bien connues des Français.

La question rhétorique sert donc d'indicateur métatextuel signalant et précisant la pragmatique textuelle (cf. Schmitt 2000): Le texte sur «La mortelle migration des abeilles tueuses» doit être lu non comme récit conventionnel, mais comme récit de fiction (comme les *Fables* de La Fontaine), il ne s'agit pas d'énonciation constative, mais d'acte performatif au sens d'Austin (1970), basé, avant tout, sur l'implicite (cf. Martin 1996) et sur l'insinuation et de nombreux sous-entendus (cf. Récanati 1979).

Nous voilà donc devant un ensemble de phrases ayant la fonction d'une parabole ou d'une allégorie, par conséquent d'un écrit qui ne correspond que matériellement au titre du texte et que son auteur qualifie de récit allégorique sous lequel se cache un enseignement; d'une narration ou d'une description métaphorique dont les éléments constitutifs suivent les règles de cohérence et d'orientation téléologique (Jeandillou 1997) et qui, pour être compris, représentent avec précision une idée générale. Mais quelle serait cette idée et pourquoi, contre toute habitude communicative, l'indication métatextuelle se trouve-t-elle à la fin du texte alors que tout titre de mode d'emploi, par exemple, est toujours antéposé par rapport au texte? L'emploi de signes métaphoriques et de signes symboliques ainsi que la métaphorisation du texte nous font comprendre que cet énoncé est fait pour cacher quelque chose. Le concours de la mémoire discursive, l'acte métatextuel et le souvenir des actions typiques attribuées au groupe de l'énonciateur peuvent nous servir de clé d'accès au texte rédigé en termes cryptiques pour cacher l'information aux non-initiés et camoufler le message qui pourrait constituer l'objet de poursuites juridiques. Le seul emploi des métaphores décelées peut constituer un grand risque pour l'énonciateur; mettons à leur place les signes appropriés et entendus par le public ciblé et un sens tout à fait différent surgira (conforme au message tel qu'il est compris par les lecteurs initiés et habituels familiarisés avec ce type de textes persuasifs):

- les abeilles africaines et européennes tiennent la place d'êtres humains de deux races différentes;
- l'hybridation des deux races, qualifiée de dangereuse, est à remplacer par «croisement entre deux races», phénomène toujours nocif dans la vue du lecteur, puisqu'il crée des êtres qui se «reproduisent beaucoup» et sont «belliqueux et agressifs» et attaquent «tout ce qui se trouve à la portée de leur dard»;
- la *surnatalité* est faite pour aggraver et agrandir le danger de l'immigration;
- dans ce contexte *immigration voulue* se transforme en reproche contre le gouvernement, responsable selon le texte du *désastre* et d'*immigrés* qui ne connaissent ni *éducation* ni *acclimatation*;
- tuer *les reines* dans les *nids d'abeilles européennes* équivaut donc à «menacer la race européenne» (cf. aussi: «la disparition des abeilles européennes»);
- la *grande invasion* constitue une des notions-clés de Jean-Marie Le Pen reprochant à la France de s'être «enfoncée dans un totalitarisme sournois qui, pour faire la chasse aux

idées violant la pensée unique, en vient à interdire l'usage de certains mots» (*Minute*, 4.4.2001, 8). Au moins, dans un récit sur les abeilles, ce mot n'aura rien de politiquement incorrect …
– (et l'on pourrait continuer en précisant cette analyse).

Il est incontestable que nous avons affaire à un discours raciste camouflé pour contourner la législation antiraciste française qui ne permet plus de «dérapages verbaux» (cf. Aubry/ Duhamel 1995, 59 et 132ss.; Jouve/Magoudi 1988, 45). Cet article s'insère parfaitement dans le système à substitutions de mots ou de rubriques pratiqué par *Minute*, publication qui se vante d'être un «*hebdomadaire politiquement incorrect*».

Traitons encore, en quelques mots, un autre exemple basé sur cette comparaison insidieuse entre le monde des humains et le monde animal: «Les pigeons et les Français» (*Présent* 21.10.2000, 4). Cette fois-ci le titre nous invite déjà à une lecture qui établit certains rapports et certaines ressemblances entre les Français et cet oiseau peu estimé que quelques-uns appellent les «rats de l'air» et que d'autres prennent, en général, pour des animaux peu intelligents:

3.2 A la tribune de «Présent»

Les pigeons et les Français

(1) Le pullulement des pigeons détériore nos immeubles et nuit à notre santé; on a décidé de les éliminer. Comment? Nous l'avons vu à la télévision (France 2, Envoyé spécial, 13 avril 2000): on les capture avec un ingénieux filet puis on les met dans la chambre à gaz. Protestations contre cette barbarie qui rappelle d'affreux souvenirs.

(2) Nouvelle formule: une fois pris, le pigeon est anesthésié et, sous contrôle de la SPA, stérilisé; il vivra castrat, tranquille comme un bœuf, mais ne se reproduira pas; un peu plus lentement mais plus proprement, le résultat sera atteint: plus de pigeon.

(3) C'est la même histoire que vit le peuple français. Les socialistes qui se disaient nationaux capturaient des Français et les tuaient dans la chambre à gaz. Ce scandale est fini. Mais maintenant, des socialistes qui ne se disent pas nationaux ont, par haine de la nation, entrepris de réduire à néant notre peuple en empêchant les Français de se reproduire.

(4) C'est plus facile qu'avec les pigeons car il est possible d'agir sur eux par le discours. Pas besoin d'anesthésistes, les médias suffiront; inutiles les bistouris, des lois feront le nécessaire. On combat la famille, on favorise l'homosexualité, on enseigne le contraception, on légalise (et paie) l'assassinat des enfants à naître; comme les pigeons, les Français ne se reproduiront plus guère.

(5) Ne dites pas que j'exagère, qu'il reste des familles françaises avec enfants. Oui, mais il reste aussi beaucoup de pigeons qu'on n'a pas «traités»; c'est pareil. Il est si vrai que le pays se vide qu'on ouvre les portes de la France. Les miséreux du monde viennent remplacer les Français sur la terre bénie qui fut la fille aînée de l'Eglise. Les Français sont des pigeons.

P.-L.M.

Pierre-Louis Mallen, l'auteur du texte, laisse ouverte la question de quels rapports entre Français et pigeons il traitera: la particule *et* est sujette à plusieurs interprétations et susceptible d'exprimer plusieurs relations (NPRob, s.v.).

Nous apprenons des choses ahurissantes et époustouflantes faites pour déconcerter tout «bon» Français aimant son pays natal, donc pour le prototype du bon Bourgeois français:
(1) les pigeons sont mis dans la chambre à gaz, cette barbarie rappelle d'affreux souvenirs;
(2) il existe une méthode plus civile, il est vrai, qui contribuera à la disparition du pigeon;
(3) l'histoire du pigeon serait celle du peuple français empêché à se reproduire par les socialistes pratiquant la haine de la nation;
(4) l'anéantissement de la nation française par la loi serait plus facile encore que l'éradication du pigeon;
(5) l'élimination des Français continuera et se fera en faveur des «miséreux du monde».

Le ton de ce message est plus rude, les sous-entendus s'avèrent plus évidents et la proposition implicite du texte, son inférence, reste plus claire. Il s'agit néanmoins d'un texte qui incite, d'une façon moins métaphorique et moins cryptique, à la haine des étrangers, au racisme et à la calomnie de l'État dirigé, à l'époque de la composition du texte, par le parti socialiste (PS).

La mémoire discursive et la connaissance des actes et de la position du journal ainsi que l'indication des équations les plus importantes nous permettent les identifications suivantes:
– les pigeons sont à remplacer par les Français, jadis mis dans les chambres à gaz, aujourd'hui anesthésiés et stérilisés;
– les actes commis contre les Français rappellent d'affreux souvenirs, ceux qui les commettent ne se distinguent guère des responsables des chambres à gaz;
– les socialistes sont les criminels responsables; ce sont eux qui réduisent à néant le peuple français;
– les lois des socialistes sont du meurtre légalisé;
– le crime contre l'humanité continuera: tous les Français seront «traités»;
– contrairement à la «préférence nationale» de l'extrême droite la gauche prône le principe du rejet et de la haine du peuple français.

Même si l'on admet que la communication est plus ouverte et que ce texte émane plutôt des querelles (peu démocratiques) des partis de la République, il faut cependant constater que même dans cet écrit il est question d'incitation publique à la haine raciste par l'opposition établie entre *Français* et *miséreux du monde* (non français). Dans une définition neutre, *miséreux* est déterminé par le NPRob (2002, s.v.) par «qui donne l'impression de la misère, d'extrême pauvreté»; cet adjectif connaît les synonymes *besogneux, famélique, misérable, nécessiteux, pauvre* et un renvoi à *crève-la-faim, besogneux, malheureux, meurt-de-faim*. De prime abord, ces équivalences textuelles ne provoquent que l'image d'un sort indigne ou digne de pitié, le malheur le plus douloureux et rappellent une extrême pauvreté pouvant aller jusqu'à la privation des choses nécessaires à la vie: c'est l'usage neutre que l'on trouve dans la presse française nationale et internationale. Mais dans la presse de l'extrême droite il s'agit là de synonymes pour «immigrés du Maghreb», de l'Afrique occidentale et d'autres parties du Tiers-Monde, groupe de personnes que l'on refuse pour raisons racistes et dont on aimerait se débarrasser. Il s'agit donc de paroles diffamatoires, et tout le monde sait que les diffamations racistes sont poursuivies (par Art. 32 alinéa 2,3 de la Loi du 29.7.1881, modifié par la Loi du 1.7.1972, complété par la Loi du 13.7.1990):

> La diffamation soit par des discours, cris ou menaces proférés dans les lieux ou réunions publics, soit par des écrits [...] soit par tout moyen de communication audiovisuelle envers une personne ou un groupe de personnes en raison de leur origine ou de leur appartenance ou de leur non-appartenance à une ethnie, une nation, une race ou une religion déterminée sera punie d'emprisonnement d'un mois à un an et d'une amende de 300 F à 300.000 F, ou de l'une de ces deux peines seulement.

La provocation publique à la haine raciste est poursuivie de la même façon (cf. Art. 23.1 et 24 de la Loi du 29.7.1981, modifié par la Loi du 1.7.1972, du 13.12.1985 et du 13.7.1990):

> Ceux qui, soit par des discours, cris ou menaces proférés dans les lieux ou réunions publics, soit par des écrits [...] soit par tout moyen de communication audiovisuelles [...] auront provoqué à la discrimination, à la haine ou à la violence à l'égard d'une personne ou d'un groupe de personnes en raison de leur origine ou de leur appartenance ou de leur non-appartenance à une ethnie, une nation, une race ou une religion déterminée seront punis d'un emprisonnement d'un mois à un an et d'une amende de 2000 F à 30 000 F, ou de l'une de ces deux peines seulement.

4. Discrimination et législation

Ces deux lois (www.perso.vanadoo.fr/mrap.76/) sont en vigueur dans l'Hexagone; le gouvernement français se vante de la législation française: «La France dispose, pour sa part, de l'une des législations antiracistes les plus avancées du monde» (www.justice.gouv.fr/vosdroits/antirac.html). Mais Birenbaum a certainement raison lorsqu'il remarque que les «dérapages verbaux» racistes ne sont pratiquement jamais poursuivis et que pour les journalistes ils ne représentent rien de plus que de simples «cicatrices subies au combat» (1992, 254) contre ce que l'extrême droite appelle la *pensée unique* (p. ex. *National Hebdo* 7.6.-13.6.1991) et dans lequel l'étranger reste et restera le bouc émissaire (Honoré 1986). L'auteur d'une de ces lois, M. Gayssot, doit même se voir discriminer comme *gay* et *sot* («D'autre part, j'ai lu que Jean-Claude Gayssot ‹bénéficie de l'avion privé du PDG de General Electric›, Mr Welsh. [...] Gay-sot ne veut pas d'avion à Bagdad», *Rivarol* du 17.11.2000, 2).

5. Résultats et perspectives

Nous voilà arrivés au terme de notre exposé. Nous croyons avoir montré la nécessité et l'utilité de l'analyse discursive pour toutes sortes de textes dont la fonction est celle de «dire l'interdit» et de cacher les intentions fascistes de leurs auteurs.

Il s'agit de décrire et d'analyser les termes marqués et connotés, l'implicite souvent exprimé par des slogans ou des lieux communs, les différentes stratégies, l'instrumentalisation de noms, de citations ou autres éléments langagiers, des questions rhétoriques (Schmitt 2000) et, avant tout, des métaphores (Bertau 1996), étant donné que ces éléments isotopiques au niveau textuel servent à créer une certaine intimité entre l'énonciateur et ses fidèles et – chose plus importante encore – contribuent à entraver ou même à minimiser la responsabilisation de l'énonciateur réclamant toujours, en cas de litige, le sens littéral et récusant l'interprétation que pourra en faire l'interlocuteur.

Commentant une reformulation de l'énoncé «Quand le mauvais conducteur fait un excès de vitesse, il paie une amende et son permis est délesté de quelques points. Quand un mauvais citoyen se rend coupable de discrimination raciale, on devrait aussi pouvoir lui retirer des points sur son ‹permis de conduire de citoyenneté›»», les rédacteurs de *Minute* qui voulaient recourir à des stratégies et stratagèmes intelligents – je dirais plutôt: produire une ‹overdose› d'esprit ironique – sont arrivés à la conclusion suivante: «La police de la pensée doit donc devenir à la réflexion ce que le gendarme est aux automobilistes» (4.4.2001, 9). L'analyse discursive ne doit pas aller jusqu'à créer une *police de la pensée* mais elle doit, par le biais d'analyses d'énonciations et d'interactions verbales dans toutes leurs polyphonies possibles, contribuer à la défense des droits de l'homme pour faire valoriser un principe que Jean-Paul Sartre a déjà réduit en formule en 1946, au sujet de l'écrivain Richard Wright:

> «Il n'y a pas de problème noir aux Etats-Unis, il n'y a qu'un problème blanc». Nous dirons de la même façon que l'antisémitisme n'est pas un problème juif: c'est notre problème. (196 s.)

Aux linguistes de décortiquer les stratégies servant à contourner le contrôle démocratique et de montrer comment les ruses discursives peuvent être mises au service de fins abjectes et inhumaines!

Références

Angenot, Marc (1982): La parole pamphlétaire. Contribution à la typologie des discours modernes. Paris: Payot.
Aubry, Martine/Duhamel, Olivier (1995): Petit dictionnaire pour lutter contre l'extrême droite. Paris: Seuil.
Austin, John L. (1970): Quand dire, c'est faire. Paris: Seuil.
Bachem, Rolf (1999): Rechtsextreme Ideologien. Rhetorische Textanalysen als Weg zur Erschließung rechtsradikalen und rechtsextremistischen Schriftmaterials. Wiesbaden: Bundeskriminalamt.
Bange, Pierre (1992): Analyse conversationnelle et théorie de l'action. Paris: Hatier-Crédif.
Berrendonner, Alain (1981): Éléments de pragmatique linguistique. Paris: Minuit.
Berrendonner, Alain/Parret, Herman (1990): L'interaction communicative. Berne: Lang.
Bertau, Marie-Cécile (1996): Sprachspiel Metapher. Denkweisen und kommunikative Funktion einer rhetorischen Figur. Opladen: Westdeutscher Verlag.
Birenbaum, Guy (1992): Le Front national en politique. Paris: Balland.
Born, Joachim (1998): Die Sprache des Front national. Faschistischer Diskurs an der Schwelle zum dritten Jahrtausend. In: Born, Joachim/Steinbach, Marion (éds.): Geistige Brandstifter und Kollaborateure. Schrift-Kultus und Faschismus in der Romania. Dresden: Univ. Press, 35-64.
Brinker, Klaus (⁵2001): Linguistische Textanalyse. Eine Einführung in Grundbegriffe und Methoden. Berlin: Schmidt.
Bronckart, Jean-Paul/Bain, Daniel (1985): Le fonctionnement des discours. Neuchâtel, Paris: Delachaux & Niestlé.
Burkhardt, Armin (1996): Politolinguistik. Versuch einer Ortsbestimmung. In: Klein, Josef/Diekmannschenke, Hajo (éds.): Sprachstrategien und Dialogblockaden. Linguistische und politikwissenschaftliche Studien zur politischen Kommunikation. Berlin, New York: de Gruyter, 75-100.
Combettes, Bernard (1992): L'organisation du texte. Metz: Université de Metz.
Cuminal, Isabelle/Souchard, Maryse/Wahnich, Stéphane (1998): Le Pen, les mots. Analyse d'un discours d'extrême droite. Paris: La Découverte.
De Nuchèze, Violaine/Colletta, Jean-Marc (éds.) (2002): Guide terminologique pour l'analyse des discours. Berne: Lang.
Ducrot, Oswald (1972): Dire et ne pas dire. Paris: Hermann.
– (1977): Présupposés et sous-entendus. In: Stratégies discursives. Actes du colloque du Centre de recherches linguistiques et sémiologiques de Lyon, 20-22 mai 1977. Lyon: Centre de recherches linguistiques et sémiologiques de Lyon, 33-43.
– (1984): Le dire et le dit. Paris: Minuit.
Erdmann, Karl Otto (1990): Die Bedeutung des Wortes. Aufsätze aus dem Grenzgebiet der Sprachpsychologie und Logik. Leipzig: Haessel.
Foucault, Michel (1969): L'archéologie du savoir. Paris: Gallimard.
Gayssot, Jean-Claude/Lederman, Charles (1996): Une loi contre l'antisémitisme militant. In: Le Monde, 26.6.1996, 14.
Guland, Olivier (2000): Le Pen, Mégret et les Juifs. L'obsession du «complot mondialiste». Paris: La Découverte.
Haroche, Claudine/Henry, Paul/Pêcheux, Michel (1971): La sémantique et la coupure saussurienne. In: Langages 24, 93-106. Repris in: Pêcheux, Michel/Maldidier, Denise (1990): L'inquiétude du discours. Paris: Cendres, 133-154.
Honoré, Jean-Paul (1986): La hiérarchie des sentiments. Description et mise en scène du Français et de l'immigré dans le discours du Front national. In: Mots 12, 129-157.
Jeandillou, Jean-François (1997): L'analyse textuelle. Paris: Armand Colin.

Jouve, Pierre/Magoudi, Ali (1988): Les dits et les non-dits de Jean-Marie Le Pen. Enquête et psychanalyse. Paris: La Découverte.
Kerbrat-Orecchioni, Catherine (1980): L'énonciation. De la subjectivité dans le langage. Paris: Armand Colin.
– (1986): L'implicite. Paris: Armand Colin.
Klein, Sigrid Michaela (1994): Les Français d'abord. Ideologische Aspekte und ihre sprachliche Inszenierung im Front national. In: Quo vadis Romania? Zeitschrift für eine aktuelle Romanistik 4, 5-32.
Maingueneau, Dominique (1991): L'analyse du discours. Introduction aux lectures de l'archive. Paris: Hachette.
Martin, Robert (1996): Sur l'implicite dans le langage ordinaire: La notion de non-dit. In: Le français moderne 64/2, 129-135.
NPRob = Paul Robert. Le Nouveau Petit Robert. Dictionnaire alphabétique et analogique de la langue française, nouvelle édition, sous la direction de Josette Rey-Debove et Alain Rey. Paris (2002): SNL Robert.
Pêcheux, Michel (1981): L'étrange miroir de l'analyse du discours. In: Langages 62, 5-8.
Récanati, François (1979): Insinuation et sous-entendu. In: Communications 30, 95-106.
Rivarol, Supplément au n° 2500, du 27 octobre 2000, 1-4.
Roulet, Eddy/Auschlin, Antoine/Moeschler, Jacques/Rubattel, Christian/Schelling, Marianne (1985): L'articulation du discours en français contemporain. Berne: Lang.
Sartre, Jean-Paul (1946): Réflexions sur la question juive. Paris: Gallimard.
Schmitt, Christian (2000): Preguntas tendenciosas y preguntas retóricas. Sintaxis contrastiva y traducción entre las lenguas alemana y española. In: Tránsitos. Etudes romanes XVI, homenaje al profesor Rodríguez Richart. Luxembourg: Centre Universitaire, 217-232.
– (2001): Textwissen und wiederholte Rede. Zu neuen Formen medialer Kommunikation im heutigen Spanisch. In: Schröder, Hartmut (éd.): Linguistik als Kulturwissenschaft. Festschrift für Bernd Spillner. Frankfurt a.M. et al.: Lang, 133-146.
– (2004): Sprachliches Handeln und Verantwortlichkeit. Ziel und Zweck linguistischer Analysen von Medienprodukten. In: Lenders, Winfried (éd.): Medienwissenschaft. Eine Herausforderung für die Geisteswissenschaft. Frankfurt a.M. et al.: Lang, 15-49.
Searle, John R. (1982): Sens et expression. Étude de théorie des actes de langage. Paris: Minuit.
Searle, John R./Vanderveken, Daniel (1985): Foundations of illocutionary logic. Cambridge: Cambridge University Press.
Sperber, Dan/Wilson, Deirdre (1989): La pertinence. Communication et cognition. Paris: Minuit.
Taguieff, Pierre-André (1984): La rhétorique du national-populisme. Les règles élémentaires de la propagande xénophobe. In: Mots 9, 113-139.
Vernant, Denis (1997): Du discours à l'action. Paris: Presses Univ. de France.
Wodak, Ruth/de Cillia, Rudolf/Reisigl, Martin/Liebhart, Karin/Hofstätter, Klaus/Kargl, Maria (1998): Zur diskursiven Konstruktion nationaler Identität. Frankfurt a.M.: Suhrkamp.

Raimund Schieß

Lights, camera, action: visualizing TV election nights across cultures[*]

1. Introduction

"Seeing is a great deal more than believing these days," writes Nicholas Mirzoeff (1998, 3) in the introduction to his *Visual Culture Reader*. The present paper focuses on the visual aspects of four recent election night broadcasts: the BBC's and CNN International's coverage of the 1997 British general elections, and the coverage by ARD German Television and by CNN International of the 1998 German parliamentary elections.[1] It analyzes and compares how the different TV channels visually realize the genre 'election night'. A number of disciplines have recently begun to pay increasing attention to the visual dimensions of 'texts'. Perhaps the best example of this 'visual turn' is the emergence of visual culture studies as a new, interdisciplinary field of study.[2] The field considers the visual "an integral part of a culture and of history, not in the sense of a static backdrop [...], but rather as a complexly activating principle" (Shohat/Stam 1998, 45). The importance of visuality and visual data is also making itself felt in some approaches to media discourse, in particular in social semiotics (e.g. Kress/van Leeuwen 1996; Kress/van Leeuwen 1998; Iedema 2001) and critical dis-

---

[*] This paper is part of the research project "Television Discourse", supported by the German Research Foundation (DFG) and directed by Gerda Lauerbach. The goal of the project is a comparative discourse analysis of election night (and, in the case of the US presidential election of 2000, post-election night) television coverage in the United States, Great Britain and Germany. For more information, see http://www.uni-frankfurt.de/zenaf/projekte/TVdiscourses/

[1] This contribution was part of a panel on *Intercultural Media Analysis*, organized for IADA 2003 by Anita Fetzer and Gerda Lauerbach. Within the panel, it was part of a workshop on the topic of *Openings of TV Election Night Broadcasts in Great Britain and Germany* in which the team of the Frankfurt *Television Discourse Project* reported on work in progress. The workshop concentrated on openings as frames which foreshadow for the recipients the content and style of what to expect and which invite preferred interpretations, identities and relations. The other papers in the workshop (all this volume) are by Gerda Lauerbach (on presenting practices), Martin Hampel (on evaluative language and metaphor) and by Annette Becker (on interviews). I am grateful to Gerda Lauerbach, Martin Hampel and Annette Becker for valuable feedback and comments on an earlier draft of this paper, and to Rirhandu Mageza for her editorial assistance.

[2] Mirzoeff (1998, 3) defines visual culture as follows: "Visual culture is concerned with visual events in which information, meaning or pleasure is sought by the consumer in an interface with visual technology. By visual technology, I mean any form of apparatus designed either to be looked at or to enhance natural vision, from oil painting to television and the Internet."

course analysis (Fairclough 1995). Still, at least with respect to television news, the visual element remains "perhaps the most under-theorised element of an otherwise well researched genre" (Graddol 1994, 137).

By concentrating on the visual properties of the election night broadcasts, the present paper also serves to contextualize and complement the three more linguistically-oriented analyses of the same data by Lauerbach, Hampel and Becker (this vol.). I focus on four selected structural elements of the broadcasts' opening phases: the title sequence, the studio setting, the graphics, and the visual management of outside broadcasts. First I briefly discuss the function and significance that each of these elements has for television newscasts in general. Then I analyze how they have been realized by the channels under consideration, given the status of the election night broadcast as a national (BBC, ARD) or an international (CNN) media event.

Title sequences (also called opening sequences) signal the beginning of a newscast and act as "boundary markers" vis-à-vis the previous TV program (Graddol 1994, 147). As Graddol (1994, 147) points out, "[t]he integrity of the [news] genre is crucial to the perception of factuality [...]. Keeping news distinct requires clear boundaries to be created." This is typically achieved by means of dramatic theme music (e.g. fanfares) and computer-animated graphics, whose speed catches the viewer's eye. Allan (1998, 130) calls attention to the "larger performative task" of opening sequences and to "their dramatic role in attracting and maintaining the interest of the viewer".

The *television studio* is the physical context in which newscasts are produced and through which the events of the broadcast are relayed. The significance of the studio, and its relevance as an object of media analysis, is summed up by media researcher Paddy Scannell as follows:

> Talk on radio and television comes from many locations but there is one that is primary and that is the broadcasting studio. [...] The studio is the institutional discursive space of radio and television. It is a public space in which and from which institutional authority is maintained and displayed.
>
> (Scannell 1991, 2)

> Audiences are required to make sense of, to make inferences about, the design, content and manner of radio and television programmes on the basis that their design, manner and content is intended for listeners and viewers to make sense of. The design, layout and lighting of the studio; the age, appearance, sex and dress of participants; the manner and style of how they talk to each other – all these give rise to warrantable inferences about the nature of the event there taking place, the character and status of participants and the relationship of event and participants to viewers and listeners.
>
> (Scannell 1991, 6)

The second part of this quotation spells out a theoretical assumption that informs not only my own paper but also the papers by Lauerbach, Hampel and Becker, which analyze the election night broadcasts from different perspectives.

Graphic displays on television have come a long way – from the handwritten cardboard held into the camera to the sleek, computer-generated 3D graphics called up at the touch of a button. Graphics have become a mainstay of newscasts, displacing the talking heads more and more often. The media's tendency to graphically represent information – whether it's the weather forecast, currency reports or the trajectory of a cruise missile – is part of a larger development – as Mirzoeff (1998, 4) observes, "human experience is now more visual and visualized than ever before". He goes on to argue that "[o]ne of the most striking features of this new visual culture is the visualization of things that are not in themselves visual" (Mirzoeff 1998, 6). Using the example of modern medicine (e.g. brain scans), Mirzoeff (1998, 7) concludes that "visualizing does not replace linguistic discourse but makes it more comprehensible, quicker and more effective." Enhanced comprehensibility, speed and effectiveness are the reasons why producers of newscasts use graphics. Yet as I will demonstrate, some state-of-the-art graphics also serve other, less information-oriented purposes.

While the studio, as Graddol (1994, 148) vividly puts it, "acts as a secure visual base from which forays into the hostile and troubled world may be made", that very world enters the studio and thus eventually the viewer's home by means of *outside broadcasts* (OBs, also called remote broadcasts, or remotes). Live or on tape, a report filed from the very place of interest communicates authenticity and suggests that the information presented has been gathered first-hand. The geographical location of the outside broadcast is often signaled by well-known monuments or buildings visible in the background behind the speaker, such as the Eiffel Tower or Big Ben for reports from Paris or London, respectively. As Morse (1985, 8) points out, visuals of this sort "may actually have no direct connection to an event, but they represent it symbolically." Another issue is the way in which the interaction between studio and outside location is mediated and how the transition from one location to another is visually managed.

Having thus briefly outlined and rendered problematic the four features of newscasts to be included in my visual analysis, I now turn to election night broadcasts in Britain and Germany. How have these four features been realized by different channels in the specific context of an election night?

2. Analysis

2.1 BBC1: *Election 97*

The BBC covered the May 1, 1997 British general elections live for some eight hours, starting at 9:55 pm, five minutes before polling stations in Britain closed. *Election 97* opens with a 50 second title sequence, a collage of images accompanied by a piece of instrumental theme music.[3] The short video clip starts with typical images of British geography, such as the White Cliffs of Dover, and goes on to show the leaders of Britain's three major parties – John Major, Tony Blair, Paddy Ashdown – as well as generic scenes from the voting process (making a cross on a ballot sheet, putting the ballot in a ballot box). After giving us a glimpse of the Houses of Parliament and of the door to No. 10 Downing Street, the sequence ends with the BBC's large 'Election 97'-logo.

The images themselves visually represent the theme of the program, elections in Great Britain, in a fairly conventional, if not stereotypical manner. What makes the title sequence appealing is the way in which these images are framed: most of them are not seen full-screen, in a direct, unmediated shot, but are shown as they appear on monitors and a video wall inside the BBC studio. Like the frame of a painting, the monitors act as a focusing device, giving viewers the impression that they are actively observing a scene through a window (cf. MacLachlan/Reid 1994, 20-21), a window which in this case is an electronic one, a product of modern technology. The images are thus not simply paraded directly in front of the viewer's eyes, but require a more active gaze. At the same time, the title sequence is not only about seeing but also about showing: self-reflexively, the segment shows the BBC showing the election, thus anticipating the BBC's role during the night and in particular the large number of interactions between studio and outside locations, mediated by the video wall. The title sequence thus combines and displays two themes: the election and the coverage of the election.

The huge studio where the BBC's election coverage originates is Studio One of BBC Television Center in London. The studio set, specially designed for the election, has a bright, modern, high-tech look. It has in fact been compared with the bridge of Starship Enterprise (Billen 1997). The studio is large and complex, featuring different specialized areas that are grouped round a circular core or round table, from where the program is anchored. Each of these areas corresponds to an individual member of the studio team and has a specific task or function within the broadcast.

---

[3] The communicative role of the theme music and sound effects used in the election night broadcasts merits a detailed analysis on its own, which is however beyond the scope of the present paper. For a recent approach to the semiotics of music and sound, see van Leeuwen (1999).

During the five minutes leading up to the 10 pm closing of the polls and thus to the presentation of the first exit poll – a moment that the BBC savors by cutting to a live shot of Big Ben striking ten – anchor David Dimbleby gives viewers a carefully choreographed tour of the studio and proudly presents the key players. Sitting on a kind of gallery above the rest of the studio is the BBC's star interviewer Jeremy Paxman, who in the course of the night will be interviewing politicians both face to face in the studio and down-the-line using the video wall. On the ground floor, stationed next to a large graphics screen, we are introduced to statistics expert Peter Snow, who will be illustrating the various results, predictions and exit polls (see below). In addition, Dimbleby introduces three further experts: polling expert Peter Kellner, standing amid several computer workstations, as well as Robin Oakley, the BBC's political editor, and Prof. Anthony King of Essex University, both of whom are sitting at the 'round table' at the center of the studio, to Dimbleby's right. In the background of the studio, we notice dozens of other people, who are not introduced: they are busily working at computers, their backs turned to the camera. These people, and in particular the numerous monitors in front of them, signify immediacy and efficiency, the transmission of up-to-the-minute information gathered by means of the latest technology – a process made seemingly transparent by placing the computer staff in front of the camera, rather than hiding them out of view.

The BBC uses a wide variety of graphics during the election night, ranging from simple tables to computer-animated maps of Britain and landslides that bury candidates. These animated graphics are the responsibility of Peter Snow, who, like Dimbleby, is a veteran of TV election night coverage. Snow is best known perhaps for operating one special instrument that is a fixture of British election night coverage: the swingometer, a device that serves to indicate the swing of the vote to or away from a particular party, illustrating the change in percentage points to the previous election. Back in the days, the swingometer was an actual physical gadget resembling a wheel or a clock, whose hand had to be moved by Snow from one side to another. But Snow, the 'King of Swing', as the *Radio Times* has termed him, has moved with the times, and so in 1997, he is operating a virtual, computer-generated swingometer.[4] Snow explicitly promises to illustrate the election "in a more adventurous and inventive way" than ever before. He thus appeals to values that do not necessarily facilitate the information process but enhance the graphics' entertainment value. In one graphics sequence, for instance, building blocks representing target seats are blown to pieces to the sound of explosions, a scenario reminiscent of video war games (cf. Schieß 2000). Hence, the role of Snow and his graphics is ambivalent: they illustrate and inform, yet they also entertain, using spectacular visual effects to hook viewers to the screens.

---

4   Four years later, for the coverage of the British elections of 2001, the BBC used a laser-beam swingometer, projected in front of Snow.

Another characteristic, prominent feature of the BBC's election coverage is the large number of outside broadcasts that feed news and reactions from key areas into the broadcast. Outside locations are emphasized from the very beginning. Anchor David Dimbleby, even before introducing any of the studio personnel, calls attention to the video wall behind him – the electronic center-piece of the broadcast – and points out some of the places the BBC will be reporting from. In Dimbleby's own words: "We are already at all the places that matter", "we'll be at the party headquarters, we'll be at the key marginal seats", "we'll be in hundreds and hundreds of places". The broadcast thus promises to become a montage of inside and outside.[5]

Formally, the BBC handles the interaction between the studio and the outside broadcast in the following manner: correspondents and interviewees on location are first seen on the video wall inside the studio, as they are addressed by Dimbleby visible in the foreground. This establishing shot is followed by a cut to a direct, unmediated shot of the outside broadcast that fills the entire screen. At the end of the segment, the speaker on location is once again framed on the studio screen, with Dimbleby in the foreground (cf. Marriott 2000, 134). During longer outside broadcasts, and especially during interviews conducted by Dimbleby down the line, the above convention is extended and produces a visual turn-taking that matches the dialogic structure of the interviews, showing the establishing shot during Dimbleby's questions and the unmediated shot of the outside location during answers. This structure, with the establishing shot contextualizing the outside broadcast, gives coherence to the spatial transitions, a coherence that is all the more necessary given the large number and often rapid succession of outside broadcasts.

2.2 ARD German Television: live coverage of the German parliamentary elections

ARD[6] covered the German elections on September 27, 1998 with a special broadcast starting at 5:45 pm – 15 minutes before polls closed in Germany – and lasting to 8 pm, with additional election specials following in the course of the evening. Unfortunately, the first 10 seconds are missing from our recording of the ARD broadcast. The portion that we do have on tape suggests that ARD opens the election special with a panoramic shot of the city of Bonn and its government district, as if seen from a helicopter. There are no additional graphic elements, titles, or theme music; the images are accompanied only by the anchor's

---

5   See Marriott (2000) for a detailed, fascinating analysis of the interplay between different locations and of the "spatiotemporal dynamics" of the BBC election broadcast.
6   ARD (also called "Channel One") is a public service broadcasting system, and its position on the German media market is comparable to that of the BBC in Britain.

live voice-over, declaring that the days of Bonn are numbered and that a touch of nostalgia has taken hold of the government district – references to the fact that at the time, the seat of the German government was about to move from Bonn to Berlin. The visual appeal of the sequence, in which the images of Bonn function as a visual metonymy for the election, stems from the unusual perspective adopted, i.e., from the bird's eye view from which we look down at the city.

The program then cuts to the interior of the election studio, or rather to the place ARD is using as a studio especially for its election coverage: the broadcast originates in Bonn, in a building called "Wasserwerk" [waterworks], which was the seat of the *Bundestag* (the lower house of the German parliament) from 1986 to 1992, while a new assembly hall was under construction. ARD thus covers the election out of a historic building and derives both prestige and authenticity from this locale and its aura. Accordingly, the producers did not have to (and probably were not allowed to) change the overall look of the Wasserwerk-cum-studio very much. Besides desks, chairs and monitors, they only added a few white and blue background panels with an election logo. The overall look of the studio is clear, sober, no-nonsense, with no gimmicks or dramatic design elements. One special decorative element that ARD was surely happy to find in place is the large metal eagle high up on one of the walls, behind what used to be the government benches. The eagle – one of Germany's national symbols – is a visual reminder of the *Wasserwerk*'s place in history as the prior seat of parliament. It might even lend ARD's election coverage a semi-official, authoritative touch.

The program is hosted by Marion von Haaren, at the time editor-in-chief of a regional ARD channel. She uses the opening phase of the program to introduce the studio team, whose members each have their own special area – as in the case of the BBC, the spatial division of the studio correlates with a functional differentiation among the participants. Interviewer Wolfgang Kenntemich is in charge of studio interviews and introduces his panel of five "high caliber" studio guests whom he will interview during the course of the evening. In the back of the studio, a studio audience can be seen at times, and it can be heard applauding while the team members and guests are introduced. The live studio audience, although never explicitly mentioned or introduced, gives the ARD's coverage an air of democracy and transparency as the channel allows average citizens or voters to be present in the studio and to monitor the election coverage. An important team member is Uli Deppendorf, sitting below the eagle, on a semicircular platform. Deppendorf is in charge of statistics and presents the results of exit polls, opinions polls and projections. The polls were commissioned by ARD and were conducted by the polling organization *infratest-dimap*, whose staff are also present in the studio, sitting in front of Deppendorf, yet remain anonymous. As with the BBC, these nameless experts visually represent part of the information process, suggesting that the information presented by Deppendorf does not come 'out of nowhere' but is the result of expert knowledge and computer technology.

The graphics that Deppendorf presents are computer-generated tables and block charts, the design is sleek, modern, 3D but has little in common with the BBC's animated sequences and "computerised pyrotechnics" (Radio Times 1997, 22). While the BBC seems to bet on the gee-whizz effect of its graphics, ARD does without any gimmicks and visualizes information in a sophisticated and modern yet solid and well-established manner.

Throughout the program, ARD reports live from a number of remote locations, though the broadcast's "spatial fragmentation" (Marriott 2000, 140) does not match that of the BBC's *Election 97*. Visually, the outside broadcasts are presented in much the same way as on BBC: the correspondent is first shown on a large monitor inside the studio, conversing with the foregrounded anchor before the program cuts to a full-size shot of the monitor image. As Morse (1985, 9) notes, this shift from mediated to unmediated shot implies that the viewer takes the anchor's position: "The gaze of the interviewee [in an unmediated shot] is frontal and directly aimed at the viewer – but it counts as being aimed at the anchor." The viewer is thus not simply an onlooker, watching two people having a conversation, but becomes, through the interviewee's direct visual address, more strongly involved in the interaction – an effect that is likely to attract viewers' attention and increase audience appeal.

2.3 CNN International: *Britain Decides* and *Germany Decides*

How does the 24-hour international news channel CNN International (CNN-I) cover Britain's and Germany's national elections? For both elections, CNN-I changed its regular programming to bring special extended live coverage. In each case, the main election special started minutes before the official poll closing time and lasted two hours.

Britain Decides starts with a 13 second title sequence, accompanied by a lively instrumental theme tune. The clip features a sequence of images, asymmetrically superimposed over a full-size fluttering Union Jack: a hand dropping a ballot in a ballot box, voters in front of a ballot box, and the leaders of the three major British parties. The sequence ends as the large banners "Britain Decides" and "the vote" appear on the screen.

Meanwhile, the 15 second sequence that opens *Germany Decides*, accompanied by a piece of solemn, dramatic instrumental theme music, is visually more intricate than the one we saw for the British elections. Superimposed over a white background is a succession of lines and squares that scroll across the screen – the overall layout is reminiscent of Malevitch's geometric abstractions. In the upper and the lower sections of the screen, the squares are filled with black-and-white images of Germany, the voting process, and German politics: the Bundestag, the candidates Schröder and Kohl, people standing in line inside a polling station, factory chimneys, the Brandenburg Gate, etc. As thin lines – some of them black, red, and yellow – move vertically down the screen, words such as "Germany", "elections" and "vote" float across the screen. At the end of the clip, below an image of a hand placing a ballot in a ballot box, a large black, red and yellow banner reading "Germany Decides" appears and announces the title of the program.

Despite the numerous stylistic differences, the two title sequences have one striking feature in common: they both use the countries' national colors or national flag as a design element – an element that is noticeably absent from the coverage by the two national broadcasters, BBC and ARD. One way of explaining this difference would be to point out CNN-I's status as an international channel with a global audience. By using national symbols (not only in the title sequence but, giving visual coherence to different segments of the program, as a part of its captions and graphic displays), CNN-I visually signals to its viewers around the world that it has temporarily focussed its coverage on one particular country. CNN-I's appropriation of national symbols also suggests that the channel is in close touch with the country in question and is thus competent to report on that country. For the BBC and ARD, the country they are covering on election day is quite obvious, it is implied by the channels' status as national broadcasters, and there is therefore less of a need to draw attention to the respective countries.[7] However, this explanation has to be reviewed if one includes in the analysis material from CNN's coverage of US elections, e.g. the way in which CNN-USA (the network's domestic channel), covers the US Presidential elections of 1996 or 2000. Here, the Stars and Stripes figures prominently throughout the program, something which can be explained by the important role that the US flag plays within the country's national culture in general. Seen against this backdrop, there emerges another possible explanation of CNN-I's use of national flags and national colors for the British and German elections: the US-based CNN-I may have transferred practices from its own national culture onto its international coverage.

The studios from which CNN-I is reporting on the elections in Britain and Germany are remarkably similar: both can be described as small, basic, unspectacular, and their design bears no special relation to the election. In London, the studio features an L-shaped desk with just enough room for anchor Richard Blystone and his two local experts. The wall behind them shows what appears to be a collage of architectural elements taken from British historic monuments, as well as a large sign reading "CNN London". In Düsseldorf, located in the buildings of CNN's German partner N-TV, the CNN studio (referred to as "German Election Center" in the captions) consists of a triangular desk where anchor Bettina Lüscher

---

[7] This difference also shows in the titles given to the BBC's and CNN-I's election night programs: in Britain, viewers of the BBC's "Election 97" readily infer from this title that the program is covering the British elections. By contrast, CNN-I and its global audience do not share the same deictic center, and it is therefore necessary to use titles such as "Britain Decides" or "Germany Decides", which explicitly name the country in question.

is joined by one local expert. In the background, we see several television monitors as well as a small office area with people working at computers. This gives viewers a glimpse of some of the activity going on behind the scenes. The logo "CNN D" (short for "CNN Deutschland" ['CNN Germany']), visible on a column behind Lüscher, refers to CNN's small German-language window. For those viewers able to understand this reference, the logo suggests that CNN-I possesses local expertise drawn from a news staff permanently based right in Germany.

CNN-I also goes local when it comes to exit polls and projections: for both elections, CNN-I relies on data provided by national channels, among them the BBC and ARD. The information presented by CNN-I is thus second-hand, yet at the same time, in a move that compromises CNN's position as the world's self-declared "news leader", the channel borrows authenticity from the national broadcasters by crediting the data to them. After all, who if not the venerable BBC could be a more reliable source of information on the British elections? The graphics that CNN-I uses to illustrate the data are mostly blockcharts overlaid on the same background that was seen during the title sequences – the British flag, and a white background with geometric shapes, respectively.

These backgrounds are also used during outside broadcasts. Unlike the BBC or ARD, CNN-I does not use establishing shots showing the anchor as s/he addresses the correspondent or interviewee on a studio screen. Instead, CNN-I has opted for another fairly common technique to contextualize the outside broadcast and to visually represent the interaction between studio and remote location: using a split-screen effect, CNN-I shows the anchor and the correspondent simultaneously in separate picture frames, superimposed over the above-mentioned backgrounds. Once the anchor has finished his/her turn, the program cuts to a full-size shot of the correspondent. This use of two simultaneous frames as a convention for representing dialogue requires a certain amount of visual literacy on the part of the viewers: both anchor and correspondent are looking directly at the camera – their gaze is aimed at the viewer but is conventionally interpreted as being aimed at each other. Whereas in the establishing shot of the type used by the BBC and ARD, the viewer is an onlooker watching the anchor address the correspondent, who is magnified on a large screen (cf. Morse 1985, 9), in the split-screen format, the viewer can escape neither the anchor's nor the correspondent's gaze.

3. Concluding remarks

The visual analysis of the four election night broadcasts presented in this paper has yielded, quite literally, many "in-sights" into the programs – notably into how they represent information, or how they attempt to capture the attention of restless viewers.

Of the four programs analyzed, the BBC's *Election 97* is the most visual and visualized – it is truly an election night *show* (which is not to say that the BBC is substituting effect for content). Broadcasting from hip, high-tech studios and using cutting-edge, computer-generated visual effects, the BBC offers its viewers quite a bit of 'eye candy', tempting them to stay tuned. Meanwhile, the visual format used by ARD is more of the quiet, discreet 'tone in tone' type. Rather than using dazzling gadgetry, the channel relies on the appeal of the historic *Wasserwerk*. CNN International is looking at the two elections through an international relevance filter and covers both events from small, static, everyday, rather inconspicuous studios. Much like ARD, CNN-I is restrained in its use of visual devices. One noticeable feature of CNN-I's coverage is the way the channel repeatedly employs national flags in order to anchor its coverage to a particular country.

The analysis given here is certainly not exhaustive. Rather, I have opted for an overview, based on different units of analysis and drawing on various methods of visual analysis. To round off the picture, further contextual information is necessary, e.g. on the economics and the politics of the media in the countries involved. The visual is, of course, just one aspect of the programs analyzed – the ultimate goal should be a truly multimodal analysis that takes into account the interplay of different semiotic resources. As Shohat/Stam (1998, 45) put it, "[t]he visual is just one point of entry [...] into a multidimensional world of intertextual dialogism".

References

Allan, Stuart (1998): News from NowHere: Televisual news discourse and the construction of hegemony. In: Bell, Allan/Garrett, Peter (eds.): Approaches to media discourse. Oxford: Blackwell, 105-141.
Billen, Andrew (1997): Beamed up, beamed down. In: New Statesman, May 1997 special ed., 28-29.
Fairclough, Norman (1995): Media discourse. London: Arnold.
Graddol, David (1994): The visual accomplishment of factuality. In: Graddol, David/Boyd-Barrett, Oliver (eds.): Media texts: Authors and readers. Clevedon: Multilingual Matters and The Open University, 136-160.

Iedema, Rick (2001): Analyzing film and television: A social-semiotic account of *Hospital: An Unhealthy Business*. In: Leeuwen, Theo van/Jewitt, Carey (eds.): Handbook of visual analysis. London: Sage, 183-204.
Kress, Gunther/Leeuwen, Theo van (1996): Reading images. The grammar of visual design. London: Routledge.
Kress, Gunther/Leeuwen, Theo van (1998): Front pages: (the critical) analysis of newspaper layout. In: Bell, Allan/Garrett, Peter (eds.): Approaches to media discourse. Oxford: Blackwell, 186-219.
Küng-Shankleman, Lucy (2000): Inside the BBC and CNN. Managing media organisations. London: Routledge.
Leeuwen, Theo van (1999): Speech, music, sound. London: Macmillan.
Leeuwen, Theo van/Jewitt, Carey (eds.) (2001): Handbook of visual analysis. London: Sage.
MacLachlan, Gale/Reid, Ian (1994): Framing and interpretation. Melbourne: Melbourne UP.
Marriott, Stephanie (2000): Election night. In: Media, Culture & Society 22, 131-150.
Mirzoeff, Nicholas (1998): What is visual culture? In: Mirzoeff, Nicholas (ed.): The visual culture reader. London: Routledge, 4-13.
Morse, Margaret (1985): Talk, talk, talk. In: Screen 26/2, 2-15
Radio Times (1997): Election 97: The night watchmen. 26 April – 2 May, 20-22.
Scannell, Paddy (1991): Introduction: The relevance of talk. In: Scannell, Paddy (ed.): Broadcast talk. London: Sage, 1-13.
Schieß, Raimund (2000): Of ballots and battlegrounds: Metaphorizing elections as war. Paper presented at the Annual Meeting of the British Association for Applied Linguistics (BAAL). Cambridge.
Shohat, Ella/Stam, Robert (1998): Narrativizing visual culture. Towards a polycentric aesthetics. In: Mirzoeff, Nicholas (ed.): The visual culture reader. London: Routledge, 27-49.
Tolson, Andrew (1996): Mediations: Text and discourse in media studies. London: Arnold.
Zettl, Herbert (^{6}1997): Television production handbook. Belmont, CA: Wadsworth.

Gerda Lauerbach

Election nights: a cross-cultural analysis of presenting practices*

1. Introduction

Television election nights are complex textual units extending over many hours of live broadcasting. They usually start shortly before the polls close and then accompany the process of projected or real election results becoming known and of a new government slowly taking shape. This paper will focus on a cross-cultural analysis of how these macro-texts are constructed in their opening stages by the presenters or anchors of these programmes.[1] In this introductory section, I will briefly address the project of mono-cultural and cross-cultural analysis of media discourse, before going on to discuss the macro-features of television election nights in section 2. The analysis is in section 3. The data are the opening stages of the programmes broadcast by the BBC on the British parliamentary elections of 1997, by the German public service channel ARD on the German parliamentary elections of 1998, and by CNN International on both of these elections. The results of the analysis will be discussed in section four.

Discourse, media and cultural studies theorists alike have argued that the news is not the objective representation of an independently given reality but the construction of a perspectivized text, all textual construction, of necessity, being grounded in a point of view. Nevertheless, texts offer a range of potential reading positions but privilege one or more of

---

* This paper is part of the research project "Television Discourse", supported by the German Research Foundation (DFG) and directed by the author. The goal of the project is a comparative discourse analysis of election night (and, in the case of the US presidential election of 2000, post-election night) television coverage in the United States, Great Britain and Germany. For more information, see http://www.uni-frankfurt.de/zenaf/projekte/TVdiscourses

1 This contribution is based on a paper presented in the panel on *Intercultural Media Analysis*, organized for IADA 2003 by Anita Fetzer and the author. Within the panel, it was part of a workshop on the topic of *Openings of TV Election Night Broadcasts in Great Britain and Germany* in which the team of the Frankfurt Television Discourse Project reported on work in progress. The workshop concentrated on openings as frames which foreshadow for the recipients the content and style of what to expect, and which invite preferred reading positions. The other papers in the workshop (all this volume) are by Raimund Schieß (on visualization), Martin Hampel (on evaluative language and metaphor) and by Annette Becker (on interviews). The paper has profited from discussions with all three. Thanks go also to Rirhandu Mageza and Vanessa Tomala for editorial assistance.

these over others. These privileged reading positions will reaffirm shared cultural coding conventions, interpretation rules, norms and values. Critical discourse analysts hold that this common ground is nothing but the naturalization of the hegemonial view, due to relations of power in a society and privileged access to the public sphere by the powerful (cf. the contributions in Bell/Garrett 1998, Fowler 1987, 1991, Fowler/Kress 1979, Fairclough 1989, 1992, 1995, Hall 1973). It is consequently the project of Critical Discourse Analysis to lay open the underlying naturalized assumptions, coding conventions and preferred reading positions, and to confront them with alternative ones that are equally possible, but not realized in a culture (see the contributions in Wodak/Meyer 2001). The cross-cultural analysis of media discourse similarly has as its goal the description of underlying common ground assumptions and coding conventions, as well as the foregrounded and the backgrounded reading positions of a culture. However, it then goes on to confront them with those of another culture. The advantages of such comparative research have been succinctly summed up by Gurevitch/ Blumer (1990, 308f.): it rests on a wide and varied data base, it counteracts any culture-centric bias in mono-cultural analysis that may remain unreflected otherwise, and it makes visible the unchallenged assumptions that are taken for granted in the analyst's own culture. Cross-cultural media analysis has the confrontation with different ways of doing the "same" thing built into its method (though not necessarily from a critical perspective).

2. Election nights

Election night broadcasts are particularly well suited for comparative analysis. They are important national media events and in spite of national differences in political systems and mass media regulations, they are highly ritualized in similar ways. They draw large audiences, they have similar goals, deal with similar topics, use similar discourse strategies and a similar variety of media formats and genres to realize them. Because they are broadcast live, these programmes are good data for a comparative analysis of unscripted but routinized discourse practices, practices through which the privileged reading positions for the event and the culturally specific identities and relations for the media, for politics, and for the public are constructed. In addition, these broadcasts are special in another way. They are probably the only news format in which the viewers are not merely unseen witnesses or overhearing audience (cf. Heritage 1995, Heritage/Clayman/Zimmerman 1988, Heritage/Greatbatch 1991, Allen 1998). On election night, the television audience is, to a considerable extent, identical with one of the major newsmakers of the day – how they have voted is after all what the programme is about.

Election nights 45

TV election nights are also different from other media events like cup finals, which are broadcast live from one location. During the broadcasts, politicians are in their constituencies all over the country, awaiting the declaration of their results (in Britain), or in their national party headquarters or local party offices (in Germany). The national channels have correspondents and camera teams "in all the places that matter" (David Dimbleby, BBC) to bring the news from these outside locations into the studio (see Schieß, this volume). It is the task of the presenters of such programmes to construct, for the television audience, a comprehensible and coherent whole from these many simultaneous and spatially dispersed happenings. They do this by commenting on live events like declarations of results, by introducing live reports by correspondents, or by interviewing newsmakers on outside locations. But the complexity does not stop there. The anchor, as the central person in the studio, interacts with participants in the studio as well. Presenters talk to experts and interviewers, may themselves interview politicians in the studio, may talk to studio guests, possibly a studio audience and, mainly in the case of things going wrong, to members of the production team, all of this for the benefit of an overhearing audience. But they also, particularly in the opening stages of the night and of media genres like reports and interviews, talk to the television audience directly. Presenters have to be able to change their footing constantly (Goffman 1981).

Fig. 1 is a representation of the components of the election night broadcasts in our data: The STUDIO, with its participants; the OUTSIDE, with its places, its events (social events, political speech events, media speech events) and its participants who, in interaction with the presenters in the studio (symbolized by the bold two-headed arrow in the graph), contribute to the construction of the night's live broadcast addressed to the TV AUDIENCE.[2] As mentioned before, this audience is partly identical with the electorate and with those who have actually voted. The grey two-headed arrow between the audience and the outside participants signifies that the latter may be part of the former. The outside participants are following the broadcast in their various locations and, when becoming active participants in the media event, e.g. by being interviewed, or just shown watching television, can be shown to react, to orient and to refer to what they have seen or heard (Marriott 2000). The two-headed broken arrow between audience and studio symbolizes the same relation between studio participants and audience: presenters and others in the studio are following the live broadcast, their own and those of their competitors, or have people who do and who prime them with relevant information that can then be replayed self-reflexively e.g. in interviewer questions (Marriott 2000, Lauerbach 2003).

Thus it is not just the television audience in the usual sense, but all other participants as well, who seem to be watching the unfolding television event all the time in order to know

---

[2] I thank Raimund Schieß for assistance with this graph.

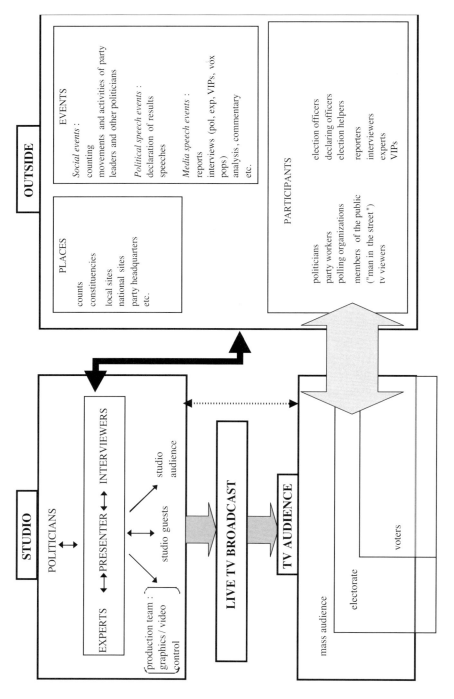

Fig. 1: Macro schema "TV election night"

Election nights 47

what is going on elsewhere and to be able to react to it if and when the occasion arises. Marriott (2000, 136) has pointed out the dynamic nature of this process, in which "the television event begins to construct itself self-referentially out of meta-discursive exchanges in and between spatially dispersed locations as encounters with successive sites impact in turn upon each other." This sounds a bit like the turn-taking machinery which, once started up, goes on and on almost of its own accord. But like the turn-taking system, election nights have to be set in motion and it is to the analysis of the presenting practices with which this is achieved that I now turn.

3. Constructing the openings

Openings are frames in the Goffmanian sense in that they put a perspective and a focus on the perception of an event (Goffman 1974, ch.2). In news interviews, they serve to present an agenda and articulate it with the current events of the day. They are also the only part of the interview that is addressed to the audience directly (Clayman 1991). This is not much different for election nights although of course their openings are much more elaborate. Based on functional criteria and due to space restrictions, I will take my analysis up to the announcement of the exit polls, although the channels involved differ formally in terms of sequence length (BBC 5 minutes, ARD 15 and CNN 3 minutes each).

The questions I shall be addressing are: (1) What kinds of audience identities and relations between channel, audience and politics are being constructed? (2) What kinds of identities are being constructed for the journalists in the studio and outside, and what kinds of relations between them and the presenters? The features that are relevant for these questions are address terms and pronouns (see Becker, this volume), referential and action descriptions, the degree of topic control imposed on outside correspondents (cf. Scollon 1998, ch.5) and the speech acts with which the floor is passed back and forth. The frameworks I will be adapting to my data are Scollon's (1998) concept of a hierarchy of channel, relationship and topic frames and of the "implicationally nested social practices" with which these are opened and closed, as well as Clayman's (1991) analysis of the openings of news interviews.

There is much uniformity across national and international channels as regards the stages of their opening sequences and, often, their content. But while the BBC has all of the following stages, the German ARD lacks (1) and (3) and both CNN broadcasts, due to their small local studios, do not have (4):

(1) Opening
(2) Lead-in
(3) Background
(4) Projecting the agenda in the studio
(5) Projecting the agenda at outside locations
(6) Announcing the exit polls/projections

(1) – (3) and (6) are spoken directly to camera/audience, (4) and (5) go from direct audience address to interaction with media personnel for an overhearing audience. The OPENING follows the title sequence, with which the channel frame was opened (see Schieß, this volume). It opens the relationship frame:

(1) OPENING FRAME

UK97 BBC	FRG98 ARD	UK97 CNN	FRG98 CNN
Good evening		Hello and welcome to our live coverage of Britain's election I'm Richard Blystone	Hello and welcome to CNN's special coverage of the German vote I'm Bettina Lüscher

The BBC's sparse *Good Evening* contrasts with CNN's more elaborate greeting, welcome and self-identification. The difference attests to the different audiences they are orienting to: the presenters of CNN International cannot take for granted the same degree of familiarity that David Dimbleby can claim from his national audience. The omission of self-identification can be taken as an in-group marker, constructing and reaffirming closeness between channel and audience. This would also hold for the German ARD, which without even a greeting goes straight from title sequence to LEAD-IN. The lead-in corresponds to Clayman's (1991) pre-headline in interview openings and serves to articulate the programme with the events of the day.

(2) LEAD-IN

UK97 BBC
For weeks we've watched the politicians slugging it out together. Tonight at last we hear the voters' verdict as they tell us who's won.

FRG98 ARD
The days of Bonn are numbered but today the city holds centre stage one more time. For a super election day is ending. Now begins the hour of the pollsters, the counters, the statisticians.

UK97 CNN
The last votes are being cast right now and, if the polls are right, an era is ending.

FRG98 CNN
In just a few moments, polling stations here will close and the first exit poll will be announced.

Together with the BACKGROUND, these early sequences set the tone for the way in which these channels will be constructing their broadcasts: the excited, hyperbolic, casual, ingroup style of the BBC (see Hampel, this volume), and the self-consciously dramatic and more formal style of the ARD contrast with the matter-of-fact way in which the CNN presenters deliver their information. Note in particular the complex and informationally dense nominal phrases in both UK97 CNN and FRG98 CNN:

Election nights 49

(3) BACKGROUND
UK97 BBC
If the opinion polls through this campaign are borne out tonight, we're likely to see one of the biggest political upsets since the Tories were swept out of office in 1945. It is at any rate going to be a very, very exciting political night.

FRG98 ARD

UK97 CNN
For the polls for weeks have said that 18 years of conservative rule begun by Margaret Thatcher, carried on by John Major is about to end in a Labour Party landslide. In those 18 years, Britain has changed profoundly.

FRG98 CNN
Four-term Christian-Democrat Chancellor Helmut Kohl has been locked in a tough campaign with Social Democrat challenger Gerhard Schröder.

The ARD presenter provides no background information at this stage. Instead, she goes straight into stage (4), which is interesting for its audience orientation:

(4.1) PROJEKT AGENDA: studio – FRG98 ARD
PRES: How YOU, dear viewers, have voted today will be revealed by Ulrich Deppendorf and the Infratest team in a few moments, and how the results are to be evaluated will be discussed by Wolfgang Kenntemich with our guests.

The address *dear viewers* [liebe Zuschauer] is quite normal on German television but totally absent in the BBC and CNN data. In combination with the preceding, emphatic *YOU*, high addressee orientation is expressed (Becker, this volume). Also, the audience is explicitly addressed in their capacity as voters, and how they have voted is construed as the important topic of the evening. Two groups are constructed: the audience, who did the voting, and the television journalists, who will be doing the reporting. Contrast this with the BBC's lead-in, in (2) above, in which *we* includes the presenter/the BBC and the audience, and where this grouping is reinforced by soliciting the audience's complicity in the presenter's negative evaluation of the politicians and their election campaigns (*slugging it out*). Presenter and audience are gathered to *hear the voters' verdict as they tell us who has won*. So here the groupings are between the BBC and its audience on the one side, and the voters on the other. Although election nights are dramatic events for the BBC, reporting on the results is a story like any other, to be presented to an audience whose role is no different from that on other news nights.

Let us now briefly look at how audience identity is constructed in relation to the channel and to the politicians and other powerful personages by the German station. Below is the continuation of the ARD excerpt above:

(4.2) PROJEKT AGENDA: studio FRG98 ARD

> WK: Yes, dear viewers ... to help you find your way in the maze of prognoses, projections, speculations, we have invited some high-calibre guests and experts for you.
> Here is Dieter Schulte, the President of the German Trade Union Council...

Again we have the emphatic orientation to an audience which here is constructed as being in need of help in comprehending the complexities of the election, and a television channel which is willing to provide that guidance and which is, by virtue of its authority, able to do this through enlisting the cooperation of powerful members of society. Contrast this with the BBC's construction of the media as watchdog over the politicians on behalf of the audience, noting again the casual tone:

(4.3) PROJEKT AGENDA: studio UK97 BBC

> PRES: All through the night, politicians will be coming here and be called to account by Jeremy Paxman (*delegation by gesture*)
> JP: Yes, (*to cam*) over the next 18 hours we shall have a succession of victors, vanquished and walking wounded up here to explain what went right, what went wrong, and what happens now in their respective parties. We'll be joined in a moment by...

This light-handed informality is also typical for the way in which the BBC presenter introduces the channel's studio experts: *Our experts up there ARE LOOKING AT ALL OF THAT and Peter Kellner WILL TELL ALL ... Robin Oakley, the BBC'S political editor, will be LOOKING AT the battles that lie ahead ...* The casual language with which complex analytical activities are referred to constructs closeness to the audience's everyday, while through this very informality simultaneously flaunting the BBC's intellectual superiority.

That this is the image the BBC wishes to project and at the same time to ironically subvert becomes clear in the first outside broadcast, which is from a helicopter:

(5.1) PROJEKT AGENDA: outside locations UK97 BBC

> PRES: And in addition to many correspondents, we have one special roving reporter tonight, Frank Skinner.[3]
> FS: Hello David! We're in MIDAIR! We're gonna get to Leeds, Manchester, Birmingham, I'm gonna get the word on the street, I'm gonna supply a sort of low-brow, down-at-heel counterpoint to your intellectual analysis in the studio. I'm sort of BBC's bit of rough for the night.

Spoken in an emphatically non-RP accent, this is designed to haul in Middle England, in the geographical as well as the social sense. Neither the German ARD nor the two broadcasts by CNN on the British and the German election even attempt to do anything comparable.

As far as delegating the floor to reporters on outside locations is concerned, the practices of the BBC and of CNN are very similar and contrast sharply with those of the ARD.

---

[3] Frank Skinner is a stand-up comedian with his own television show.

Election nights 51

The differences are in each of the components of delegation frames: the identification of the reporter by name, the degree of constraint in functional and topical terms on the reporter's contribution, and the actual passing of the floor (cf. Scollon 1998,ch.5). Compare the excerpts in (5.2), which are typical of the respective channels:[4]

(5.2) PROJEKT AGENDA: outside locations
 FRG98 ARD
 PRES: It's a tight scrape, dear viewers, whether things will work out for Gerhard Schröder at the SPD. And there ... I now greet Rolf-Dieter Krause. What are the bets there?
 R-DK: (reports)
  Back to the *Wasserwerk* for the time being.
 PRES: Thank you very much, Rolf-Dieter Krause.

UK97 CNN	UK97BBC
PRES: Now at Conservative Central Office we'll hear from CNN's Siobhan Darrow. Hello Siobhan.	PRES: And two battle-hardened correspondents back at the front line tonight. John Simpson in Sedgefield with Tony Blair, and Kate Adie with John Major in Huntingdon.
SD: Hallo Richard (reports) Richard	John!
PRES: Siobhan	JS: (reports)
	PRES: and Kate Adie
	KA: (reports)
	PRES: Thanks, Kate.

The ARD delegation frame is fully elaborated: The reporter is being introduced with first and last name in an explicit performative speech act of greeting, and the floor is passed to him with a question which imposes strict topical constraints on his contribution. At the end of his report, he explicitly passes the floor back to the election studio, and is elaborately thanked by the presenter. The CNN delegation frame introduces the reporter with location, full name and channel affiliation. The delegation however uses first names only and is achieved with an adjacency pair of greetings, and the closing of the delegation frame with an adjacency pair of vocatives. The BBC's actual delegations are the most minimal, making do with a bare first name vocative, except where the reporter is re-introduced with first name and last name, which also serves as delegation (*and Kate Adie*). Also, they are unilateral – there is no acknowledgment of the floor by the reporters and no passing back of the floor to the presenter. The impression is one of a smoothly-functioning, closely-knit team – but there is no doubt about who is in charge. Regarding topical control, it might seem that CNN and BBC impose none at all, but their presenters rely of course on the normative expectations of what a reporter can tell the audience in this discursive position. The difference

---

[4] For the way in which the channels construct visual coherence in the delegations, see Schieß, this volume.

is that the German channel spells these out. With respect to audience and channel roles, these are again neatly separated with the ARD (*dear viewers – there I now greet*). CNN on the other hand casts channel and audience together as recipients of the outside correspondent's report (*We'll hear from*. Other delegation formulae favoured by CNN are *let's go now to, we're joined by*). The BBC's audience meanwhile has disappeared into the invisible onlooker role.

4. Concluding remarks

Some interesting differences have emerged in this analysis which will enable us to formulate more precise hypotheses about cross-cultural variation in the rest of our data. Compared to the presenting practices of the BBC and CNN International, those of the German ARD are generally more formal, both in its relations with the audience and in its interactions with experts and channel personnel. Specifically with reporters, they are more hierarchical, controlling and explicit than those of the Anglo-Saxon channels. With respect to relations between channel and audience, there is a clear division between the two in the German channel. The BBC starts with channel-audience inclusion in the lead-in, but casts the audience as overhearers in the delegations to outside reporters. In CNN this is the other way round. Only the German channel addresses the audience as voters.

When comparing the channels with respect to the relations between audience, media personnel and politicians, it may be helpful to refer to Blumer/Gurevitch's (1995, 15) proposal of the following four sets of complementary participant roles:

Audience	Media Personnel	Politicians
(1) partisan	editorial guide	gladiator
(2) liberal citizen	moderator	rational persuader
(3) monitor	watchdog	information provider
(4) spectator	entertainer	actor/performer

We can hypothesize at this stage that the German ARD, with its paternalistic formality has features of 1 and 2. CNN, with its professional service-orientation to an international audience, corresponds most closely to the features in 2. The BBC is firmly established at the lower end of the table, combining a commitment to the watchdog role with a tendency towards sophisticated verbal (and visual[5]) entertainment.

---

5   See Schieß, this volume.

References

Allan, Stuart (1998): News from NowHere: Televisual news discourse and the construction of hegemony. In: Bell, Allan/Garrett, Peter (eds.): Approaches to media discourse. Oxford: Blackwell, 105-141.
Becker, Annette (this volume): Interviews in election night broadcasts: A framework for cross-cultural analysis.
Bell, Allan/Garrett, Peter (eds.) (1998): Approaches to media discourse. Oxford: Blackwell.
Blumler, Jay. G./Gurevitch, Michael (1995): The crisis of public communication. London: Routledge.
Clayman, Stephen (1991): News interviews openings – Aspects of sequential organization. In: Scannel, Paddy (ed.): Broadcast talk. London: Sage, 48-75.
Fairclough, Norman (1989): Language and power. London, New York: Longman.
– (1992): Discourse and social change. Cambridge: Polity Press.
– (1995): Media discourse. London: Edward Arnold.
Fowler, Roger (1987): Notes on critical linguistics. In: Threadgold, Terry/Steele, Ross (eds.): Language topics: Essays in honour of Michael Halliday. Amsterdam: Benjamins.
– (1991): Language in the news: Discourse and ideology in the press. London: Routledge.
Fowler, Roger/Kress, Gunther (1979): Critical linguistics. In: Fowler, Roger/Hodge, Bob/Kress, Gunther/Trew, Tony (eds.): Language and control. London, Boston, Henley: Routledge and Kegan Paul, 185-213.
Goffman, Erving (1974): Frame analysis – An essay on the organization of experience. Boston: Northeastern University Press.
– (1981): Footing. In: Goffman, Erving (ed.): Forms of talk. Oxford: Blackwell, 124-157.
Gurevitch, Michael/Blumler, Jay G. (1990): Comparative research: The extending frontier. In: Swanson, David L./Nimmo, Dan (eds.): New directions in political communication. A resource book. Newbury Park, London, New Delhi: Sage, 305-325.
Hall, Stuart (1973): A world at one with itself. In: Cohen, Stanley/Young, Jack (eds.): The manufacture of news. London: Constable, 85-94.
Hampel, Martin (this volume): Intersubjective positioning in election night discourse. A cross cultural analysis.
Heritage, John/Clayman, Steven/Zimmerman, Don (1988): Discourse and message analysis – The micro-structure of mass media messages. In: Hawkins, R.P./Wiemann, John M./Pingree, Suzanne (eds.): Advancing communication science: Merging mass and interpersonal processes. Newbury Park: Sage, 77-109.
Heritage, John/Greatbatch, David (1991): On the institutional character of institutional talk: The case of news interviews. In: Boden, Deidre/Zimmerman, Don (eds.): Talk and social structure. Cambridge: Polity Press, 93-137.
Heritage, John/Roth, Andrew L. (1995): Grammar and institution: Questions and questioning in the broadcast news interview. In: Research on Language and Social Interaction 28/1, 1-60.
Lauerbach, Gerda. (2003): Voicing and ventriloquizing – The constructive role of discourse representation in political interviews. In: Zeitschrift für Interkulturellen Fremdsprachenunterricht 8/2-3 (Sonderheft). Festschrift für Juliane House zum 60. Geburtstag, 176-186.
Marriott, Stephanie (2000): Election night. In: Media, Culture & Society 22, 131-150.
Schieß, Raimund (this volume): Lights, camera, action: Visualizing election nights across cultures.
Scollon, Ron (1998): Mediated discourse as social interaction – A study of news discourse. Harlow, Essex: Addison Wesley Longman.
Wodak, Ruth/Meyer, Michael (eds.) (2001): Methods of critical discourse analysis. London et al.: Sage.

Martin Hampel

Intersubjective positioning in election night discourse
A cross cultural analysis*

1. Introduction

The subject of this paper is the cross-cultural analysis of television election nights, focussing on the micro-level of linguistic and discourse analysis. The data examined was broadcast by BBC and CNN International covering the 1997 British General Election and the 1998 German Parliamentary elections (ARD and CNN International).[1] For the analysis, I draw on the model of Critical Discourse Analysis as developed by Norman Fairclough (e.g. 1995), taking a multi-functional view on language as a means to represent, as well as to establish and maintain social relations and identities, based on the division of ideational, interpersonal and textual meta-functions of language (cf. e.g. Halliday 1994). As Fairclough (1995, 17) puts it, "this [division] ties in with my suggestion that representations, relations and identities are always simultaneously at issue in a text: the ideational function of language is its function in generating representations of the world; the interpersonal function includes the functioning of language in the constitution of relations, and of identities. (The textual function relates to the constitution of texts out of individual sentences.)"

---

* This paper is part of the research project "Television Discourse", supported by the German Research Foundation (DFG) and directed by Gerda Lauerbach at the University of Frankfurt a.M. The goal of the project is a comparative discourse analysis of election night (and, in the case of the US presidential election of 2000, post-election night) television coverage in the United States, Great Britain and Germany. For more information, see http://www.uni-frankfurt.de/zenaf/projekte/TVdiscourses/

[1] This contribution was part of a panel on *Intercultural Media Analysis*, organized for IADA 2003 by Anita Fetzer and Gerda Lauerbach. Within the panel, it was part of a workshop on the topic of *Openings of TV Election Night Broadcasts in Great Britain and Germany* in which the team of the Frankfurt *Television Discourse Project* reported on work in progress. The workshop concentrated on openings as frames which foreshadow for the recipients the content and style of what to expect and which invite preferred reading positions. The other papers in the workshop (all this volume) are by Raimund Schieß (on visualization), Gerda Lauerbach (on presenting practices) and by Annette Becker (on interviews). I am grateful to all three for valuable comments on earlier drafts of this paper. I also would like to thank Rirhandu Mageza for her editorial assistance.

For the purpose of this analysis, I will focus on appraisal systems, which have been developed as methodological tools to categorize evaluative language (Martin 1992, 2000, 2003; White 1999, 2001, 2003), distinguishing between the attitudinal, dialogistic and intertextual positioning of speakers/writers. Appraisal theory is a recent development,[2] which concentrates on the representational and ideational meta-functions of language as suggested by Halliday (e.g. 1994). The appraisal framework facilitates the exploration of evaluative language, which is used "to evaluate, to adopt stances, to construct textual personas and to manage interpersonal positioning and relationships" (White 2001).

Three categories, which I outline briefly, are used to achieve this goal: attitude, engagement and graduation.

The first category, ATTITUDE, covers the set of linguistic devices with which speakers or writers indicate positive or negative assessments of people, objects and situations. The speaker's attitudinal positioning can be subdivided in three subtypes, namely judgement, affect and appreciation:

JUDGEMENT refers to appraisal on the grounds of social norms and values. White (2001) describes this as "normative assessments of human behaviour typically making reference to rules of behaviour" (White 2001), e.g. *This man is cruel*.

AFFECT is to be defined as evaluation by means of the writer/speaker indicating how they are emotionally disposed to the people, situations or things they are speaking or writing about, or characterizing their imputed affective state, e.g. *The crowd is cheering*.

APPRECIATION means "assessments of the form, appearance, composition, impact, significance etc of human artefacts, natural objects as well as human individuals (but not of human behaviour) by reference to aesthetics and other systems of social value" (White 2001), e.g. *This is a beautiful picture*.

Martin (2000, 2003) argues that the categories of judgement and appreciation are institutionalised forms of affect, as each type of attitude "involves positive and negative feeling" (e.g. Martin 2003, 173). Moreover, appraisal theory is concerned with the range of resources with which speakers negotiate the propositional content of their utterances. These resources are called ENGAGEMENT, which form the second category of appraisal, and have been previously analysed under headings such as modality, voicing, and evidentiality. Engagement is further subcategorized into heteroglossic and monoglossic modes of expression (after Bakhtin e.g. 1981). The statement "*Tony Blair is Prime Minister of Great Britain*" is in monoglossic mode, also referred to as bare assertion, since only the speaker's voice is involved. However, the statement "*Tony Blair may be re-elected as Prime Minister of Great Britain*" would be a heteroglossic mode of expression, as it is inherently dialogic since it allows the possi-

---

[2] That the appraisal framework is emerging as an important field in linguistic research is underlined by the fact that the journal TEXT issued a special issue on appraisal in 2003.

bility of other opinions (White 1999, 11). The appraisal framework also distinguishes between intra-vocalisation and extra-vocalisation, the latter displaying at least one voice within the heteroglossic mode which is not the speakers's voice, e.g. "*Some experts suggest that Tony Blair may be re-elected as Prime Minister...*", whereas the intra-vocalised mode does not involve voices other than the speaker's.

The third category of appraisal used for the purpose of analysis is GRADUATION. Graduation are "values by which (1) speakers graduate (raise or lower) the interpersonal impact, force or volume of their utterances (force), and (2) by which they graduate (blur or sharpen) the focus of their semantic categorisations" (White 1999, 4). The latter is usually indicated by words such as *exactly*, *kind of*, *a little bit*.

This paper focuses on affect as part of the attitudinal system, on graduation and on engagement. It scrutinizes how these three categories correlate in the language use of the journalists during election night broadcasts from different cultural backgrounds. It particularly focuses on the presentation of the first poll results by looking at the journalists' use of engagement and force, as well as examining their attitudinal stance towards situations outside the studio as presented in outside broadcasts. A further section concentrates on the use of evoked affect and the construction of historical significance.

Besides linguistic manifestations of appraisal, the paper examines the use of metaphors in the data. I explore the question whether coherent conceptual metaphors are used, as defined by Lakoff/Johnson (1980), which determine the discourse of election night. The thesis is that if a particular metaphor is consistently used throughout the coverage, the underlying conceptual metaphor is likely to determine the way in which the viewers perceive the discourse. Following Montgomery/Tolson/Garton (1989) my paper focuses on the use of metaphors of the semantic domain of war and the military. These authors examined the 1987 British General Election campaign and noted a tendency to metaphorize the campaign as war. Likewise, in his analysis of newspaper articles on drug abuse Fairclough (1995, 71) found the "war metaphor [...] also significant in terms of the newspaper's implicit claim to a relationship of solidarity and common identity with the audience. It draws upon war as an evocative theme of popular memory and popular culture, claiming to share that memory and culture."

2. Engagement and evaluation

The channels under investigation show notable differences in the ways in which they display the results of the exit polls. In both the UK and Germany, these results are not allowed to be publicised until the polls close, which is at 1800 CET in Germany and at 2200 GMT in the UK. The differences between the networks can be found in the choice of appraisal, the use of metaphors and the way in which certain speech events which appear to be obligatory in the discourse of election coverage, i.e. outside broadcasts or the presentation of the poll results, are evaluated. This section particularly focuses on the use of engagement and graduation.

BBC presenter David Dimbleby announces "Ten o'clock and we say: Tony Blair is to be Prime Minister and a landslide is likely", thereby at least partly extra-vocalising the propositional content of his statement ("we say"). The mode of expression is heteroglossic, as the statement is inherently dialogic and points at a construed diversity of possible meanings, one of which is foregrounded via "we say". On the other hand, the interpersonal impact is raised since "we say" leaves little space for negotiation, as opposed to e.g. *We think Tony Blair is to be Prime Minister*. White (2001) refers to this phenomenon of a heteroglossic mode paired with raised interpersonal impact as proclamation. Only seconds later, Dimbleby repeats the statement, in a monoglossic mode of expression, "Tony Blair will be Prime minister and this is why". In appraisal terms, he refrains from using graduation and leaves no space for negotiation of the facts he asserts in the latter statement.

Like all presenters in the data analysed, Dimbleby repeatedly notes during the coverage that he is referring to exit poll results. He thus constantly extra-vocalizes his assertions and increases the negotiability of the propositional content of his statements. However, Dimbleby gives a statement about who is to be Prime Minister at a very early stage, instead of reading the poll results. He uses two statements, the latter as a bare assertion and the earlier as one which maintains the possibility of negotiating the propositional content of the utterance.

BBC's statistics analyst Peter Snow combines style of hyperbole with different forms of engagement, depending on how safe the prognoses are: "It'd be something quite unique for the Labour Party and a record certainly since 1945." Note, that Snow seems to be certain of the precision of the announced poll results, as is evident in his use of the term "certainly". It functions both on a level of graduation to sharpen the focus and on the level of engagement, opening only little space to negotiate the content of the statement. However, the certainty is modified by being made dependent on the subjunctive *would* (*It'd*). In other utterances as well, Snow mixes heteroglossic mode in terms of engagement on the one hand with hyperbole style, strong force and sharpened focus on the other hand. In terms of appraisal, he thus signals via engagement that his position is negotiable, while making his statements sound colourful and sensational by means of hyperbole style and strong force: "And it's even worse (*force: strong*) than that for the Tories if our exit poll is anywhere near right. (*engagement, heteroglossic mode*)". In this example, Snow leaves very much space for negotiating the content of his utterance in connecting it to the condition that the poll is "anywhere near right".

The German channel ARD reports on the elections 1998 in a more neutral way. Analyst Ulrich Deppendorf hardly positions himself attitudinally when presenting the results. Engagement and graduation are only used once, when Deppendorf starts to interpret and discuss the numbers he has presented previously: "Deutliche Verluste [considerable losses]".

Interestingly, the strategy of combining hyperbole and extra-vocalization as displayed by David Dimbleby and Peter Snow is used by other presenters as well. This is the strategy which Jonathan Dimbleby employs, who presents the result on the British commercial channel ITN. The sequence is embedded in CNN International's coverage of the British General elections, where Dimbleby states: "[our prediction] based on the poll (*engagement, heteroglossic mode*), is that Labour will win this election with a huge (*force: strong*) majority".[3]

CNN presenter Richard Blystone comments on the embedded ITN sequence: "All right, that was ITN and the bottom line after all that flash and filigree was this, and it sounds very bad for the ruling Conservative Party." Schieß (this volume) argues that the CNN International coverages use less high-tech graphics and broadcast in a plainer style than the domestic channels do. Blystone's characterization of the computer graphics as "flash and filigree" would seem to support this position. In summing up the ITN sequence, however, Blystone also uses the combination of hyperbole and heteroglossic mode: "Their political expert was saying this is a decisive turn." He quotes the hyperbole and superlative segments of the ITN coverage, thereby not claiming responsibility for the propositional content of the assertion.

The same channel uses different linguistic resources when presenting the results of the 1998 German Parliamentary elections. CNN reporter Bettina Lüscher constantly reminds the viewers that the results are drawn from exit polls and that these polls were not conducted by CNN International: "[figures] that the ARD and ZDF networks are providing". Lüscher gives the figures of five parties (CDU, SPD, FDP, the Greens and PDS) and mentions four times that the numbers are provided by networks other than CNN International. The language style Lüscher uses is neutral. She refrains from using metaphors or attitudinal positioning: "CDU thirty-five percent, this is the first exit poll coming in. SPD, according to

---

[3] The ITN sequence is embedded in the CNN International coverage, but as the analysis focuses on differences between the channels ARD, BBC and CNN, the paper does not put too much emphasis on the ITN-sequence.

ZDF, gets forty-one percent. The Greens, according to the exit polls from ZDF, get six point five percent. The FDP, according to ZDF, six point five percent, the PDS five percent."

3. Inscribed affect and graduation

The channels also show considerable differences in reporting on the participants' emotional responses. This notion of affect is most often used by the reporters in broadcasts from outside the studio, for instance from the parties' headquarters when describing the reactions of the politicians and party members. However, there appears to be a tendency of combining specific types of appraisal, particularly graduation and affect.

Reports in the national channels are very frequently introduced with strong affect, mainly drawing on mental states of either depression or excitement ("rather more somber scenes" (BBC) or "gloomy atmosphere" (CNN International) as opposed to "Feierstimmung [party mood]" (ARD).

This combination of strong force and sharpened focus on the one hand and positive affect on the other hand can be noticed particularly often in the BBC's coverage. John Simpson, who reports from Labour headquarters, notices that the crowd is "extremely excited, no doubt, a big celebration". Presenter David Dimbleby, after having read the results, looks at his monitor and watches the crowd at the Tory headquarters, commenting that he sees "rather more somber scenes" as opposed to the Labour club, where "all [are] applauding there". A correlation of graduation and affect becomes visible. Negative emotional notions appear to be mitigated and juxtaposed to positive notions by drawing on linguistic devices of graduation.

The thesis, that there is this specific correlation of affect and force, is further supported by the ARD data on the German elections. German reporter Rolf-Dieter Krause at the SPD headquarter states: "Sie haben gejubelt, als das CDU-Ergebnis kam, und dann erst recht, als das SPD-Ergebnis kam. [They cheered, when the CDU-result came, and then even more when the SPD result came.]" ARD correspondent Martin Schulze reports from the headquarters of the Christian Democratic Union, who lost the election, noting "eine etwas gedrückte Stimmung [a slightly depressed mood]".

CNN International's reporters covering the same elections make use of a slightly different combination of appraisal categories: Jim Bittermann at the CDU headquarters reports a "kind of stunned silence" and later, "it's kind of glum I mean it's kind of silent", thereby mitigating the negative affect, too. Likewise CNN reporter Jonathan Mann draws on reinforcers and rhetorical devices like alliterations to describe and evaluate the situation at the

Social Democratic Parties' headquarter: "there was already a cheer in the air. They look like very good numbers for the supporters of Gerhard Schröder. The crowd outside is excited and expectant and waiting to hear more" and, seconds later, "we should stress, these are very, very early numbers but they look very good for the supporters of Gerhard Schröder". The positive affect of "cheer" is enhanced in the context of the "very good numbers" as stated by Mann.

The exception to the rule briefly outlined here is displayed in CNN International's coverage of the British General Election. Correspondent Christiane Amanpour rarely uses affect at all, but draws on metaphors which are meant to underline the supposed historical relevance of the election: "A new generation, a new era", she remarks. This might be considered as implicit or indirect affect and/or judgment, which in appraisal theory is referred to as evoked (cf. section 4) as opposed to inscribed attitude. The notion of evoked affect will be discussed in the next section.

CNN reporter Siobhan Darrow draws on different resources than her colleagues, too. She does nothing to mitigate the depression at Tory headquarters, but enhances the negative affect. Although she uses the subjunctive, "this would be a complete massacre" [if the polls were right], the negative affect ("massacre") is combined with a reinforcer ("complete"). Moreover Darrow has witnessed a "very gloomy atmosphere", thus sharpened focus ("very") is used again in combination with the negative affect ("gloomy").

4. Evoked attitude

Beside the explicit, or inscribed, attitude, here is a form of evoked attitude which functions on an implicit level. The channels seem to want to make the viewers feel that they are witnessing an event of historic significance. Both affect and judgement are involved. The presenters repeatedly refer to either historical figures or attribute historical significance not only to the elections they are reporting on, but to the very moment of the broadcasting. BBC's David Dimbleby for instance states: "If the opinion polls through this campaign are borne out tonight, we're likely to see one of the biggest political upsets since the Tories were swept out of office in 1945." This is in addition one of the cases in which, as outlined in section 2, the hyperbole style is combined with low force and a heteroglossic mode of expression.

The German channel ARD uses the same linguistic strategy, which is further enhanced by the fact that the ARD studio is located inside the "Wasserwerk", which used to house the German parliament for a number of years (cf. Schieß, this volume). Hence, presenter Marion von Haaren reports "ein Hauch von Nostalgie [an air of nostalgia]", and relates this to the move of the German Capital from Bonn to Berlin planned at that time. "[Die] Tage Bonns sind also gezählt [the days of Bonn are numbered]" is meant to give the broadcast further significance that exceeds the bare reporting of results. Viewers are invited to witness a unique broadcast, as the parliament is moving.

Another topic which relates to history is introduced as presenters and reporters refer to change in the political landscape. As stated above, Christiane Amanpour notes "a new generation, a new era" when reporting from the Labour headquarters. The old era is ending at the very moment of the coverage.

We see the same linguistic device in CNN International's coverage of the German election in 1998. Affect is once more evoked by inviting the viewers to witness radical challenge and change: Jonathan Mann reports from the SPD headquarters: "Schröder is trying to achieve something that others before him found impossible: Unseat an icon and jump German politics forward a generation". Reporter Jim Bittermann at the CDU headquarters explicitly refers to the historical significance of the situation, too: "One way or another, it is going to be an historic evening here. We're either going to see a four term Chancellor get elected a fifth term and that'll be surprising, or we're going to see a Chancellor turned out of office [...] after being one of the longest serving democratic leaders in history". Either way, the viewer witnesses historical change live from his/her living room.

5. The use of metaphors

The networks vary in their lexical choice in metaphorical expressions. The BBC has the clearest strategy in terms of using metaphors. In the opening sequence of the BBC broadcast, the presenter and the reporters use 18 war metaphors as opposed to only one metaphor of sports and two of body and/or nature. It is not only the election ("battle for power"), which is described in terms of war, but even the staff. The outside reporters Kate Adie and John Simpson are referred to as "battle hardened correspondents at the frontline", which would have been a literal description for the latter when he worked as BBC reporter in Iraq during the second Gulf War.

In contrast, the ARD reporters and correspondents tend to use metaphors very rarely, with only three exceptions to this rule in the opening sequence of broadcasting (one metaphor of sports, betting and nature each)

The CNN International British election coverage employs the greatest variety of metaphors, although the semantic field of military and war is prevalent here too. They employ metaphors from the domains of literature (e.g. "election drama") and medicine (e.g. "a deep stream of socialism in their blood"). However, the same Channel rarely uses metaphorical language in reporting on the German elections. In the opening sequence of the broadcast, the reporters only used four metaphors, all of them from the semantic domain of sports (e.g. "the race is too close to call"). Thus, at least in this small sample, it looks as if CNN International tends to adapt to the metaphorical strategy and tradition which the domestic channels (BBC and ARD) make use of.

6. Concluding remarks

The coverages analysed to some extent display the use of identical linguistic devices, which however differ considerably in the detail of their use. Presenters and reporters regularly operate with affect, in the largest parts of the data both positive and negative affect is used. Hyperbole style is common too, as is the tendency of the participants to extra-vocalise their argument by means of engagement in order to make their assertions negotiable. This happens commonly when the polls are read, as they might be inaccurate and the outcome cannot be guaranteed. Most of the journalists tend to use the combination of inscribed affect and force/focus. Negative affect tends to be downgraded with low force and blurred focus (CNN Internationals' reporter Jim Bittermann notes "it's kind of glum"), whereas positive affect is enhanced with high force and/or sharpened focus, e.g. BBC's John Simpson, who remarks that the crowd is "extremely excited". The use of these combined appraisal categories can be noticed in data from every channel under investigation.

The differences in the use of linguistic and rhetorical devices as well as in the use of metaphors lie mainly in the extent to which these resources are drawn on. Some channels may prefer their journalists to rely on implicit or evoked affect like the German ARD, while other networks like BBC prefer their staff to draw on drastic and dramatic language in order to provide a rather spectacular broadcast.

References

Bakhtin, Michail (1981): The dialogic imagination. Ed. by Holmquist, M., transl. by Emerson, C./Holmquist, M. Austin: University of Texas Press.
Eggins, Suzanne/Slade, Diana (eds.) (1997): Analysing casual conversation. London: Cassell.
Fairclough, Norman (1995): Media discourse. London: Edward Arnold.

Halliday, Michael (1994): An introduction to functional grammar. London: Edward Arnold.
Lakoff, George/Johnson, Mark (1980): Metaphors we live by. Chicago: University of Chicago Press.
Macken-Horarik, Mary/Martin, Jim R. (eds.) (2003): Text 23/2. Special Issue: Negotiating heteroglossia. Social perspectives on evaluation. Berlin: de Gruyter.
Marriott, Stephanie (2000): Election night. In: Media, Culture & Society 22, 131-150.
Martin, James R. (1992): English text: System and structure. Philadelphia, Amsterdam: Benjamins.
– (2000): Beyond exchange: Appraisal systems in English. In: Eggins, Suzanne/Slade, Diana (eds.): Analysing casual conversation. London: Cassell, 142-175.
– (2003): Introduction. In: Macken-Horarik, Mary/Martin, James R. (eds.): Text 23/2. Special Issue: Negotiating heteroglossia. Social perspectives on evaluation. Berlin: de Gruyter, 171-181.
Montgomery, Martin/Tolson, Andrew/Garton, Greg (1989): Media discourse in the 1987 general election: ideology, scripts and metaphors. In: ELR Journal (New Series) 3, 173-204.
White, Peter (1999): Appraisal and a grammar of solidarity: new developments in the theory of modality, evidentiality and hedging. Paper for the International Systemic Functional Congress, Singapore.
– (2001): Appraisal. An Overview. In: http://www.grammatics.com/appraisal/AppraisalGuide/Framed/Frame.htm

Annette Becker

Interviews in TV election night broadcasts: a framework for cross-cultural analysis*

1. Introduction

In TV election night broadcasts, there are two major subtypes, or sub-genres of interviews: interviews with politicians and interviews with experts. Both kinds of interviewees can be interviewed either by the anchor, or by other journalists. The interviews can be face-to face or down-the-line. In this paper, I will present the multi-disciplinary framework I have developed for the cross-cultural analysis of questioning strategies in election night interviews, combining methods from pragmatics, appraisal theory and conversation analysis.[1] Firstly, I will give a general overview over the distribution and function of interviews with politicians and experts during the national and international election night coverages of the U.K. General Election in 1997 and the F.R.G. *Bundestagswahl* in 1998. Secondly, I will demonstrate how the framework can be applied for both the qualitative analysis of single interviews and the quantitative analysis of a larger corpus.

---

* This paper is part of the research project "Television Discourse", supported by the German Research Foundation (DFG) and directed by Gerda Lauerbach. The goal of the project is a comparative discourse analysis of election night (and, in the case of the US presidential election of 2000, post-election night) television coverage in the United States, Great Britain and Germany. For more information, see: http://www.uni-frankfurt.de/zenaf/projekte/TVdiscourses/

[1] My contribution was part of a panel on *Intercultural Media Analysis*, organized for IADA 2003 by Anita Fetzer and Gerda Lauerbach. Within the panel, it was part of a workshop on the topic of *Openings of TV Election Night Broadcasts in Great Britain and Germany* in which the team of the Frankfurt *Television Discourse Project* reported on work in progress. The workshop concentrated on openings as frames which foreshadow for the recipients the content and style of what to expect and which invite preferred reading positions. The other papers in the workshop (all this volume) are by Raimund Schieß (on visualization), Gerda Lauerbach (on presenting practices), and by Martin Hampel (on evaluative language and metaphor). I am grateful to Gerda Lauerbach, Martin Hampel and Raimund Schieß for valuable feedback and comments on earlier drafts of this paper, and to Rirhandu Mageza for her editorial assistance.

2. National and international election night broadcasts

Television channels cater to their national or international audiences' expectations from the very beginning of an election night broadcast. In the U.K. General Election in 1997 and the F.R.G. *Bundestagswahl* in 1998, the overall majority of interviews broadcast by the major national channels BBC and ARD were interviews with politicians, while CNN International showed almost exclusively expert interviews. This distribution has to do with the relevance of the event for a national or international audience, and also with the different functions, or communicative goals of each type of interview. When politicians are interviewed, we get to hear and see the persons who might be ruling the country in the coming years, or the persons who used to rule it and are now being held to account. For a national audience, this is, of course, much more vital than anything an expert could ever say. Experts are there to give background information, impartial analyses and commentaries, and, especially in national election night broadcasts, sometimes simply to bridge time between results. Their role is more important during international election night broadcasts, where an international audience cannot be expected to be familiar with the peculiarities of a nation's election system, like the British 'marginal constituencies', in which elections tend to be won by very small margins, or the German *Überhangmandate*[2]. Accordingly, during the opening phase of the BBC election night broadcast, BBC anchor David Dimbleby conducted two down-the-line interviews with political representatives of the two major parties: the winning Labour Party and the losing Conservative Party. Interviewees were shown on a video wall (for a description of the studio settings, see Schieß, this volume). ARD anchor Marion von Haaren and co-anchor Wolfgang Kenntemich interviewed representatives of the winning SPD and the losing CDU. They also interviewed representatives of the three smaller but central parties, the F.D.P., Bündnis 90 – Die Grünen, and the PDS, who, as is characteristic of German politics, play an important part as potential coalition partners for the major parties. These interviews were conducted face-to-face in the studio. Both national channels did not interview experts until much later. In the opening section of its coverage of the U.K. election for an international audience, CNN showed a brief expert interview taken over from the British commercial channel ITV (and distributed by ITN, the channel network ITV is part of), as well as a debate agenda interview between two opposing British experts, moderated by CNN anchor Richard Blystone. In the corresponding section on the German election in 1998, CNN anchor Bettina Lüscher interviewed one German expert in the CNN studio. All experts interviewed were leading journalists from political or financial magazines. Even in this small

---

[2] Translated as 'overhang mandates' on the homepage of the German Bundestag (http://www.bundestag.de). Other translation attempts are 'surplus mandates', and 'adjustment seats'.

corpus of data, remarkable differences between interviewer styles could be observed on several linguistic levels. To capture at least some of them, I have developed a multi-disciplinary set of tools to describe, analyse and cross-culturally compare the various questioning activities in interviews with politicians and experts, using insights from pragmatics, appraisal theory and conversation analysis. This kind of multi-disciplinary approach is inspired by the contributions of the critical discourse analysts in Wodak/Meyer (2001), who explicitly advocate theoretical diversity for analysing a particular discursive reality in a multi-dimensional way.

3. A framework for analysing questions in interviews

An interviewer (IR) asking questions in an interview has a multitude of meaningful choices on various linguistic levels. My choice of analytic criteria was influenced by the need for quantifiable features in the cross-cultural analysis of a larger data corpus. Therefore, I have concentrated on the linguistic levels from macro to micro and back, where the interview questions from the election night corpus showed the most striking cross-cultural differences. In the following paragraphs, I will explain my framework's categories in an exemplary analysis of the core sequences (without opening or closing sequences) of two election night interviews from the opening sections of the two national channels. Data will be taken from the first interview between BBC anchor David Dimbleby and Dr Brian Mawhinney, the Conservative Party's Chairman, and from the first ARD interview between Wolfgang Kenntemich and Jürgen Rüttgers, the CDU's former Minister of Future.

3.1 Turn structure and addressee orientation

Questioning turns contain at least one questioning activity, realised by various syntactic forms like grammatical questions, declaratives as questions, tag-questions, sub-sentential or elliptic formats (Heritage/Roth 1995). Questioning activities within turns may come single or in series. They may be prefaced and/or postfaced. Very often, communicative effort of this kind is used to mitigate the negative impact of a face-threatening-question regarding an unfavourable state of affairs (Brown/Levinson 1978). In his initial turn, BBC anchor David Dimbleby does not confront Brian Mawhinney directly with his observation that his party has obviously lost the election. Instead, he precedes it with the preface "it is not a very good exit poll for you":

(1) DD: Dr Mawhinney, er, it's not a very good exit poll for you, it does look as though you've lost.

Similarly, his German colleague Wolfgang Kenntemich prefaces his first question to Jürgen Rüttgers:

(2) WK: Die Zukunft für die Koalition sieht *nicht* gut aus nach dieser Prognose. Bei allem Vorbehalt. Hat es an Kanzler Kohl gelegen, dass er doch nicht mehr die Wähler hat ziehen können? [The coalition's future does *not* look good, according to this forecast. With all reservations: Was it Chancellor Kohl's fault that he could no longer attract the voters?]

But the turns differ significantly in other respects. Generally, English and German native speaker discourse tends to show characteristic phenomena in five central dimensions of cross-cultural difference (House 1996):

English		*German*
Indirectness	↔	Directness
Orientation towards Other	↔	Orientation towards Self
Orientation towards Addressees	↔	Orientation towards Content
Implicitness	↔	Explicitness
Verbal Routines	↔	Ad-Hoc-Formulation

For the purpose of this analysis, I have combined the dimensions of "Orientation towards Other/Self" and "Orientation towards Addressees/Content", distinguishing between HIGH, MEDIUM and LOW ADDRESSEE ORIENTATION.[3] A HIGH degree of addressee orientation is represented in discourse by 2nd person reference *and* the use of an address term[4] (3). MEDIUM addressee orientation involves 2nd person reference *or* the use of address terms (4), whereas LOW addressee orientation is associated with 1st or 3rd person reference, and no use of address terms (5):

(3) DD: Dr Mawhinney, er, it's not a very good exit poll for you […]

(4) DD: […] it does look as though you've lost.

(5) WK: Die Zukunft für die Koalition sieht *nicht* gut aus nach dieser Prognose. [The coalition's future does *not* look good, according to this forecast.]

---

3   Cf. Simon-Vandenbergen (2000) on the "power/solidarity function of pronominal choices" in talkshows. I do not use the term INVOLVEMENT (Eggins/Slade 1997, Martin 1997) for this dimension of interpersonal meaning because INVOLVEMENT is more complex and includes resources like technicality, swearing, slang or anti-language, which are rare to non-existent in the election night interviews.

4   This is what Eggins/Slade call a "redundant vocative", as opposed to a "targeting vocative". Redundant vocatives are used "when there is already sufficient contextual information for the nominated person to be assumed next speaker". Their use "would tend to indicate an attempt by the addresser to establish a closer relationship with the addressee, implying some exclusion of the other participants" (Eggins/Slade 1997, 145).

As examples (3) and (4) show, Dimbleby exhibits significantly higher addressee orientation in his opening turn than his German colleague Kenntemich, who opens the interview with Jürgen Rüttgers using 3rd person reference only (5), like his colleague Marion von Haaren does in her lead-in to the ARD election night broadcast as a whole (cf. Lauerbach, this volume). One might speculate whether this remarkable cross-cultural difference on addressee orientation is also due to the different settings of the interviews. The Dimbleby-Mawhinney interview is conducted down-the line, whereas Kenntemich interviews Rüttgers face-to-face in the studio. Therefore, one might conclude that Dimbleby has to invest more effort in facework because he has to bridge a larger physical distance than Kenntemich. On the other hand, Marion von Haaren exhibits medium to high addressee orientation in the interviews she conducts face-to-face in the same setting as Kenntemich. At this point, one may only speculate whether this might also have to do with the gender of the interactants.[5] Such questions would be a task for quantitative analysis.

3.2 Appraisal

To analyse the interpersonal potential of questioning turns in more detail, I have used categories from appraisal theory, a theoretical approach developed during the last fifteen years by systemic-functional linguists, and one of the theoretical orientations of the Frankfurt *Television Discourse Analysis* Project (cf. Hampel, this volume). Appraisal Theory seeks to describe the linguistic resources speakers or writers use for evaluative purposes, always bearing in mind at least one real or virtual person as a co-active recipient. Central to appraisal theory is the Bakhtinian perspective that all texts, either written or spoken, are dialogic in nature. This dynamic perspective has been adopted by e.g. Eggins and Slade (1997), Martin (1992, 1997), and White (2001a, 2001b). As appraisal theory is constantly being cross-checked against empirical data, it is currently undergoing noticeable changes (for an overview see Martin 2003). For my analysis of election night interviews, I have used the three main systems of appraisal theory as outlined by White (2001a; 2001b). These are ENGAGEMENT, ATTITUDE, and GRADUATION. The system of engagement, "includes values which have been analysed in the literature under headings such as attribution, modality, hearsay, concession, polarity, evidentiality, hedges, boosters and metadiscursives" (White 2001b). Engagement, or SOURCE, "covers resources that introduce additional voices into a discourse, via projection, modalisation, or concession; the key choice here is one voice (MONOGLOSS), or more than one voice (HETEROGLOSS)" (Martin/Rose 2003, 54). Originally, these categories were developed for the analysis of monologic genres, not for dialogic genres like interviews.

---

5   For the influence on IR and IE gender on the style of media interviews see Giora (1995).

However, questions are not per se heteroglossic, as interviewers strategically choose between opening up, or limiting the range of options for an interviewee's answer. When Wolfgang Kenntemich asks Jürgen Rüttgers: "Hat es an Kanzler Kohl gelegen, dass er doch nicht mehr die Wähler hat ziehen können? [Was it Chancellor Kohl's fault that he could no longer attract the voters?]" (cf. section 3.1, ex. (2)), this would count as a monoglossic question, were it not for the initial concession "bei allem Vorbehalt [with all reservations]". If a question is modified through items like ' a little' or ' certainly' , this belongs to the appraisal system of GRADUATION. Graduation refers to "[v]alues by which speakers graduate (raise or lower) the interpersonal impact, FORCE or volume of their utterances, and by which they graduate (blur or sharpen) the FOCUS of their semantic categorisations." (White 2001b). While Kenntemich raises force only once and not even lexically, but merely via prosodic stress, Dimbleby combines high force and blurred focus to modify the negative evaluations "not good" and "you have lost" (cf. section 3.1, ex. (1)).[6] Such evaluations are discussed within the appraisal system of ATTITUDE. Attitude is concerned with reactions to reality on a moral, aesthetic, or emotional level. The corresponding sub-types of attitude are labelled JUDGEMENT, APPRECIATION, and AFFECT. Appreciation refers to the evaluation of objects or facts according to normative values. Judgement is associated with the evaluation of persons and their actions according to normative values, whereas affect is a resource for expressing subjective emotional reactions to either persons or facts (White 2001a, 2001b). In their initial questioning turns, both Dimbleby and Kenntemich use negative appreciation in their prefaces, followed by negative judgement in their questions. They modify the bad news through heteroglossic engagement and graduation in a face-saving way. However, as intricate as the interplay of turn structure, addressee orientation and appraisal qualities of single interviewer turns may be, it is also important for a more comprehensive understanding of their interpersonal potential to consider their functions within the turn sequence.

3.3 Function of IR turn within sequence

Strategic sequencing of questioning activities is an important discursive resource for interviews (Lauerbach 2001, Clayman/Heritage 2002), which is also explicitly recommended in handbooks for journalists like Friedrich/Schwinges (1999). Within a sequence of questioning turns, turns are used to accomplish different goals. Using an approach developed by Lauerbach, I will discuss the functions of QUESTIONS, FORMULATIONS, CHALLENGES and FOLLOW-UPS in the Dimbleby-Mawhinney interview and the Kenntemich-Rüttgers interview,

---

[6] The ironic understatement in the litotes "it's not a very good exit poll" is an interesting example for the interaction of engagement and graduation.

starting with the British interview and then turning to its German equivalent. Both interviews begin, as all interviews do, with a QUESTION (6). QUESTIONS are defined as, "[a]ny topic-initiating turn by IR, asking for information or yes-no-response" (Lauerbach 2001, 201):

(6) DD: Dr Mawhinney, er, it's not a very good exit poll for you, it does look as though you've lost.
BM: Well the country has made its decision, David (clears throat), we have a new government, we simply have to wait to deter- [interruption of sound/problem of transmission, 1 sec] government, that is, which choice the British people have made.

When Brian Mawhinney does not admit the Conservatives' defeat, Dimbleby metadiscursively (Ilie 2003) sums up his answer in the following FORMULATION (7):

(7) DD: Er are you saying (.) that you accept that Labour has won?

FORMULATIONS "preserve relevant features of a previous utterance while also recasting them" (Heritage 1979, 129), thus providing "a candidate reading for a preceding stretch of talk" (Heritage 1979, 138). Such a reading may or may not be accepted. Mawhinney's answer to Dimbleby's FORMULATION is another evasive answer (8)[7]:

(8) BM: No, I'm saying that er (.5) when the polls closed, (.5) all of those votes and ballot boxes up and down the country constitute a new Parliament, they constitute a new government, that may be a government led by John Major or it may be a government led by Tony Blair. Er all the speculation in a sense is over, we will find the result er fairly soon, I'm a patient man.

Dimbleby reacts to this with a CHALLENGE (9):

(9) DD: But er, a/are you saying you think there's a chance Mr Major has won, surely your own polls tonight a/ are/ are telling you that's not possible, aren't they?

Like FORMULATIONS, CHALLENGES are also responding turns, with the IR "questioning aspects of (interviewees) IE's response" (Lauerbach 2001, 201).[8] This is typically indicated by ' but'. Challenges are the most face-threatening type of questions. They are met most frequently with dispreference markers like hesitations at the beginning of the answering turn, and are very often rejected (10):

---

[7] For a discussion of answers, see Blum-Kulka (1984), Harris (1991), Clayman (1993) and Fetzer (this volume).
[8] Bell/van Leeuwen define challenges as confrontations with statements contradicting or weakening an IE's position. "[C]hallenges always formulate objections to the interviewee's position as stated in the interview. They always involve a 'but' or, a bit stronger a 'but surely'. They always force the interviewee in a defensive position. The interviewee is always the batsman, never the bowler" (1994, 141).

(10) BM: No, I'm saying that er the people have *already* decided. We simply don't know the er judgement that they have passed, but we will know it soon enough and I'm happy to wait until that judgement has become clear.

In his next turn, Dimbleby subtly introduces the new topic 'campaign' by embedding it into a FOLLOW-UP (11):

(11) DD: So you're satisfied with the way you fought the campaign and/ and with the outcome?

FOLLOW-UPS are IR utterances "[c]ontinuing" (Lauerbach 2001, 201) or elaborating a previous question on a topic. Dimbleby uses this format to expand the topic from 'election result' to 'election result and campaign' , but Mawhinney only takes up the topic 'election result' , rejecting it as before (12):

(12) BM: (1.0) Er, (.5) you're asking me to speculate on the result. As I've said, I think we should now wait until all of those ballot papers are counted, we will know soon enough who is going to be governing this country for the next five years.

Dimbleby's last turn in this interview is a FOLLOW-UP to the previous FOLLOW-UP, this time taking up and returning to the topic 'campaign' (13):

(13) DD: Looking back on the campaign, Dr Mawhinney, were you happy with the way it went all the way through, are there things you like to have done differently?

Like Dimbleby, Kenntemich also begins his interview with a QUESTION (14):

(14) WK: Die Zukunft für die Koalition sieht *nicht* gut aus nach dieser Prognose. Bei allem Vorbehalt. Hat es an Kanzler Kohl gelegen, dass er doch nicht mehr die Wähler hat ziehen können? [The coalition's future does *not* look good, according to this forecast. With all reservations: Was it Chancellor Kohl's fault that he could no longer attract the voters?]
JR: Also, man muss den Vorbehalt natürlich machen. Äh die/ wir haben unser Wahlziel nicht erreicht. Äh die Koalition der Mitte hat ihre Mehrheit nach dieser Prognose verloren. Ich/Wir haben einen guten Wahlkampf gemacht, äh, unsere Leute vor Ort haben unglaublich gut gekämpft, das werden wir genauer [...] müssen. [Well, you've got to treat that with some reservation, of course. We have not reached our election goal. The coalition of the centre has lost its majority, according to this forecast. I / We've run a good election campaign, our people out there have fought unbelievably well, we'll have to [...] that more precisely.]

But when Rüttgers only admits the party's failure without commenting on Chancellor Kohl, as Kenntemich asked him to do, Kenntemich challenges him immediately (15), followed by another challenge in (16):

(15) WK: Aber lag es an Personen? [But was it due to individuals?]
JR: Nein, das lag nicht an Personen. Wir haben gesamt/ äh gemeinsam gekämpft, und da gibt's jetzt keine Schuldzuweisungen. [No, it was nobody's fault. We've been fighting together, and there's not going to be any finger-pointing now.]

(16) WK: Aber Trend zum Wechsel war da. Das hat man auch in den Umfragen gesehen, vorher. [But the tendency towards change was apparent. You could see that in the opinion polls, beforehand.]
JR: Ja gut, äh, die Leute haben sich für eine andere Regierung entschieden, wenn das so kommt, obwohl ja noch nicht klar ist, ob's eine Rot-Grüne Mehrheit im deutschen Bundestag gibt. [Well, OK, the people have decided in favour of a different government, if that is what comes to pass, although it is not yet clear whether there will be a Red-Green majority in the German Bundestag.]

Kenntemich's last question is a follow-up on Rüttgers' topic 'party coalitions' (17):

(17) WK: Mhm. Ist die Große Koalition auch noch ein Thema? [Mhm. Is the Grand Coalition still an issue?]
JR: Das werden wir im Laufe des Abends sehen. [We'll see that in the course of the evening.]

Obviously, Kenntemich seems to see unmitigated challenges as unproblematic interviewing strategies needing no preliminary formulation in the preceding question. However, after his second challenge, he briefly departs from his neutralistic stance (Clayman 1988) as an interviewer by acknowledging Rüttgers' answer with the response token "Mhm". This practice is common in casual conversation, but uncommon within institutional communication in general and interviews broadcast to mass media audiences in particular (Heritage 1985). It is not altogether improbable that Kenntemich wishes to counterbalance the negative impact of his challenges by briefly departing from the institutional routine. Dimbleby, on the other hand, chooses to maintain his neutralistic stance throughout. Generally, within the election night corpus, politicians' answers were formulated and challenged more frequently than the answers of experts, irrespective of the level of broadcasting, be it national or international. This corresponds to the different functions, or communicative goals, of each type of interview as outlined above.

4. Summary and conclusion

The analysis of interviews from the openings of British and German election night broadcasts has shown how interviewers strategically combine the interpersonal potential of turn structure, appraisal systems, and sequencing to shape their questioning activities. At the same time, even in this small set of data, noticeable cross-cultural differences emerged, similar to those described in Fetzer (this volume). Whereas the initial turns of the Dimbleby-Mawhinney interview and the Kenntemich-Rüttgers interview show remarkable similarities, their interpersonal properties in general differ significantly. In their initial turns, Dimbleby and Kenntemich each ask a prefaced question. Both prefaces are heteroglossic and use negative appreciation to foreground the negative judgement contained in the likewise heteroglossic question. Whereas Dimbleby keeps offering Mawhinney little appetisers already spiced with judgement, appreciation, or even affect, employing the whole range of attitudinal resources, Kenntemich's linguistic repertoire in the course of the interview seems pretty bland in comparison. This reluctance regarding the multiplication of meanings goes along with a preference for single-question turns and low addressee orientation. Likewise, Kenntemich is more reluctant regarding the intensification of force, whereas Dimbleby repeatedly verbalises high force. As a result, a clear distinction becomes apparent between the comparatively elaborate, more person-oriented questioning style preferred by the British journalist and the more direct and matter-of-fact style preferred by his German colleague. However, this style is not merely an individual choice. It is determined by British and German audience expectations. In this, it is also determined by what is seen as acceptable behaviour towards either British or German politicians as interviewees. A quantitative analysis of one or more of the levels outlined above would seek to investigate and interpret the frequency in which certain options are chosen within a larger number of interviews. This will be the aim of further research.

References

Bell, Philipp/van Leeuwen, Theo (1994): The media interview: Confession, contest, conversation. Kensington NSW: University of NSW Press.
Blum-Kulka, Shoshana (1983): The dynamics of political interviews. In: Text 3/2, 131-153.
Brown, Penelope/Levinson, Stephen (1978): Universals in language usage: Politeness phenomena. In: Goody, Esther (ed.): Questions and politeness: Strategies in social interaction. Cambridge: CUP, 56-311.
Clayman, Stephen (1988): Displaying neutrality in television news interviews. In: Social Problems 35/4, 474-492.
– (1993): Reformulating the question: A device for answering/not answering questions in news interviews and press conferences. In: Text 13/2, 159-188.
Clayman, Stephen/Heritage, John (2002): The news interview. Journalists and public figures on air. Cambridge: CUP.
Eggins, Suzanne/Slade, Diana (1997): Analysing casual conversation. London: Cassell.
Fetzer, Anita (this volume): Non-acceptances in political interviews: British styles and German styles in conflict?
Friedrichs, Jürgen/Schwinges, Ulrich (1999): Das journalistische Interview. Opladen: Westdeutscher Verlag.
Giora, Rachel (1995): Female interviewing styles in the Israeli media. In: Millar, Sharon/Mey, Jacob (eds.): Form and function in language. Proceedings of the First Rasmus Rask Colloquium, Odense University, November 1992. Odense: Odense UP, 171-191.

Hampel, Martin (this volume): Intersubjective positioning in election night discourse. A cross-cultural analysis.
Harris, Sandra (1991): Evasive action: How politicians respond to questions in political interviews. In: Scannell, Paddy (ed.): Broadcast talk. London: Sage, 76-99.
Heritage, John (1985): Analysing news interviews. Aspects of the production of talk for an overhearing audience. In: van Dijk, Teun (ed.): Handbook of discourse analysis 3: Discourse and dialogue. London: Academic Press, 95-117.
Heritage, John/Roth, Andrew (1995): Grammar and institution. Questions and questioning in the broadcast news interview. In: Research on Language and Social Interaction 18/1, 1-60.
Heritage, John/Watson, D.R. (1979): Formulations as conversational objects. In: Psathas, George (ed.): Everyday language. Studies in ethnomethodology. New York: Irvington, 123-162.
House, Juliane (1996): Contrastive discourse analysis and misunderstanding: The case of German and English. In: Hellinger, Marlis/Ammon, Ulrich (eds.): Contrastive socioliguistics. Berlin: Mouton de Gruyter (Contributions to the Sociology of Language 71), 345-361.
Ilie, Cornelia (2003): Discourse and metadiscourse in parliamentary debates. In: Journal of Language and Politics 2/1, 71-92.
Jucker, Andreas (1986): News interviews. A pragmalinguistic analysis. Amsterdam: Benjamins.
Lauerbach, Gerda (2001): Implicit communication in political interviews: Negotiating the agenda. In: Weigand, Edda/Dascal, Marcelo (eds.): Negotiation and power in dialogic interaction. Amsterdam: Benjamins, 197-214.
– (this volume): Election nights: a cross-cultural analysis of presenting practices.
Martin, Jim R. (1992): English text. System and structure. Philadelphia: Benjamins.
– (1997): Analysing genre: Functional parameters. In: Christie, Frances/Martin, Jim R. (eds.): Genre and institutions. Social processes in the workplace and school. London: Cassell, 1-39
– (2003): Introduction. In: Macken-Horarik, Mary/Martin, Jim R. (eds.): Text 23/2. Special Issue: Negotiating heteroglossia. Social perspectives on evaluation. Berlin: de Gruyter, 171-181.
Martin, Jim R./Rose, David (2003): Working with discourse. Meaning beyond the clause. London: Continuum.
Schieß, Raimund (this volume): Lights, camera, action: Visualizing TV election nights across cultures.
Simon-Vandenbergen, Anne-Marie (2000): Towards an analysis of interpersonal meaning in daytime talk shows. In: Ungerer, Friedrich (ed.): English media texts past and present. Language and textual structure. Amsterdam: Benjamins, 218-240.
White, Peter R.R (2001a): An introductory tour through appraisal theory. In: http//www.grammatics.com/appraisal/AppraisalGuide/Framed/Frame.htm.
– (2001b): Appraisal. An overview. In: http://www.grammatics.com/appraisal/AppraisalGuide/ Framed/Frame.htm.
Wodak, Ruth/Meyer, Michael (eds.) (2001): Methods of critical discourse analysis. Introducing qualitative methods. London: Sage.

Marjut Johansson

Represented discourse as a form of mediation from a contrastive point of view

1. Introduction

Political discourse can be considered as a form of action. Moreover, discourse and action are the components of the social exchange of verbal interaction (Charaudeau 2002, 161f.). Several types of political discourse are media bound, that is, they only exist in and through the media. The political interview is one of the genres in which the representatives of two separate, but closely linked institutions meet. Without the media, many instances of political life would not be mediated to the public. Their interconnectedness and other links to public space in general result in the clear intertextuality of political talk.

In this paper, I am interested in the interactional contributions of the politician in this institutional media genre, the political TV-interview. The main focus of interest is the way the politician relates to and represents public space and expresses his or her opinions. I propose to focus on them from a specific point of view, through a linguistic device I term *represented discourse* (abbreviation RD), or, as it is called in traditional approaches, *reported speech*. I will be looking at instances that are constituted of two parts – the representing (underlined) and the *represented* (in italics) parts such as these in the following example:

> IE: <u>when Mr Major said</u> *he'd get the ban lifted within weeks of the beef war* <u>then he came back and said</u> *it would be lifted by the end of Nov/ by the beginning of November* and here we are six months on not a thing has been done

My approach to RD as a form of mediation is anchored in a dialogical framework in which the cognitive and social dimensions are taken into consideration. First, in section 2, I undertake an explanation of *mediation* and define represented discourse. Then, in section 3, I discuss the premises of contrastiveness and the method used in this paper and, in section 4, describe the data. Finally, in section 5, I present a pilot analysis of the use of RD in French and English interviews from a contrastive perspective.

2. Mediation and represented discourse

2.1 Mediational means

In his account of mediated action, Wertsch considers mediation to be a very broad concept. He sees that almost everything in life is mediated in the sense that social communicative processes are linked to psychological ones (Wertsch 1998, 13). That is why mediated action is also action situated in cultural, historical and institutional settings (Wertsch 1998, 15). This is based on Vygotski (1978, 39f.), who sees meaning as built up through mediated action in the learning process. The social actors acting at a certain moment in social space use semiotic devices what Wertsch (1998) calls *cultural tools* and Scollon (2001) renames *mediational means*. It is by these that actions are carried out or through which everything holds together. Here I prefer the latter term.

The importance of mediational means lies in the fact that they constrain actions and enable them to create links to sociocultural and sociopolitical history (Scollon 2001, 115; Wertsch 1998). Mediational means can be concrete objects such as money, a coffee cup, the pole in pole vaulting or a pen in drawing, or they can be representations of objects. Language and speech are also mediational means.

Mediational means have several properties. For instance, they are linked to the (political, economic, social, cultural, etc.) world in a *historical* sense and they are always *partial* (Scollon 2001, 120f.). All these properties can be examined in relation to RD.

2.2 Represented discourse

Several researchers have analyzed RD – or *reported speech* – from different points of views. For instance, Fairclough (1995) gives an analysis of *voices* in media discourse, and Clayman (1992) and Clayman/Heritage (2002) use the notion of *footing* when discussing various functions of what they call *third party attributed statements*. The following approach differs somewhat from these and is based on my earlier studies of RD and its functions in French political interviews (Johansson 2000, 2002).

In the title of the paper, the term *mediated* is used to refer to the object of study. It is based on Wertsch (1998, 78-80), who sees that a narrative is a cultural tool that can be used to represent for instance the past. Here, I propose to treat RD in a similar way. RD is considered to be a form of *mediated action* that is used as a specific discursive and representational device in interaction. The focus will be on narrative mediation.

The following theoretical explanation of RD is based on Johansson (2000, 2002). First, the voice anchors the consciousness of the speaker in a certain previous context. In recontextualizing something from this context, the voice functions as the anchor of the speaker's consciousness and in this way reflects his or her experience. As the speaker constructs an instance of RD in his or her discourse, he or she, on the one hand, in a most obvious way, links him- or herself to other discourses and other social agents; that is, the RD functions as one indicator of *intertextual* or *interdiscursive chaining* (for the definition of these notions, see Fairclough 1992). In other words, it mediates sociocultural representations from public space. The RD can also refer to the ongoing context; in that case it creates *intratextual links*.

Secondly, RD is a *recontextualization* through the enunciation of the speaker in a certain discursive and interactional context. In the interview, this recontextualization takes place in an institutional context and it has a double addressee, the interviewer and the public. The functions of RD in different types of sequence vary according to the different speaker roles as the interviewer and the interviewee negotiate.

In all, I believe that RD contributes to the construction of the identity and subject position of the politician at the same time as the *political* (Charaudeau 2002, Chilton/Schäffner 2002) emerges in the discourse. On the level of the co-construction of meaning, RD is used as a mediational means in order to anchor and objectify something from the sociocultural, interactional and cognitive contexts into the ongoing frame of action. Here I will focus on the politicians who use it not only to develop the factual and referential aspects of their answers, but also to construct their own standpoint on the topics, or to show their attachment to persons or ideas.

3. Contrastiveness and research questions

In this analysis, the method will be contrastive, which refers to a very broad notion of cross-linguistic comparison on a pragmatic level. As I will be comparing political pragmatic phenomena, the basic assumption, according to Gurevitch/Blumer (1990, 306) is that different features will "promote or constrain political communication roles and behavior in given systems". By comparison, when more than one case of national political communication is analyzed one draws attention to different features and their meaning (cf. Gurevitch/Blumer 1990, 309).

There are several possible ways of carrying out this kind of work. Traditionally, contrastive approaches have started with comparison of differences between two languages, taking one of them as a frame of reference (Hellinger/Ammon 1996, 5). According to Krzeszowki (1989, 57), there are three steps in contrastive studies, which are description, juxtaposition, and comparison. He says that the choice of the platform of reference, or, to put in more traditional terms, the *tertium comparationis*, is a determining factor in finding out similarities or differences. As my object of study is a pragmatic one, the remark of Verschueren (1996, 590) has also to be taken into account. In contrastive pragmatics, one should not consider certain categories, such as requests, to be stable phenomena. The negotiation the interactants produce "does not allow for fixed form-function relationships" (Verschueren 1996, 590). In other words, in the analysis of the narrative use of RD, it is the variation that will be examined (see section 5).

Finally, I agree with Chesterman (1998, 54-61), who says the comparison that starts with perceived similarity of any kind between two languages, leads to a general problem: "what is the nature of this similarity?" and to the initial hypothesis: "X and Y are identical". The kind of similarity we are looking is the one Chesterman (1998, 7) calls *similarity-as-attribution* or *subjective similarity*, that is, an observer perceives that some entities in the world are similar. In this case, the direct or indirect form of RD is the basis on which we identify the formal entities, but we are looking for the functional similarities (see Chesterman 1998, 35; Hellinger/Ammon 1996, 6; Jaszczolt 1995, 562) of one linguistic device between the two languages.

I formulate my research questions as follows:
– What kind of variation is there in the use of represented discourse?
– What are the functions fulfilled by represented discourse in these positions?
– Are these functions similar in two different languages?

By asking these questions, we will find out how the RD functions as a narrative mediational means.

4. Data

As basic data I use four full length French interviews recorded at the beginning of the 1990's from two interview programs, *7 sur 7* and *L'heure de vérité*. The politicians interviewed are from different political parties, but all have occupied the position of minister in the past. The politicians are Martine Aubry, Jack Lang, Michèle Barzach and Bernard Tapie with different interviewers (Anne Sinclair in *7 sur 7* and several others one at a time in *L'heure de vérité*). These interviews are from 36 to 47 minutes long.

These data will be contrasted with four British interviews of Tony Blair by different interviewers on different programs (David Frost, Jonathan Dimbleby, Jeremy Paxman and

David Dimbleby) in 1997 and 1998. All the interviews are approximately from 24 to 30 minutes long.

All the interviewees – the French and the English – share the same political position: that of the opposition. Despite the differences in the length of the interviews, all the interviews can be characterized as dyadic.

5. Analysis

5.1 Delimiting criteria of RD

The analysis started with the identification of the linguistic object by its two main formal features: the syntactic form of direct or indirect RD, and the explicit voice. In this analysis, the voice is a singular or plural, animate (*my dad, the Conservatives*) or inanimate (*contract*) 3rd person voice. On these criteria, 53 instances of RD were found in the French data and 43 in the English data.

Then, the discursive and interactional context of emergence was examined. This was done along three different lines of *sequentiality* (see Johansson 2002), namely *turn-taking*, *topic progression* and the production of *textual sequences* in answers. In other words, the positioning of RD in answers was examined together with the kind of textual sequences in which RD emerges. Here, the notion of *textual sequence* is used in the sense in which it is defined by Adam (1992). Instead of starting with a typology concerning a text, Adam distinguishes several kinds of prototypical textual sequence that can be found *within* a text. There are five types of textual sequence, namely *dialogical, narrative, descriptive, explicative* and *argumentative* (Adam 1992). Their status can vary from dominant to embedded. The political interview is a dialogical, that is, interactional text. As for the other types of textual sequence, it is the explicative and argumentative ones that are dominant. Narrative and descriptive sequences are most often embedded within the explicative and argumentative sequences. In the following, the narrative functions of represented discourse will be examined.

5.2 Types of RD and narrativity

According to Adam (1992, 70f.), a textual sequence can be characterized as *narrative* if it contains a unity of action that is marked on the surface level by temporal organization, thematic unity and succession of events. In other words, a narrative contains temporal and causal features. Unlike ordinary conversations, political interviews rarely contain narrative sequences, and this is precisely the reason why it is interesting to take them as an object of study.

In the present data, there is only one interview that contained narrative sequences in the sense defined by Adam. This interview was highly conflictual and its topics concerned more the private or professional domains of the politician (French politician Bernard Tapie) than the public sphere. The politician was asked to explain the incidents and the scandals he was believed to be involved in. In this case, the RD was used to represent dialogues within a short narrative or story he told. The stories contained the characteristics described above. We can formulate the first case in the following manner:

(1) RD can constitute (several) turns of a dialogue and represent one or several voices speaking in a complete narrative sequence (story).

However, there are also narrative elements embedded in explicative and argumentative sequences. These were found in both French and English interviews. Here, the characteristics of RD are mainly twofold. On the one hand, it resembles the first case, as the representing utterance can contain some scene setting and there can be one or two turns of dialogue that are recontextualized, but unlike the first case, this type does not contain all the phases of a story (with a beginning or an end, for instance). On the other, RD remains a narrativized utterance representing mainly one piece of speech from public space without specification of the scene of original utterance or all the narrative features. We can summarize these types as follows:

(2) RD can represent a part, usually one turn, of a dialogue with some scene setting and certain narrative features.

(3) RD represents a piece of speech in public sphere with certain narrative features but without specific scene setting in the representing utterance.

It needs to be added that in cases 1) and 2), the speaker describes him- or herself as present in the situation in which the RD was originally uttered. In case 3), there is no indication of the presence of the speaker in the situation with the voice.

5.3 Comparison of English and French RD

(1) RD can constitute (several) turns of a dialogue and represent one or several voices speaking in a complete narrative sequence (story).

It was only the French data that contain *stories or short narratives* that contained a recontextualization of more than one turn of dialogue. In the following, there is an incident that is related by the politician in three different turns:

IE: Dans les questions que posait euh ce journaliste à mon assistante qui était tourmentée je la voyais. elle transpirait à grosses gouttes et et je passais à ce moment-là **je lui dit** *qu'est-ce qui se PASSE Noelle* **elle me dit** *ils font une* [*enquête*]
[...]

IE: [*ils sont en train de*] *faire une enquête sur votre fortune personelle*

IR: ah

IE: alors je le prends et et je le sentais bien **aux questions qu'il me posait me disant** *mais DITES-MOI vous êtes quand même très ENDETTE* et j'ai compris que ça lui faisait plaisir + que je lui dise que j'étais ruiné {riant}+ [...]

In these questions that the journalist asked my secretary who was upset I saw her she was perspiring heavily and I was passing at that moment and **I said to her** *what is going on Noelle* **she said to me** *they are carrying out an investigation*
[...]

they are carrying out an investigation of your personal property

oh

then I take [the phone] and I sensed what he meant by **the questions he was asking saying to me** *but tell me you must be very much in debt* and I realized it would make him happy if I told him I was ruined {laughing}+ [...]

In this excerpt, the politician is relating a conversation with his secretary and a phone conversation he has had with a journalist. Here the RDs are preceded by a piece of scene setting, a contextualisation of the situation by means of a perception of the politician *je la voyais elle* [*I saw her*] and by means of a description of his own actions: *et et je passais à ce moment-là* [*I was passing at that moment*]. This is followed by the first instance of RD, which forms the first question turn in a dialogue he has had with his secretary, the first voice being his own and the secretary answering him in the second turn. The last instance of RD is a recontextualization of the questions a journalist has asked him over the phone. At the end, the politician relates his own evaluation of the questions he has been asked to answer. In all, by telling this story the politician declares why he has answered in a certain way in a phone interview and reveals his implicit attitude towards journalists.

(2) RD can represent a part, usually one turn, of a dialogue with some scene setting and certain narrative features.

In both sets of data, the English and the French, there are instances in which a turn recontextualized by the politician is preceded or followed by the description of the situation. In the following excerpt, Tony Blair is setting out what he can promise for the Health Service when he comes up with an RD which is situated in the past.

IE: Well I look I believe that we will end that situation but if you re saying to me are you going to commit yourself to saying that everything in the Health Service is going to be put right I can't do that what I can say is that we will start the process and I believe people in this country see er **I I when I was doing this meeting now with those people that had come over the Labour Party a woman put a point to me I thought was a very good point she said** *all I want is for you to make promises that you can keep don't tell us you can do everything* and the people in this country want that they know that we can't put eighteen years right in eighteen days

The RD contains a rather long description of the situation pointing out the scene (*meeting*), the actors involved in it (*people, a woman*). The voice, the *woman*, is left anonymous. What characterizes this instance is that it is framed before and after by the politician's evaluation. First, in describing his reaction, the politician uses the first person (*I*), modal verb *think* in the past tense and adjective *good* (*I thought it was a good point*). The RD constitutes support for his way of taking action in politics (reforms take a long time) and shows that his action has the understanding of the people. In other words, this is an indirect way of not making a promise of any kind.

(3) RD represents a piece of speech in public sphere with certain narrative features but without specific scene setting in the representing utterance.

In the following excerpt, there is an RD which contains two parts embedded in an argument concerning the opposing party. The RD emerges in the middle of the answer and it functions as a example in the argument.

> IE: Well there are no major steps of integration that we intend to agree to I mean we've made that absolutely clear and again just so I can knock down a bit of Conservative propaganda (…) so any Conservative propaganda that is saying the opposite it's simply not true what we do have to do is though in Europe and this is the issue of Europe it's about leadership if you look at what's happened to Britain over the beef war look here we are a year on from the imposition of that ban **when Mr Major said** *he'd get the ban lifted within weeks of the beef war* **then he came back and said** *it would be lifted by the end of Nov by the beginning of November* **and** here we are six months on not a thing has been done now we have to get into a position with Britain in Europe where we start to shape and lead the agenda for change (…)

The politician is taking a position against the Conservatives and setting out his own political program for the place of Britain in Europe. The RD is initiated by a hypothetical utterance beginning with *if* and mediates criticism of the Prime Minister of the time and his incapacity to take action in a certain situation. The instance contains time deixis (*a year on from*, *within weeks*, *by the end of Nov*, *by the beginning of November*, *six months on*) anchoring the incident temporally. In comparison with the second case, here the utterance seems – even though this is not explicitly specified – to have been made in the media. In the French data, there is a different kind of use of RD of this type.

6. Conclusion

I have distinguished three different types of RD use which have narrative features. The first type is a narrative sequence which was found only in the French data. The stories were told in a conflictual situation about personal topics or about topics belonging to the professional life of the politician, not to politics. The politician recontextualized dialogues in which he had taken part.

The two other types are found in both sets of data. They are narrativized RDs which are embedded in explicative or argumentative sequences. The second type is also one in which the politician put marks of his presence in the original situation of utterance, but this type contains only one turn of dialogue functioning as a starting point for an evaluation or as the support the politician needed in his or her argument. The third type of RD represents something uttered in the public sphere with certain narrative features but without specific scene setting in the representing utterance. The functions fulfilled by RD in the two latter cases are similar in both languages.

Overall, there is some variation in the use of RD in the data, but this needs to be tested with a larger set of data to discover if it is a cultural difference. The RD is a linguistic device that can be used to give an example, to act as an anchor for comparison, to supply a fact from the public space or to lend support to an argument. This is the way in which the politician links him- or herself to public space and to the ongoing topics in which he or she is taking part or on which he or she is commenting.

References

Adam, Jean-Michel (1992): Les textes: types et prototypes. Récit, description, argumentation, explication et dialogue. Paris: Nathan.
Charaudeau, Patrick (2002): A quoi sert d'analyser le discours politique? In: Lorda, Clara U./Ribas, Monserrat (eds.): Anàlisi del discurs polític. Producció, mediació i recepció. Barcelona: Universitat Pompeu Fabra, 161-176.
Chesterman, Andrew (1998): Contrastive functional analysis. Amsterdam, Philadelphia: Benjamins.
Chilton, Paul/Schäffner, Christina (2002): Themes and principles in the analysis of political discourse. In: Chilton, Paul/Schäffner, Christina (eds.): Politics as text and talk. Analytic approaches to political discourse. Amsterdam, Philadephia: Benjamins, 1-41.
Clayman, Steven (1992): Footing in the achievement of neutrality: the case of news interview discourse. In: Drew, Paul/Heritage, John (eds.): Talk at work. Interaction in institutional settings. Cambridge: University Press, 163-198.
Clayman, Steven/Heritage, John (2002): The news interviews. Journalists and public figures on the air. Cambridge: University Press.

Fairclough, Norman (1992): Discourse and social change. Cambridge: Polity Press.
– (1995): Media discourse. London: Edward Arnold.
Gurevitch, Michael/Blumer, Jay G. (1990): Comparative research: Extending frontier. In: Swanson, David L./Nimmo, Dan (eds.): New directions in political communication. London: Sage, 305-325.
Hellinger, Marlis/Ammon, Ulrich (1996): Contrastive sociolinguistics: An introduction. In: Hellinger, Marlis/Ammon, Ulrich (eds.): Contrastive sociolinguistics. Berlin, New York: de Gruyter. 1-13.
Jaszczolt, Katarzyna (1995): Contrastive analysis. In: Verschueren, Jef/Östman, Jan-Ola/Blommaert, Jan (eds.): Handbook of pragmatics. Manual. Amsterdam, Philadelphia: Benjamins, 561-565.
Johansson, Marjut (2000): Recontextualisation du discours d'autrui. Discours représenté dans l'interview médiatique politique. Turku: Université de Turku.
– (2002): Sequential positioning of represented discourse in institutional media interaction. In: Fetzer, Anita/Meierkord, Christiane (eds.): Rethinking sequentiality. Amsterdam, Philadelphia: Benjamins, 249-271.
Krzeszowki, Tomaz P. (1989): Towards a typology of contrastive studies. In: Oleksy, Wieslaw (ed.): Contrastive pragmatics. Amsterdam, Philadelphia: Benjamins, 55-72.
Scollon, Ron (2001): Mediated discourse: the nexus of practice. London: Routledge.
Verschueren, Jef (1996): Functioning in a multi-cultural world. Contrastive ideology research: aspects of a pragmatic methodology. In: Language Sciences 18/3-4, 589-603.
Vygotsky, Lev S. (1978): Mind in society. Cambridge, Mass., London: Harvard University Press.
Wertsch, James V. (1998): Mind as action. New York, Oxford: Oxford University Press.

Anita Fetzer

Non-acceptances in political interviews: British styles and German styles in conflict?

1. Introduction

Political interviews have been investigated from different perspectives: the conversation-analytic approach focuses primarily on the interactional organization and reconstruction of a political interview as regards the context-sensitive employment of the turn-taking system and the interactional organization of neutralism (cf. Greatbatch 1998). Of relevance to this analysis of non-acceptances in political interviews is their premise that a communicative genre is interactionally organized locally on the micro domain and globally on the more remote level of genre and its constitutive opening, closing and topical-sequence sections (cf. Luckmann 1995). The critical-discourse-analysis approach (cf. Fairclough 1998) examines the role of language regarding medialization, conversationalization and ideology. The social-psychology paradigm (cf. Bull 2003) focuses on political equivocation and face. Pragmatics (cf. Blum-Kulka 1983, Fetzer 2000, Wilson 1990) concentrates on the participant's rights and obligations, which are deduced from a speech act's felicity conditions. It also examines *hedging* and *evasiveness*, which are anchored to the dichotomy of *what is said versus what is meant*. The distinction is the foundation of the differentiation between direct speech acts and an explicit use of language, and indirect speech acts and an implicit use of language: direct speech acts do not seem to cause any communication problems as the speaker unambiguously says what s/he means. By contrast, indirect, implicit or speaker's meanings are anchored to the speaker's communicative intentions and must be inferred from an utterance in its social, sociocultural, linguistic and cognitive contexts. For this reason, implicit meaning is indeterminate – to some degree. In the integrative approach to political interviews adopted here, the frameworks are seen as supplementary rather than mutually exclusive. So how are non-acceptances seen in this integrated perspective?

Non-acceptances comprise the communicative acts of denial, rejection, disagreement and challenge, which can be realized both implicitly and explicitly. From a sequential-organization viewpoint, a non-acceptance is a responsive act, and its communicative function can be (1) to deny the truth of a prior communicative act, (2) to reject its appropriateness and (3) to reject its sincerity. Furthermore, non-acceptances refer locally to the domain of a communicative act and its presuppositions, and they refer globally to the domain of communicative genre and its presuppositions. Since communicative performance is anchored to sociocultural competence (cf. Saville-Troike 1989), every speech community has culture-specific preferences for the linguistic realization of non-acceptances regarding particular levels of directness and indirectness, and their more process- or more product-oriented interactional organization.

Against this background, a contrastive analysis of non-acceptances has been conducted. It is based on short dyadic interviews (2 to 5 minutes) between professional journalists and the losers of the general election in Britain (1997) and Germany (1998). The German data and the British data share almost identical external parameters and very similar contextual features. Moreover, the coparticipant's argumentation is based on nearly identical premises, namely that they are not in a position to comment on their situation as their defeat has not yet been assigned an official status. In spite of the contextual similarities, the linguistic realizations of the British and German non-acceptances differ significantly.

The following section presents the definition of a non-acceptance, which is informed by Habermas's notion of *validity claim* from his *theory of communicative action*. Section 3 examines non-acceptances in British election-night interviews and presents a taxonomy based on their referential domains, section 4 analyses non-acceptances in German election-night interviews and categorizes them accordingly. Section 5 summarizes the results obtained.

2. Non-acceptances: a definition

The communicative act of a non-acceptance is defined within a sociopragmatic frame of reference. Adopting Habermas's (1987) theoretical outline and terminology, communication is based on the premise that coparticipants negotiate the communicative status of their validity claims. Of relevance is his premise that a dyadic setting is a necessary condition for communication: a speaker postulates a validity claim and directs it towards an addressee, who ratifies the act by accepting it and assigning it the status of a plus-validity claim, or by rejecting it and assigning it the status of a minus-validity claim. Another necessary condition for felicitous communication, which is defined as the negotiation of validity claims, is their ratification. Departing from Habermas's macro approach, plus/minus-validity claims are defined by their references to context. This comprises the notions of (1) social and sociocultural contexts, (2) linguistic context, cotext and (3) cognitive context, which are conceived of as an onion with its constitutive layers, metaphorically speaking (cf. Sperber/Wilson 1996). Naturally, the different sets of contexts are administered in their own particular ways.

As regards linguistic and social contexts, the contextual references of a validity claim are systematized in a tripartite system of objective, social and subjective worlds, which is schematized in figure I:

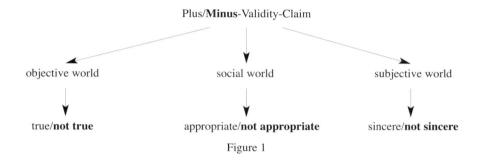

Figure 1

In the communication framework, non-acceptances are explicated as follows:
- The objective world is defined by truth, which is based on reference and predication, and on their presuppositions. False validity claims comprise the non-acceptance of reference, of predication or of their presuppositions.
- The subjective world is defined by sincerity, which is based on a coparticipant's communicative intention meant as uttered and uttered as meant. Insincere validity claims comprise the non-acceptance of the speaker's or hearer's sincere intentions.
- The social world is defined by the appropriateness of the communicative act, which is based on another tripartite system of interpersonal, interactional and textual presuppositions. This is schematized in figure II:

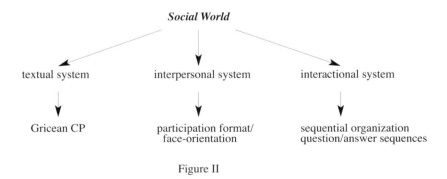

Figure II

A non-acceptance referring to the social world and its presuppositions is defined as follows:
- The textual system is based on the Gricean cooperative principle (CP), the maxims of

quality, quantity, relation and manner, and the conversational implicature (cf. Grice 1975). Inappropriate validity claims are defined by the non-acceptance of a communicative act as being in accordance with one or more of the maxims or with the calculation of the implicature. Not acting in accordance with the CP does not result in an inappropriate validity claim. Instead, not adhering to this fundamental premise means not communicating at all.

– The interpersonal system is based on Brown and Levinson's (1987) conception of a model person, its face needs and face wants, and on Goffman's conception of footing (cf. Goffman 1974). Inappropriate validity claims are defined as not being in accordance with the contextual constraints and requirements regarding face and participation.

– The interactional system is based on sequentiality and sequential organization. Inappropriate validity claims are defined as not being in accordance with the basic premise of adjacency and the contextual constraints and requirements of the turn-taking system (cf. Levinson 1983).

Non-acceptances do not only express that a validity claim is considered as inappropriate, untrue or insincere on the local domain of discourse. They also express that a validity claim is inappropriate or insincere on the global domain of genre. Here, they express violations of genre-specific norms and expectations. In the framework of political interviews this means that there is an inappropriate performance with regard to its guiding principle of neutralism (cf. Greatbatch 1992), its constitutive coparticipant-specific question-and answer sequences, its genre-specific ratified participation status, and its media-specific constraints and requirements. For instance, an interviewee might choose to ask questions instead of answering them, an interviewer might ask questions about the politician's personal domains, or an interviewer and interviewee might only talk amongst themselves and not to the audience.

In the following, the linguistic representation of non-acceptances in British election-night interviews is examined in detail.[1]

3. Non-acceptances in British election-night interviews

In the interviews with the losers of the 1997 election, there are numerous negotiation-of-validity-claim sequences and thus a high degree of negotiation of meaning. This is due to the fact that the conservatives did not want to focus on the present moment of the interaction which entailed their defeat and loss of power. Instead, they talked in detail about the merits

---

[1] I would like to thank Gerda Lauerbach and her team for sharing their data with me.

of their former government. The negotiation-of-validity-claim sequences display a higher frequency of verbs of cognition used with an epistemic function, such as *think* or *believe*, a higher frequency of cohesive links, for instance *so* or *so you're saying*, a larger number of references to media-specific constraints and requirements and a larger number of references to the inappropriateness of questions and presuppositions than a ratifying sequence would do. While the verbs of cognition signify subjectification and reduce the pragmatic force of the argument, the cohesive links function as textual signposts and generally indicate some incoherence. More precisely, textual-meaning references to one's own argument have the communicative function of making it stronger, while textual-meaning references to other's argument indicate that it has not been fully conclusive. This also holds for references to media-specific constraints and requirements, which are frequently used as a reason for locally opting out (cf. Lauerbach in press).

In the following, non-acceptances of the election-night interviews are systematized with regard to their inappropriate referential domains.

3.1 Non-acceptances of the appropriateness of a validity claim's content

All of the following examples are responses to the interviewer's questions, in which s/he intends to elicit a statement about who is to blame for the defeat of the conservatives. All responses display metapragmatic devices, which intensify the pragmatic force of the argument. In example (1), Stephen Dorell (SD), the Health Secretary, boosts the pragmatic force of his minus-validity claim by the adverbial phrase *by any means* and explicitly rejects the interviewer's implicit presupposition that the outcome of the general election has been decided. In (2), which is performed implicitly, the force is attenuated by the negated verb of cognition *don't think*:

(1) SD: *I don't accept by any means* that the results of the election has yet been decided or at least that it is yet known ...

(2) SD: *No I don't think* that we need to get into speculations about what the lessons are from a result we don't know yet

The same line of argumentation is employed by William Hague (WH), the leader of the conservatives, who rejects the interviewer's validity claims implicitly in (3), and by David Evans (DE), who explicitly rejects the validity claim that John Major, the former Prime Minister, is to be blamed in (4):

(3) WH: *Well I don't think* we should *I don't think* there is any point in apportioning blame around the party ...

(4) DE: *No it's not his fault*. Nice man, sincere, wonderful ...

The strong pragmatic force of explicit non-acceptances is reinforced by an additional negative evaluation. This is discussed in the following section.

3.2 Non-acceptances of a validity claim's appropriateness with an explicit negative evaluation

Non-acceptances of a validity claim's appropriateness with an explicit negative evaluation do not focus on the content of a prior validity claim. Instead, they explicitly refer to its sequential status, for instance by the explicit term *question* or by the implicit pronominal expression *it*; these references are evaluated by the strong negative adjectives *ridiculous* by Alan Clark (AC) in (5), *not sensible* by Michael Howard (MH) in (6), by Stephen Dorrell (SD) in (7) and by John Redwood (JR) in (8), and *secondary* by SD in (9):

(5) AC: oh that's a *ridiculous question*

(6) MH: I do*n't* think that's *a very sensible question*

(7) SD: ... and I do*n't* think it's *very sensible* to speculate about *it* when all we know that the result the true result is gonna be available within a few hours

(8) JR: Well I want to look at the overall results in the light of the morning and think what would be right to say. I do*n't* think *it's sensible* to rush off tonight with all sorts of explanations ...

(9) SD: Well I think the *leadership* question is frankly *a secondary question*

An explicit negative evaluation can close a topical sequence, or it can close a short interview, as is the case with the data examined here. In the following, another strategy to close a sequence is discussed.

3.3 Non-acceptances of a validity claim's appropriateness by explicitly opting out

The strategy of *opting out* is adopted from the Gricean CP, which is the foundation of the social world's constitutive textual system. That is, coparticipants can opt out locally if higher-order principles provide good reasons for doing so. They over-rule the fundamental requirement that coparticipants should make their contribution "such as is required, at the stage at which it occurs, by the accepted purpose of direction of the talk exchange" (cf. Grice 1975, 45). In the British data, the strategy is quite frequent and often based on the claim that one should not speak on behalf of and for a colleague. However, references to the moral principle of loyalty, as is the case with John Redwood (JR) in (10), are not a necessary requirement for opting out. Interviewees can also opt out by simply stating that they are not commenting on a validity claim thereby implicating that the claim in question lacks validity, as is the case with JR in (11), and Ian Lang (IL) in (12) and (13):

(10) JR: *I'm not commenting on anything like that.* John Major is the leader of the conservative party and you should allow him time to consider what is best for the conservative party

(11) JR: *I have no further comments ...*

(12) IL: *I'm not gonna talk about that now*

(13) IL: *I'm not gonna talk about that either* that's a hype/ a hype/ a hypothesis ...

Validity claims are not only rejected on the micro domains. They are also rejected on the macro domain of genre regarding their genre- and media-specific constraints and requirements. This is examined in the following.

3.4 Non-acceptances of the macro validity claim's appropriateness

Political interviews are defined as both public discourse and media event (cf. Fetzer 2000). As a consequence of this, the appropriateness of validity claims referring to the two domains can be rejected. In the election-night interviews, there is not a single instance of a non-accepted reference to the public domain. Media-specific references and constraints, however, are challenged by Brian Mawhinney (BW) in (14), and by Michael Heseltine (MH) in (15):

(14) BM: I have spoken to the prime minister er on a number of occasions during the course of the evening and you would erm expect me to give him any advice that he might or might not seek in private *not in front of the television*

(15) MH: Well those are the sort of questions we'll have to ask ourselves and, as I said, I don't myself go for the sort of pealing technique within hours of the polls closing I think these will require mature reflection ... *a way which is very fascinating to the media* but it is not the best interest of the conservative party

In both cases, the appropriateness of a communicative act as mediated communicative action, such as giving advice in (14) and analysing an election defeat in (15), is not accepted. Rather, the interviewer's request to perform such an act is rejected as inappropriate.

3.5 Summary and conclusion

In the short election-night interviews investigated, non-acceptances are classified with regard to their domains of rejection, namely the appropriateness of a validity claim's content, which can be supplemented by an explicit negative evaluation. Furthermore, the communicative strategy of opting out anchored to the social world's textual system is frequently employed to reject the appropriateness of a validity claim. In addition to the local non-acceptances, media-specific macro requirements are rejected and signify an inappropriate interviewer performance. There are further non-acceptances, which are not discussed in detail here as they are anchored to longer sequences, such as the communicative strategy of avoiding the question, where an interviewee blatantly fails to respond thus signifying that s/he does not intend to respond in the interviewer-intended manner, not even if challenged in a follow-up sequence. Additionally, there are negotiation-of-validity sequences and negotiation-of-meaning sequences, where the appropriateness of lexical items, pronominal references and presuppositions is at stake.

4. Non-acceptances in German election-night interviews

The German data also consist of short election-night interviews with the losers of the 1998 general election, the Christian Democrats and its Bavarian sister party. Analogously to the British conservatives, they talk about the merits of their former government rather than commenting on their defeat. In spite of the content-based similarities, the non-accepted domains of reference and the strategies employed differ. In the German sociocultural context, the linguistic realization of rejecting the appropriateness of a validity claim's content is different; the same is true for the communicative strategy of opting out and for the non-acceptance of the macro validity claim's appropriateness. This is examined in the following.

4.1 Non-acceptance of the appropriateness of the validity claim's content

In the British data, rejecting the appropriateness of a validity claim's content is realized quite explicitly and sometimes accompanied by an explicit negative evaluation; and in all of the examples, the pragmatic force of the claim is intensified. In the German data, there is one instance of rejecting the appropriateness of a validity claim's content, example (16) by Peter Hinze (PH), which is implicit:

(16) PH: also mein demokratieverständnis ist ... [Now my conception of democracy is ...]

Not only is this type of non-acceptance realized implicitly, the communicative strategy of opting out is also performed implicitly, as is discussed in the following.

4.2 Non-acceptances of a validity claim's appropriateness by implicitly opting out

In the British data interviewees frequently opt out in an explicit manner. Or, they simply state that they intend to close a topical sequence. In the German data, opting out is performed implicitly. In (17), Norbert Blüm (NB), opts out non-verbally by shaking his head thus signifying that he does not intend to respond in the interviewer-intended manner. The non-compliance is supplemented by opting out implicitly. That is, NB provides reasons for not responding in the requested manner:

(17) NB: Also ich bin nicht jetzt der äh Besitzer der Gedanken der Wähler Aber richtig ist es gibt nie ne fehlerlose politik ... [Now I do not own the electorate's thoughts. But it is true that there is no politics without any flaws ...]

4.3 Non-acceptances of the macro validity claim's appropriateness

In the British data, references to the macro validity claim's appropriateness are anchored to the genre's constitutive domain of media. In the German data, there is only one reference to the genre-specific requirement of the turn-taking system. Again, this is realized implicitly. In (18), Theo Waigel (TW) asks the interviewer to let him finish his turn thereby implicating that he has been interrupted:

(18) TW: ja kleinen moment. Lassen sie mich einen satz nach dem anderen sagen. Wenn wir nun die absoluten zahlen nehmen ... [A tiny moment. Let me say one sentence after the other. If we take the absolute figure ...]

4.4 Summary and conclusion

In the German data there is less variation in the employment of communicative strategies for non-acceptances, and there is a preference for implicit linguistic realizations. However, we also find the strategy of avoiding the question.

5. Conclusions

The British and German short election-night interviews with the losers of the general elections have an almost identical content: the politicians do not want to give reasons for their failure and therefore talk about the merits of former governments. The content is, however, formulated differently. As a consequence of that, the following culture-specific ways of expressing non-acceptances are not only found in unmarked everyday talk, but also in political discourse: first, the British sociocultural context makes more references to both interpersonal and information domains. Compared to the German sociocultural context, the interpersonal domain is stressed. Second, the British sociocultural context prefers a process-oriented setting, where the institutional identities of interviewer and interviewee are interactionally organized in a more dynamic manner with more interpersonal needs. The German sociocultural context prefers a product-oriented setting, where the identities are interactionally organized in a less dynamic manner with less interpersonal needs.

References

Blum-Kulka, Shoshana (1983): The dynamics of political interviews. In: Text 3/2, 131-153.
Bull, Peter (2003): The microanalysis of political communication: Claptrap and ambiguity. London: Routledge.
Brown, Penelope/Levinson, Stephen (1987): Politeness. Cambridge: Cambridge University Press.
Fairclough, Norman (1998): Political discourse in the media: an analytical framework. In: Bell, A./Garret, P. (eds.): Approaches to media discourse. Oxford: Blackwell, 142-162.
Fetzer, Anita (2000): Negotiating validity claims in political interviews. In: Text 20/4, 1-46.
Goffman, Erving (1974): Frame analysis. New York: Harper & Row.
Greatbatch, David (1992): The management of disagreement between news interviewees. In: Drew, P./Heritage, J. (eds.): Talk at work. Cambridge: Cambridge University Press, 268-301.
– (1998): Conversation analysis: Neutralism in British news interviews. In: Bell, A./Garret, P. (eds.): Approaches to media discourse. Oxford: Blackwell, 163-185.
Grice, H. Paul (1975): Logic and conversation. In: Cole, P./Morgan, L. (eds.): Syntax and semantics. Vol. 2: Speech acts. New York: Academic Press, 41-58.
Habermas, Jürgen (1987): Theorie des kommunikativen Handelns. Frankfurt a.M.: Suhrkamp.
Lauerbach, Gerda (in press): Opting out of the media-politics contract. Discourse practices in confrontational television interviews. In: Bondi, M. (ed.): Selected papers from the 8th IADA conference Bologna 2000. Tübingen: Niemeyer.
Levinson, Stephen (1983): Pragmatics. Cambridge: Cambridge University Press.
Luckmann, Thomas (1995): Interaction planning and intersubjective adjustment of perspectives by communicative genres. In: Goody, E. (ed): Social intelligence and interaction: Expressions and implications of the social bias in human intelligence. Cambridge: Cambridge University Press, 175-188.
Saville-Troike, Muriel (1989): The ethnography of speaking. Oxford: Blackwell.
Sperber, Dan/Wilson, Deidre (1996): Relevance: Communication and cognition. Oxford: Blackwell.
Wilson, John (1990): Politically speaking. Oxford: Oxford University Press.

Dominique Desmarchelier

Argumentative strategies: the French debate about immigration

We will attempt to show the thematic movements and the dissemination of opinions in the public arena in France by comparing the types of arguments used during sessions on immigration at the French National Assembly with arguments used on TV debates, or amongst citizens in public places.

Political oratory

In book I (part.3) of *Rhetoric*, Aristotle establishes three kinds of rhetoric: political, forensic and ceremonial. Of the first one, he writes:

> Political speaking urges us either to do or not to do something: one of these two courses is always taken by private counsellors, as well as by men who address public assemblies.[...] These three kinds of rhetoric refer to three different kinds of time [...] The political orator is concerned with the future: it is about things to be done hereafter that he advises, for or against.

In a few lines, everything seems to have been quickly laid down by the Greek philosopher. In the following chapter, Aristotle even gives a list of the matters on which all men deliberate (and about which political speakers make speeches): ways and means, war and peace, national defence, imports and exports and legislation. A hasty conclusion could lead us to believe that the debate on immigration is only a matter of law. However, it becomes clear when studying discussions, that speaking of immigration and therefore of immigrants, also refers to ways and means, national defence, security and threats of war.

Places of debate

This presentation is based on a report to the Region Rhône-Alpes in 2001 on parliamentary debates, televised debates, legal documents on schooling of immigrants' children, articles from Encyclopaedia Universalis, Internet websites' discussions amongst students and conversations heard at a newsagents. The above mentioned document involved 2 teams of researchers: on the one hand, a team specialised in "argumentative discourse analysis", and a team specialised in "discourse analysis and lexicometry", on the other hand. In this presentation, we will only look at different types of arguments used in the various places for debate and their circulation.

Argumentation in the public places

In the preface of the new edition of "Espace public", Habermas brings up the idea of "public spaces" as a "place for exchanging points of view as well as for circulating ideas either personal or borrowed from journalists, politicians, experts or other people". It is no longer a place where only the elite discuss and debate.

A first examination of the various themes mentioned in relation to immigration will allow us to bring to light similarities and differences related to the place of debate and the situation in which the debate took place. According to the corpora (and according to their size), we have either used tools from lexicometry or from a more qualitative analysis whereby we have noted the themes mentioned during the discussion. We felt it would be less appropriate to apply statistical calculations to corpora containing a few thousands occurrences.

Comments on table 1

Some of the corpora, more specifically DEP/CES reports, only mention a few themes (schooling and cultural issues). On the contrary, discussions taking place at the French National Assembly, on TV or via forums on the Internet allow the participants to mention a majority of the themes in the table.

Reading across the table, looking at the themes, we notice that the most frequently occurring themes appear in 5 out of 7 corpora (culture, unemployment, legal status, delinquency, religion, daily life). We also notice that problems linked to daily life (proximity) are present in both debates at the French National Assembly and discussions at the newsagent. It will therefore be interesting to see whether the nature of the arguments used is similar or not.

Argumentative strategies

Themes \ Corpora	RESEDA National Assembly	Encycl. ALIS ALIA	CES/DEP Reports	Media	Internet	Students	Newsagent
1. People of different cultures	+	+	+	+	+	+	+
2. Workers = economic necessity	+	+		+		+	
3. Advantages for France brought by immigration	+	+		+	+	+	
4. Tradition = "immigrant friendly" land	+			+		+	+
5. Reseda text	+			+	+	+	+
6. French nationality	+			+	+		+
7. Unemployment problems	+	+		+	+	+	
8. Legal status Legalised/illegal	+	+		+	+	+	+
9. Daily life, proximity	+	+		+	+	+	+
10. Demography, birth-rate	+	+		+	+	+	
11. Religions, conflicts, fundamentalism	+	+		+	+		+
12. Delinquency	+			+	+	+	+
13. Racism toward immigrants	+						
14. Anti-Semitism							+
15. Play the French National Front's game	+			+	+		+
16. Education, Problems in school			+				
17. Political force Lobbying	+						+

Table 1: Themes mentioned in the different corpora

To illustrate this, let us compare an extract of discussion about polygamy taking place at French National Assembly, to a discussion taking place at the newsagent.

> CH. COVA (RPR): Pour épouser des femmes là-bas et les ramener en France!
> CH. COVA (RPR): Vous les connaissez mal, ils ramènent des minettes de quinze ans!
> B. ACCOYER (RPR): Ils sont plus vigoureux que vous!

---

[1] Corpus by Marianne Doury (A.D.I 2001).

Maison de la presse (Press House):[1]

    F1: ah: rue des Envierges | (...) rue des Envierges y a (.) y a (.) y a quat' femmes (.) pour le mâle (.) le
    C4: | ah oui rue des Envierges y en a beaucoup
    F1: mâle et y a vingt gosses dans (.) dans un quat'pièces
    F2: non (.) c'est vrai (.) | elle a raison
    F1: | alors::
    C4: y en a quelques uns comme ça | (..) oh pas beaucoup hein
    C: | ouais:: mais c'est pas la majorité:
    F2: non (.) y en a pas beaucoup
    F1: si (.) dans (.) dans mon immeuble y a une famille de noirs qui sont arrivés i sont très propres (..) y a deux femmes (...) et (.) et y en a une qui en fabrique l'autre elle est stérile paraît-il (.) y a elle a déj- et ça | elle est mariée depuis (..) elle est elle est mariée depuis six
    C: | <u>c'est une jumente alors</u> [riant]
    F1: ans (..) elle a six enfants déjà (..) maint'nant (.) elle entame le septième (.) alors ma gardienne qui a pas sa langue dans sa poche (.) elle lui a dit mais (.) vous allez en avoir combien comme ça (.) alors | (.) elle elle a dit
    F2: | ça ça s'dit pas ça
    F1: mais oh:: huit peut-être dix douze enfin (.) c'est celle celle qui est stérile qui a répondu pour
    C: <u>quatorze</u> [riant]

The noticeable difference is that whereas members of the Assembly use generic terms (*they, them*), customers at the newsagent use personal experiences (*in my apartment building, there's a family* ...).

In the next extracts, it is the difference between illegal and legal immigration, which is mentioned by MPs and students:

National Assembly, Conference 8 (8. 4. 98):

>THIERRY MARIANI (RPR): [...] Le certificat d'hébergement est un instrument de lutte contre *l'immigration irrégulière*, mais c'est aussi un outil qui permettait aux étrangers de bénéficier de conditions de résidence décentes sur notre sol. Pourquoi donc voulez-vous le supprimer? Je vous citerai cette phrase du président Fabius, que vous trouverez page 1334 du Journal officiel du 25 février 1997: "Les certificats n'avaient qu'un but: préserver la dignité de l'étranger accueilli sur notre sol, lui garantir un toit, assurer sa santé physique et morale, mettre fin à l'exploitation de la misère des plus pauvres à laquelle se livrent les marchands de sommeil."

Discussions in the media:[2]

>CHARLES PASQUA: Oui. J'crois que (*traîne*) le problème de l'immigration c'est avant tout celui de l'immigration (*pause*) *irrégulière*, de l'immigration (*pause*) *clandestine*. C'est cela qui pose problème. Et c'est cela qui pose problème notamment heu par rapport à ceux qui heu sont entrés légalement et qui sont installés *régulièrement* sur notre sol. Parc'que quand les gens entrent heu, sont dans une situation *irrégulière*, ou y deviennent heu la proie des esclavagistes c't-à-dire des gens qui font travailler à bas prix dans des conditions inhumaines etc., ou bien alors heu ils tombent entre les mains des, des, des trafiquants de drogue etc. (Et) du même coup se fait l'amalgame (*pause*) entre (*pause*) immigré(s), délinquant(s) et ça

---

2   Corpus by Christine Barats (A.D.I 2001).

c'est extrêmement préjudiciable (*pause*) pour la démocratie. Alors j'crois que le, global'-ment heu la France a réussi, et elle continue à réussir d'ailleurs, (*pause*) l'intégration. 80% des gens ne posent aucun problème.

Discussion among students:[3]

LAURENT [22,35]: *l'immigration clandestine*
on est allé là-bas on est allé dans ces pays là sans aucun sans aucun droit en fait finalement on leur a imposé plus ou moins notre culture notre façon de vivre et cetera
y rêvent de notre pays et cetera je comprends tout à fait moi qu'il y ait de l'immigration clandestine et cetera mais c'est nous qui l'avons créée finalement quelque part donc heu::

AHMED [23,45]: *nous*
les étrangers que la France a fait appel tous les étrangers à qui la France a fait appel les personnes qui sont intégrées ici les personnes étrangères et qui vivent ici qui sont peut-être heureux d'être ici peut-être souhaitent aussi amener leurs proches leurs proches venir vivre avec eux ici et:

Internet Forum:[4]

PASQUIER GUILLAUME (étudiant): Malgré les prises de position démagogique des partis de gauche durant la campagne des dernières législatives, on constate, maintenant qu'ils sont au pouvoir, que leur position sur le problème de l'immigration clandestine n'est pas si éloignée de celle de leur prédécesseurs de droite. Du moins en ce qui concerne la gauche non-extrémiste.

GORJESTANI TEYMOURAZ (lycéen): 17.09.97 11h26 *Mensonges: il y a eu abrogation*
Les lois Pasqua-Debré ont été abrogées au contraire de ce que peuvent dire les hommes politiques. En effet, de nombreuses mesures inscrites dans ces lois seront effacées par le nouveau projet de loi Chevènement. C'est ine honte. En effet, coment veux-t-on lutter contre le chomage et la précarité si l'on fait un appel d'air à l'immigration. […]
L'angélisme, incarnée par la gauche n'a pas de place en cette fin de 20e siècle. Il faut lutter le plus efficacement possible contre l'immigration. […] Je lance donc un appel au gouvernement de ne rien supprimer des lois Pasqua-Debré mais au contraire de combattre plus fortement l'immigration clandestine. C'est l'avenir de la France qui se joue.

Towards a classification of arguments

Our answer will be based on the classification suggested by Philippe Breton, "Autorité, analogie, cadrage et communauté". We will consider the transmission of the arguments between the different places of debates, either official (National Assembly, Official texts), in the media (TV, Internet) or public (university, shops).

---

3 Corpus by Christian Plantin (A.D.I 2001).
4 Corpus by Michel Marcoccia (A.D.I 2001).

The group of arguments for analogy uses classical structures, such as the example, the 4-terms analogy or the metaphor, giving them an argumentative power. [...] The group of arguments of authority covers any strategies in which an authority is established, whether pro or contra the motion, who is accepted by the audience and defends his opinion, which one may be for or against.

(Breton, 2001, 43)

	Types of Arguments	RESEDA National Assembly	Encycl. ALIS ALIA	CES/ DEP Reports	Media	Internet	Students	Newsagent
caution	Expert[5]	x	x	x	x	x		
	Personal Experience	x			x	x	x	x
	Testimony	x			x	x	x	x
	Negative[6] authority	x			x	x		x
analogy	Analogy	x				x		
	Example[7]	x	x		x	x	x	x
	Metaphor	x						
	Illustration[8]		x	x	x			

Table 2: Types of arguments used in the different corpora

Comments on table 2

Arguments of caution

a) One should not be surprised to see the arguments of competence (expert) in institutional or media debates. They are favoured by either the status of some of the participants or the use of approved authority's speech.

---

[5] Breton establishes a distinction between competence and experience. The expert (who has an acknowledged status in society), has competence in a certain domain or area, where competence has a more theoretical and institutional character. The individual, on the contrary, has acquired experience, which has not modified his status in society.

[6] The authority is given by the status in society. It is negative when used to illustrate an opposite point of view.

[7] Some testimonies are used as examples.

[8] We would like to point out that, according to Perelman, argumentation through example implies some disagreement regarding the subject of the rule the example is used to exemplify, whereas illustration is here to strengthen an already known and recognized rule.

b) On the contrary, personal testimonies of experiences are more common in discussions between students, on the Internet or at the shop.
c) Arguments of a negative authority's nature are used to discredit the opponent on the text in question.

Arguments of analogy

a) The use of analogy and metaphor seems restricted to institutional or Internet debates, however, the use of example is more widespread with the exception of the CES and DEP reports.
b) The aim of illustration is to update an acknowledged position and it is used mainly in official texts as encyclopaedia as well as occasionally in media debates.

Conclusion

Rather than a clear-cut difference, we note a continuum from more formal written language (encyclopaedia, official texts) to more spontaneous spoken language (discussions between students or customers), with various stages between the two (prepared speech or verbalised writing). The structure of the exchanges presents obvious differences due to the variations of spoken and written language, however, it is in the nature of the arguments used that different strategies come to light.

The oppositions established by Aristotle such as general/specific; affirmation/negation; accomplished/prospective reappear. Whereas similar themes on immigration are used, there is a variation in the types of arguments according to the different places of debates.[*]

---

[*] I am grateful to Julie Desmarchelier for translation of this paper.

References

Bonnafous, Simone/Desmarchelier, Dominique (2001): L'argumentation des députés des quatre principaux partis à l'Assemblée Nationale sur le projet de loi RESEDA. In: GRIC (CNRS et Lyon II) et ANACOLUT (ENS Fontenay/Saint-Cloud) (eds.): L'argumentation dans l'espace public contemporain: le cas du débat sur l'immigration. Lyon, mars 2001, 49-77.
Breton, Philippe (1996/2001): L'argumentation dans la communication. Paris: La Découverte/Repères.
Desmarchelier, Dominique/Doury, Marianne (ed.) (2001): L'argumentation dans l'espace public contemporain: le cas du débat sur l'immigration. GRIC (CNRS et Lyon II) et ANACOLUT (ENS Fontenay/Saint-Cloud) Rapport pour l'ARASH, mars 2001.
Heiden, Serge (1999): Encodage uniforme et normalisé de corpus: application à l'étude d'un débat parlementaire. In: Mots 60, 113-132, Presses de Sciences Po., version HTML (avec liens internes vers le site http://lexico.ens-lsh.fr)
– (2001): Manuel Utilisateur de WEBLEX, v 2.3, UMR8503, CNRS – ENS Lettres et Sciences humaines. Lyon, http://weblex.ens-lsh.fr/doc/*weblex*/index.html
Plantin, Christian (1990): Essais sur l'argumentation. Introduction à l'étude de la parole argumentative. Paris: Kimé.
– (1995): Fonction du tiers dans l'interaction argumentative. In: Kerbrat-Orecchioni, Catherine/Plantin, Christian (eds.): Le trilogie. Lyon: P.U.L, 108-133.

Anne-Marie Simon-Vandenbergen / Karin Aijmer

The discourse marker *of course* in British political interviews and its Dutch and Swedish counterparts: a comparison of persuasive tactics

1. Introduction

Research on the discourse marker *of course* has revealed that it is a multifunctional word which is used for various strategic purposes (e.g. Holmes 1988; Simon-Vandenbergen 1992). The discourse marker appears to be particularly favoured by political speakers in interviews, which tend to be adversarial in nature and which therefore require the use of persuasive tactics on the part of the interviewee (see Simon-Vandenbergen 1992). The aim of this paper is to examine the argumentative value of *of course* in contrast with that of similar devices in Dutch and Swedish in the same registers. The data which are used for this comparative study are British, Flemish and Swedish political interviews and debates.

The equivalents of *of course* in Dutch and Swedish have been gathered from translation corpora and are described extensively in Simon-Vandenbergen and Aijmer (2003). We hope to show in this way that the findings from contrastive corpus research can serve as a basis to provide further insight into intercultural similarities and differences, in this case in the genre of broadcast political argumentation.

Starting from an examination of the strategic uses of the most common translation equivalents, however, we have found that such words are part of a much larger field of markers of 'obviousness', which is systematically exploited by political speakers. We hope to show that political speakers in the data make use of various strategies to present propositions as non-negotiable. We argue that, while this paper can only lay bare the types of strategies which are part of the genre in the three cultures concerned, further research in this area promises to be rewarding from the point of view of intercultural genre analysis.

2. *Of course* in British political interviews

While *of course* is very frequent in several registers, including casual conversation (see Biber et al. 1999, 861), it appears to be particularly favoured by political speakers. Simon-Vandenbergen (1988) found that it was the most frequently used modal adverb in her corpus of radio political interviews. In order to explain this finding, Simon-Vandenbergen (1992) examined what functions *of course* has in conversation and in political interviews. More specifically, the aim of that study was to determine whether the difference was purely one of relative frequency or whether the two genres put the word to different uses.

It appeared that *of course* is used in quite different pragmatic contexts in the two genres. The main differences can be summed up as follows. The most important function of *of course* in conversation is to contribute to the basic purpose of speakers in such contexts, which is the establishment of sociability. One of the ways in which this goal can be reached is by maintaining a balance of power. In different contexts this balance is achieved in different ways. For instance, in the context of an exchange of services, the speaker formulating a request should not be 'dependent' on the requestee. In such contexts it is therefore polite to suggest that granting the request is to be expected as normal and certain. *Of course* can hence be used by the requestee to signal his or her agreement to comply with the request and moreover to present that agreement as 'obvious'. In general, it appears that *of course* is typically used in casual conversation in accordance with the politeness principles as formulated by Leech (1983) (Simon-Vandenbergen 1992).

In contrast, the conventions governing the social roles in political interviews are completely different. The nature of the genre is such that the politeness maxims do not apply in the same way. Since speakers are engaged in a type of institutionalised discourse in which they represent groups, the rules are different. In Goffman's terms the speaker as 'principal' is communicating "as a member of a group, office, category, relationship, association, or whatever, some socially based source of self-identification" and this often means that "the individual speaks, explicitly or implicitly, in the name of 'we', not 'I'" (Goffman 1981, 147). In political debates this social role determines the rules of interaction in the sense that both speaker and hearer are acting as representatives of groups and exclusively acting as 'we' (though 'ad hominem' arguments may for instance change the footing). As Levinson points out (1988, 211), in media political discussions

> simply by an identification of participants with political parties, accusations of political incompetence (etc.) can readily pick out a representative of a political party as a non-addressed recipient, or indirect target.

One consequence of the difference in rules, for instance, is that the modesty maxim ('minimum praise of self/maximum praise of others') does not apply. On the contrary, the guiding principle is that what is 'good for us' is focused on, and what is 'bad for us' is played down. Mutatis mutandis this also applies to 'them' (cf. van Dijk 1998; Simon-Vandenbergen 1997). This means that *of course* will typically be used to present claims which are positive from one's own point of view as non-negotiable. In the same way, claims which are negative to the opponent's face are also presented as 'obvious' by such words as *of course*.

In sections 4 and 5 we discuss the Flemish and Swedish political data from the point of view of these findings. In the following section we first briefly explain the method used in defining the equivalents of *of course* in Dutch and in Swedish.

3. Equivalents of *of course* in Dutch and in Swedish

By looking at translation equivalents in electronic corpora one finds what can be considered more or less prototypical equivalents of a particular item in the source language. By subsequently looking at sources of the correspondences one is further able to determine with greater precision to what extent particular items are each other's cross-linguistic equivalents. This method was used to establish the Dutch and Swedish equivalents of *of course* by Simon-Vandenbergen/Aijmer (2003).

As far as Dutch is concerned, it was found that there is one word which can be said to be the prototypical equivalent of *of course*, namely the word *natuurlijk*. In both fiction and non-fiction texts it was by far the most frequent translation equivalent. In second place but far behind came the word *uiteraard*. Other translation equivalents turned out to be negligible in terms of frequency (for details see Simon-Vandenbergen/Aijmer 2003). The list of equivalents gave us, however, a reliable basis to start looking for similarities and differences between British and Flemish politicians' tactics in this respect.

The Swedish data showed a slightly different pattern. In contrast with Dutch, it does not have an equivalent which has all the functions that *of course* fulfils. The Swedish *naturligtvis* as a translation of *of course* is less frequent than *förstås*. As a source of *of course*, *naturligtvis* behaves very differently in fiction and in non-fiction. In fiction it comes in third position only, the most frequent sources being *förstås* and *ju*. In non-fiction, *naturligtvis* is the most common source. This suggests that there may be a marked difference between conversation (reflected in fiction) and other genres of writing. The question is which, if any, of these words politicians tend to favour.

4. The Flemish Dutch data

The analysis of the Dutch data is based on two political debates broadcast on Flemish television on 7 and 8 February 2003. The following features appeared to be recurrent in the political speakers' utterances.

First, it was quite striking that the prototypical equivalent of *of course*, the word *natuurlijk* occurs very frequently, and with the same rhetorical functions as the English word. Its basic function is to present particular propositions as self-evident, as part of common knowledge, as presupposed. The types of propositions which are thus presented as beyond negotiation are those which fit the 'us' versus 'them' framework: 'good for us' and 'bad for them' propositions are presented as self-evident. In example (1) below, the MP for the Flemish Bloc (rightwing party in the opposition) presents a negative value judgement of the government as self-evident, as 'to be expected'. The term 'purple-green' refers to the then coalition between Socialists, Liberal Democrats and the Green Party:

(1) Mag ik er toch op wijzen dat dit voor paars-groen <u>natuurlijk</u> een beetje een alibidecreet is. [May I however point out that this is for purple-green <u>of course</u> a bit of an alibi decree.]

(Filip Dewinter, Flemish Bloc)

In the same vein, a Liberal Democratic MP presents positive value judgements of the government policy as what is to be expected:

(2) Dit neemt niet weg dat <u>natuurlijk</u> de regering een investeringsplan op lange termijn heeft goedgekeurd. [This does not take away that <u>of course</u> the government has approved an investment plan in the long term.]

(Rik Daems, Flemish Liberal Democrats)

When we look more closely, however, we find that the tactic of presenting propositions as common knowledge is one of the most salient strategies used by political speakers in argumentation, and that these strategies take various forms. Examples of structures which are used in this way include subordination in a *that*-clause following a factive verb (example 3), backgrounding through embedding as a relative clause (example 4):

(3) en sommige mensen <u>zagen blijkbaar niet dat ze</u> daarmee de schwung van de vernieuwing en de campagne die rond de vernieuwing moet draaien, dat ze dit eigenlijk aan het ondermijnen waren. [and some people <u>did apparently not see that they</u> were thereby actually undermining the verve of the renewal and the campaign which should revolve around the renewal.]

(J.-L. Dehaene, Christian Democrats)

By saying that *some people apparently did not see* the speaker is presenting his own evaluation, namely that they were undermining the renewal, as if it were an objective fact, not open to negotiation.

In the following exchange, Rik Daems (Flemish Liberal Democrats, government party) is talking to Herman Van Rompuy (MP for the Christian Democrats, opposition party). The issue is the feeling of unsafety (a key political issue) and Rik Daems (RD) ascribes the cause of this feeling to Mr Dehaene (Christian Democrat and former Prime Minister), who is implicitly accused of wilfully instigating fear among the people. Note that this proposition, which is 'bad for them', is embedded as a relative clause and thus presented as non-negotiable. However, the opponent, Herman Van Rompuy (HVR) challenges the presupposition:

(4) RD: Ja maar <u>natuurlijk</u> als je in de politiek, collega Van Rompuy, belangrijke mensen zoals mijnheer Dehaene een belangrijk man is, krijgt, <u>die de indruk willen wekken bij de bevolking dat het onveiliger wordt</u>//
[Yes but <u>of course</u> if in politics, colleague Van Rompuy, you get important people such as Mr Dehaene is an important man, <u>who wish to create the impression among the population that unsafety increases</u>]
HVR: Oh, het is mijnheer Dehaene?
[Oh, it's Mr Dehaene, is it?]
RD: // dan vind ik het erg. Waar het om g//
[// then I think it's bad. What m//]
HVR: Olala, mijnheer Dehaene die zorgt voor de onveiligheid.
[Oh dear, Mr Dehaene who creates unsafety]
RD: Waar het om gaat is de realiteit//
[What matters is reality]
HVR: Dat is dat is//
[That is that is]
RD: En ik geef u een ander voorbeeld.
[And I'll give you another example]
HVR: zeer nieuw voor ons, dat is zeer nieuw//
[very new, that is very new]
INTERVIEWER: Ja, u moet afronden, mijnheer Daems//
[Yes, you have to conclude, Mr Daems.]
HVR: Dat is zeer nieuw.
[That is very new.]

Striking in the above extract is the large amount of overlap, due to the fact that the opponent, HVR, wants to challenge the presupposition in the embedded clause. It will be noted that the speaker, RD, in this case combines various devices for presenting a subjective statement which is negative to the opposition as presupposed: backgrounding in an *if*-clause, embedding in a relative clause, use of *natuurlijk*, and explicit comment *then I think it's bad*. What gets highlighted is the value judgement "it is bad", the object of evaluation is presented as common knowledge. The opponent, however, picks up the so-called 'old information' and explicitly comments *that is new*.

5. The Swedish data

The Swedish political debate which served as the basis for the following analysis was broadcast on 21 March 1980. The topic is nuclear energy and the participants represent three different lines. Line one is in favour of nuclear energy, line three argues against it, and line two takes a middle position. As there is a chairman assigning speakers' turns there is relatively little overlap and interruption. The whole debate consists of 17,600 words, and the word *ju* was used 90 times (i.e. with a frequency of 51 per 10,000 words). In contrast, there is no instance of another adverb which was found in the translation corpus as an equivalent of *of course*. The question then arises whether the word *ju* fulfils the same strategic functions as the English and Dutch words. It appears from the analysis that it does.

Ju is a word whose main function in conversation is to create sociability, rapport and informality. It does so by appealing to common ground as the basis for feelings of solidarity (see e.g. Simon-Vandenbergen/Aijmer 2003). Just like *of course*, however, it can also be used to create an imbalance of power by presenting a proposition as an undisputed truth. In all instances in this debate speakers indeed use the word *ju* as a rhetorical ploy to persuade. Example (5) illustrates this:

(5) ni måste ju komma ihåg att alla maskiner fungerar sämre när dom blivit gamla och slitna// och det gäller ju allting från bilar och kylskåp till kärnkraftverk [you must of course remember that all machines function less well when they get old and worn out// and this concerns of course everything from cars and refrigerators to nuclear reactors]

(Lennart Daleus, line 3)

The speaker uses *ju* here in what is actually common knowledge, namely that machines function less well when they are old, and starts from there to claim that the same applies to nuclear reactors. The rhetoric resides in the implication that the opponent somehow does not remember this or does not take this fact into account. In other words, the speaker creates an imbalance of power by suggesting lack of sound reasoning on the part of the opponent. In example (6) below, *ju* is used to underline the naturalness of 'what is good for us', as well as to contrast the opponent's 'surprise' with what is self-evident. Hence, the speaker again contrasts his own knowledgeability with the lack of knowledge of the opponent (see Simon-Vandenbergen 1996 on politicians' strategies to come across as knowledgeable):

(6) LD var förvånad över att jag talade om oljan i folkomröstningskampanj om kärnkraften/ skälet är ju,/ att vi bestämt oss för att använda våra kärnkraftverk för att därigenom ge oss möjlighet att pressa ett oljeberoende som är på väg att gå oss alldeles ur händerna [LD was surprised that I spoke about oil in a referendum campaign about nuclear energy/ the reason is of course, that we have decided to use our nuclear reactors in order to give us a possibility not to make further demands on a dependence on oil which is getting out of hand]

(Per Unckel, line 1)

The Swedish data further contain a large number of expressions which emphasise the truth or the importance of the proposition. The list includes the following expressions:

(7) Faktum är ju att [The fact is of course that]
Sanningen är ju den [The truth is of course that]
Poängen här är ju [The point is of course that]
Den väsentliga skillnaden är ju just [The essential difference is of course that]
Skälet är ju [The reason is of course that]
och en viktig fråga är ju [and an important question is of course that]

Such expressions are comments on the proposition which take the form of subjects in relational process clauses, in which the actual proposition is the complement. A clause is thus embedded as a nominalisation with the function of an Identifier (Halliday 1994, 266). In addition, as Halliday points out (1994, 267), there is in such clauses no mental process and no implication of a conscious participant who is involved in the judgement. For example:

(8) sanningen är ju den att satsar vi på kärnkraft som linje ett och linje två vill / då måste vi satsa ytterligare minst femton miljarder kronor// [the truth is of course that if we go in for nuclear energy as line one and line two want/then we must invest at least fifteen billion crowns//]

(Lennart Daleus, line 3)

Finally, it appears that the same strategies as discussed for Dutch were used in the Swedish data, including the subordination of propositions in order to present them as non-negotiable. Example (9) illustrates this:

(9) vi vill avveckla dom här kärnkraftverken medan linje ett och linje två vill köra reaktorerna tills dom är helt slut [we want to shut down these nuclear reactors while line one and line two want to run the reactors until they do not function any longer]

What is presented as self-evident is in the 'while' clause, namely that the opponents want to run the reactors until they are used up.

6. Conclusions

Starting out from an examination of the use of one word, *of course*, and its equivalents in Swedish and Dutch we found that the strategy of presenting certain types of propositions as presupposed, common knowledge and hence beyond negotiation, is pervasive in political discourse. This suggests that political speakers, at least in the three languages looked at here, make use of the same tactics, by means of very similar lexical and grammatical choices. We would like to suggest as a hypothesis for further research that political debate is conventionalised to a large extent on the interpersonal level, and that the conventions are similar in the three cultures examined. It would be interesting to look for similar tactics in the language of politicians belonging to more different cultures. We believe that a cross-linguistic comparison of the genre of political debate must proceed via very detailed analysis of the kind illustrated in this paper.

A second finding was that the tactics used by speakers are actually recognised as such by the opponents in the debate. In other words, what is presented as non-negotiable is constantly challenged by the opponent. The question arises why speakers should use a tactic which does not seem to work. The answer lies in the nature of the genre: speakers are not trying to persuade their interlocutors but the home audience. They are performing in front of their (potential) electors and want to come across as strong and convincing (Simon-Vandenbergen 1996). By using the strategies discussed in this paper they recruit expressions from the arsenal which contributes to the creation of a power imbalance. The fact that the same tactic recurs frequently, not only in one language but across languages, suggests that it is part of the genre and 'learnt on the job'.

References

Biber, Douglas/Johansson, Stig/Leech, Geoffrey/Conrad, Susan/Finegan, Edward (1999): Longman grammar of spoken and written English. London: Longman.
Goffman, Erving (1981): Forms of talk. Oxford: Blackwell.
Halliday, M. A. K. (^{2}1994): An introduction to functional grammar. London: Edward Arnold.
Holmes, Janet (1988): *Of course*: A pragmatic particle in New Zealand women's and men's speech. In: Australian Journal of Linguistics 2, 49-74.
Leech, Geoffrey N. (1983): Principles of pragmatics. London: Longman.
Levinson, Stephen C. (1988): Putting linguistics on a proper footing: Explorations in Goffman's concept of participation. In: Drew, P./ Wootton, A. (eds.): Erving Goffman: Exploring the interaction order. Cambridge: Polity Press, 161-227.
Simon-Vandenbergen, Anne-Marie (1988): What 'really' really means in casual conversation and in political interviews. In: Linguistica Antverpiensia, XXII, 206-225.
– (1992): The interactional utility of *of course* in spoken discourse. In: Occasional Papers in Systemic Linguistics 6, 213-226.
– (1996): Image-building through modality: the case of political interviews. In: Discourse and Society 7/3, 389-415.
– (1997): Modal (un)certainty in political discourse: a functional account. In: Language Sciences 19/4, 341-356.
Simon-Vandenbergen, Anne-Marie/Aijmer, Karin (2003): The expectation marker *of course* in a cross-linguistic perspective. In: Languages in Contrast 4/1, 13-49.
van Dijk, Teun A. (1998): Opinions and ideologies in the press. In: Bell, A./Garrett, P. (eds.): Approaches to media discourse. Oxford: Blackwell, 21-63.

Richard W. Janney / Andriy Yakovlyev

Cyberwar perception management in the Middle East:
A view from pragmatics

1. Introduction

Three decades after the Six-Day War, Israel, the West Bank, and the Gaza Strip continue to be areas of bloodshed and tragedy, and the so-called Israeli-Palestinian 'vicious circle of violence' continues to spiral upwards. Since the collapse of peace talks in 2000 and the beginning of the second Intifada, reports of Palestinian terror attacks and Israeli reprisals (and vice versa) have appeared on an almost daily basis in the world's media. In 2002, the Israeli government attacked the Jenin refugee camp in the West Bank, signaling the beginning of 'Operation Defensive Shield', which was hailed by Israeli government officials as "an important stage in the Israeli war against terrorism"[1] and simultaneously condemned by Palestinian leaders as a further escalation of "apartheid policies in the Occupied Palestinian Territory."[2]

Today, parallel to the fighting, a virtual war of words and images rages between official and unofficial websites of the two sides in the Internet. This paper focuses on this latter aspect of the crisis: its virtual extension into cyberspace. In the cyberwarfare scenario, the Israeli-Palestinian conflict is fought out as a public debate (albeit an oddly nonreciprocal one, as will be shown below), in English, as opposed to Hebrew or Arabic, before a global Internet audience. The goal of the debate, rather than to attack the enemy's military capabilities, is to undermine its credibility and mobilize world opinion in one's favor. The relative ease of access to the Internet tends to encourage information warfare. It counteracts imbalances of power, enabling actors of various strengths, types, and sizes (state, non-state, ratified, semi-ratified, unratified, etc.)[3] to compete on more nearly equal footing. Since the Gulf War, we have increasingly experienced war as its own virtual *depiction* in the electronic media, and increasingly, we have found combatants using their points of view as weapons of *perception management* (see section 3) (cf. Molander et al. 1996, 24).

It is not unusual in the long history of propaganda for nations at war to try to influence public perceptions of themselves and their enemies. What is unusual in the Israeli-Palestin-

---

[1] Prime Minister Ariel Sharon to the Knesset, May 2002.
[2] Abed Rabbo, Palestinian Minister of Culture and Information, June 2002.
[3] On participation frameworks in polylogues, see Kerbrat-Orecchioni (forthcoming).

ian conflict is the sheer immensity, interactivity, and multimediality of the arena in which attempted perception management takes place, and the cacophonous, *polylogal* conditions under which the warring sides attempt to assert their points of view.[4] In the cavernous, echoing, virtual spaces of the Internet, arguments between Israeli and Palestinian websites resemble shouting matches in loud halls cheered on by supporters and booed by enemies against the yelling objections of peace activists in the presence of millions of helpless bystanders.

The Internet, with its global network of interconnected documents, is without doubt the most powerful, least controllable medium of multiparticipant information proliferation in human history. Websites participating in the Israeli-Palestinian conflict communicate intense, appellative, multimedia messages intended to encourage their random recipients to perceive, think, and act in certain ways. Both sides propagate biased information and employ manipulative verbal, pictorial, graphic, and videomatic rhetorical techniques, and their reports compete for attention and impact with those of many other information providers. Many of the electronic documents produced by websites on both sides of the conflict can be regarded as heavily loaded pragmatic weapons leveled at the chance visitor (cf. Bolinger 1980).

2. The parallax phenomenon

A typical skirmish in the Israeli-Palestinian cyberconflict might unfold somewhat as follows: (Gaza City, July 22, 2002) a missile fired by an Israeli jet strikes an apartment building in a Palestinian residential area, killing 15 people, including 8 children, 4 women, and 3 men, one of whom is an important Hamas military commander. The Israel Defense Forces website (IDF) issues an electronic press release depicting the action as a successful military operation and describing the terroristic history and importance of the Hamas commander. The Palestine Media Center (PMC) issues a press release depicting the action as a savage attack on the civilian residents of the neighborhood and lists the names, ages, and family relationships of the victims. Although the designated facts in each case are essentially correct, the two official websites' *depictions* of the event differ radically. The IDF release fails to mention the deaths of civilians and the original PMC release fails to mention the dead commander's connection to Hamas.

---

[4] On polylogues, see Kerbrat-Orecchioni (forthcoming); on Internet polylogues, see Marcoccia (forthcoming).

Without access to further information, a chance reader of two such conflicting releases experiences what we will call a *parallax effect* (see below). Exposure to large amounts of conflicting information in the Internet over long periods of time, we will argue, results in epistemological uncertainty and ends in a new kind of perceptual paralysis that is characteristic of today's cyberspace information war (see section 5).

The astronomical term *parallax* (rooted in Gr *pará* to one side, beyond, amiss) refers to perceived differences in the positions of stars when observed from different points on the earth, or when observed from one place on earth at different points in its orbit around the sun. Hence, a given star (●) appears to be located in a different position relative to the stars beyond it (o) when viewed from point A in Figure 1 than when viewed from point B.

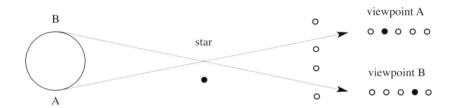

Figure 1: The parallax phenomenon

In his book *The language parallax*, Paul Friedrich (1986) points out analogies to this phenomenon in discourse. Things expressed 'in other words' often are perceived as 'other things'. Every instance of discourse, he says, contains the built-in coordinates of an implicit observer's perspective: an authorial viewpoint encoded into, and subtly coloring, the representation of 'the facts of the matter' expressed. Hence, strictly speaking, the commonsense intuition that the *same* things can be said 'in other words' is pragmatically misleading, because this actually applies only to designation (denotation). We can designate the same things with different words: 'Nigel', 'son', 'husband', 'Daddy', 'Brit', 'soldier', 'member of the Coalition Forces', 'prisoner of war', etc. may all denote the same individual. But to assume that the main function of words is only this indexical function of naming things or pointing them out is to leave the depictive pragmatics of words out of the picture altogether (cf. Janney 1999a). In fact, it makes a big difference whether a designated participant in a military skirmish is depicted as a 'soldier', 'fighter', 'activist', 'fanatic', 'terrorist', 'assassin', 'killer', etc., or whether a particular designated military event is depicted as an 'operation', 'strike', 'attack', 'ambush', 'atrocity', 'war crime', or so forth. Depictive perspective establishes important conceptual coordinates for the interpretation of designated content. The 'hows' of discourse shape our pragmatic understandings of the 'whats' (cf. Janney 1999b).

3. Cyberwar perception management

Of course, in itself, the idea that perceptions of designated events in discourse depend largely on how the events are depicted is neither new nor particularly interesting. This truism of the rhetorical tradition is an underlying principle of all persuasive discourse – in politics, diplomacy, deliberation, litigation, psychotherapy, advertising, propaganda, and elsewhere. But "the conceptual casting of events", as Aristotle (ca. 330 BC) called it, takes on disturbing new pragmatic meaning (or rather, *lack* of meaning, as we will argue later, which is even worse) in connection with cyberwarfare. A simple Google check of *Gaza City, July 22, 2002*, for example, turns up 53,800 Internet documents depicting the apartment building bombing described above, some including complex, multimedia combinations of texts, photographs, audio recordings, and video images, in only 0.15 seconds. What effect does this type of information overload have on human perception and understanding?

Strategic studies point out revolutionary changes in 'classical war' taking place through new information technologies (cf. Fitschen 2002; Freedman 1998) and refer increasingly to the "expanded role of perception management" in modern information warfare (Molander et al. 1996, xiv).[5] Analysts of this so-called 'new face of war' emphasize the importance of the Internet for disadvantaged parties like the Palestinians in asymmetrical wars like the Israeli-Palestinian conflict (cf. Shalikashvili 1996; Shelton 2000). The ability to mobilize world opinion with instantaneous, up-to-the-minute information contradicting one's enemy's official information is a new form of political empowerment with considerable catalytic potential. In this connection, live, on-the-scene reports of events sent at real-time speed via the Internet by eye witnesses and alternative news providers can become what information strategists call 'military force multipliers' with immediate impact on the course of events.

This makes the perception-manipulating potential of the Internet virtually unlimited, not only for disadvantaged parties but also for powerful government agencies, mainstream and alternative news providers, activist groups, and non-state actors of all political persuasions. A consequence of the expanded role of perception management in information warfare, Molander et al. (1996, 24) say, is that large amounts of conflicting information and mis- and disinformation can dramatically cloud and complicate decision-making processes. With the monopoly on credibility of the traditional mass media increasingly called into question by contradictory information, people dependent on information from the Internet –

---

[5] Schwartau (1994, 13) defines *information warfare* as "electronic conflict in which information is a strategic asset worthy of conquest or destruction [and] information systems become attractive first-strike targets." The concept of *strategic information warfare* is described by Molander et al. (1996, 1-2) as "the intersection of evolving information warfare and post-cold war 'strategic warfare' concepts."

everyday news consumers and military decision-makers alike – may no longer be able to determine in all cases what is *real* – much less what is *right*.

4. A thought experiment: Bill's unguided tour of the Web

With this situation in mind, let us conduct a thought experiment. We will send a mock user named Bill on an unguided tour of the World Wide Web. Bill is an everyday European citizen with moderate interest in international politics, whose political judgements are in general impartial. Let us imagine that Bill's assignment is to search the Internet for information about the Israeli-Palestinian conflict and its main actors.

Bill begins by checking the Google search engine for *Middle East*, and in a fraction of a second, he receives the results of his query: a list of the first 10 of more than 4,560,000 links to Internet documents on web servers around the world referring to the Middle East. There is naturally also an intimidating amount of information about the two main protagonists in the conflict, Yasser Arafat and Ariel Sharon (257.000 and 113.000 documents respectively). So already at the beginning, Bill faces an almost infinite-seeming labyrinth of interrelated documents about the Middle East that vastly surpasses his human brain's modest neurobiological processing capacities.

4.1 The conflict in Israeli and Palestinian websites

Let us assume, however, that he ignores this and persists in his assignment, clicking the first link on the first list, where he is connected to the *Israeli Defense Forces* (IDF) homepage. It has been designed by Internet specialists to appear just in this first position. The IDF website, Bill discovers, is available in four languages (English, Hebrew, French, and Russian), and it quickly directs him to the version in his mother tongue. The languages of the site suggest the importance of communicating the IDF view of the conflict to particular parts of the Western world, and to particular segments of the Israeli population. Interestingly, there is no version in Arabic. Although the IDF fiercely attacks Palestinians whenever possible, it does not address them directly and in fact seems to ignore them as potential visitors.

Browsing through the IDF website, Bill is witness to an unusual angry cyberdialog in the form of a mock debate, where the positions of both sides are acted out by the IDF before the Internet audience. This mock debate, of course, is designed to mobilize support for the IDF position. Bill soon finds out, for example, that from the perspective of the IDF, all

Palestinians fighting for their land are "criminals" and "terrorists", and that their actions are "inhuman atrocities" and "terrorist activities" punishable by law. Palestinians are purported to use ambulances "to transport weapons to terrorist activists", who, in turn, use these "in planned terror attacks" against "Israeli civilians". An "Islamic Jihad terrorist" is arrested by "an IDF force", Palestinian "armed terrorists" "infiltrate" an "Israeli Home Near Hebron, Killing Husband and Wife," and so forth. Like most military information providers, the IDF website is not very ingenious at inventing negative depictions of their "enemy number one".

As can be imagined, the depictive picture brightens in those IDF documents providing information about *Israeli soldiers* and *civilians*. Here, Bill finds pictures of amiable Israeli soldiers distributing food among refugees, giving words of encouragement to Christian priests, leaning over babies in cradles, posing humbly with their shining weapons etc., and pictures of soldiers being shocked by Palestinian atrocities. In defense of Israel's honor and credibility, the IDF "tells the truth" about "Palestinian lies", deconstructing old and new Palestinian accusations in a mock dialogical way. Finally, Bill comes across the IDF casualty statistics for the conflict, and discovers interestingly that only the Israeli losses are reported, making it appear almost as if Palestinians have been killing Israelis since the beginning of the conflict with impunity.

Having thus surveyed this official Israeli view of the conflict (obviously incompletely, because of the many documents and the fact that the IDF site is only one of many official Israeli information providers), Bill now clicks the *Electronic Intifada* (EI). This website, which purportedly receives about one quarter of a million visits per month, depicts itself as publishing news, commentary, analysis, and reference materials about the Israeli-Palestinian Conflict "from a Palestinian perspective." Significantly, here, there is neither a Hebrew version nor one in Arabic, and the only language of the site is English. From this, one could hypothesize that that EI has a different information targeting strategy than the IDF. Whereas the IDF site, with its larger number of languages, appears to be broadly aimed at *image-making* both outside and inside Israel ('military public relations'), the EI website seems to be directed more specifically toward *mobilizing opinion against the occupation of Palestinian Territory*

The first thing Bill sees at the EI site is a picture of a small Palestinian boy throwing stones at a huge Israeli tank.[6] The caption reads: "Against the Israeli Machine: Sending tanks to refugee camps to 'fight terrorism'". The appellative force of this multimodal message is enormous. The photograph is tantamount to visual *proof* of what the Israelis are doing in the Occupied Territories from the Palestinian perspective. The caption and the image direct perceptions of each other, depicting the Israelis, via the tank, as ruthless aggressors, and 'terrorism', via the boy, as an empty claim. The courageous resistance of the small boy in the face of the 'Israeli machine' suggests a David vs. Goliath scenario.

---

[6] Interestingly, a similar picture can be found on the website of the Palestine National Authority.

Interestingly, the EI website, in addition to claiming to be "the leading Palestinian portal for information about the Israeli-Palestinian conflict", also declares its active interest in the representation of the conflict in the media, particularly by Israeli websites. And it too engages in a sort of one-sided dialog with Israel. Like the IDF website, the EI site deconstructs its enemies' accusations, often quoting official Israeli sources and then disqualifying their statements as lies by providing further information. Israeli accounts of a "massacre of worshippers" in Hebron (November 15, 2002) are depicted as purposeful disinformation. An EI article provides long quotes and screenshots of web pages of official Israeli sources reporting that Palestinian terrorists in the occupied West Bank city of Hebron had killed innocent Jewish worshippers. The EI points out contradictions and inconsistencies in Israeli media accounts of this incident, claiming that, in fact, there had been no massacre of civilians. The Israeli government, according to the EI, misrepresented the incident, depicting "an ambush which killed only Israeli soldiers and 'armed paramilitary settlers'" as a "Sabbath Massacre".

Another example of the EI website's dialogical strategy is a document entitled *Debunking 6 Common Israeli Myths*, in which well-known Israeli claims (here again often presented as quotations from official Israeli sources) are subjected to severe criticism. Like the IDF, the EI takes advantage of its captive audience to have the last word in the dialog before the visitor moves on. To give one example: according to the EI, Israel claims that "there is no moral equivalence between suicide bombings on the one hand, and Israel's killing of Palestinians on the other". To this, the EI comments: "What needs to be added, and what is almost always missing in American media commentary, is a similar condemnation of Israel's deliberate targeting of Palestinian civilians."

Finally, Bill turns to the EI casualty statistics page. The figures represent the same state of affairs as the IDF figures for the period from September 29, 2000 to December 8, 2002, but they differ from the official Israeli statistics insofar as casualties on both sides are reported, making it possible to compare the relative suffering of the Israelis (691 deaths, 4.900 injuries) to that of the Palestinians (1.926 deaths, 21.240 injuries). But again, as in all the preceding examples, there are few means of judging the credibility of the information found independently from the contexts in which it is found.

No matter where Bill goes in the part of cyberspace permeated by Israeli-Palestinian antagonism, the same controversial, contradictory picture presents itself. On Palestinian websites he is deluged with pictures and reports of Israeli "massacres" and "daily aggression". The official website of the city of Nablus greets the visitor with pictures of heavy explosions and city buildings destroyed by Israeli tanks and bulldozers. Yasser Arafat's homepage condemns "heinous crimes" committed by Israelis and decries "the suppressive and racial nature of the Israeli government, which will not bring peace to the Israelis". The Palestinian Ministry of Information publishes lists of children and women martyrs and provides evidence of "the Israeli official policy of killing and assassination" in reports, memoranda, and press releases.

The Israeli Ministry of Foreign Affairs does the same thing, publishing full lists of Israeli victims and explaining that Israeli retaliations are only answers to Palestinian atrocities. One Israeli website says that "it is important to [...] understand the profound moral and legal differences between Palestinian terrorism, which is always deliberately barbarous and indiscriminate, and Israeli retaliations, which are always consciously designed to AVOID civilian casualties." Another Israeli website calls the al-Aqsa Intifada "an engineered tragedy", and yet another accuses Arab media of spreading anti-Semitism.

4.2 Arafat and Sharon in Israeli and Palestinian websites

The depictions of the main *dramatis personae* in the conflict, Yasser Arafat and Ariel Sharon, are no less contradictory. Bill finds that Yasser Arafat on Palestinian websites is depicted as a champion of the Palestinian struggle and a peacemaker, statesman, and recipient of the Nobel Peace Prize. In photographs, he often appears dressed in an unassuming, plain military uniform and black-and-white headscarf, with a thoughtful look on his face, and with his hands clasped piously, looking like the living embodiment of the Palestinian people and their cause ("Mr. Palestine"). There are pictures of Arafat donating blood, visiting the injured, meeting with foreign politicians. etc. Official Palestinian sites uncritically reproduce his speeches, report on his meetings and political decisions, publish his official statements, and, so forth.

On Israeli websites, Bill finds quite a different Yasser Arafat. The Israeli Foreign Ministry, quoting from live speeches and interviews, depicts Arafat as a blood-thirsty fanatic who is guilty of "terrorism against Israel, corruption, and crime". The website claims to provide "clear-cut hard evidence" of Arafat's "direct responsibility for the cold-blooded murder of Israeli citizens." Arafat's blood donation is depicted as a "prick for propaganda". There are pictures of him embracing Saddam Hussein, surrounded by belligerent militants, and so forth.

Indeed, as Bill is forced to realize, Arafat functions as a powerful icon for both official sides in the conflict: as the embodiment of all that is good from a Palestinian perspective, and as the embodiment of all that is evil from an Israeli one. Interestingly, even his birthplace has iconic significance, and the argument about whether he was born in Jerusalem, the Gaza Strip, or Egypt is at a higher ideological level an argument not only about the legitimacy of his role in Palestinian politics but also about the legitimacy of the underlying Palestinian claim to a homeland itself.

Bill discovers that there are confusing 'electronic faces' of Israeli Prime Minister Ariel Sharon as well. Sharon's biographies on Israeli websites contain no mention of the "war crimes" and "massacres" frequently attributed to him in biographies on Palestinian websites,[7] and Palestinian sites engage in various forms of dialogical deconstruction of Sharon's Israeli biographies. The Electronic Intifada's biography of Sharon, for example, is not simply a depiction of his life from a Palestinian point of view, but in fact a sophisticated dialogical deconstruction of the Israeli Ministry of Foreign Afairs' official version of his biography, combined with the EI's commentaries on specific events in Sharon's life. The result is a sort of annotated biography, or meta-biography, in which, one by one, Sharon's presumably legally sanctioned actions as military commander or Prime Minister (e.g., "retaliatory operations" of Special Commando Unit 101 lead by Sharon in the 1950s) are turned into crimes against the Palestinian people (e.g., "attacks on Palestinian villages in which women and children were killed").

5. The internet and the crisis of common knowledge

How, we will now ask, turning back to issue of the *parallax effect* raised at the beginning of the paper, does the conflicting information gathered by our Internet surfer Bill from documents like those above help him *understand* the Israeli-Palestinian 'vicious circle of violence'? Or, put the other way around, how does the knowledge Bill acquired during his cyber-travels help him interpret the many conflicting representations of events in the Middle East that he found in Israeli and Palestinian websites in the Internet? These are important pragmatic questions, even if posed only hypothetically in the context of our thought experiment. Because Bill, in order to understand the Israeli-Palestinian conflict, requires *knowledge*: a framework of relatively stable assumptions of various kinds about the way things happen and what they mean in this particular context. A stable assumptive framework is a prerequisite for interpreting conflicting information.

---

[7] There is a website called "Indict Sharon", which accuses the Israeli PM, among other things, of being "responsible for the massacre, killing, rape and disappearance of civilians that took place in Beirut between 16 and 18 September 1982 in the camps of Sabra and Shatila and the surrounding area."

5.1 Knowledge, expectation, and interpretation

Knowledge, expectation, and interpretation are complexly interrelated, as Charles Sanders Peirce pointed out long ago in his discussions of inductive, deductive, and abductive reasoning (see Figure 2). As individuals, he said, we acquire knowledge of the world inductively, in a bottom-up manner, experiencing things, inferring relationships between them, and finally concluding that the inferred relationships hold true. Hence, what we 'know', from this perspective, can be regarded as something we assume on the basis of something we have inferred about something we have perceived. Perception is viewed as the basis of knowledge. Expectations, on the other hand, Peirce said, work the other way around – deductively, top-down, in a predictive manner. Given what we assume we know, we hypothesize what we are likely to perceive next. Finally, interpretations of all types (inferences, hypotheses, pragmatic implicatures, etc.), Peirce claimed, depend on abductive reasoning and stem reflexively from what we assume we know and what we perceive. On the basis of our knowledge and our perceptions, we infer that what we have just perceived is a token of a particular 'known' type. In doing this, we postulate a relationship between these two givens that we regard as 'meaningful'.

Modern techniques of information warfare interfere with these reasoning processes, altering the very basis of knowledge, and hence affecting expectations and interpretations as well, by manipulating the perceptual *input* to the inductive process behind it (Figure 2, second column from left). This is the goal of modern *perception management*.

	knowledge	expectation	interpretation
what we know	then ↑	given	given ↓
inference/hypothesis	if	if ↓	then ↑
what we perceive	given	then	given

Figure 2: Knowledge, expectation, interpretation

5.2 Common knowledge?

Prior to the appearance of the Internet, perception management was possible on a large scale (as traditional propaganda) mainly only for political, religious, corporate, and other organizations powerful enough to control the content of the mass media. The rise of the Internet, however, has complicated the propaganda situation considerably. Greater ease of access, a steadily growing global usership, and a proliferation of information from uncontrollable providers have changed the dynamics of perception management for information strategists. As we have seen in this paper, it is no longer possible for a single perspective to dominate the media. The perceptual input of media consumers like our Bill has become increasingly *parallaxical*. With information dissemination steadily accelerating, Shelton (2000, 10) remarks, "there is a risk of outstripping our ability to capture ideas, formulate operational concepts, and develop the capacity to assess results."

Even from the simplified account of perception and knowledge above, it should be clear that if 'what we perceive' is perpetually *parallaxical*, as it was for Bill, about all we can assume that we 'know' about our perceptions is that they are inconsistent, confusing, or unreliable. And if our knowledge of 'what we perceive' is only that it is unreliable, this can paralyze our capacity to interpret perceived events and predict what might hypothetically happen next on the basis of our perceptions. Given this dilemma, it might seem legitimate to ask whether *knowledge*, in any useful sense, is acquired at all by collecting contradictory Internet information about a complex, controversial issue like the Israeli-Palestinian conflict.

The status of the pragmatically central concept of *common knowledge* (shared knowledge, shared assumptive frameworks, common grounds, etc.) in the Internet seems even more problematical. Despite optimistic predictions of early media philosophers like Marshall McLuhan (1964) that a global electronic information network could potentially unify the world, the facts seem to suggest that it presently unifies mainly only special interest groups. The vast majority of the Internet's users participate in it as isolated individuals. The virtually unlimited mass of unfiltered, unanalyzed information stored in the Internet, the global (and perspectival) diversity of its information providers, and the almost autistic isolation of its individual users are not conducive to the emergence of shared information, much less common knowledge or assumptive frameworks. As much as we may wish to view our Bill as an active member of the global community sharing his concern about the Israeli-Palestinian conflict with other concerned members of the community on the basis of shared information (see Figure 3), we are forced by the user-dynamics of the system to recognize that he is in fact an isolated individual randomly excercizing choice in a network that more than anything is a projection of his own curiosity (see Figure 4).

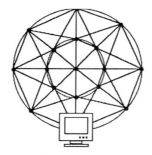
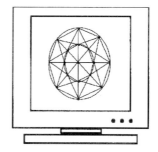

Figure 3: Bill as a 'member of a network'   Figure 4: Bill as an isolated user

The information, of course, is *there*. But is it immediately clear whether Bill can really find what he needs, properly interpret it, use it to better understand the Middle East crisis, and share it assumptively with others concerned about humane solutions to the Israeli-Palestinian 'spiral of violence'? In the context of the Internet, these questions seem to be pragmatically difficult indeed.

References

Ariel Sharon's Office (http://www.pmo.gov.il/english)
Electronic Intifada's Homepage (http://electronicintifada.net/new.shtml)
Electronic Intifada's Casualty Statistics page (http://electronicintifada.net/v2/casualtystats.shtml)
Electronic Intifada's Biography of Ariel Sharon (http://electronicintifada.net/forreference/keyfigures/sharon.html)
Electronic Intifada's Article "Debunking 6 Common Israeli Myths" (http://electronicintifada.net/v2/article865.shtml)
Indict Sharon (http://indictsharon.net/)
Israeli Defense Forces' Homepage (http://www.idf.il)
Israeli Defense Forces' Casualty Statistics page (http://www.idf.il/english/statistics/statistics.stm)
Israeli Foreign Ministry (http://www.mfa.gov.il/mfa/home.asp)
MidEastTruth.com (http://www.mideasttruth.com)
Palestine Media Center (http://www.palestine-pmc.com)
Palestine Ministry of Information (http://www.minfo.gov.ps)
Yasser Arafat's Office (http://www.p-p-o.com)

Aristotle (1932): The rhetoric of Aristotle. Ed. and transl. by Cooper, L. New York: Appleton.
Bolinger, Dwight (1980): Language: The loaded weapon. London, New York: Longman.
Fitschen, Patrick (2002): Revolution in military affairs. Neue Form der Kriegführung und strategische Doppelasymmetrie. Kiel: ISUK (Kieler Analysen zur Sicherheitspolitik 1).
Freedman, Lawrence (1998): The revolution in strategic affairs. London: The International Institute for Strategic Studies (Adelphi Paper 318).

Friedrich, Paul (1986): The language parallax: Linguistic relativity and poetic indeterminacy. Austin: University of Texas Press.
Janney, Richard (1999a): The whole truth and nothing but the truth. Linguistic avoidance in the O.J. Simpson transcripts. In: Falkner, W./Schmid, H.J. (eds.): Words, lexemes, concepts – approaches to the lexicon. Studies in honour of Leonhard Lipka. Tübingen: Narr, 259-272.
– (1999b): Words as gestures. In: Andersen, F./Hoye, L./Wagner, J. (eds.): Pragmatics: The loaded discipline. Special issue of Journal of Pragmatics. Oxford: Pergamon, 953-972.
– (2002): Cotext as context. In: Fetzer, A./Akman, V. (eds.): Contexts of social action. A special issue of Language and Communication. Oxford: Pergamon, 457-475.
Kerbrat-Orecchioni, Catherine (forthcoming): Introducing polylogue. In: Journal of Pragmatics.
Marcoccia, Michel (forthcoming): On-line polylogues: Conversation structure and participation framework in Internet newsgroups. In: Journal of Pragmatics.
McLuhan, Marshall (1964): Understanding media: The extensions of man. New York: McGraw-Hill.
Molander, Roger C./Riddile, Andrew S./Wilson, Peter A. (1996): Strategic information warfare: A new face of war. Santa Monica: RAND.
Peirce, Charles S. (1935): Collected Papers I-VII. Cambridge, Mass.: Harvard University Press.
Schwartau, Winn (1994): Information warfare: Chaos on the electronic superhighway. New York: Thunder's Mouth Press.
Shalikashvili, John M. (1996): Joint vision 2010. Washington, D.C.: The Joint Chiefs of Staff.
Shelton, Henry H. (2000): Joint vision 2020. Washington, D.C.: The Joint Chiefs of Staff.

Christoph Sauer

Christmas Messages 1998 by heads of state on radio and TV: pragmatic functions, semiotic forms, media adequacy

1. Introduction: The setting of a Christmas Message

UK memories of Christmas Day – in autobiographical texts (Jeyes 1997), literature and even in nostalgic excursion advertisements (BH Tours 2002) – are often related to the King's or Queen's voice delivering a Christmas Message. This was first on radio, then on television. Since British children normally were not allowed to open the gifts after Christmas dinner until they had listened to the Message, which began (and still begins) at 3 p.m., a link between speech and gift-giving is established. It influences the way British people look back on their childhood and particularly on Christmas Day.

In his novel "Out of the Shelter", David Lodge (1970) describes from the perspective of his protagonist Timothy, a post-war English adolescent who travels to Germany and visits Frankfurt still covered with ruins, the associations that were produced when Timothy unexpectedly hears the sounds of *God Save the King*. Timothy automatically couples this moment with other moments:

> – It was queer hearing it in this place, said Timothy. I connect it with home.
> Standing self-consciously in the aisle of the local cinema, turning sheepishly to face the Union Jack flattering on the screen, furtively buttoning up your coat. Listening to the radio on Cup Final day, the strains of a military band floating across a hushed Wembley. Or sitting at the table in the dining-room on Christmas Day as the yellow December light faded outside the window, miming requests for mince-pies and a second helping of pudding, while the thin faltering voice of the King enunciated vague syllables of hope and goodwill: *at this season... people of every nation... Empire and Commonwealth... hope and pray... united effort... peace*. And, as the strains of the National Anthem died away, mother saying, *I thought he was better this year. Poor man, it must be a strain.*
>
> (Lodge 1970, 220f.)

In such a way, Lodge's Timothy mediates between a typical Christmas Day situation forty years ago and the Christmas Message setting nowadays; it is still functioning in a comparable manner, albeit transmitted by television and adapted to television features. There are of course differences between the European countries. In Britain, the Christmas Message is delivered in the early afternoon of Christmas Day and finishes with the national anthem (repeated at 9 p.m., subtitling and sign language interpreting added). In the Netherlands, Queen

Beatrix's voice could only be heard on radio (until 2000, when she began using TV too), framed by sacred music before and after her text, at 1 p.m.; in conformity with calvinistic traditions, after returning from the church, this is a dead moment before the Christmas dinner begins. The Message text is always published by the national press, the following day. No link to gift-giving exists since gifts are normally offered on 5 December (St. Nicholas). In Germany, the President delivers his Christmas Message on TV at prime time (8 p.m.) without music and national anthem (German children get their Christmas gifts earlier on Christmas Eve).

Concerning their forms and functions, the three Christmas Messages have in common:
- their delivery as an exceptional programme on a special occasion,
- their comparable main function of reflecting the last year and wishing a merry Christmas,
- their format as an exclusive 'live' broadcast (however recorded earlier),
- and their setting that is well-known to the audience and traditional in character, referring to national customs.

It is, in particular, the sociocultural practice of addressing the domestic public and the use of media features that needs scrutiny. It will be analysed below.

2. Christmas Messages as representative discourses

A Christmas Message is a strange discourse. It combines a pagan ritual (of midwinter) with Christian traditions and political morality. A Christmas Message is one of the unique occasions on which heads of state address directly their nation exclusively on radio and/or television. Its only function is that addressing on Christmas Day: heads of state allude to norms and values, express wishes and convey Christmas greetings. The strangeness of such a message comes to the fore if we look at other public addresses by heads of state. Normally, they represent their countries in the context of a state visit or an (inter)national meeting. Even if their speeches are transmitted by television, their – in Goffmanian terms – *ratified recipients* are present during the speech: an assembly, etc. In such a way, a head of state delivers his or her speech in front of a 'real' public, and in a multi-party setting. This 'real' public unavoidably influences the quality of performance, at least as far as rhythm, gaze or articulation is concerned.

A Christmas Message, however, is a full speech, delivered during the dark winter times (which is often referred to), addressing the domestic public outside the studio and broadcast as an exceptional programme. There is no 'real' public in the orator's vicinity. A Christmas

Message resembles a *sermon* more than a political speech. There are no other programmes, with the exception of jubilees or times of crises, in which a head of state directs a speech of a certain length – ten minutes – solely to his or her nation with no other purpose than this addressing, eventually wishing 'Merry Christmas to you all'. Therefore, it is the words of the speech, the organisation of its structure, the concatenation of the speech acts and their adaptation to media features that provides the means to constitute their very public.

The rhetorical main function of a Christmas Message is that of a *eulogy*: heads of states praise their people for virtues, deeds and attitudes. By doing so, they establish and re-establish the community (Sauer 1996, 2002). This is one of the main tasks of a head of state, and on this specific Christmas occasion, his of her role can be associated with a pope-like speaking and representing behaviour (like the papal *Urbi et Orbi* in Rome, also on Christmas Day). In the context of a Christmas Message, references may be made to historic events and recent problems. Therefore, a *critical* note might be added to the general line of the laudatory speech. In sum, a Christmas Message contributes to the social fabric of the community.

3. Discourse and its adaptation to the delivery situation

Each discourse has to be accompanied by a *shadow discourse*, so to speak, an underlying discourse that provides, dependent on the media possibilities, *understanding* and *comprehension support* (Ehlich 1994). In face-to-face situations, for instance, participants have a wide range of possibilities available in order to make the understanding smooth and easy and to signal potential problems including already realised comprehension: a high verbal flexibility, body language, facial expressions, tonal variation, interjections, "uh huh" and other minimal responses – summarised as minimising risk in communication. In Functional Pragmatics (Ehlich 1994, Sauer 2002), this constellation is seen as the *anchoring* of utterances in the speech situation itself. It runs by deixis, by orienting the participants to specific knowledge operations (by morpho-syntactic means) and by focussing the participants' attention according to the needs of the very moment. These descriptions have in common that the *simultaneity* of speech is the dominating feature: it determines the discursive quality and intensity.

Assuming that content and tenor of a message do not change, when another medium – other than that of *orality* – is used, many features of the face-to-face situation have to be modified. The *lasting* quality of *written communication*, for instance, alters completely the access to the transmitted content. Because the reader may go back and forward intermittently the written text has to carry all means that compensate for the absence of 'on line' reactions and steerings. The reading process integrates semiosis with verbal cognition. The anchoring in the communication situation, then, depends only on what the text offers to the reader – and what this reader experiences as support in relating textual and visual features to comprehension and understanding. Content parts of the text (propositions and illocutions) and supportive elements (anchoring means) must collaborate.

A Christmas Message may, at face value, also be considered a *written text*: as such it is designed by the head's of state staff and provided via official web sites (and in Holland also via the press). Its delivery is the *adaptation* of this text to the chosen medium: radio and/or television. Thus, the broadcast resembles to a certain extent the re-oralisation of an already written text. This adaptation results in what is often referred to as 'secondary orality' (see Holly 1995): orality framed by media features. The anchoring of the speech in the delivery situation reflects the dynamics of media discourses: *evanescence* and (*determined*) *rhythm* which are characteristic of both radio and television. Both kinds of discourse are not fully controllable by the audience inasmuch as a later piece of the message may overrun or cancel out the earlier pieces. This problem is solved, in classical rhetoric, by advising that the most essential part of the message should be offered at the very end of the speech so that the public may easily remind it.

Such sort of problem-solving calls for a clear *media adequacy* of the message. For instance, the re-oralisation and mediation of the (written) text have to supply the audience with adequate means that establish a 'common ground' of understanding and comprehension. Adequately anchored in the (ideal typical) recipient setting is a Christmas Message that:
– has a clear organisation (offers a 'logical' sequentialisation),
– uses non-sophisticated formulations (adopts concretisations if possible),
– reflects in structure and wording the public's expectations (not too much, not too less),
– gives room for repetition (compensates thus for the absence of permanent access),
– and guides gradually the assembly of the overall meaning by providing identification.

The *invisibility* that applies to radio and the *combination of sounds and pictures* in the case of television ask for special measures. A radio message is fully concentrated on the orator's voice and has to offset the absence of comprehension support by visuals. It is in particular the *intensity* of speaking and the quality of *articulation* that matters. The risk of ambiguity and misunderstanding is fully related to *how* that voice is mediating. Radio in general appeals to the imagination (more than audio-visual media) and, at the same time, has a 'fictional tendency' in that it urges the audience to 'picture' the person 'behind' the voice (see Crisell 1986). Focussing upon a Christmas Message on radio, it is the audience's imaginative work the *Dutch Queen's* voice has to activate: the listeners may grasp the message content, if accentuation, rhythm, pauses etc. evoke the textual meanings by adequate support and guidance. In such a way, the re-oralisation of the written text causes its anchoring in the delivery setting.

A 'televisualised' (Atkinson 1984) Christmas Message, however, confronts the audience with less businesses of imagination in that certain visual signals are determined in advance, for instance, concerning clothes, hairstyle, physical appearance in general, low-key communicating behaviour, avoidance of being seen as eccentric, etc. The TV constellation as such reduces considerably the degree of imaginative picturing. For so much is already pictured: the place that is shown, the room from which the broadcast is recorded, the arrangement of Christmas symbols like tree, flowers, candles or decoration, the distance to the camera (normally medium, medium close-up and close-up shots) etc. The performance, then, depends on the way of speaking, acting and showing, according to representativeness (Ensink 1996). The teleprompter technology allows the speaker to look directly into the camera while speaking. Yet, a 'script-bound' behaviour prevails as long as a head of state relies heavily on the written text – as does the *German President* who performs chiefly like a preacher.

Only if other sequences are added or inserted which show the speaker talking and chatting with *other* people, and thus interrupt the delivery of the very Christmas Message, signals are given to the audience that the head of state wants to act, at least to a certain extent, according to how other representatives may be exposed to a mass public. If Atkinson (1984, 171) is right in his conclusion that the "secret of successful television lies in the presentation of events in such a way that viewers can feel they are *eavesdropping* on a scene, rather than being spoken to directly from the screen", then the *English Queen* is an example for this shift. Her presentation style consists of a blend of genres, viz. a Christmas Message and video reports (showing her talking to people), resembling a year's review.

There follows a short characterisation – in terms of text organisation and content description – of the three Christmas Messages, for convenience of reference translated into English (by Titus Ensink [Beatrix] and Gisela Redeker [Herzog]). The way media features are dealt with will be discussed.

4. Dutch Queen Beatrix: radio message 1998

[Announcement, sacred music (motet *All unser Schuld*, text Martin Luther, music Hans Leo Hassler)] [Calm and a bit flat articulation, no accelerations] [No form of address]
During Christmas time a ray of light breaks through the dark clouds above human existence. The birth of the Christmas child is a sign of reconciliation and peace. In a world full of contradictions many people feel themselves oppressed by hostility and violence between the inhabitants of this world.
We hear daily stories about what people do to each other, both on a small scale and on a large scale. However, it gives hope to see how people everywhere do efforts to restore disturbed rela-

tions and shocked confidence. All of us may feel encouraged by that, the more so when we seek reconciliation in our private lives as well.

In countries where prolonged injustice and oppression have come to an end, people are looking more and more for ways to go on to live together peacefully. This requires a painful process of opening the truth and facing the harm that has been done. This way the bad habit of renouncing the past is broken with. We may learn a lot from this, also in small-scale associations and in our own environment, where relations sometimes are completely disturbed and where human dignity is affected. Christmas, the celebration of Peace on earth, calls for reconciliation between people [lit. humans].

[...]

Only reconciliation may result in a lasting peace. This requires a real effort from all of us. The world would be a worse place if not everywhere people were willing rather to bear injustice than to do injustice themselves: people who were willing to make the first step themselves in breaking through the downward spiral of hostility and violence. We may thank God that there are people who have the courage and tenacity for making peace. Blessed are the peacemakers, Jesus says.

In our world peace seems sometimes far away. But the striving for reconciliation and restoration of hope which takes place in so many countries now gives hope and may inspire each of us to celebrate Christmas also this year as occasion for peace on earth.

I wish you all a Merry [lit. Blessed] Christmas.

[Christmas Carol *Peace, gentle peace*, closure by radio presenter]

Framed by sacred music, the message is religiously coloured and augmented by some vague biblical associations. This starts from the very beginning: "The birth of the Christmas child is a sign of reconciliation and peace". The topics *reconciliation* and *peace* both determine the text, which, in general, is worded in as abstract formulations as possible. It is not offering to the audience more than a clue to the potential meaning. What appeal to the imagination – as applies to the medium radio – is adopted by Beatrix? The message stimulates a *guessing* habit. People must unceasingly ask themselves what exactly Beatrix has referred to and which circumstances are focussed on. The mainly passive sentences have no real actors and depersonalise political meanings so that the listeners have to complete the utterings with their own assumptions. Confronted with a solemn voice that shows not much tonal variation, the audience is guided to combine the traditional Christmas topic 'peace on earth' with the rejection of 'hostility and violence' – all over the world, including Holland. Identification – unavoidable in the case of an invisible voice – is given only by the rare use of an ambiguous 'we', referring to orator *and* public. Although addressed as essential participants in a ceremony, the audience never exactly knows whether that 'we' points to Holland or other countries. In such a way, Beatrix acts distantly, according to the overall written text format. Her behaviour of avoiding concretisations, however, matches perfectly her style of performance – and her style of representativeness in general, being a *royal* head of state rather than a *political* voice. In sum, an ambivalence is established by the *Christian* content of the Message (her *moral narration*) and the fact that it is Queen Beatrix in her function as head of state who refuses to link her speech to political events and developments other than by means of vagueness and abstraction.

5. German President Herzog: television message 1998

[Announcement, picture of presidential building *Palais Bellevue*, then room where Herzog is seated, next to a table with a candle, a Christmas tree lighted in the background. Medium shot]
Good evening, [lit. Dear TV watchers], from here in Berlin, at Bellevue Palace, I am greeting all citizens, and also all those who have found a home, hospitality, or asylum in our country.
Behind us lies a year in which – more than in other years perhaps – we have been gripped by a feeling of change. There is the change in government, executed in democratic normality, and the move of the Government to Berlin, which has now begun to be carried out. There is the European Monetary Union that will begin with the New Year, which will lead to the farewell to the trusted Deutsche Mark. There are of course the turbulences of the global economy, which make us all wonder about the consequences for our future. And maybe it is also the approach of the turn of the century that makes us take account of this century and also of all our personal life. Christmas is not a bad occasion to quietly reflect and to ask oneself what is really important.
[...]
In the last four years of my office, I have got to know our country from many perspectives. I saw of course also negative things. Tonight, however, I want to stress that I am confident with respect to our country's future. Germany has made a very great effort during the last years. By this, I do not only refer to the reconstruction of East Germany, even if the positive changes there are the most obvious ones. Our businesses have widely introduced new technologies and new structures – also in West Germany – and in doing so have asked much of those who have been affected. But through this the German economy has once more become one of the most modern and most competitive in the world. To those who are now profiting from that, I say: Now is the time to make good on the social promise of our market economy. Now is the time to also think of those who need employment.
It is crucially important for the future how we treat each other as humans. I have seen how many citizens stand up for each other. I have had opportunity to see countless actions, initiatives, and projects. Many people have written to me about this. I have seen that we are not just an elbow society, as is so often claimed. Many people make sure that we are *also* a caring society.
Hardly any other country sends as many gifts to the far and farthest away. Hardly any other country admits as many foreigners and refugees as Germany. That too makes me optimistic for the future.
There is an old saying: All the darkness in the world does not suffice to extinguish the light of a single candle.
My wife and I wish you all a Merry Christmas.
[Close-up candle, closure by presenter]

Herzog's Message resembles a *protestant sermon* which is a heritage of antique culture and rhetoric. He performs in high speed, although sitting uncomfortably in his chair, looking constantly into the camera. His Message is rhetorically well structured: he wants to persuade the Germans (not only them, but also all people who live in Germany) into changing their general mood of wait-and-see. He takes on the role of 'political therapist', especially by saying the Germans need not being so sober; he tries to encourage them to have more 'fun'. In such a way, he is admonishing the public. He stresses some problems of the community in order to play down nervous demeanour and dissatisfaction. Herzog relates all his descriptions of the state of the German mind to experiences and competences he himself in his role as *witness* (*observer*) possesses. As a witness he has sources to relate on, which are consecutively listed. This way of listing influences even the syntax. Herzog favours rather simple clause combinations and prefers parallel structures. As mannered as he is in his preaching style (his sentences seem to stem from a percussionist), its goal is to focus the public's attention on its content, which is realistic and definite. Herzog thus shows that he knows about which he is speaking to the Germans. There is a great discrepancy between the textual content, which is well organised and has a clear discussing and persuading tenor, and the way TV features are used. What you get is not what you see. Herzog's – mainly motionless – preaching habit is not at all translated into TV frames that grip, even if one admits that one may not expect a lot of staging work or camera movements. It is static in character, in contrast with the convincing mood of the address. The Message's end is surprising since Herzog suddenly mentions his wife: this is accompanied by a camera movement (close-up of the candle). Then the slightly 'stormy atmosphere' of the address is over. Herzog finishes as the 'father' of all Germans.

6. English Queen Elizabeth II: television message 1998

[Beginning sequence: text *The Queen*, while members of the Royal Family are decorating a Christmas tree, music: Christmas carol]
- [voice-over]

Christmas is a time for reflection and renewal. For Christians the year's end has a special and familiar significance, but all faiths have their calendars, their sign-posts, which ask us to pause from time to time and think further than the hectic daily round. We do that as individuals, with our families, and as members of our local communities.
- [talking directly into the camera (Medium Close Shot)]

It is not always easy for those in their teens or twenties to believe that someone of my age – of the older generation – might have something useful to say to them. But I would say that my mother has much to say to me.
- [v-o (video sequence: scenes from Queen Mother's birthday)]

Indeed, her vigour and enjoyment of life is a great example of how to close the so-called generation gap. She has an extraordinary capacity to bring happiness into other people's lives, and her own vitality and warmth is returned to her by those whom she meets.
- [v-o (video sequence: scenes from Remembrance Day)]

But there are many of my mother's generation still with us. They can remember the First World War. Prince Philip and I can recall only the Second.
- [inserted video report from Remembrance Day]
  QUEEN: You'd better sit down again, I think
  VETERAN: Thank you
  QUEEN: It's really impressive coming here today

- [v-o (video sequence: Remembrance Day)]

I know that those memories of ours define us as old, but they are shared with millions of others, in Britain and the Commonwealth, people who often feel forgotten by the march of time. They remember struggles unknown to young people today, and which they will not forget. Nor should their countries forget them.

- [talking directly into the camera (Medium Close Shot)]

And in recent days we have had another reminder of the courage and dedication shown so often round the world by our armed forces in the cause of peace. Memories such as these are a consequence of age, and not a virtue in themselves. But with age does come experience, and that can be a virtue if it is sensibly used. Though we each lead different lives, the experience of growing older,

- [v-o (video sequence: Charles' birth, than scenes from his 50th birthday)]

and the joys and emotions which it brings, are familiar to us all. It is hard to believe that a half century has passed since our son Charles was christened, and now, last month, he has celebrated his fiftieth birthday. It was a moment of great happiness and pride on our part in all he has achieved during the last three decades.

[...]

- [talking directly into the camera (Medium Close Shot)]

These organisations [volunteers' organisations already shown in the birthday video sequence], and those who serve them so selflessly, provide the bridges across which the generations travel, meet and learn from one another. They give us, with our families, our sense of belonging. It is they that help define our sense of duty. It is they that can make us strong as individuals, and keep the nation's heartbeat strong and steady too. Christmas is a good time for us to recognise all that they do for us and to say a heartfelt thank you to each and every one of them.

[With a shy smiling] Happy Christmas to you all.

[National Anthem sung, text of the Anthem showed, TV scenes from the last year, Windsor flag]

The Queen's Christmas Message is realised as a blend of TV genres: video sequences that are 'commented' by herself as voice-over, direct addressing, scenes that picture her (and members of the royal family) talking with other people, in sum: a year's review from the perspective of the head of state. What you get is considerably more than what you hear. The choice of visualisations seems to be influenced by the will to show as many actions of the Queen (and other royals) in representative tasks as possible. In doing so, the Queen legitimises her political and societal role and her privileged function. As voice of the nation, she thanks her people for doing volunteer work, praising them by at the same time showing her own commitment. Her Message job here is very much TV oriented in that she avoids the description of facts and the mentioning of events which cannot be framed by TV pictures. Even the (remains of) the religious meaning of Christmas are stressed in such a way: symbols in connection with the royal family, carols sung when one sees the Queen, and the direct address of "Happy Christmas to you all" that is not, as might be expected, the climax of the Message, but the beginning of the National Anthem, which proves to be a 'summary' of representative actions during the last year. These features altogether function as the *predominantly visual anchoring* of the Christmas Message in the TV setting.

7. Concluding remarks: a short comparison

In figure 1, a synopsis of the three Messages presents the pragmatic realisations, as discussed above, related to the functions of anchoring and media adaptation.

means / level	BEATRIX	HERZOG	ELIZABETH
provision of comprehension support	written language style, minimal support, calls for re-reading the text	rhetoric, sequentiality, using lists, overtly oriented towards expectations	sequentiality, text content is supported by pictures and inserted video footages
knowledge-centred operations	conundrums, creating astonishment	'political therapy', argumentative moves, knowledge depends on observations	documentation in words and pictures, pictorial confirmation of existing knowledge
concretisations	not really (yet: some characteristic post-war lexemes, definitely not WW II)	acknowledges shortages and worries, points out that he knows the situation	video footages: scenes and documented talks with those concerned (and other royals)
guiding of reception	low key (relies on press publication), very formal manner, metaphor ('light')	announcements, listing style (but high speed performance)	time-related structure, year's review, from personal (family) to social (offical tasks)
references to contextual information	biblical and religious allusions, reference to Christmas, no persons mentioned	political developments, reference to Christmas, public discussions	references by pictures, Christmas and national context (visits and invitations)
verbal actions (apart from: to wish, to praise, to describe)	moral narration, stimulates mysterious meanings	paradoxical request for more 'pleasure' and for normality, admonishing	in words and pictures: thanking, explaining, (less) admonishing

Figure 1: Realisation means and media features

What is more, the realisation of the delivery of the Christmas Messages by Elizabeth (E), Beatrix (B) and Herzog (H) may contribute to the following sociocultural practices:
– representing the nation in a common-sense way (E and H),
– constructing solemnity (B),
– producing popularity (E) or just avoiding it (B),
– opting for authority (H and B),
– demonstrating knowledge about what is going on (E and H).

Pragmatic functions, semiotic forms and media adequacy collaborate in order to compose the meaning of a specific Christmas Message. An analysis without taking into consideration this constellation would not suffice, since the recipient's perspective requires at least a basis comprehension of the medium features and a reconstruction of their uses.

As has been shown, however very shortly, the three Christmas Messages have in common that they are related to actual problems of political representation by heads of state in 1998, albeit mainly tempered by abstraction. The radio characteristics are fully used by the Dutch Queen who invites her listeners to apply conundrum related knowledge operations. She inclines to mysterious meaning building, which, in fact, functions as a mystification device. Her moral narration matches perfectly the possibilities of radio presentations in that she opts for stimulating guessing behaviour. Because Beatrix tries to avoid text fragments that might be heard as political statements she excludes potential criticism. She herself was already object of criticism since she was involved in critical opinions with respect to the Dutch people's behaviour during the Second World War on the occasion of the fiftieth anniversary of the War's end, in 1995. Once bitten twice shy.

President Herzog met criticism, since he, in 1998, overtly reversed his own earlier uttered intention to stay in office no longer than one term (i.e. five years) and was toying with the idea of being re-elected. His Message is – therefore? – full of political statements (or clauses that could be heard as ones) formulated by someone who must no longer perform carefully in order not to provoke counterproductive actions by others. His disinterest in 'televisuality' is in conformity with other German Presidents' TV presentation styles, relying heavily on oratory features. Herzog's Christmas Message is strictly rhetorically framed and uses TV only as transmission means.

Queen Elizabeth II shows strategic insights concerning exposure to a mass public. Her Christmas Message is embedded in video reports and embeds itself several reported sequences of earlier representation actions by herself. Although semiotic and verbal meanings thus coincide, her specific blend of TV genres might cause the danger of 'exaggeration', i.e. too much 'impression management', and too less appeal to content oriented processing. Critics of her recent style of Christmas Messages considered it related to the renewal of the *pr strategy* of the House of Windsor after numerous reproaches that were published in the context of her reactions to Lady Diana's death.

Media discourses, like the ones investigated here, need an adequate anchoring in the media setting. The comparison of three different examples of Christmas Messages shows that the application of media features may provoke intertextual and intermedial 'extra' meanings.

References

Atkinson, J. Maxwell (1984): Our masters' voices. The language and body language of politics. London, New York: Methuen.

BH Tours (2002): Christmas in England. In: http://www.britishheritage.com/tourscie.htm (accessed on 19 November 2002).

Crisell, Andrew (1986): Understanding radio. London, New York: Methuen.

Ehlich, Konrad (1994): Funktion und Struktur schriftlicher Kommunikation. In: Günther, H./Ludwig, O. (eds.): Handbuch Schrift und Schriftlichkeit. Vol 1. Berlin, New York: de Gruyter, 18-41.

Ensink, Titus (1996): The footing of a royal address. In: Current Issues in Language and Society 3/3, 205-232.

Holly, Werner (1995): Secondary orality in the electronic media. In: Quasthoff, U.M. (ed.): Aspects of oral communication. Berlin, New York: de Gruyter, 340-363.

Jeyes, Billie F. (1997): Christmas at the manor. In: http://www.citybeat.com/archives/1997/issue403/coverarticle10.html (accessed on 19 November 2002).

Lodge, David (1970): Out of the shelter. London: Macmillan.

Sauer, Christoph (1996): Echoes from abroad – speeches for the domestic audience: Queen Beatrix's address to the Israeli Parliament. In: Current Issues in Language and Society 3/3, 233-267.

– (2002): Ceremonial text and talk. A functional-pragmatic approach. In: Chilton, P./Schäffner, C. (eds.): Politics as talk and text. Analytic approaches to political discourse. Amsterdam: Benjamins, 111-142.

Zohar Livnat

"Like in the movies": Dialogue between different voices in the public discourse in Israel*

1. Introduction

The premise of this paper is that a discourse of any kind is a site of a struggle (Seidel 1985, 44). In particular, a newspaper report is a story that cannot be disassociated from its historic, political, social and cultural context. Events are exploited by different writers for various purposes, and the journalist always has a position and has a purpose and agenda, and his or her text is very frequently part of an overt or covert public debate. The aim of the paper is to demonstrate the various voices in Israeli society and the dialogue held among them in the context of the public discourse in Israel. This will be done by describing the manner in which a specific event was presented in the Israeli press by different writers, assuming that "a powerful way of examining ideological structure is through the examination of language" (Kress 1985, 30).

The analysis is based on a single image that appeared in very many texts at that time. The positions of the various writers and voices in Israeli society are presented through an analysis of texts containing this image. The analysis demonstrates and emphasizes the dialogic aspect of the public discourse.

On a January night in the year 2002, an elite commando unit of the Israeli army seized an arms ship making its way from the Persian Gulf to Israel in a dramatic raid. No one was injured in the operation. The government of Israel maintained that the large cache of various types of arms found on the ship had come from Iran and was on its way to the Palestinian Authority. It presented this as proof positive that the peaceful intentions of the Palestinian leadership could not be trusted. When the ship arrived in the Israeli port of Eilat, the arms were displayed on the dock and a press conference was held in the presence of the Israeli prime minister, defense minister and chief of staff. The Palestinian Authority denied any connection to the ship.

On the first day of the report the two largest newspapers – *Ma'ariv* and *Yedioth Ahronoth* – devoted 15 entire pages each to the subject, including huge pictures of the arms dis-

---

* I would like to thank Deirdre Wilson for her useful comments on an early version of this paper. Mistakes, needless to say, are mine.

played on the dock, a map of Israel with all the locations that would have lain within the range of the missiles on the ship had they fallen into the hands of the Palestinian Authority and an illustration showing all the stages of the seizure of the ship by the Israeli commandos.

By and large, the report reflected the official position of the government of Israel – that the arms were on their way to the Palestinian Authority; that Yasser Arafat, the chairman of the Palestinian Authority, had known about the ship and authorized it, and that the arms had apparently come from Iran. The Israeli press also presented reports that did not agree with the official Israeli version, such as that of the United States that the arms had in fact been on their way to the Hezbollah in Lebanon rather than to the Palestinian Authority, and of the Palestinians that claimed that the operation was in fact an Israeli provocation and an attempt by Israel to evade negotiations with the Palestinians and thereby cause the mediation attempts by the American General Anthony Zinni, who had just arrived in the region, to fail.

During the following week, the debate over the facts continued – where the arms had come from, who they were intended for, and whether or not Arafat had known about them. But one may find in the Israeli press not only a debate over the facts of the case, but also over its general context. Some claimed that it was the policies of the government of Israel that were driving the Palestinians to take action of this kind because Israel was not giving the Palestinian people sufficient incentive to abandon the battlefield, that it was the diplomatic deadlock that was intensifying the violent dynamic. Voices were heard to claim that it was not difficult to understand why the Palestinians would want to arm themselves, and that what they were doing was in fact no different than what the Israelis had done during their fight for independence.

2. Presentation of the event: Different voices

When reviewing the articles that appeared in the press at that time, one is struck by a single continually repeated image – that the "operation was like something out of a Hollywood movie". The seizure of the ship was repeatedly compared to a scene out of a movie. I would like to use this image to demonstrate the positions and views of the various writers and the different voices within Israeli society. This image is exploited in each of the various texts as a medium to present each journalist's particular position. At first, the image is used to express praise and amazement. Later on, reservations are expressed about it and it is used to level criticism, and finally, it is used for the purpose of refutation.

2.1 Voice No. 1 – Praise and amazement

The source of this image is in something stated by an Israeli officer:

(1) A swift action, **classic James Bond**, as one of the members of the General Staff put it.

(*Yedioth Ahronoth*, January 6)

This image appeared in the headline on the same day and in the same newspaper:

(2) Like **in the movies**

(Headline, *Yedioth Ahronoth*, January 6)

In the editorial:

(3) [...] Operation carried out with high-quality performance, **of the type that goes beyond any special effects produced by a Hollywood scriptwriter**.

(*Yedioth Ahronoth*, January 6)

and in the commentary:

(4) [...] A successful military action, à la **James Bond**.

(*Yedioth Ahronoth*, January 6)

The next day we find it in the competing newspaper too:

(5) The operation looked as if it had been taken from a **Hollywood action movie**. But it really happened, early Thursday morning at high sea, 500 kilometers from Israeli shores.

(*Ma'ariv*, January 7)

This is the voice that is reflected by the manner in which the event was reported in the popular press. It is related to the fact that this event gave Israelis the opportunity to look back and see themselves as they once did – in the 1940's, 1950's and early 1960's – as a small state surrounded by enemies, fighting for its life in a just war that employed mainly ingenuity and resourcefulness. This operation had all the features needed to uphold this image: huge quantities of arms depicting Israel as the victim; the report on the missile ranges reminds the reader how small the State of Israel is. The gathering of intelligence over a long period, the operations of an elite unit at night, far from Israeli shores all required ingenuity and resourcefulness. And what is especially important about this operation is what did not happen – no one was injured. This, in my opinion, is the Israeli consensual context surrounding the event and this is what is reflected in the major stories as reported in Israel's two largest newspapers.

2.2 Voice No. 2 – Reservation and criticism

The second voice expresses reservation and criticism, and the criticism uses the very same image, exploiting it for its own ends.

The next day, *Ha'aretz*, Israel's third largest circulation newspaper, considered to be of a higher quality than *Ma'ariv* and *Yedioth Ahronoth*, published an article that expressed reservation with the Hollywood image:

(6) I hope the reader will forgive me if I am not swept up in waves of enthusiasm at the "**James Bond operation right out of the movies**", as the seizure of the Karine A was described in the media headlines that triggered a national erection. The seizure of the large amount of arms was important in itself, but also as a public relations instrument that was squeezed like a lemon, with the entire security establishment hitching a ride on it. For a moment, we were allowed to feel like **Israel of yesteryear** – Israel of the Entebbe rescue[1], which nothing resembles in planning and daring; Israel that demolished the nuclear reactor in Iraq, for which the world thanks it to this day, or Israel preparing to get as far as Iran and perhaps to return to Iraq. The problem is that between **the glory of yesteryear** and the preparation for the dangers of the future, we have been unable to find a solution to the immediate danger at our doorstep and our leaders have no idea what is going to happen the day after "**the daring raid taken right out of a Hollywood action movie**".

(Yoel Marcus, *Ha'aretz*, January 8)

The reservation expressed in this text is related to the claim that the current operation does not resolve any real problem. Expressions such as "the glory of yesteryear", and "Israel of yesteryear" hint that the time for military solutions has passed, and they are worthless if not backed up by political ones. The author's reservation with the image is related to the fact that it diverts the debate from its truly important aspects. This text especially reflects the recognition that these images belong to the past and are no longer compatible with Israeli reality.

From a linguistic point of view, this is a simple case because of the fairly standard usage of the quotation marks for both expressions – the "**James Bond operation right out of the movies**", and "**the daring raid taken right out of a Hollywood action movie**". We can use here the relevance theory's account of irony, as was presented in Sperber/Wilson (1981) and Wilson/Sperber (1992), according to which ironic interpretation of an utterance is achieved mainly by recognition of an "echoic mention" (or "echoic interpretation")[2] –, that

---

[1] "Entebbe rescue" = Entebbe is a city in Uganda. In 1976, an Air-France plane on its way from Tel Aviv to Paris was hijacked and landed in Entebbe. An Israeli commando unit was flown 4.000 kilometers to Uganda, and successfully freed the hostages. Two Hollywood films were made depicting this event.

[2] The term 'echoic mention' was used by Sperber/Wilson in their 1981 paper and in the first edition of their book (1986), but they have abandoned it later in favor of the more general term 'echoic interpretation', which refers to "the use of a propositional form to represent not itself but some other propositional form it more or less closely resembles" (see Sperber/Wilson 1986, notes to first edition, footnote 25, 289-290).

is, the ironic utterance echoes and is dissociated from another use of the same proposition. Thus, what we have here is a clear case of irony. The ironic interpretation is based on dissociative echoic mention of the utterances that at first were used to express praise and amazement. The victim of the irony is anyone who uses, or even accepts, this image. Since irony is a major device for expressing criticism, using these recognizable statements in quotation marks is a standard way of achieving a strong effect of criticism.

However, example 7 presents a more complex and fuzzy case. We return to *Ma'ariv*, one of the two large newspapers, but this time the quote is from a personal column published in the weekend supplement a full week after the event. Example 7 includes excerpts from a much longer article entirely turning on the movie metaphor. Even the title is the name of an old movie:

(7) The Ship of Fools

Last week, one of the satellite stations showed an action-packed film about the American commando unit, *Navy Seals*, Cast with handsome, testosterone-saturated actors – Michael Biehn, Billy Paxton and Charlie Sheen – who entered and exited violent Beirut in an attempt to destroy Stinger missiles that terrorists managed to lay their hands on. The Seals jumped out of helicopters, slide down ropes and used state-of-the-art technology to complete their mission, leaving their dead behind, rendezvousing with a submarine waiting for them opposite the coast of Lebanon. This cartoon-action picture is worth taking in at the end of the hard day's work. Since *You Only Live Twice* with Sean Connery as James Bond, we have seen commando units sliding down ropes to get the bad guys as they fitfully doze hundreds of times.

On the background of the manner in which the much admired the art of guerilla warfare has been translated into cinematic language in dozens of films, and on the light of background that American and British forces slide down ropes into Taliban caves and, on the background of the reality in which the world is sick of its media-hyped representatives slipping in to slit the throats of villains in their sleep in the name of an obscure idea, on the background of the recognition that all violence, even that which serves the most noble ideas to eradicate terror is an unnecessary appendage, left over from the previous millenium – it was difficult not to smile in pity at the pathetic and foolish attempts, completely lacking any media acumen, by official Israel to market – in installments, and like **three Indiana Jones sequels** – the seizure (**thunder of drums grows louder**) by the naval commando unit (**trumpets**), that is Flotilla 13, on board the Karine A, **the fishing boat whose sailors all slumber**, that belongs to the Palestinian Authority. [...]

Even if today, tomorrow or next week the IDF Spokesman's film unit releases archive shots of **our fine young men** seizing the Karine A at high sea, a movie about the Navy Seals will always be more fascinating and convincing. Moreover, in a world and state overflowing with far more serious and painful problems, which yearns to lay down its weapons, the raw footage, like the repeated presentation of the weapons that were seized, turned into **an item devoid of viewers or clients**.

(Ron Meiberg, *Ma'ariv*, January 11)

The main claim in this text is that the world of today is sick of this type of movie just as it is sick of this type of action and this type of thinking. The situation that we are living in has changed dramatically and this requires a radical change in our perception of the conflict too.

This is a dispute, and the event described here is right in the middle of it. On the one hand, there is a yearning to return to the "Israel of yesteryear", to the days when the conflict was not a matter of controversy, and the belief in the justice of our cause was shared almost by all. But on the other hand, we find the recognition and realization that all this in fact belongs to the past. That is the other voice, and one might say that the combination of both voices reflects the predominant dispute dividing Israeli society today.

As for the linguistic style of example 7, can we use again the notion of "echoic mention"? Sperber/Wilson use it in quite a broad sense and allow "an implicit mention of propositions" (1981, 306), and echoic mention of many different degrees and types. If, in example 6, we can easily point at the mentioned propositions, in example 7 there is no such direct echo and no quotation marks. The writer quite vaguely refers to the image of a "movie", which had been "in the air", that is, had been the subject of public discourse during the previous week. Ironic, dissociative or hostile tone is evident especially in the second paragraph ("Three Indiana Jones sequels") and perhaps in the title too. We can also refer to the phrases "our fine young men" and "the fishing boat whose sailors all slumber" (a line from a famous Hebrew folk song) as cases of echoic mention which carry an ironic tone. It seems that here, the author himself accepts this image, therefore the victim of the irony is not the one who thinks that the operation was "like a movie" but rather the one who cannot see that it is an inferior, old movie that no one wants to watch anymore.

However, not every reference of the "movie" image is ironic. For instance, the "item devoid of viewers or clients" in the last sentence makes an immediate connection to the world of film and television (the English word "item" is used in Hebrew only in this context). It endorses the analogy between the actual event and an action movie, but it does not imply dissociation from this analogy. We can also suggest that what we see in the first paragraph of example 7, which starts as a review, is an echo of style, an echo of the conventional style of the genre of a movie review.[3] But again, it in itself does not create an ironic effect. We should also take into account the very fact that this writer chose to build his entire article around the theme of action movies. Assuming that this choice is not accidental, it may also be considered as a response or a reaction to statements already heard in the previous week, but there is nothing ironic about it in itself. Thus, what we see in this text is a mixture of different kinds of phenomena, not all of them fit the strict concept of "echo" in relevance theory. This conclusion should lead us to a search for a looser, more general description of the case at matter.

One path we can take is referring to notions developed for the analysis of interpersonal conversation, such as "repetition" (as in Tannen 1989) or "resonance" (as in DuBois 2001).

---

[3] Fairclough (1992, 104-105), discussing intertextuality (see below), following Bakhtin (1981, 1986), makes a clear distinction between intertextual relations of texts to specific other texts, on one hand, and intertextual relations of texts to linguistic and discursive conventions (genres, discourses, styles, etc.), on the other hand. Thus, the idea of echo of genre or echo of style is not a new one.

These kinds of approaches describe the interpersonal dialogue as "a joint production", in which each of the speakers advances the dialogue, or moves it forward, by means of components used by the interlocutor. Although these approaches focus on the use of the same words or the same syntactic structures, they allow in principle an application to various kinds of linguistic phenomena: "Resonance is a process of activating relationships between comparable linguistic elements at any level: structures, words, morphemes, phonemes, features, meanings, referents, illocutionary forces, etc." (DuBois 2001, 9). The main idea is that an effective way to construct a dialogue of any kind is to use elements used by the interlocutor. In our case, the reader, as a third party which is familiar with the public atmosphere and the recent public discourse, can recognize connections between various texts based not only on words and propositions but also on meanings, styles, images and even less explicit elements.

Another path we could take is to take a step back to a higher level of generalization and to allow the term "intertextuality" into the discussion. In this level, we may think about any text as a "mosaic of quotations", to use Kristeva's words (1986, 37), or as Bakhtin (1986, 91) put it: "Each utterance is filled with the echoes and reverberations of other utterances to which it is related by the communality of the sphere of speech communication" and "Each utterance is a link in the chain of speech communication". If this is true, then what we see here is only a fancy example of a general phenomenon. And what our examples show is that in the public discourse, the "polyphonic nature" of utterances enables the speaker to express support for ideas expressed in the public discourse, or relate to them ironically, presenting them as ridiculous, thereby expressing reservation and criticism in a more or less explicit fashion, and even, as we shall immediately see in example 8, to expressly refute them and present a totally opposed position.

2.3 Voice No. 3 – Refutation

Example 8 will represent the third voice. It comes from an article by an Israeli journalist named Uri Avneri and was published on the Internet that very same weekend. Once again, here are excerpts from a much longer text:

(8) "The Ships on the Way"

> The chiefs of the three big parties in Israel – the *Likud*, the Labor party and the army – were sitting **on the stage**. They were frustrated. It was already clear to them that they had not succeeded in selling **the major performance** they had prepared so carefully – the capture of the arms ship belonging to **the villain in the heroic epic Entebbe 2**. [...]
> It is also clear that the information was supplied by agents that managed to plant themselves **in the center of the plot**. But where? In the Hizballah headquarters? In Iran? Among the arms merchants? On the ship itself? And if there was a collaborator on the ship, who was he? [...]

> The captain was very happy to tell all to the Israeli reporters, the hand-picked darlings of Army Intelligence, who **played the role of the reporters in the show**. During the evening, I saw the captain on TV three times. The first time I saw something that was omitted later. At the end of the interview, the captain requested: "Tell my daughter that I am a fighter!" Then he broke into tears and hid his face between his hands. What caused this outburst? Was he afraid that his daughter might think he was a collaborator? A traitor? […]
>
> The whole story does not make sense. It smells of improbability. The more so since all this happened, of course, exactly on time, **as if a supreme director had orchestrated everything with amazing precision**. Anthony Zinni was due in the country in order to impose a cease-fire to which Sharon strenuously objects (because it would oblige him to freeze all settlement activity). Hocus pocus – and here is a new pretext for continuing the war against Arafat. […]
>
> (Uri Avnery, *Gush-Shalom* website, January 12)

This text presents numerous reservations with the official Israeli version of the events, in fact all the reservations voiced by Palestinians in the Israeli press. The possibility proposed here is that this was an operation launched by Israel to cause Zinni's mission to fail, and in order to prove that Arafat and the Palestinian Authority cannot be viewed as partners to an agreement. This possibility is supported by the image of the film, or play. There are a number of hints scattered throughout the text, all of which I have emphasized in bold. Some of them may be interpreted as dissociative echoic mentions, for instance "the major performance" and "the villain in the heroic epic Entebbe 2" where an ironic tone is clearly heard. However, other examples, such as "played the role of the reporters in the show" are not cases of echo, and it is unlikely to discuss them under this term. Again, a more general description is required, and according to this, we can only assume that the references to the movie metaphor are a reaction and a response to the salience of this image in the Israeli press during the previous week.

How does this image function here? What the author is in fact saying is that if the event was "like a movie", then it is not real, not true. The people involved are only characters playing roles that have been written for them. Consequently, we may say that the image is used here for the purpose of refutation, to deny the truth of the official Israeli version and support the version that conforms to the views of the writer. Whereas in examples 6-7 the writers express criticism but basically accept the consensual version, i.e. the facts as they were presented, here the writer does not accept the consensual version, and uses the movie image in order to reject the description of the event, i.e. to refute the validity of the facts themselves.

3. Summing up quickly

When we look at the way in which a specific event is reported and discussed by different writers, we can see the reflection of the various voices in the public discourse and the dialogue held among them. This analysis can demonstrate and emphasize the dialogic aspect of the public discourse.

Using the strict notion of "echo" or a more general concept as "intertextuality" we can show how, by using the same image, a speaker can support another's position, criticize it and express reservation towards it, and even refute it and propose a totally different position.

References

Bakhtin, Michael (1981): The dialogical imagination. Ed. by Holquist, M. Transl. by Emerson, C./ Holquist, M. Austin: University of Texas Press.
– (1986): Speech genres and other late essays. Ed. by Emerson, C./Holquist, M. Transl. by McGee, V.W. Austin: University of Texas Press.
DuBois, John W. (2001): Towards a dialogic syntax. Manuscript, UC Santa Barbara.
Fairclough, Norman (1992): Discourse and social change. Cambridge: Polity Press.
Kress, Gunther (1985): Ideological structure in discourse. In: van Dijk, T.A. (ed.): Handbook of discourse analysis. London u.a.: Academic Press, 27-42.
Kristeva, Julia (1986): Word, dialogue and novel. [Transl. by Jardine, A./Gora, T./Roudiez, L.S.]. In: Moi, T. (ed.): The Kristeva Reader. New York: Columbia University Press, 34-61.
Livnat, Zohar (2004): On verbal irony, meta-linguistic knowledge and echoic interpretation. In: Pragmatics and cognition 12/1, 57-70.
Seidel, Gill (1985): Political discourse analysis. In: van Dijk T.A. (ed.): Handbook of discourse analysis. London u.a.: Academic Press, 43-60.
Sperber, Dan/Wilson, Deirdre (1981): Irony and the use-mention distinction. In: Cole, P. (ed.): Radical pragmatics. New York: American Press, 295-318.
– (1986/1995): Relevance: Communication and cognition. Oxford (UK), Cambridge (USA): Blackwell.
Tannen, Deborah (1989): Talking voices: Repetition, dialogue, and imagery in conversational discourse. Cambridge: Cambridge University Press.
Wilson, Deirdre/Sperber, Dan (1992): On verbal irony. In: Lingua 87, 53-76.

Jana Hoffmannová

Interviews in Zeitungen und Zeitschriften: Frage- und Antwortbeziehungen

1. Einleitung

In diesem Beitrag befasse ich mich mit dem Genre Interview, das heute in der tschechischen Presse (und in der tschechischen medialen Sphäre überhaupt) in unterschiedlichster Gestalt realisiert wird – was auch aus den Beispielen sichtbar wird. Dieses Genre gründet sich auf die Beziehung zwischen Fragen und Antworten; es handelt sich um ein linguistisches Problem, dem schon einige Aufmerksamkeit gewidmet wurde (z.B. Conrad 1978; Schegloff 1990; Freed 1994; im Rahmen der IADA Likomanova 1998; Štícha 1998; für das Tschechische vgl. z.B. Müllerová 1982; Mluvnice češtiny 3, 1987, 649-655; u.a.); hier jedoch wird speziell dessen Profilierung im konkreten Texttyp verfolgt.

Alle Interviews, mit denen ich gearbeitet habe, wurden im Jahr 2002 veröffentlicht und das Quellenrepertoire ist verhältnismäßig breit gefächert, es handelt sich um die meistgelesenen tschechischen Tageszeitungen, verschiedene Fernseh- und andere Magazine bis hin zu Frauenzeitschriften (wie Xantypa). In großem Maße sind das Gespräche, die zur Popularisierung bekannter Persönlichkeiten und zur Präsentierung ihrer Ansichten dienen; Interviews, die im Rahmen verschiedener Meinungsbefragungen realisiert wurden, lasse ich hier beiseite (Darüber haben wir bei anderen Gelegenheiten berichtet: Müllerová 1994, Hoffmannová 2000). Weiter muss ich vorausschicken, dass ich nur mit klassischen Interviews gearbeitet habe, die in Zeitungen und Zeitschriften als Folge von gegenseitig abgetrennten Fragen und Antworten präsentiert wurden.

Zur Einleitung noch etwas beinahe Selbstverständliches: im Genre Interview vielleicht mehr als anderswo muss eine »Frage« bei weitem keine Frage im eigentlichen Sinn des Wortes sein, d.h. mit den entsprechenden grammatischen Parametern; und eine »Antwort« muss nicht eine Antwort unter dem Aspekt des Grades der gewährten Informationen sein, aber auch nicht unter anderen Aspekten. Oft handelt es sich hier um eine sehr freie Beziehung beider Redebeiträge: Der Fragesteller bietet einen bestimmten Impuls an und gibt sich damit zufrieden, dass er den Partner »zum Sprechen anregt«, d.h. er gibt sich eigentlich mit jedweder Reaktion zufrieden (sei es eine eher indirekte, implizite »Echo«-Antwort oder eine andere). Vielleicht ist es nur für Politikerinterviews typisch, dass der Redakteur – u.U. wiederholt – eine wirkliche, informative, genaue Antwort einfordert.

Bei meiner Analyse der Fragen und Antworten in einem verhältnismäßig umfangreichen Interview-Ensemble werden syntaktische Fragestellungen nicht im Zentrum stehen (auch wenn ich selbstverständlich einige Erkenntnisse der Textsyntax nutze). Ich werde mich also nicht mit schon detailliert beschriebenen Fällen befassen (obwohl deren Klassifizierung gewiss immer noch zu verfeinern wäre), wo die Verknüpfung der Frage mit der Antwort sehr eng ist, wo die Antwort von der Frage abhängig ist, von ihr das syntaktische Schema übernimmt und auf ihrer Grundlage verschiedene Typen von Ellipsen und Reduktionen realisiert, von ihr einzelne Elemente der lexikalischen Besetzung übernimmt und diese entweder wiederholt oder durch Synonyme, Hyponyme, Hyperonyme, Paraphrasen ersetzt... Im Vordergrund wird auch nicht der Aspekt der aktuellen Gliederung stehen. Ich konzentriere mich vielmehr auf etwas weniger Erforschtes, nämlich auf die lockeren Beziehungen zwischen Fragen und Antworten. In diesem Falle bietet es sich an – ohne dass wir dabei die syntaktischen Aspekte der Analyse vernachlässigen –, eher beim stilistisch-pragmatischen Ende zu beginnen. Und so fesseln mich vor allem individuelle Stile, die Art und Weise, wie einige der Interviewten ihre Antworten formulieren und sie mit den Fragen verbinden.

2. Der stilistisch-pragmatische Zugang zum Interview

2.1 Koreferenz in Topikketten (Isotopieketten)

In den Antworten einer der befragten Persönlichkeiten herrscht z.B. die lexikalische Kohäsion vor, die sehr diszipliniert gebildet ist: der Sprecher reagiert präzise auf die Frage, allmählich erschöpft er alle darin enthaltenen »Hauptmotive« und wiederholt deren Bezeichnung entweder wortwörtlich oder mit geringen Abweichungen:

(1) *Rybařina* mi vždycky přišla jako dosti *osamělé posedávání* na břehu s *pokuřováním* cigárka. Je to tak?
V posledních deseti letech jsem opustil *sedavou rybařinu*, jezdím na pstruhy – většinou na Šumavu [...]. Člověk brouzdá řekou, neustále musí nahazovat, střídat mušky, snadno urazí pár kilometrů a o *poklidném pokuřování* nemůže být řeč. Navíc nemyslím, že by *rybařina* byla vyloženě *osamělá*. Jezdíme chytat s kamarády, vytahujeme se před sebou a je to prima.
[*Angeln* kam mir immer wie ein ziemlich *einsames Sitzen* und *Zigarettenrauchen* am Ufer vor. Ist das so?
Im letzten Jahrzehnt habe ich das *Angeln, bei dem man nur sitzt*, aufgegeben, ich fange jetzt Forellen – meistens im Böhmerwald [...]. Man watet durch den Fluss, ständig muss man die Angel auswerfen, den Köder auswechseln, leicht legt man ein paar Kilometer zurück und vom *gemütlichen Zigarettenrauchen* kann nicht mehr die Rede sein. Darüber hinaus glaube ich nicht, dass Angeln ein ausgesprochen *einsamer* Zeitvertreib sei. Wir fahren mit den Kameraden zum Angeln, spinnen Anglerlatein und das ist prima.]

Interviews in Zeitungen und Zeitschriften 151

Ganz anders verhält sich ein anderer Sprecher. Ein temperamentvoller, eruptiver Schauspieler bildet seine Antworten nicht so präzise und auf so erschöpfende Weise, mit auf Wiederholung gegründeter Kohäsion. Sein Stil ist kreativ und lebendig. Es herrscht auch hier lexikalische Kohäsion vor, aber die einzelnen Ausdrücke in den Fragen werden in den Antworten wiederholt und vielfältig variiert, es leiten sich davon weitere Isotopieketten ab, die sich verschiedenartig kreuzen und durchdringen; ins Spiel kommt ein ganzes Gewebe semantischer Zusammenhänge, gebildeten nicht selten auch auf spielerische Weise; dazu treten noch Gegenfragen, Ausrufe und unmittelbar benutzte Kontaktmittel. Das folgende Beispiel für diese reichhaltige, spontan gebildete Kohäsion der Antwort zeigt, wie der Vergleich des Torwarts mit dem populären Schauspieler, der in der Frage aufgeworfen wurde, in zwei sehr blumigen, sich ständig kreuzenden Ketten entfaltet wird:

(2) Mluvili jsme o Evaldu Schormovi, s jehož jménem je spojeno i úspěšné monodrama, které s vámi nastudoval…
Osamělost fotbalového brankáře.
A je *osamělejší brankář*, nebo *populární herec*?
Teda vy máte otázky! Já nejsem osamělý! Ba ne, já vám rozumím. Máte pravdu, popularita je hrozná věc. [...] *Co si s vámi dnes dokážou udělat novináři, je neuvěřitelné. Už nejsou dány žádné mantinely. Můžou cokoli – a vy jste jako kopací míč. A jsme u toho brankáře: každý si může kopnout. Brankář má výhodu, že buď chytne, nebo ne. Vy se ale nechytáte. I bulvár má mít svoje mantinely* [...].

[Wir sprachen über Evald Schorm, mit dessen Namen auch das erfolgreiche Monodrama, das er mit Ihnen einstudiert hat, verbunden ist …
Einsamkeit des Torwarts.
Und sind Sie ein *einsamer Torwart* oder ein *populärer Schauspieler*?
Sie stellen aber Fragen! Ich bin nicht einsam! Durchaus nicht, ich verstehe Sie. Sie haben Recht, die Popularität ist eine schreckliche Sache. [...] Was heutzutage die *Journalisten* fertig bringen mit ihnen anzustellen, ist unglaublich. Es sind keine *Schranken* gesetzt. Sie können alles und sie sind wie ein *Fußball*. Und da sind wir bei diesem *Torwart*: Jeder kann *schießen*. Der *Torwart* hat den Vorteil, dass er den Ball entweder *fängt* oder nicht. Sie *fangen* sich aber *nicht*. Auch die *Regenbogenpresse* soll ihre *Schranken* haben [...].]

Wiederum völlig unterschiedlich ist der Stil eines Sprechers, der permanent auf die spaßhafte Geringschätzung der Beziehung zwischen Frage und Antwort orientiert ist. Die Hypertrophie der lexikalischen Kohäsion in seinen Antworten ist gegründet auf die konsequente und mechanische Wiederholung der Ausdrücke aus der Frage, die zweifellos durch Ironisierung motiviert ist – durch Lächerlichmachen der Frage, des Fragenden, der eigenen Person, der ganzen Situation, des ganzen Interviews:

(3) *Bylo to zadostiučinění?* – Ano. *Bylo to zadostiučinění.*
[*War das Genugtuung?* – Ja. *Das war Genugtuung.*]

Vy jste se seznámili už za účelem vzniku kapely, nebo to bylo opačně? – *Už jsme se seznámili za tím účelem.*

[*Sie haben sich schon mit dem Ziel kennen gelernt*, eine Band zu gründen, oder war das umgekehrt? – *Wir haben uns schon mit diesem Ziel kennen gelernt.*]

Das Frage-Antwort-Kohärenzmuster einer weiteren bekannten Persönlichkeit ist verhältnismäßig einfach, aber zugleich interessant: Der Sprecher wiederholt immer wortwörtlich (respektive fast wortwörtlich) den wesentlichen Teil der Frage, aber nicht gleich am Anfang seiner Antwort, sondern erst viel später, im zweiten Satz oder sogar erst am Ende der Antwort:

(4) Kdy *jste do Olympiku přišel*?
Vždycky mě představují jako vynálezce Olympiku nebo zakladatele, a to není pravda. Byla to kapela, která už hrála, a *já jsem do ní přišel* koncem srpna roku 1963.
[Wann *sind Sie zu Olympic gekommen*?
Immer stellt man mich als Erfinder oder Gründer von Olympic vor, das stimmt aber nicht. Das war eine Gruppe, die schon spielte, und *ich bin dazu* Ende August 1963 *gekommen*.]

První éra Olympiku byla spojena se sólovými zpěváky. Proč jste se najednou *rozhodli jít jinou cestou*?
Tehdy to byl světový trend. Obdivoval jsem Beatles, Rolling Stones, Animals a další kapely šedesátých let. *Chtěli jsme jít jejich cestou.*
[Die erste Ära von Olympic war verbunden mit Solosängern. Warum *haben Sie sich* auf einmal *entschlossen, einen anderen Weg zu gehen*?
Damals war das ein Trend in der Welt. Ich bewunderte die Beatles, Rolling Stones, Animals und weitere Gruppen der sechziger Jahre. *Wir wollten deren Weg gehen.*]

Wieder durch einen anderen Individualstil (respektive durch ein individuelles »Kohärenzmuster«) zeichnet sich der Schauspieler aus, der ganz regelmäßig inmitten der umfangreichen Antwort zu einem völlig anderen Thema springt und dieses entfaltet, ohne irgendwie zum ursprünglichen (von der Frage abgeleiteten) Thema zurückzukehren. Wird er z.B. gefragt »Díváte se na zprávy?« [Schauen Sie sich *Nachrichten* an?], tritt in der Mitte der Antwort ein Sprung ein »A těším se na telenovely [...]« [Und ich freue mich auf die *Telenovellen* [...]]. Führt die Frage zu Filmen, in denen er einen Cowboy spielte, geht er inmitten der Antwort plötzlich zu einem anderen, dem Lustspielgenre über. In diesen Fällen finden wir noch Hyperthemen, von denen einzelne Themen abgeleitet sind (›was er im Fernsehen verfolgt‹, ›in welchen Filmtypen er spielte‹). Ein noch größerer Sprung tritt im Rahmen der Antwort ein, die mit dem Gespräch über die eigenen Filmrollen beginnt und mit der Erzählung über die Kinder des Schauspielers endet:

(5) Když jste ten televizní divák, díváte se i na sebe?
To už méně, mám z toho trému. Spíš na reprízy starých *filmů*, to jsem byl větší fešák. Závidím si, jak jsem vypadal. *Děti* pak říkají – táto, tys byl dobrej, a já mám radost. [...] *Kluk* je mi podobný, takže v něm vidím svého nástupce, a *holka*, Klára, je vyloženě hezká. Je tak řádná, že je to až hrozné. Je bakalářkou barcelonské univerzity a ještě bude pokračovat ve studiu. *Synáček* má dva reparáty na diplomatické škole [...].

Interviews in Zeitungen und Zeitschriften 153

[Wenn Sie dieser Fernsehzuschauer sind, schauen Sie sich auch selbst an?
Das schon weniger, ich habe Lampenfieber dabei. Eher die Reprisen alter *Filme*, da war ich noch ein fescherer Kerl. Ich beneide mich, wie ich ausgesehen habe. Die *Kinder* sagen dann – Vati, du warst gut, und ich freue mich. […] Der *Junge* ist mir ähnlich, so dass ich in ihm meinen Nachfolger sehe, und das *Mädchen*, die Klara, ist ausgesprochen hübsch. Sie ist so anständig, dass es direkt schrecklich ist. Sie hat das Bakkalaureat der Universität Barcelona und wird noch weiter studieren. Das *Söhnchen* hat zwei Wiederholungsprüfungen an der Diplomatenschule […].]

2.2 »Auftakte« der Antworten

Im Aufsuchen der Spuren individueller Stile könnten wir noch lange fortfahren, auch wenn wir nicht immer das charakteristische Kohärenzmuster entdecken, sondern eher nur bestimmte Teilspezifika. Es ist sicher kein Zufall, wenn die Fernsehmoderatorin im Gespräch so oft in der Antwort lapidar, mit einem Wort beginnt (auch wenn sie dann nach diesem extrem reduzierten Beginn ihre Antwort weiter entfaltet):

(6) Jak jste trávila prázdniny? – *Neuvěřitelně*. […]
    [Wie haben Sie die Ferien verbracht? – *Unglaublich*. […]]

    Je pro vás moře důležité? – *Určitě*. […]
    [Ist für Sie das Meer wichtig? – *Bestimmt*. […]]

Die Antworten einer anderen Interviewten verraten wiederum innere Unsicherheit – beginnen sie doch oft mit »Myslím, že…« [Ich denke, dass…]; »Ale přesto si myslím, že…« [Aber dennoch denke ich, dass …]; »Nevím, jestli…« [Ich weiß nicht, ob…]; »Možná…« [Vielleicht…]; »Kdoví, třeba…« [Wer weiß, vielleicht…]; »Doufám, že…« [Ich hoffe, dass …]. Für ihre Antworten ist übrigens kennzeichnend, dass sie niemals in medias res beginnen, immer sind sie durch irgendetwas eingeleitet – entweder durch die oben angeführten Äußerungen der Unsicherheit oder durch andere »Auftakte«: »Je pravda, že…« [Es ist wahr, dass…]; »Musím se přiznat, že…« [Ich muss zugeben, dass …]; »Pamatuji si, že…« [Ich erinnere mich, dass…].

Vorzeichen, Auftakt der Antworten können aber bei verschiedenen Sprechern unterschiedliche Funktionen haben; sie müssen nicht nur Unsicherheit signalisieren, sondern im Gegenteil zum Beispiel das Bemühen des Sprechers, sich selbst – und zugleich den Leser des Interviews – von etwas zu überzeugen, in etwas zu bestärken: »Je pravda, že…« [Es stimmt, dass…]; »Ale je fakt, že…« [Aber es ist Tatsache, dass…]; »Vím moc dobře, že…« [Ich weiß sehr gut, dass…]; »Vím zcela jistě, že…« [Ich weiß ganz sicher, dass…]. Die Anfänge der Antworten eines weiteren Interviewten verraten seine Bedächtigkeit, Besonnenheit – er erwägt, ob er damit einverstanden sein kann, was der Fragende in seiner Frage andeutet, er gibt kund, dass er nur bedingt zustimmt, bis zu einem gewissen Grad, dass er die angedeutete Möglichkeit zulässt: »Tak nějak.« [So ungefähr.]; »Něco na tom je.« [Da ist etwas dran.] ; »I tak se to dá říct.« [So kann man das auch sagen.]; »Řekl bych, že ano.« [Ich würde sagen, dass das so ist.].

2.3 Expressive und Kontaktdimensionen der Antworten

Ich habe bereits auf den Umstand hingewiesen, dass die Kohärenz der Redebeiträge einiger Antwortender nicht darauf gegründet ist, dass ihr Text mit dicht besetzten Topikketten gespickt ist; die Reaktivität ihrer Antworten ist eher in der expressiven oder in der Kontaktdimension angesiedelt. Dabei können in den verschiedenen Fällen unterschiedliche tragende Ausdrucksmittel überwiegen; bei einer älteren Schriftstellerin finden sich zum Beispiel unerwartet lebendige Ausrufe am Anfang der Antworten, die ihre außerordentliche Vitalität verraten. Beim Lesen dieser Antwortanfänge kann man sich des Eindrucks nicht erwehren, dass die alte Dame dem Fragesteller ins Wort gefallen ist:

(7) Nebojíte se, že se vám něco stane? – *Ale ono se stalo*!
[Haben Sie keine Angst, dass Ihnen etwas passiert? – *Aber es ist ja passiert*!]

Vždyť hrajete klasiku: Chopina, Beethovena, Janáčka… – *Přeháníte*!
[Sie spielen doch Klassik: Chopin, Beethoven, Janáček… – *Sie übertreiben*!]

Je ještě něco, co byste chtěla dosáhnout? […] podívat se někam […] najít si třeba ještě chlapa? – *Chlapa ne*!
[Gibt es noch etwas, das Sie erreichen möchten? […] irgendwohin zu fahren […] vielleicht noch einen Mann zu finden? – *Einen Mann nicht*!]

Bei weiteren Gesprächen wird die Verbindung zwischen Frage und Antwort, respektive zwischen Antwortgeber und Fragesteller, hauptsächlich durch die Benutzung der 2. Person bewirkt. Die »Arbeit« mit diesem Mittel lässt sich aber weiter differenzieren. Manchmal handelt es sich um den wirklich persönlichen, authentischen Kontakt der interviewten Persönlichkeit mit dem Fragesteller (in dem Falle duzen sich beide Partner gewöhnlich):

(8) U tebe se skoro nerozezná obraz od litografie.
Ale to není pravda, špatně se *díváš*. Dokonce je dobře, že ten rozdíl *nevnímáš*.
[Bei dir unterscheidet man kaum das Bild von der Lithographie.
Aber das stimmt nicht, *du guckst* schlecht. Es ist sogar gut, dass *du* den Unterschied nicht *bemerkst*.]

Ein anderes Mal wendet sich der Antwortende in Wirklichkeit nicht an den momentanen Partner und die 2. Person wird allgemein angewendet, als Vertreter (im Sinne von *Mensch, man*), oder sie ersetzt eher die erste Person, also »ich« des Antwortenden, der so in den Hintergrund tritt. Dann pflegt die zweite Person mit dem Siezen verbunden zu sein (und auch bei dieser Anwendungsweise erhöht sich stark die Dringlichkeit der Antwort):

(9) Byla jste na to připravena?
 Ale to si *můžete* tisíckrát říkat, že *jste* na to *připravená*! Když se to ovšem realizuje – *zůstanete* zaskočená a bezradná... *nevíte*, odkud *máte* ten nový život začít [...].
 [Waren Sie darauf vorbereitet?
 Aber *Sie können* sich tausendmal sagen, dass *Sie* darauf *vorbereitet waren*! Wenn das allerdings realisiert wird – *bleiben Sie* überrascht und ratlos... *Sie wissen nicht*, von welcher Stelle aus *Sie* das neue Leben beginnen *sollen* [...].]

In informellen Antworten eines weiteren Sprechers wechseln sich sogar beide unterschiedliche Verwendungsweisen der 2. Person (authentisch und als Vertreter) ab:

(10) Jak ses dostal do Perníkové věže?
 Normální konkurs. Přijde spousta lidí a *ty se probíjíš* těma kolama. Upřímně řečeno, já to nemám moc rád. *Musíš* dělat něco, o čem nic *nevíš*, *nemáš* přečtenej text, navíc se to někdy *musíš* na místě učit, když to režisér chce.
 Jak ty jsi viděl Šteindlerův film?
 Jestli *jsi viděl* nějaké Milanovy filmy, tak *víš*, jaký humor má rád.
 [Wie bist du in den »Pfefferkuchenturm« gekommen?
 Eine normale Ausschreibung. Es kommen eine Menge Leute und *du schlägst dich* durch diese Räder *durch*. Aufrichtig gesagt, ich habe das nicht sehr gern. *Du musst* etwas tun, wovon *du* nichts *weißt*, *du hast* den Text nicht *durchgelesen*, darüber hinaus *musst du* das manchmal auf der Stelle lernen, wenn das der Regisseur will.
 Wie hast du den Film von Šteindler gesehen?
 Wenn *du* Filme von Milan *gesehen hast*, dann *weißt* du, welchen Humor er gern hat.]

2.4 In der Antwort ausgedrückte Haltungen zur Frage; die »diskursiven« Antworten

Schon aus den vielen vorangegangenen Beispielen ist zweifellos (mehr oder weniger) ersichtlich, welche Haltung die gefragte Person zur Frage einnimmt. Nun erinnern wir noch an einige ausgewählte Typen der Exteriorisierung dieser Haltungen in den Antworten. Manchmal reagiert der Sprecher auf die Frage zustimmend und identifiziert sich direkt mit dem Vorschlag oder der Alternative der Antwort, die ihm in der Frage angeboten wurde:

(11) Jak je vidět, důležitější než prošlapávat potomkovi cestu je stát při něm, i když s jeho konáním docela nesouhlasíme...
 Přesně tak. To pro mě bylo nejdůležitější.
 [Wie zu sehen ist, ist wichtiger als dem Nachkommen den Weg zu ebnen, bei ihm zu stehen, auch wenn wir mit seinem Tun nicht ganz einverstanden sind...
 So ist es. Das war für mich am wichtigsten.]

In anderen Fällen akzeptiert die interviewte Persönlichkeit die Frage nicht; entweder bemüht sie sich um deren Korrektur oder verwahrt sich dagegen, lehnt die Frage ab, kritisiert die Art und Weise der Fragestellung, eventuell ironisiert sie diese (sei es hauptsächlich ihr Sinn oder eher die benutzten Ausdrücke):

(12) Nestane se, že zpěvák, který hraje v muzikálu, se tak trochu rozmělní na úkor své sólové kariéry? [...] *Nemyslím si*, že bych muzikálem ohrožovala nějakou svou sólovou »kariéru« . Navíc *to slovo nemám ráda*. Mě to divadlo opravdu baví.
[Passiert es nicht, dass ein Musicalsänger sich ein bisschen auf Kosten seiner Solokarriere zerreibt? [...]
Ich glaube nicht, dass ich durch ein Musical irgendwie meine »Solokarriere« gefährdet habe. Darüber hinaus *habe ich dieses Wort nicht gern*. Mir macht dieses Theater wirklich Spaß.]

Eine eigenständige Kategorie bezüglich der Einnahme einer Haltung zu den Fragen bilden offensichtlich Gespräche mit Politikern. Niemand ist so vorsichtig wie sie. Ihre Antworten sind nicht nur ausweichend, oft unbestimmt, sondern sie analysieren auch ständig die Fragen, drehen sie um, werten sie, berichtigen sie, lehnen sie ab, machen sie lächerlich, polemisieren, stellen Gegenfragen, streiten sich über einzelne Wörter. Ihre Antworten beginnen z.B. »Takhle to není možno říci...« [So kann man das nicht sagen...]; »Takhle bych si to netroufal říct...« [So würde ich mir nicht erlauben es zu sagen...]; »Taková spekulace mi nepřísluší...« [Eine solche Spekulation steht mir nicht zu...]; »Takovou otázku jsem si nepoložil...« [Eine solche Frage habe ich mir noch nicht gestellt...]; »Asi nejsem úplně správný adresát této otázky...« [Wahrscheinlich bin ich nicht der ganz richtige Adressat dieser Frage...]; »K tomu se těžko mohu vyjádřit...« [Dazu kann ich mich nur schwer äußern...]; »Tento výrok nechci ani potvrzovat, ani zpochybňovat...« [Diesen Ausspruch will ich weder bekräftigen noch bezweifeln...].

Es treten auch ausgesprochen metasprachliche Polemiken auf:

(13) Nemáte strach, že Klaus bude politiku ODS z pozadí neblaze ovlivňovat?
Neblaze ovlivňovat – to mi připadá jako termín, který nemohu přijmout.
[Haben Sie keine Angst, dass Klaus die Politik der ODS aus dem Hintergrund verhängnisvoll beeinflussen wird?
Verhängnisvoll beeinflussen – das scheint für mich ein Terminus zu sein, den ich nicht annehmen kann.]

Manchmal erscheint vor der Antwort – wenn es überhaupt dazu kommt – eine vollständige Analyse der Frage, verbunden mit einer Belehrung des Fragestellers; hier setzt sich allerdings schon der ausgeprägte Individualstil des konkreten Politikers durch. Es ist ersichtlich, dass die Haltungen der Politiker in den Antworten sehr deutlich exponiert zu sein pflegen und meistens sind sie, falls sie nicht ablehnend sind, zumindest vorsichtig.

Davon unterscheidet sich der Stil der Antworten einiger außerordentlicher künstlerischer Persönlichkeiten: sie verhalten sich lebendig und unkonventionell, ihr Stil ist stark

Interviews in Zeitungen und Zeitschriften 157

diskursiv – sie beziehen in ihre Antworten die Gesprächssituation direkt ein, wenden sich an den Partner, haben zu ihm unmittelbaren Kontakt, stellen ihm »ergänzende Fragen", untermauern ihre Antworten mit Zitaten und der Reproduktion fremder Aussprüche. Vielleicht kann das der Auszug aus einem Interview mit einem berühmten Regisseur wenigstens ein bisschen illustrieren:

(14) Když nevěříte na d'ábla, proč o něm děláte filmy?
A vy věříte na upíry? Já ne, a dělám o nich filmy. Pak se nedivte, že se zabývám také d'áblem.
[Wenn Sie nicht an den Satan glauben, warum drehen Sie dann über ihn Filme?
Und Sie glauben an Vampire? Ich nicht, aber ich mache darüber Filme. Dann wundern Sie sich bitte nicht, dass ich mich auch mit dem Satan beschäftige.]

Podle čeho se rozhodujete, jestli text, který čtete, zfilmujete?
Když vidíte hezkou dívku, uvažujete, proč se ve vás rodí touha vyspat se s ní? Analyzujete ten stav? V restauraci si rovněž vybíráte, na co máte chut'. [...] Čtu knížku a cítím, že bych se do toho chtěl pustit, napsat na ten námět scénář.
[Wonach entscheiden Sie sich, ob Sie den Text, den Sie lesen, verfilmen werden?
Wenn Sie ein hübsches Mädchen sehen, erwägen Sie, warum in Ihnen die Sehnsucht erwacht, mit ihm zu schlafen? Analysieren Sie diesen Zustand? Im Restaurant wählen Sie ebenfalls aus, worauf Sie Appetit haben [...] Ich lese ein Buch und fühle, dass ich mich hineinstürzen möchte, dass ich zu diesem Sujet ein Drehbuch schreiben möchte.]

Diese Antwortentypen lassen sich, auch wenn sie von Reaktivität durchdrungen sind, schwerlich in irgendein »Kohärenzmuster« hineinpressen; sie sind eher Reaktionen auf den Partner und auf den globalen Sinn seiner Frage als auf ihre wortwörtliche Gestalt. Daher zum Schluss ein Beispiel für ein Extrem, wo sich ein aggressiver Filmstar der Leitung des Gesprächs bemächtigt, den »Fragesteller« in Verlegenheit bringt, mit seiner Dominanz eine Inversion der Rollen bewirkt und die Führung des Gesprächs zeitweilig auf eine unerwartete Schiene bringt:

(15) [...] Co tak na mě koukáte? Není něco v pořádku?
Promiňte. Nechtěl jsem. Zrak mi náhodou padl na...
Na má prsa? Náhodou? Myslel jste, že mám větší, vid'te?
Prosím? Nikoli, já vůbec...
Viděla jsem váš pohled. Zklamán? [...]
[[...] Was schauen Sie mich so an? Ist etwas nicht in Ordnung?
Entschuldigen Sie. Das wollte ich nicht. Mein Blick fiel zufällig auf...
Auf meinen Busen? Zufällig? Sie haben geglaubt, ich hätte einen größeren, nicht wahr?
Bitte? Keinesfalls, ich habe überhaupt...
Ich habe Ihren Blick gesehen. Enttäuscht? [...]]

3. Schlussbemerkung

Ich habe bis jetzt nur eine Grobanalyse von ungefähr 50 umfangreicheren Gesprächen mit tschechischen, aber auch ausländischen Politikern, Schriftstellern, Schauspielern, Musikern, Sängern, Moderatoren, bildenden Künstlern, Sportlern und weiteren bekannten Persönlichkeiten durchgeführt. Ich wollte darauf hinweisen, dass es sich lohnt, ein syntaktisches Problem (respektive das Problem der Textsyntax) stilistisch-pragmatisch zu beleuchten und die Forschung speziell auf ein konkretes Genre zu richten. Dabei sollte unbedingt die Spezifik der individuellen Stile berücksichtigt werden: Der Grad der Initiative unterscheidet sich, wie wir gesehen haben, darin, inwieweit die Antwortenden Themen und Motive aus der Frage übernehmen und davon die Topikketten der Antworten ableiten, oder inwieweit sie selbst eigene, nicht geforderte Themen als Ausgangspunkt weiterer Ketten einführen. Wenn dies mitbeachtet wird, können wir das Repertoire der textsyntaktischen »Schemata«, »Muster« um neue Möglichkeiten und zahlreiche Details bereichern und so ein differenzierteres Bild gewinnen.

Literatur

Conrad, Rudi (1978): Studien zur Syntax und Semantik von Frage und Antwort. Berlin: Akademie-Verlag (Studia grammatica 19).
Freed, Alice F. (1994): The form and function of questions in informal dyadic conversation. In: Journal of Pragmatics 21, 621-644.
Hoffmannová, Jana (2000): »Podskazyvanije«, »poddakivanije« i drugije vidy strategii preodolenija kommunikativnych bar'erov. In: Ješič, B.M./Kořenský, J./Neščimenko, G.P./Nikol´skij, L.B./ Tarasov, Je.F./Smeškovskaja, Ju.R. (Hgg.): Jazyk kak sredstvo transljacii kul'tury. Moskva: Nauka, 132-153.
Likomanova, Iskra (1998): Some features of Slavic dialogic exchanges (on material from the Bulgarian, Polish and Czech languages). In: Čmejrková, Světla/Hoffmannová, Jana/Müllerová, Olga/ Světlá, Jindra (Hgg.): Dialoganalyse VI. Referate der 6. Arbeitstagung Prag 1996. Teil 1. Tübingen: Niemeyer (Beiträge zur Dialogforschung 16), 493-500.
Mluvnice češtiny (1987) [Grammatik der tschechischen Sprache]. Teil 3. Hg. v. Daneš, František/ Grepl, Miroslav/Hlavsa, Zdeněk. Praha: Academia.
Müllerová, Olga (1982): Otázka a odpověd' v dialogu [Frage und Antwort im Dialog]. In: Slovo a slovesnost 43, 200-212.
– (1994): Podmínky úspěšnosti rozhovoru jako metody sociálně psychologických výzkumů [Das Interview als Methode der sozial-psychologischen Forschung und die Bedingungen seines Erfolgs]. In: Gajda, Stanisław/Nocoń, Jolanta (Hgg.): Kształcenie porozumiewania sie. Opole: Uniwersytet Opolski, 265-271.
Schegloff, Emanuel A. (1990): On the organization of sequences as a source of »coherence« in talk-in-

interaction. In: Dorval, B. (Hg.): Conversational organization and its development. Norwood, NJ: Ablex (Advances in Discourse Processes 38), 51-77.

Štícha, František (1998): *Ich weiss es nicht*. Ein deutsch-tschechischer Vergleich einer Antwort. In: Čmejrková, Světla/Hoffmannová, Jana/Müllerová, Olga/Světlá, Jindra (Hgg.): Dialoganalyse VI. Referate der 6. Arbeitstagung Prag 1996. Teil 1. Tübingen: Niemeyer (Beiträge zur Dialogforschung 16), 481-485.

Laura Sergo

Die Wiedergabe von bewertenden und metasprachlichen Elementen in der Übersetzung von Zeitungsinterviews

1. Die Textsorte Zeitungsinterview

Unter den journalistischen Textsorten nimmt das Interview einen besonderen Stellenwert ein. Die Stimme einer Persönlichkeit aus der Welt der Politik, der Kultur oder der Unterhaltung soll einerseits die im Presseorgan behandelten Themen ergänzen, andererseits den Eindruck von Unmittelbarkeit und Authentizität der Information vermitteln.

Schon die Entstehungsgeschichte eines gedruckten Interviews zeigt jedoch, daß es sich lediglich um simulierte Authentizität oder Spontaneität handelt (vgl. Haller 1997, Sergo 2002), da vor der Veröffentlichung beträchtliche Eingriffe in die ursprüngliche Interviewaufnahme durchgeführt werden, wobei u.a. auch ein großer Teil der Oralitätsmerkmale getilgt wird. So finden sich im gedruckten Text keine Anakoluthe, Aposiopesen, Wiederholungen, Redundanzen, Reparaturen und sonstige Elemente, die gegen die standardsprachliche Norm verstoßen. Mit wenigen Ausnahmen werden sogar die meisten Partikeln ausgelassen. Auf der makrostrukturellen Ebene kann außerdem die Aufmerksamkeit der Empfänger durch eine Verlagerung der Gewichtung des thematischen Materials gesteuert werden (vgl. Holly 1992, 25). Nach dieser redaktionellen Revision bleibt von den ursprünglichen Merkmalen nur die dialogische Form beibehalten, bei der manchmal die Frage berechtigt erscheint, ob nicht bestimmte Oralitätsmerkmale absichtlich wieder eingeführt worden sind, wie z.B. die Punkte zur Bezeichnung einer Turnunterbrechung, um den Eindruck der Authentizität wieder herzustellen.

Solche Eingriffe in einen mündlichen Text weisen Ähnlichkeiten mit den von Heinze (1979) beobachteten Prozeduren zur Verschriftlichung von Bundestagsreden auf. Der mündliche Sprachgebrauch, auch beim von Heinze erwähnten »schriftnahen Sprechen« (1979, 36), ist z.B. durch umfangreiche Satzstrukturen, Gefügesätze mit mehreren abhängigen Gefügeteilen und weitverzweigte Subordination charakterisiert. In den verschrifteten Texten sind solche komplexen Perioden im Sinne einer Simplifizierung in kürzere und überschaubare Einheiten segmentiert.

Damit läßt sich das Presseinterview in die Tradition des Protokolls situieren (Schlieben-Lange 1983), und tatsächlich wird der Ursprung der Textsorte auf die Berichterstattung von Prozessen zurückgeführt, wobei der Journalist den Verlauf des Prozesses in der Abfolge von Fragen und Antworten nachahmte, wie es in den Journalistenhandbüchern zu lesen ist (Haller 1997).

Die Analogie der kommunikativen Situationen läßt auch an den dramatischen Dialog denken, denn in beiden Formen wird der Dialog nicht aus privaten kommunikativen Bedürfnissen der unmittelbaren Beteiligten heraus geführt. Seine Funktion ist vielmehr auf die Rezeption durch ein Publikum ausgerichtet. Ein weiterer Berührungspunkt betrifft die Redundanz der Information im Spiel von Frage und Antwort.

2. Das Corpus

Die hier untersuchte Textsorte ist in italienischen Zeitungen, insbesondere in Tageszeitungen, besonders stark vertreten: Neben Interviews mit einheimischen Persönlichkeiten werden oft, vor allem bei besonders aktuellen Anlässen wie Wahlen und anderen wichtigen Ereignissen, auch Interviews mit ausländischen Vertretern der Bereiche Politik, Kultur und Unterhaltung veröffentlicht. Solche Interviews werden entweder von italienischen Korrespondenten direkt durchgeführt und übersetzt (d.h. es gibt keinen Hinweis auf eine zusätzliche übersetzerische Tätigkeit von anderen) oder sie werden ausdrücklich als Übersetzungen gekennzeichnet, wobei in der italienischen Zeitung meistens sowohl die Quelle als auch die Übersetzer genannt werden. Gegenstand der Untersuchung sind ausschließlich solche Texte, von denen eine ausgangssprachliche Version vorliegt.

Das dieser Untersuchung zugrundeliegende Corpus besteht aus Interviews mit Persönlichkeiten, die hauptsächlich zur Welt der Politik und der Kultur gehören und in folgenden Zeitungen und Zeitschriften erschienen sind: *Bild am Sonntag*, *Stern*, *Süddeutsche Zeitung*, *Die Welt*, *Welt am Sonntag*, *Die Zeit*. Die italienischen Wiedergaben sind in den Tageszeitungen *Corriere della Sera* und *La Repubblica* veröffentlicht worden. Außerdem wurden zum Vergleich auch Paralleltexte, d.h. original italienische Interviews berücksichtigt, die ebenfalls in den beiden erwähnten Blättern erschienen sind.

3. Die Wiedergabe von Zeitungsinterviews

Vor der Veröffentlichung wird der Zielsprachen(ZS)-Text, wie sich aus einem ersten Vergleich von Ausgangssprachen(AS)- und ZS-Interviews leicht feststellen läßt, einer weiteren redaktionellen Bearbeitung unterzogen. Bei solchen Modifikationen handelt es sich in den meisten Fällen um Umstellungen und Tilgungen, die sowohl die Makrostruktur als auch die Mikrostruktur betreffen. Fortgelassen bzw. umgestellt werden einzelne Lexeme, Satzteile, Teile von Frage-Antwort-Sequenzen sowie ganze Serien von Fragen und Antworten. Solche umfangreichen kürzenden Eingriffe (Thome, im Druck) betreffen vor allem Themen, die den ZS-Textempfänger vermutlich nicht unmittelbar interessieren, wie z.B. bei Politikerinterviews Details zur Steuer- oder Rentenpolitik, sie sind also empfängerorientiert.[1]

In der vorliegenden Untersuchung wird von der in der Übersetzungswissenschaft vertretenen Auffassung ausgegangen (vgl. u.a. Albrecht 1990, Gerzymisch-Arbogast 1994, House 1997, Koller [5]1997, Reiß [3]1993, Thome, im Druck), nach welcher Äquivalenz als Beziehung zwischen Ausgangs- und Zieltext und Übersetzung als »Ausdruck der Bindung [...] sowohl an die ausgangssprachliche als auch an die zielsprachliche Linguakultur und deren je spezifische kommunikativen Bedingungen« (Thome, im Druck) betrachtet wird. Die Übersetzungsbewertung erfolgt daher aus einer Gegenüberstellung von Originaltext und dessen Wiedergabe in die Zielsprache.

Die Ergebnisse unserer Analysen lassen sich grundsätzlich in zwei Gruppen unterteilen:

1. Es findet vor allem bei Politikerinterviews ein Übergang von einem überwiegend appellbetonten Text, wie etwa einer mehr oder weniger expliziten Wahlwerbung oder dem Verfechten der eigenen (Partei- oder Regierungs-)Politik, zu einem überwiegend darstellungsbetonten Text statt (vgl. Reiß [3]1993, 91). Die Gründe für diesen Funktionswechsel sind die veränderten textexternen Gegebenheiten, d.h. der durch die Übersetzung herbeigeführte Adressatenwechsel. An die ZS-Textempfänger kann sich kein derartiger Appell richten, denn bei allem Interesse an der deutschen Politik wird der italienische Leser doch nicht aktiv daran teilnehmen können.

2. Der ZS-Text bleibt appellbetont, aber angesichts des Adressatenwechsels werden im ZS-Text nicht alle Inhalte oder Themen des Originals aufgenommen und wiedergegeben, sondern nur diejenigen, die sich, vermutlich in den Augen der Redaktoren, für die Realisierung einer solchen entsprechend modifizierten Funktion auch bei den neuen Adressaten eignen: Das Interview mit der ausländischen Persönlichkeit kann z.B. als

---

[1] Eine nicht unbeträchtliche Rolle spielen dabei auch redaktionelle Gründe wie der verfügbare Platz auf der Zeitungsseite.

Unterstützung der eigenen politischen Linie dienen oder ein gezielt gestaltetes Bild der interviewten Person oder deren Landes geben.

Nunmehr sollen anhand eines Vergleichs von deutschen Originalinterviews mit ihren in italienischen Zeitungen erschienenen Übersetzungen und Paralleltexten, d.h. italienischen Originalinterviews, Veränderungen von pragmatischen Funktionen im Zieltext erfaßt werden. Exemplarisch wird dies anhand der Analyse der Wiedergabe von bewertenden und metakommunikativen Elementen dargestellt.

3.1 Wiedergabe von bewertenden Elementen

In Texten wie Interviews, die vielfach eine mehr oder weniger stark ausgeprägte appellative Komponente aufweisen, spielt die Bewertung eine besonders wichtige Rolle. »Bewertung« ist Gegenstand verschiedener linguistischer Untersuchungen: Sandig und ihre Saarbrücker Projektgruppe befassen sich mit dem Themenkomplex aus einer sprechaktorientierten Perspektive (1979, 1991) mit dem Ziel, ein operationalisierbares Begriffsinstrumentarium zu erstellen (vgl. Thiel/Thome 1998).

Eine erweiterte Konzeption von Bewertung wird in der *Linguistique de l'énonciation* vertreten (Kerbrat-Orecchioni [4]2002). Bewertung oder *évaluation* steht im engen Zusammenhang mit dem Begriff der Subjektivität, die jeden Äußerungsprozeß in unterschiedlichem Maße charakterisiert. Es stellt sich dabei die Frage, auf welche Art sich die Subjektivität des Sprechers manifestiert und welche ausschlaggebende Rolle neben den eigenen semantischen Merkmalen der Lexeme auch außersprachliche und situationelle Faktoren bei der Bewertung spielen. Gerade bei den in der vorliegenden Arbeit untersuchten Texten, in denen Bewertung nicht immer explizit, sondern oft implizit und durch Argumentation erfolgt, bietet sich dieser Analyseansatz als wertvolles Instrument zur Erfassung der axiologischen Dimension in Texten im Zusammenhang mit der Sprechereinstellung an.

Was die Übersetzung betrifft, so läßt sich die Vielfalt der in den Texten angewendeten Verfahren in folgende Gruppen einordnen, die jeweils anhand besonders repräsentativer Beispiele dargestellt werden:

3.1.1 Wörtliche Übersetzung

Als »wörtlich« werden nach Thome (1975, 43) solche Übersetzungen bezeichnet, in denen »ein AS-Satz oder Teilsatz in der Weise in die ZS übertragen wird, daß seine Glieder vollzählig und gleichartig, d.h. mit gleicher syntaktischer Funktion, mit gleicher Wortklassenzugehörigkeit und unter Beibehaltung der wesentlichen Komponenten ihrer AS-Bedeutung, jedoch in einer den zielsprachlichen Strukturgesetzen entsprechenden Reihenfolge wieder-

Die Wiedergabe von bewertenden Elementen 165

kehren«. Das wird in Beleg (1) gezeigt, in dem die bewertende Aussage in der Antwort der zitierten Definition entspricht:

(1) F: Aber sicher ist, dass Sie für die SPD Partei ergreifen werden?
     A: Für Rot-Grün! Ich halte die Grünen nach wie vor für eine mutige Partei, die zu Unrecht dauernd abgestraft wird.
     F: Sicuramente però a favore della Spd.
     A: Per i rosso-verdi! Continuo a considerare i verdi un partito politico coraggioso che viene costantemente a torto penalizzato.

(Grass, *Stern/La Repubblica*, 14.2.2002)

3.1.2 Kürzung

Die Wiedergabe erfolgt durch Kürzungen, d.h. quantitative Veränderungen, in denen bewertende Elemente weggelassen wurden (vgl. Schreiber 1993, 314 ff.). Fortgelassen werden einzelne lexikalische Einheiten, vor allem Adjektive, wie in den Belegen (2) und (3), aber auch ganze Sätze oder Satzteile wie in (4):

(2) F: [...] Glauben Sie, die ARD oder das ZDF ziehen nach?
     A: Nein, das sind alle unglaublich feige Leute. Die trauen sich nicht, aus *blöder* Quotenangst. [...].
     F: [...] Non dovremmo fare lo stesso in Germania con le notizie delle nostre reti pubbliche?
     A: No, da noi sono terribilmente vili. Hanno troppa paura dell'indice d'ascolto, non avrebbero mai il coraggio di farlo. [...]

(Enzensberger, *Welt am Sonntag*, 2.7.2000/*La Repubblica*, 3.7.2000)

(3) F: Sir Simon, hat das Symphonieorchester, diese *ehrwürdige* Institution aus dem 19. Jahrhundert, noch eine Zukunft?
     F: Sir Simon, pensa che l'orchestra sinfonica, questa istituzione ottocentesca, abbia ancora un futuro?

(Rattle, *Die Zeit/La Repubblica*, 19.4.2000)

(4) F: Wann würden Sie zurücktreten: *Wenn die Zahl der Arbeitslosen fünf Millionen erreicht?* Oder wenn Deutschland am Ende der Irakdebatte im UN-Sicherheitsrat neben Syrien ganz alleine steht?
     F: Cancelliere Schroeder cosa aspetta a dimettersi, che al termine del dibattito sull'Iraq in seno al Consiglio di sicurezza dell'Onu la Germania si ritrovi isolata accanto alla Siria?

(Schröder, *Stern/La Repubblica*, 13.2.2003)

Die Auslassung des axiologischen Adjektivs in Beleg (2) bewirkt eine deutliche Abschwächung der negativ konnotierten Aussage. In Beispiel (3) ergibt sich durch das Fehlen des affektiven Adjektivs »ehrwürdig« im ZS-Text außerdem eine Verschiebung der Gesamtkonnotation der Apposition in die Richtung einer eher negativen Bewertung im Sinne von »altmodisch«, »überholt«. In Beleg (4) wird in der Frage auf zwei mögliche Argumente für den Rücktritt verwiesen, die beide eine negative Bewertung von Sachverhalten seitens des Sprechers aufweisen: In der ersten Aussage bestimmt das im Lexem »Arbeitslosen« enthaltene negative Merkmal die Bewertungsrichtung, in der zweiten wird das durch das Verbalgefüge »ganz alleine stehen« sowie das dem aktuellen außersprachlichen Kontext entnommene Wissen bewirkt. Anders gestaltet sich die ZS-Version: Hier wurde die erste Aussage weggelassen und damit nicht nur die argumentative Struktur verändert, sondern auch der Bezug auf die den deutschen Leser unmittelbar betreffenden Probleme. Damit ist die negative Bewertung der aktuellen Situation des Bundeskanzlers deutlich abgeschwächt und der Hinweis auf seinen eventuellen Rücktritt für den italienischen Leser auch nicht nachvollziehbar, denn die mögliche außenpolitische Isolation dürfte allein keinen ausschlaggebenden Grund dafür liefern, zumal die Mehrheit der deutschen Bürger diese politische Linie unterstützte.

3.1.3 Konnotative Abschwächung

Die Bezeichnung Konnotative Abschwächung wurde in Anlehnung an Koller (^{5}1997, 240ff.) gewählt und bezieht sich auf die Fälle, in denen bewertende Elemente im AS-Text durch unmarkierte Ausdrücke im ZS-Text wiedergegeben werden. Dies läßt sich auf Wort-, Lexem- und Satzebene beobachten, wie folgende Belege zeigen:

(5)   F: Was ist denn das Bedrohliche an Edmund Stoiber?
      A: Na, seine ganze Einstellung zur Einwanderung beispielsweise. Er war es doch, der vor der »*Durchrassung* des deutschen Volkes« gewarnt hat.
      F: Che cosa vede di pericoloso in Edmund Stoiber?
      A: Beh, tutto il suo atteggiamento rispetto all'immigrazione, ad esempio. E' stato lui a lanciare l'allarme per *la perdita di identità* del popolo tedesco.

(Grass, *Stern/La Repubblica*, 14.2.2002)

(6)   A: [...] Aber wir haben zunehmend einen rechten Populismus in Europa, der sich nicht scheut, *in dieser trüben Brühe von Stimmungen nach Stimmen zu fischen*.
      A: [...] Sta montando però, in Europa, un populismo di destra che *va a caccia di voti nel malcontento popolare*, ed è collegata ad un crescente antieuropeismo.

(Fischer, *Welt am Sonntag/La Repubblica*, 26.5.2002)

Die Einheit »Durchrassung« von Beleg (5) befindet sich auf der axiologischen Skala gut – schlecht des Prozeßagens Stoiber auf einer extrem negativen Stufe und entspricht damit dessen Einstellung zur Einwanderung. Die Übernahme als Zitat durch den Sprecher Grass signalisiert als Begründung der Gefährlichkeit des bayerischen Politikers ein ausgeprägt negatives Werturteil bezüglich der Verwendung dieses Begriffes.[2] In der ZS wird das fast

---

[2] Eine umfassendere Darstellung der hier angedeuteten Problematik der Redewiedergabe würde den Rahmen dieses Beitrages sprengen.

Die Wiedergabe von bewertenden Elementen

tabuisierte Lexem durch das harmlosere »perdita di identità« wiedergegeben. In (6) wird die durch die Entwicklung des konventionalisierten »im Trüben fischen« entstandene und durch ein Wortspiel angereicherte okkasionelle ausgangssprachliche Metapher durch eine konventionalisierte Metapher in der Zielsprache ersetzt.

Sowohl Kürzungen als auch konnotative Abschwächungen werden in mehr als der Hälfte der analysierten ZS-Stellen vorgezogen, obwohl auch in der Zielsprache eine wörtliche Übersetzung durchaus möglich gewesen wäre. Es scheint, als ob die Verantwortlichen für die Veröffentlichung der ZS-Fassung eine gewisse Scheu vor »spitzen Tönen« hätten. Dies ist um so überraschender, wenn man bedenkt, daß die als Paralleltexte berücksichtigten italienischen Zeitungsinterviews durch eine besondere Vielfalt von bewertenden Ausdrücken gekennzeichnet sind.

Da diese Verfahren eindeutig auf Varianzforderungen zurückgehen, kann man in bezug auf die analysierten Teiltexten von interlingualer Bearbeitung sprechen (Schreiber 1993, 314), deren Auswirkung eine bedeutende Verringerung der Appellativität ist.

3.2 Wiedergabe von metakommunikativen Elementen

Eine metakommunikative Aussage wird von Franceschini (1998, 99) in Anlehnung an Meyer-Hermann (1978, 1983) wie folgt definiert:

> Un enunciato metacomunicativo è un enunciato il cui tema – cioè l'oggetto al quale l'interlocutore si riferisce e sul quale fa delle predicazioni – è un'interazione verbale (o un suo aspetto verbale) che precede o segue l'enunciato metacomunicativo e che fa parte della stessa unità d'interazione come l'enunciato metacomunicativo stesso.

Da sie zu den typischen Merkmalen oraler Diskurse (Schlieben-Lange 1975, 192) gehören, sind metakommunikative Elemente jedoch in verschrifteten Interviews eher spärlich vertreten.[3] In dieser Hinsicht weist also das Presseinterview keine Ähnlichkeit mit Theatertexten auf, bei denen gerade die Metakommunikation – als Imitation des Gesprochenen – eine wichtige Rolle spielt. Das Vorkommen von metakommunikativen Sequenzen beschränkt sich im allgemeinen auf folgende Fälle:

Als Eröffnung einer Sequenz kündigen sie entweder einen Themawechsel an oder signalisieren eine Antwortverweigerung:

---

3 Nur in Interviews mit Helmut Kohl kommen metakommunikative Sequenzen etwas häufiger vor, und zwar auch als Träger anderer Funktionen, wie z.B. Verständnissicherung. Sie scheinen sozusagen zu seinem im journalistischen Sinn »persönlichen« Stil zu gehören: »So hätte ich mir nie träumen lassen, dass, wie es in diesen Tagen geschieht, Ergebnisse der verbrecherischen Praktiken der Stasi – *ich spreche von den Abhörprotokollen* – als so genanntes Beweismaterial gegen mich verwendet werden« (Kohl, *Die Welt*, 3.4.2000).

(7) F: *Kommen wir zur Außenpolitik*: Wie fühlen Sie sich als Regierungschef, der von den USA in einem Atemzug mit Castro und Gadhafi genannt wird?

(Schröder, *Stern*, 13.2.2003)

(8) F: Könnten auch deutsche Soldaten an einer Blauhelm-Mission im Irak teilnehmen?
    A: *Für mich empfiehlt es sich nicht, auf derart theoretische Fragen zu antworten.*

(Schröder, *Stern*, 13.2.2003)

Vereinzelt erscheinen die typischen »ritualisierten« metakommunikativen Formen (Franceschini 1998, 85):

(9) F: Es gibt Pläne, sie in die Verantwortung des Bundes zu verlagern, ein – *wenn man so will* – Staatsorchester aus ihnen zu machen. Würden Sie das begrüßen?
    A: Ich glaube, das ist keine schlechte Idee.

(Rattle, *Die Zeit*, 19.4.2000)

Häufiger treten Anführungszeichen auf: Die Anführungszeichen ersetzen in der schriftlichen Kommunikation einen metakommunikativen Ausdruck, gehören also, im Gegensatz zu den anderen hier besprochenen metakommunikativen Elementen, zur Schriftlichkeit:

(10) F: Kern Ihres Vorschlags ist auch die »*uneingeschränkte Waffenruhe*«. Eine solche ist aber nie eingehalten worden.

(Fischer, *Die Zeit*, 14.2.2002)

Italienische Originalinterviews weisen im Vergleich zu deutschen Interviews etwas häufiger Oralitätsmerkmale, und daher auch metakommunikative Elemente, auf, was für eine entsprechende Textsortenkonvention sprechen könnte. Beleg (11) soll dies exemplarisch darstellen:

(11) F: Lei è soprattutto il frutto della sua storia: un grande editore – vogliamo dirlo? – un po' incazzato con il mondo intero.

(Garzanti, *La Repubblica*, 26.1.03)

Im vorliegenden Corpus sind zur Wiedergabe dieses Aspekts im Italienischen verschiedene Lösungen vertreten:

3.2.1 Beibehaltung der metakommunikativen Elemente

Diese Lösung wird vor allem bei Anführungszeichen und selbstverständlich bei Eröffnungssequenzen oder Antwortverweigerungen gewählt, wie in Beleg (12) zu sehen ist:

(12) F: Könnten auch deutsche Soldaten an einer Blauhelm-Mission im Irak teilnehmen?
     A: *Für mich empfiehlt es sich nicht, auf derart theoretische Fragen zu antworten.*

Die Wiedergabe von bewertenden Elementen

F: Alla missione dei caschi blu in Iraq potrebbero partecipare anche soldati tedeschi?
A: *A domande teoriche come questa non conviene rispondere.*

(Schröder, *Stern/La Repubblica*, 13.2.2003)

3.2.2 Auslassung von Sequenzen metasemantischer und metapragmatischer Art

Nach Stati (1982, 225f.) dienen solche Sequenzen zur Klärung der Bedeutung oder der pragmatischen Funktion der Aussage und befinden sich vor allem in der Turn-Mitte, wie im nächsten Beispiel:

(13) Ja, die Fehler, die ich bei der Spendensache gemacht habe, bedaure und bereue ich. *Aber ich glaube, dies ist nicht der Kern Ihrer Frage.* Wenn man so viele Jahre Verantwortung getragen hat, dann muss man sich schon die Frage stellen, ob man den Menschen immer korrekt begegnet ist.

Sì, per gli errori che ho commesso sulla questione delle tangenti. Ma se ci si assume responsabilità importanti per così tanti anni, allora ci si deve porre la domanda se ci si è comportati sempre correttamente nei riguardi delle persone, dei collaboratori.

(Kohl, *Die Welt/Il Corriere della sera*, 3.4.2000)

3.2.3 Anwendung von metasprachlichen Kommentaren als Übersetzungsverfahren

Eine solche Verfahrensweise wird vor allem bei Lücken im System der Zielsprache angewendet (vgl. Koller [5]1997, 232ff.), besonders zur Wiedergabe von AS-Kulturspezifika. Die metasprachlichen Kommentare sind oft auch graphisch als solche gekennzeichnet:

(14) F: Was kommt bei Ihnen auf den Tisch?
    A: »Himmel und Erde«, Sauerkraut, Kartoffelpüree.
    F: A casa sua cosa viene messo in tavola?
    A: *Himmel und Erde* (ingredienti: patate schiacciate e purea di mele calda guarniti con cipolle e sanguinaccio fritti, *ndr*), crauti e purè di patate.

(Merkel, *Bild am Sonntag/La Repubblica*, 2.4.2000)

Die geringe Frequenz und die beschränkte Auswahl von metakommunikativen Elementen im Corpus erlaubt bisher keine definitive Aussage über ihre Wiedergabe in der Zielsprache. Angesichts der in Paralleltexten festgestellten häufigeren Anwendung solcher Sequenzen könnte man jedoch bei den übersetzten Interviews von einem Verstoß gegen eine zielsprachliche Textkonvention sprechen. Wie bei der Wiedergabe von Bewertungen orientiert sich die Übersetzerin/die Zeitungsredaktion bei der Option zwischen zwei gleichermaßen akzeptablen Lösungen vielfach nicht an den Präferenzen der italienischen Sprache. Insgesamt dürfte daher der ZS-Textempfänger u.U. den Text im Vergleich zu entsprechenden italienischen Originalinterviews als »distanzierter« empfinden.

Schlußbetrachtung

Aus der vorliegenden Untersuchung ergibt sich, daß in anscheinend so stark standardisierten Texten wie Presseinterviews in Wirklichkeit vielfach interkulturelle, durch eigene Präferenzen und Textkonventionen gekennzeichnete Unterschiede vorhanden sind. Bei der Wiedergabe bewertender und metakommunikativer Elemente, die vorwiegend die stilistische Ebene betreffen, werden jedoch solche kulturellen Spezifika nicht berücksichtigt und eher neutrale und damit unverfänglichere Lösungen vorgezogen, die zu einer Verschiebung der pragmatischen Funktion der zielsprachlichen Texte führen.

Literatur

Albrecht, Jörn (1990): Invarianz, Äquivalenz, Adäquatheit. In: Arntz, Reiner/Thome, Gisela (Hgg.): Übersetzungswissenschaft. Ergebnisse und Perspektiven. Festschrift für Wolfram Wilss zum 60. Geburtstag. Tübingen: Narr, 71-81.
Franceschini, Rita (1998): Riflettere sull'interazione. Un'introduzione alla metacomunicazione e all'analisi conversazionale. Milano: Franco Angeli.
Galatanu, Olga (2002): La dimension axiologique de l'argumentation. In: Carel, Marion (Hg.): Les facettes du dire. Hommage à Oswald Ducrot. Paris: Kimé, 93-107.
Gerzymisch-Arbogast, Heidrun (1994): Übersetzungswissenschaftliches Propädeutikum. Tübingen: Franke (UTB 1782).
Haller, Michael ([2]1997): Das Interview. Ein Handbuch für Journalisten. Konstanz: UVK Medien.
Heinze, Helmut (1979): Gesprochenes und geschriebenes Deutsch. Vergleichende Untersuchungen von Bundestagsreden und deren schriftlich aufgezeichneter Version. Düsseldorf: Schwann.
Holly, Werner (1992): Holistische Textanalyse. Anmerkungen zur »Methode« pragmatischer Textanalyse. In: Stati, Sorin/Weigand, Edda (Hgg.): Methodologie der Dialoganalyse. Tübingen: Niemeyer (Beiträge zur Dialogforschung 3), 15-40.
House, Juliane (1997): Translation quality assessment: a model revisited. Tübingen: Narr.
Kerbrat-Orecchioni, Catherine ([4]2002): L'énonciation. Paris: Armand Colin.
Koller, Werner ([5]1997): Einführung in die Übersetzungswissenschaft. Wiesbaden: Quelle & Meyer (UTB 819).
Kotschi, Thomas (1986): Procédés d'évaluation et de commentaire métadiscursifs comme stratégies interactives. In: Cahièrs de linguistique française 7, 207-230.
Lüger, Heinz-Helmut ([2]1995): Pressesprache. Tübingen: Niemeyer.
Meyer-Hermann, Reinhard (1978): Aspekte der Analyse metakommunikativer Interaktionen. In: Meyer-Hermann, Reinhard (Hg.): Sprechen – Handeln – Interaktion. Tübingen: Niemeyer, 103-142.
– (1983): Vers une définition (non fonctionnelle) de la métacommunication. In: Langage et société XXIV, 4-35.
Reiß, Katharina ([3]1993): Texttyp und Übersetzungsmethode. Der operative Text. Kronberg i.Ts.: Scriptor.
Sandig, Barbara (1979): Ausdrucksmöglichkeiten des Bewertens. Ein Beschreibungsrahmen im Zusammenhang eines fiktionalen Textes. In: Deutsche Sprache 7, 137-159.

– (1991): Formeln des Bewertens. In: Palm, Christine (Hg.): EUROPHRAS 90. Akten der internationalen Tagung zur germanistischen Phraseologieforschung, Aske/Schweden, 12.-15.6.1990. Stockholm: Almquist & Wiksell International, 225-252.
Schlieben-Lange, Brigitte (1975): Metasprache und Metakommunikation. In: Schlieben-Lange, Brigitte (Hg.): Sprachtheorie. Hamburg: Hoffmann und Campe, 189-205.
Schreiber, Michael (1993): Übersetzung und Bearbeitung. Zur Differenzierung und Abgrenzung des Übersetzungsbegriffs. Tübingen: Narr.
Schwitalla, Johannes (1979): Dialogsteuerung in Interviews. München: Hueber.
Sergo, Laura (2002): »Europa vor dem Ziel« – »Schröder ha sbagliato tutto«. L'intervista scritta: traduzione o elaborazione? In: Bauer, Roland/Goebl, Hans (Hgg.): Parallela IX. Testo – variazione – informatica/Text – Variation – Informatik. Atti del IX Incontro italo-austriaco dei linguisti (Salisburgo, 1-4 novembre 2000)/Akten des IX. Österreichisch-italienischen Linguistentreffens (Salzburg, 1.-4. November 2000). Wilhelmsfeld: Egert, 373-387.
Stati, Sorin (1982): Il dialogo. Considerazioni di linguistica pragmatica. Napoli: Liguori.
– (1986): Cinque miti della parola. Lezioni di lessicologia testuale. Bologna: Pàtron.
Thiel, Gisela/Thome, Gisela (1998): Aspekte der Bewertung im Wissenschaftsjournalismus. In: Lebende Sprachen XLIII/4, 149-155.
Thome, Gisela (1975): Die Übersetzungsprozeduren und ihre Relevanz für die Ermittlung des translatorischen Schwierigkeitsgrades eines Textes. In: Nickel, Gerhard/Raasch, Albert (Hgg.): Kongreßbericht der 6. Jahrestagung der GAL, Bd. I: Wilss, Wolfram (Hg.): Übersetzungswissenschaft. Heidelberg: Groos, 39-51.
– (1998): Printmedien und Übersetzung. Zur deutschsprachigen Ausgabe von Le Monde Diplomatique. In: ZfAL 28, 53-71.
– (im Druck): Bearbeitung in Übersetzungen als Kriterium für die Bewertung der translatorischen Leistung. In: House, Juliane/Baumgarten, Nicole (Hgg.): Übersetzungskritik. Modelle und Methoden. St. Ingbert: Röhrig Universitätsverlag (Arbeitsberichte des Advanced Translation Research Center (ATRC) an der Universität des Saarlandes).
Tiittula, Liisa (1994): Implizites Bewerten in finnischen und deutschen Leitartikeln. In: Moilanen, Markku/Tiittula, Lisa (Hgg.): Überredung in der Presse. Texte, Strategien, Analysen. Berlin, New York: de Gruyter, 225-240.

Lawrence N. Berlin

Media manipulation

1. Introduction

In a democracy, the worlds of media and politics are expected to function independently of one another. Indeed, the purpose of journalism in its ideal form is to provide information without biased language, uninfluenced by political agendas. Unfortunately, this has not always been the case. Discourse studies are replete with examples of how individual politicians and/or whole regimes use the media for advancing their own policies (Bell 1991; Caldas-Coulthard 2003; Kress/van Leeuwen 1996; Lakoff 1990; van Dijk 2003). For instance, in a discussion of the student uprising at Tiananmen Square of 1989, Lakoff (1990) likens the Chinese government's censorship of local media reporting of the event as totalitarian, ultimately denying that the event ever took place.

Though such an intrusion into the working of the 'free' press would be deemed unthinkable in a western democracy with freedom of speech and the press held sacrosanct, we have, of late, witnessed parallel occurrences in the U.S. media. The media coverage during the U.S. invasion of Iraq stands out as extremely informative. While American media sources showed 'embedded' reporters and aerial views of bombings, Middle Eastern news agencies presented images of the Iraqi people and their suffering during the war. In each case, the sociocultural context was manipulated to serve separate goals: in the former, to maintain a general trend of patriotism within the U.S. toward the Bush administration and, in the latter, to fuel anti-American sentiment among the peoples of the Middle East (Dajani 2003).

Underlying the shift in the functioning of the media, the past few decades have witnessed news networks and periodicals become components of major corporations. According to Lakoff (1990, 301), "If those who already hold excessive power wish to consolidate their strength still further, they will seek to do so through control of language at its source: the media." Examples can be seen in the mergers of the American Broadcasting Company and the Disney Corporation, the National Broadcasting Company and Microsoft, and the mega-conglomerate America Online Time-Warner, parent company of Cable News Network (CNN). By choosing which news is fit to print and by placing a 'spin' on the way language is presented, ways of thinking have been manipulated to construct an acceptable public discourse.

In the current study, news media are examined as a source of promotion for the U.S. government's passage of Title I, the No Child Left Behind Act of 2001 (NCLB). This legislation was adopted in the wake of the World Trade Center bombings of September 11, 2001, when a frightened public put an almost blind faith in the government without considering the consequences of the law. In effect, NCLB requires extensive testing of students, claiming to maintain educational standards while negating the very nature of a pluralist society in favor of a more traditional definition of education: one that posits an idealized learner modeled after the dominant group and denigrates all other forms of knowing. Though the xenophobic aspect of the ratified legislation did not escape the notice of educators, the news media immediately began constructing a 'we-they' dialogue between the general public and the educational system. This paper, specifically focusing on headlines in the news, thus provides a clear example of 'dialogue in the grip of the media' (Weigand 1999) insofar as the media do not present the facts in a balanced form, but tend to be biased in favor of the government's position.

2. Theoretical perspective: Critical discourse analysis

Within a critical discourse analysis, there are several theoretical perspectives that seem appropriate here. Kumaravadivelu (1999) provides a productive framework for the exploration of dialogue in context. Dividing the analysis into three levels – the sociopolitical, the sociocultural, and the (socio)linguistic – media headlines are examined within the immediate, or local, context and the wider, or global, context. In effect, the language of the media serves to link the various and interacting contexts, presenting language in a specific form that ties together the dominant rhetoric of the sociopolitical context with the day to day interactions of the sociocultural context in a compelling way so as to indoctrinate the populace to a particular viewpoint. In other words, choices in the representation of the language of headlines can subsequently manipulate the ideological stance of the people in a way that favors the hegemony of the government.

Lakoff (1990) distinguishes between two types of users in the language of public persuasion: "economic" and "political". In other words, there are those who stand to gain economically and those who stand to gain politically; however, in a capitalist system where money equals power and large corporations contribute to political campaigns (and own various media sources), the lines become blurred between the divisions. Taking the framework a step further, Lakoff separates political persuaders into the "legitimate" and the "illegitimate" – those who are recognized as duly elected officials versus those who deliberately aim to manipulate through propaganda. Within the current situation, though, my objection is that without adequate representation of differing viewpoints, a democratic society cannot make an informed choice for itself. Even as the public becomes aware of manipulation, a good persuader will deftly redirect attention, much like an illusionist. "One thing both advertisers and politicians know too well is that the public becomes wise to their tactics remarkably fast; they have to keep replacing techniques to keep them working at all" (p. 16). This has been the case in the United States, first with the passage of the NCLB and more recently with its attempts at implementation. Furthermore, I would contend that a pluralistic society cannot and should not be forced to adhere to only one way of doing things, especially in the case of the education of its people. Such a position would be repressive of the very differences it purports to value.

Finally, Caldas-Coulthard (2003) focuses on the discourse of media in its representation of 'otherness'. She posits three roles embodied in the presentation and interpretation of 'news'. These are the political, social, and educational roles. Through these roles, the media function to construct a national identity, in a sense by establishing a 'we-they' dichotomy where readers recognize what a 'good citizen' should believe. Herein, the power of the press to ascribe an ideological stance through the presentation of text and images is undeniable as it attributes positive self-representation to the stated position (van Dijk, 1992). Thus, the interconnectedness of the various roles – Caldas-Coulthard's (2003) political role and Kumaravadivelu's (1999) sociopolitical context – advances the dominant view from a global or national, top-down position. The social role is evident within the local sociocultural context by examining how the media connects to the daily lives of the people, setting up the 'we' by showing concern for the interests of the readers (i.e., the education of their children). "Newsgivers have come to adopt the position of mediators, figures who cultivate 'characteristics which are taken to be typical of the 'target' audience' and a relationship of solidarity with it" (Fairclough 1995, 62). Simultaneously, the educational role tends to be precisely what serves the political agenda of the powerful inasmuch as the media only present one side of the issues of current affairs, typically those favoring the government.

3. Context

3.1 Sociopolitical context: Legislation and political climate

In the United States, major laws, especially those as controversial and all encompassing as NCLB rarely pass through the House of Representatives and the Senate without at least some public debate. Typically, information is disseminated to the American public through the mass media. This was not the case with NCLB. In the wake of the attacks on the World Trade Center on September 11, 2001 with public attention focused on matters of security, the Bush administration took the opportunity to pass several pieces of legislation that might not have otherwise become law. NCLB was one such piece of legislation presented during the first session of the 107th Congress on December 13, 2001. It was ratified by both houses of Congress and passed into law in January 2002, unopposed and largely unnoticed by the public (i.e., uncovered by the media).

Only now that educators have been required to implement systemic changes has there been a good deal of attention given NCLB in the local press. The central focus of the news, however, has been turned against the educational system while claiming to be interested in "improving the academic achievement of the disadvantaged" (NCBE 2001, 17).

3.2 Sociocultural context: Press coverage

In many cases, school administrators and teachers have had to become accomplices in the promotion of the new law as they scramble to help their students meet minimum standards or run the risk of losing federal funding. In one example, a local school with an exemplary performance record was put on probation as its already comparatively high scores failed to achieve the minimum percentage for improvement established by the government.

Though the new legislature has initiated a frenzy of discussion, debate, and maneuvering within the educational system, most forms of the media have left the issue relatively ignored, save one: print media. In Chicago, one of the major daily newspapers, *Chicago Sun-Times*, published a series of articles that coincided with the commencement of the school year in which it blasted Chicago Public Schools on everything from a lack of qualified teachers to a lack of materials to poor facilities. The attention-grabbing headlines, an attack on Chicago's schools, framed a local context that primed citizens to believe the current situation of schools was virtually untenable and the new law could be not only a viable option, but also a likely panacea.

The headlines, in bold and large print across the front of the newspapers, not only dominate in their appearance, but also in the way they shape the opinions of readers. Indeed, the contemporary media have become more focused on headlines, trying to keep apace with the preoccupation of time in modern Western society. Television news programs like *Headline News* (a branch of CNN) and newspapers like *USA Today* are essentially little more than a series of headlines accommodating the time constraints of the people while claiming to provide the most essential news. According to van Dijk:

The proposition expressed by the headline is also a strong strategic suggestion to the readers to construct this as the top macro proposition of their mental model of the event to be represented – or to add or modify an opinion already formed in an earlier model when readers heard about this case...the actual formulation of the headline is also a function of the context model, in particular of the social and political aims of the editorial and the newspaper.

(van Dijk 2003, 99)

In other words, the 'spin' the media place on a particular piece of information serves to further a particular point of view rather than provide unbiased coverage of an event.

4. (Socio)Linguistic context: Data & analysis

For the data, I extracted headlines related to NCLB published between January and April 2003 from the websites of three major American newspapers: the *New York Times* (*NYT*), *Chicago Tribune* (*CT*), and *Chicago Sun-Times* (*CST*). The first paper, while not "local" to Chicago, the focus of the study, has a bearing in that it is considered a national newspaper and is available in its daily form around the country. It was considered that the headlines contained therein would establish a baseline which could potentially suggest that different opinions were, in fact, being represented, or support a standard, 'unilateral' approach to presenting news in the print media. A total of 48 headlines from articles about NCLB were utilized for the analysis: 8 from *NYT*, 6 from *CT*, and 34 from *CST*. In cases where a headline consisted of two units of analysis, each was counted and categorized individually. Thus, despite the 48 headlines analyzed, the total number of units of analysis presented in the findings equals 52.

Headlines were categorized according to their propositional content and form after a suggestion by Fairclough (1995) regarding the benefit to more firmly grounding results through the interplay of intertextual and textual analyses. Propositional semantic content, referred to by Fairclough as the 'signified', included direct or indirect references in the headlines to objects of particular import to the inquiry at hand; that is, teachers (e.g., "teach", "teacher", "educator"), schools (e.g., "school", "district", "education"), testing (e.g., "test", "testing"), the law (e.g., "law", "policy", "bill"), and students (e.g., "students", "pupils", "kids"). The forms, or 'signifiers', were derived from the actual headlines. The consequent syntactic categories found were as follows:

1) Independent Clauses (IC), complete with the possible exclusion of some function words, such as articles;
2) Reduced Independent Clauses, complete except for the deletion of a copular verb (IC-cop);

3) Interrogative Independent Clauses (int IC) containing an initial question word and subject-verb inversion;
4) Adverbial Clauses (Adv Cl) comprise a complete IC preceded by a subordinating adverb;
5) Noun Phrases (NP);
6) Verb Phrases (VP); and
7) Prepositional Phrases (PP).

Propositional Content / Form	IC	NP	IC-Cop	Int IC	Adv Cl	VP	PP	TOTALS
"teacher" only	7/13%	2/4%	4/8%	2/4%	0/0%	0/0%	1/2%	16/31%
"school" only	4/8%	3/6%	0/0%	0/0%	0/0%	0/0%	0/0%	7/13%
suggestive of teacher/school	3/6%	2/4%	0/0%	1/2%	0/0%	0/0%	0/0%	6/12%
"teacher" & "test"	2/4%	1/2%	0/0%	1/2%	0/0%	0/0%	0/0%	4/8%
"law" & "test"	3/6%	0/0%	0/0%	0/0%	0/0%	0/0%	0/0%	3/6%
"law" & "school"	1/2%	1/2%	1/2%	0/0%	0/0%	0/0%	0/0%	3/6%
"school" & "teacher"	0/0%	0/0%	2/4%	0/0%	0/0%	0/0%	0/0%	2/4%
"teacher" & "student"	1/2%	0/0%	0/0%	1/2%	0/0%	0/0%	0/0%	2/4%
"student" only	1/2%	0/0%	0/0%	0/0%	1/2%	0/0%	0/0%	2/4%
"student" & "test"	2/4%	0/0%	0/0%	0/0%	0/0%	0/0%	0/0%	2/4%
"law"	1/2%	1/2%	0/0%	0/0%	0/0%	0/0%	0/0%	2/4%
"test" only	0/0%	1/2%	0/0%	0/0%	0/0%	0/0%	0/0%	1/2%
suggestive of teacher & "test"	1/2%	0/0%	0/0%	0/0%	0/0%	0/0%	0/0%	1/2%
suggestive of teacher & student	0/0%	0/0%	0/0%	0/0%	0/0%	1/2%	0/0%	1/2%
TOTALS	26/50%	11/21%	7/13%	5/10%	1/2%	1/2%	1/2%	52/100%

Table 1. Headlines' propositional content & forms in numbers & percentages

5. Findings & discussion

5.1 How do the media represent the 'we'?

The findings for the analysis are reported in Table 1. Perhaps the most striking finding of all is the relatively little attention in the headlines given to the students, the purported benefactors of the new law. Only 6 headlines (12%) even mention students directly with one additional headline alluding to them. Moreover, the law itself is only referred to 8 times (15%). To approach this analysis from another perspective, it might be argued that since the name of the law incorporates a reference to students – "No Child Left Behind" – and the fact that "law" and "students" never co-occur, the propositional content can be claimed as co-referential; however, even a combined interpretation only accounts for little more than one quarter of the data obtained.

Interestingly, nearly all headlines referring to students fall into the IC classification, providing a syntactic frame that is not ambiguous at all for readers. Additionally, they are ostensibly positioned as victims, thereby producing a situation where the news is taking on the educational role (Caldas-Coulthard 2003) and, suggestive of the social role, or sociocultural context (Kumaravadivelu 1999), where the media appear to take sides with the public by championing its cause (1-2).

(1) Poorest Kids Often Wind Up with the Weakest Teachers (*CST*)
(2) More Intensive Reading Program Is Added for Struggling Pupils (*NYT*)

Similarly, other headlines that make references to students are presented in an unreduced form; that is, Int IC and Adv Cl also contain complete ICs which remain unambiguous as in the following examples (3-4).

(3) Who's Teaching Our Children (*CST*)
(4) When a Student Prefers Learning of the Hands-On Variety (*NYT*)

As stated in section 3.2, *CST* seems to clearly delineate the 'we' and the 'they' in the local, sociocultural context, positioning itself in the 'we' camp with the general population against the educational system. This co-opting of the 'we' position is even further emphasized in Headline 3 by the use of 'our' in the reference to 'our children'. Furthermore, Headline 5, reminiscent of Headline 1, shows that even absent any direct reference to teachers or students, a proposition can still be unambiguous in the establishment of a 'we-they' dichotomy.

(5) Short-Changing the Neediest (*CST*)

Indicating whose agenda is being advanced, only two headlines (6-7) stand out because of their divergence between content and form; that is, both share in their clarity of content yet vagueness of form.

(6) A Pervasive Dismay on a Bush School Law (*NYT*)
(7) Bush Lessons (*CT*)

In examples where the governmental propositional content reference is not so obvious, the 'signified' is supported by a more accessible 'signifier', an IC or one merely reduced by the omission of the copula, as in 8 and 9.

(8) Thousands of Schools May Run Afoul of New Law (*NYT*)
(9) Schools Meeting Rules – In a Way (*CT*)

In both cases, however, the proposition of the headlines places the onus of any fault squarely upon the educational system, reconfirming the 'they' status of the schools.

Propositional Content / Form	IC	NP	IC-Cop	Int IC	VP	PP	TOTALS
"teacher" reference	10/24%	3/7%	4/10%	4/10%	0/0%	1/2%	22/52%
"school" reference	5/12%	4/10%	1/2%	0/0%	0/0%	0/0%	10/24%
"teacher" & "school" combined	0/0%	0/0%	2/5%	0/0%	0/0%	0/0%	2/5%
suggestive of teacher and/or school	4/10%	2/5%	0/0%	1/2%	1/2%	0/0%	8/19%
TOTALS	19/45%	9/21%	7/17%	5/12%	1/2%	1/2%	42/100%

Table 2. Headlines focusing on the educational system

5.2 How do the media represent the 'they'?

Schools, especially teachers, have been made the scapegoats in the depiction of the 'we-they' dichotomy by the media, ostensibly the cause for what's wrong with the current educational system. While this conclusion may seem intuitive – which is, in itself, a strong basis for the popular belief that the press is fomenting – it is a crime of omission that the media are responsible for. In fact, as the dialogue of the media usurps the presumed educational role (Caldas-Coulthard 2003), the media become guilty of bias by highlighting one side of an issue and giving a negative 'spin' to the other, or by only presenting one side. In either case, the media influence public opinion by sanctioning the sociopolitical context as inseparable from the sociocultural. With regard to NCLB, then, headlines obtained during the first quarter of 2003 negatively position schools and teachers while drawing battle lines in the 'we-they' discourse. Thus, the aims of the government are fulfilled by positing 'dialogue in the grip of the media' (Weigand 1999).

In reporting on a law that is supposed to focus on children, 22 headlines (42%) retrieved from the three major newspapers refer to teachers, 10 headlines (19%) refer to schools, and an additional 2 headlines (4%) name both. These references account for 65% of the propositional content identified in the headlines, compared with only 12% that mention students. Furthermore, indirect reference to teachers and/or schools (i.e., "suggestive") adds 8 more headlines (15%) to the already high total accounting for 81% of the data obtained.

Table 2 provides an overview of the headlines with direct or indirect reference to the educational system. In examples where the linguistic context is greatly reduced – only NPs or PPs – adjectives with a negative meaning frame the attitudes being advanced (10-14).

(10) Failing Teachers (*CST*)
(11) Teachers Who Barely Passed the Basic Skills Test (*CST*)
(12) Chicago Schools with the Most Flunkers[1] (*CST*)
(13) Districts with the Most Flunkers (*CST*)
(14) In Poor School for Long Haul (*CST*)

What remains most remarkable, though, is that all but one of the headlines making use of one of the reduced linguistic contexts come from *CST*. In the headlines above, the naming of the 'culpable' demonizes the educational system. This type of 'public shaming' has historical significance in the representation of 'otherness' in the United States. Reminiscent of McCarthyism, schools are made virtual criminals by the press (15-17).

(15) Tips for Parents Who Want to Know about a Teacher's State Certificate (*CST*)
(16) Failing Teachers Spur Hearings (*CST*)
(17) Substandard Teachers Under the Microscope (*CST*)

In its 'purging' of the local educational system, *CST* utilizes interrogative forms to suggest a tactic most commonly associated with corruption: the 'cover up' (18-19).

(18) Why are Teacher Tests Secret? (*CST*)
(19) Should Parents Worry about Teachers? (*CST*)

The effect of this form of discourse can be traced in subsequent headlines where the media incite the public into developing mistrust in educators (20-23). In fact, the only recourse seemingly available in such a purported state of affairs is governmental intervention (24-26).

(20) Teacher Colleges Turn Out Poorly Trained Graduates (*CST*)
(21) 5,243 Illinois Teachers Failed Key Exams (*CST*)
(22) City Begins Informing Parents About School-Transfer Rights (*NYT*)
(23) Over 16,000 Seek Transfers from Failing Schools (*NYT*)
(24) House Raises Bar for Teaching (*CST*)
(25) Basic Skills Test Bill Moves to Senate Floor (*CST*)
(26) Private Tutoring Firms Can Use Chicago Public School Buildings (*CT*)

In each of the preceding examples, clarity is achieved in both the 'signified' and the 'signifier'. The propositional content consists of straightforward language, unambiguous in meaning, and syntactic form is represented by ICs.

---

[1] The "flunkers" in the headlines 11 and 12 refer to results presumably obtained on teachers' performance on the Illinois State Test of Basic Skills. Once again, however, the choice to present only enough of the information to advance a particular viewpoint dominates. Issues not mentioned by the media include the areas tested, the teachers' disciplines, the recent redesign of all components of the test in 2002, and the status of the test-takers (i.e., many current teachers are in the process of completing their degrees while working under a special government-sanctioned program that recognizes the severe lack of teachers).

6. Conclusion

It seems a foregone assumption in the United States that the same law that provides for freedom of the press also guarantees impartiality of the press. Instead, a critical discourse analysis illustrates how several factors combine to create a situation in which the media act as a partner in the promulgation of the ideology of the governmental hegemony. Thus, the current sociopolitical context dominates every component of the news as the headlines mediate the sociocultural context through manipulation of the propositional content and form of the language being used.

Through textual and intertextual analysis, it becomes evident that the print media, as exemplified in the *NYT*, *CT*, and *CST*, align themselves with the government and utilize the power of language to establish a fellowship with the general population at the expense of schools and teachers. In such an environment, the current educational system has little choice but to accept "No Child Left Behind" or remain an unwilling adversary and ultimate loser in the 'we-they' discourse battle over education.

References

Bell, Allan (1991): The language of news media. Oxford: Blackwell.
Caldas-Coulthard, Carmen R. (2003): Cross-cultural representation of 'otherness' in media discourse. In: Weiss, Gilbert/Wodak, Ruth (eds.): Critical discourse analysis: Theory and interdisciplinarity. Hampshire (UK): Palgrave Macmillan Ltd., 272-296.
Dajani, Jamal (Producer) (2003): Mosaic special report: Aftershock Iraq – America and the new Middle East [Film; broadcast May 7, 2003. Available from Link TV, Inc., San Francisco, CA. http://www.linktv.org].
Fairclough, Norman (1995): Critical discourse analysis: The critical study of language. London, New York: Longman.
Kress, Gunther R./van Leeuwen, Theo (1996): Reading images: The grammar of visual design. London: Routledge.
Kumaravadivelu, B. (1999): Critical classroom discourse analysis. In: TESOL Quarterly 33/3, 453-484.
Lakoff, Robin T. (1990): Talking power: The politics of language. San Francisco: Basic Books.
NCBE [National Clearinghouse for Bilingual Education] (2001): No Child Left Behind Act of 2001: Title I: Improving the academic achievement of the disadvantaged. Washington: The National Clearinghouse for Bilingual Education.
van Dijk, Teun A. (1992): Discourse and the denial of racism. In: Discourse & Society 3/1, 87-118.
– (2003): The discourse-knowledge interface. In: Weiss, Gilbert/Wodak, Ruth (eds.): Critical discourse analysis: Theory and interdisciplinarity. Hampshire (UK): Palgrave Macmillan Ltd., 85-109.
Weigand, Edda (1999): Dialogue in the grip of the media. In: Naumann, Bernd (ed.): Dialogue analysis and the mass media. Tübingen: Niemeyer (Beiträge zur Dialogforschung 20), 35-54.

Stefanie Schnöring

Personnel advertisements as a form of mediated dialogic interaction

1. Introduction

Recruiting employees is a complex communicative process which comprises different phases. The purpose of this article is to investigate the way companies present themselves to potential employees in the media. Even if the proliferation of new media forms has added new dimensions to advertisement and recruiting strategies, this article focuses on the print media. It will be emphasized that dialogic interaction, being central to methods of e-recruitment, can also be considered a feature of personnel advertisements in the print media. The advertisements chosen for analysis do not promote special jobs. They belong to the form of an image advertisement and as such address a group of people, in this case young and highly qualified graduates (also called 'High Potentials').

My analysis is based on a model of dialogic interaction as developed by Weigand (2000). This model allows for the integration of different communicative means. The article demonstrates that verbal, perceptual and cognitive means are used integratively to reach the communicative goals of the advertising company.

2. Setting

Central to the notion of the Dialogic Action Game is the presumption that human communication is culturally embedded (cf. Weigand 2000). Phenomena of the wider socio-economic context as well as functional characteristics of the action game as a whole have to be considered before turning to the theoretical premises and the method of analysis.

2.1 Developments on the labour market

Middle- and long-term developments on the labour market indicate that there is competition for certain groups of qualified employees and that it is expected to continue (cf. Dostal/ Reinberg 1999). Due to declining population and changes concerning work itself political economies have to manage an increase in qualified jobs as well as a decrease in qualified employees. The transformation of an industrialized society in what might be called a 'service society' calls for seemingly new qualifications such as self-empowerment/-responsibility, flexibility as well as communication and presentation skills. 'Human capital' is of the outmost importance for companies competing in today's globalized economy.

Various surveys show that people with high qualifications tend to make high demands.[1] Payment does not play a major role for them. Rather, the 'employer of choice' should be able to offer flexibility in terms of working conditions (e.g. flexible working hours, forms like job enlargement or job enrichment). Graduates are interested in jobs that allow for a high degree of personal-development and -fulfillment. Moreover, they decide in favour of a corporate culture marked by values and norms with which they can identify.

2.2 The recruiting process

> Recruitment performs the essential function of drawing an important resource – human capital – into the organization. The success of later human resource efforts, such as selection, training and compensation, depends in part on the quality and quantity of new employees identified and attracted through the recruitment process.
>
> (Barber 1998, 1)

This definition highlights the function of recruiting with regard to employment conditions. It emphasizes that recruiting represents the first part of an on-going process which does not stop with the applicant selection but also comprises further personnel management functions. Many companies have formed special functional departments such as 'personnel marketing' that take care of the first part of the process linking the presentation of the company (to potential employees) to the following selection phase.

All aspects of personnel marketing depend on communication and can be distinguished as forms of face-to-face communication on the one hand and mediated communication on the other hand. Methods of personal and direct communication include conversations between potential employees and representatives of a company, e.g. on a job fair (which has become a popular form of recruiting) or a special event arranged by the firm.

Apart from these forms of personal recruiting most companies address a more or less anonymous group of potential employees by advertisements. There are two basic forms: the specific job advertisement, promoting a particular job, and image advertisement (abbreviated as 'image ad').

---

[1] Cf. surveys by Universum Communications, Modalis, or the VDI (Verband deutscher Ingenieure).

2.3 The function of images

An image can be defined as a scheme of cognitive and emotive structuring (cf. Merten 1994, 206). It can also be defined as a 'mental picture'. As such it reflects what people think and feel about an object or topic. Even if it represents a subjective construct it depends on socialization, and in our times particularly on the way media influences human dialogic interaction.

Thus, the image of a company refers to the assessment of the company by the public, particularly by its target groups or stakeholders. Certain variables such as the reputation of the firm, its size, its products, its internationality and its success establish an image of the company. For potential employees this image represents a cognitive construct with the functions of orientation and substitution (cf. Beba 1993, Schneider 1995). It can be shown that people more likely tend to apply for a job at a company if it is well-known and successful. But more relevant for the purposes of my study is the fact that missing information is substituted by the image formed in one's mind. It is important to emphasize that the image is not only the result of a communicative process such as recruiting but also a decisive presupposition for communication itself.

Personal image advertisements help to create a positive image of a company as a potential employer. In this respect they are functionally equivalent to methods of public relations aiming at promoting a company in the public sphere. Nevertheless *creating* a positive image does not work like a stimulus-response-model might suggest. It rather has to be considered as an *interactive* process depending on individual and social assumptions.

3. The dialogic action game *War for Talent*

A linguistic perspective on the question "How do companies recruit new staff?" shifts the focus to the integration of different communicative means and their functional features. The question is how to take this into account in an analysis. The model of the dialogic action game as developed by Weigand (2000) may serve as a theoretical basis. It considers interaction taking place in cultural units (so-called action games) in the centre of which are different human beings. As an open model the model of the dialogic action game allows for rules and conventions of language use but regards principles of communication as constitutive features of dialogic interaction. Dialogue cannot be described as a fixed pattern, it is rather a process of negotiation of meaning and understanding which is guided by purposes and interests (Weigand 2001). This negotiation process depends on the situation, i.e. the interlocutors' knowledge and the abilities of visual, cognitive and emotional perception.

"The action game is not constituted as a type of situation but determined by its interactive purpose" (Weigand 2000, 7). Following this premise, the process of recruitment is considered as the action game *War for Talent* because it has the interactive purpose of winning high potential employees. This allows for a functional distinction from other forms of advertisements like advertisement for products. The Action Principle implies that "taking communicative action means pursuing specific dialogic purposes with specific dialogic means" (Weigand 2000, 9). It does not only serve as a technique of orientation for the interlocutors but also for communication analysis in general. In addition to verbal and perceptible means cognitive means such as mental pictures have to be taken into account as far as possible.

One might raise the objection that 'real' dialogic interaction is not given with advertisements in the print media. But as Weigand clearly emphasizes, dialogue is not a formal feature but a *functional* interdependence of different types of speech acts (Weigand 2000, 10). Even in face-to-face communication the dialogic sequence is not calculable in advance. Instead, there is a rational basis implied in the initiative speech act itself, "in its pragmatic claim which is to be negotiated in dialogue" (Weigand 2000, 10). As relationships between initiative and reactive speech acts represent expectations, they are subject to negotiation and one has to be aware of the fact that there are open points in the process of dialogic interaction. In this respect the possibility of leaving things open has to be regarded as a constitutive strategy of the dialogic action game *War for Talent*.

Companies which are engaged in the *War for Talent* are expected to present themselves as attractive employers. But attracting the attention and interest of potential employees is not enough as "the recruiting organization must [.] set out to persuade individuals to apply" (Barber 1998, 32). Persuasion is a central aspect of the action game *War for Talent* and that is why it corresponds with the way a company *persuades* people to apply through their advertisement presentation.

4. Methodology

As Weigand emphasizes, methodology has to be derived from the object of study (Weigand 2000, 2). Having outlined constitutive features of the dialogic action game *War for Talent*, this article aims at presenting a model developed for the analysis of personnel advertisements and some results from a more comprehensive analysis. Taking the interactive purpose as a starting point there are three different aspects of analysis which correspond to sub-goals in this action game. First, 'presentation of the company' refers to general information about the company and to information about the company as employer. Second, 'selection of employees' specifies abilities and characteristics of the kind of employee the company is interested in. Third, 'motivation of employees' refers to the aspect of persuasion in at least two respects: On the one hand, offers made by the firm should have a motivating effect. (This also includes the long-term function as employees demand and receive benefits when they are already members of the company.) On the other hand, potential employees should be motivated to immediate and continuous interaction. This can be the beginning of the recruiting process with an application and a job interview following. It should be emphasized that the three dimensions are distinguished for heuristic purposes. To reach the communicative goal of 'winning high potential employees' they are integrated in the whole of the action game.

5. Sample analysis

The personnel image advertisements chosen for analysis were launched by the automobile manufacturer DaimlerChrysler and the media company Bertelsmann, two *global players* as they employ people worldwide. Both companies are particularly interested in graduates and rank with the most popular employers in Germany (cf. Sievers/Wozniak 2001).

The image ads presented here were published in career magazines whose target groups are university students and graduates. Apart from advertisements, these magazines contain journalistic articles on companies and give advice on how to get ahead with one's career.

5.1 DaimlerChrysler: Steer your career

At first sight the viewer's attention is drawn to the visual means by a futuristic steering wheel.[2] It represents a central motif of the image campaign and also appears again on the websites and on the front page of the image brochure. As it only slightly resembles a traditional steering wheel the question "What do you say to an engineer who wants to make a car *with no steering wheel*?" fits the first impression. It directly connects the recruiting process with the products of the company: cars.

The beginning of the text placed below the picture refers to the company's past, present and future stating: "Once it was horseless carriages, then cars with gullwings or diesel-powered motor cars. Now it is our F200 Imagination prototype; which really has no steering

---

[1] Unfortunately due to copyrights it was not possible to print the image ad in the context of my article. I try to describe it by verbal means.

wheel". Innovation is a key word in the text (cf. the name of the prototype "F200 Imagination" or the sentence "Innovators are always the best in their business") and it is presented as being in line with the tradition of the company. Thus, a continuous corporate culture/corporate identity is presented to the potential employee from the beginning. With the use of representative speech acts there can be no doubt that DaimlerChrysler presents itself as a truly innovative company. It certainly takes advantage of its corresponding product image – cars of high quality, developed according to up-to-date standards.

The characteristic features of the company are clearly set, as well as the qualifications demanded from potential employees. With the image ad DaimlerChrysler addresses "engineers with outstanding graduate qualifications". One can presume that this advertisement goes over well with engineers as they are usually interested in activities in research and development. The pun *conceiving the inconceivable* as well as the metaphorical idiom *to refuse to recognise boundaries in one's mind* deviate from the short and explicit style and offer variant readings. The viewer raises the question "Do I fit into this working environment?" and is motivated to imagine situations where he/she has demonstrated creativity, self-confidence and courage (to name but a few personal traits implicitly referred to). Nevertheless, DaimlerChrysler does not promote jobs for mavericks, stating that: "Great things can only come through teamwork, in collaboration with colleagues around the world".

Analysis of the motivation-dimension demands a closer look on the way the company addresses its potential employees. The viewer is addressed directly three times. First, by the question "What do you say to an engineer who wants to make a car with no steering wheel?", second by the following directive "Climb aboard!"; third, by the directive "Apply to DaimlerChrysler AG". In the immediate context the first two speech acts serve as an invitation to have a closer look at the image ad as a whole. Moreover, they refer to further actions such as applying to the company and working with DaimlerChrysler. At the same time the directives do not carry the central message with regard to the sub-goal motivation/persuasion. As explained before particularly verbal and cognitive means (i.e. the 'image') make it quite clear that DaimlerChrysler is a company which offers excellent development opportunities (in more than one sense: concerning product development as well as career development). The mentioning of core competences of DaimlerChrysler together with the positive image is expected to fulfill the motivating function sufficiently.

Looking at the image ad as a whole after this first cursory analysis, the central message could be summarized as following: The employee DaimlerChrysler is looking for should be able to take charge of his/her career. Consequently, activity and commitment are not only important selection criteria but also represent motivating factors for the target group. Graduates are persuaded to apply by a reference to the image they have of DaimlerChrysler and the image they have of themselves.

Personnel advertisements 189

5.2 Bertelsmann: myfuture@bertelsmann

In the image ad launched by Bertelsmann verbal means are kept to a minimum. Therefore the analysis has to focus on the combination of different communicative means.

Central topics of the image campaign are media, internationality and creativity. With pictures of young people, obviously from different nationalities, busy with different media, Bertelsmann presents the image of a global media company. Graduates are addressed directly with the utterance "If your ideas revolve around a management career in the most international media company...". The if-clause refers to an ambition necessary for those seeking to work with Bertelsmann. As presuppositions for a management career, creativity and international thinking are mentioned rather implicitly by use of the collocation *ideas revolve around* (note the comparability to the DaimlerChrysler ad). Whereas the if-clause corresponds with the sub-goal 'selection of employees', the second half of the sentence, a directive speech act, refers to the motivational aspect. The directive *go to* can be completed in two ways: either by the address of the website, printed in bold-type below the pictures, or, by the company logo *Bertelsmann media worldwide*. With regard to the first alternative graduates interested in the company as an employer are invited to visit the career websites. The code of the websites is interesting as it includes the viewer explicitly by use of the possessive pronoun *my*. (The corresponding e-mail-address is myfuture@bertelsmann.com; literally read: my future *at* Bertelsmann.) Thus, the actual situation of the graduate is linked to a future perspective as an employee of Bertelsmann, which corresponds to the second variant reading, the rather explicit directive "Go to Bertelsmann media worldwide". In this way, creativity as a qualification demanded in the media business is reflected by the way the company presents itself in the media.

Bertelsmann has decided to focus its recruiting strategy on the WWW. This might also explain why the address of the website has such a dominant position in the context of their image ads. Those interested in working for Bertelsmann should visit the website where they can get more information. Persuasion in this respect refers to a central functional feature of the 'traditional' image advertisement: it serves to convince the viewers that further (inter)action is worthwhile.

6. Conclusion

Although only two image ads could be examined and presented in this paper, it has become obvious that we have to approach our object of study in a holistic way taking into account verbal, visual and cognitive means. Personnel image advertisements normally do not contain much information. Not everything is stated explicitly, drawing inferences is of central importance. Companies such as DaimlerChrysler or Bertelsmann can rely on a positive image due to manifold factors, advertising being certainly one of them. Nonetheless, companies have to keep in mind that crisis and bad news spread quickly in our media society and that might also have an impact on the image of a company as an employer.

Competing in the *War for Talent* is a balancing act in more than one respect. On the one hand, companies present themselves as attractive employers, on the other hand, they have to meet the demands of qualified and self-confident graduates. Thus, personal address is very important. As this analysis has shown the ways of addressing can be rather subtle. Even if directives are used they are often based on the self-motivation expected from the potential employee. The focus of attention is placed on the viewer. This is also reflected in the communication process itself: the viewer has to ask him-/ herself if he/she is a person who fits into the company, he/she has to use the abilities of perceiving and drawing inferences. All different speech acts become subject to a process of negotiation. In this respect the graduates may also ask themselves "Is this claim acceptable and consistent with the image I have of the company?" From the very beginning the characteristic feature of human dialogic interaction, the negotiation of interests, also becomes obvious in the dialogic action game *War for Talent*. Both, the companies and the employees and their specific interests and abilities have to be taken into account. Thus, recruiting can be considered to be an interactive process even in its mediated forms.

References

Barber, Alison (1998): Recruiting employees: Individual and organizational perspectives. Thousand Oaks: Sage Publications (Foundations of Organizational Science).
Beba, Werner (1993): Die Wirkung von Direktkommunikation unter Berücksichtigung der interpersonellen Kommunikation: Ansatzpunkte für eine Kommunikationsstrategie des Personal-Marketing. Berlin: Duncker und Humblot (Schriften zum Marketing 35).
Dostal, Werner/Reinberg, Alexander (1999): Arbeitslandschaft 2010 – Teil 2: Ungebrochener Trend in die Wissensgesellschaft. Nürnberg: Bundesanstalt für Arbeit.
Merten, Klaus et al. (eds.) (1994): Die Wirklichkeit der Medien. Eine Einführung in die Kommunikationswissenschaft. Opladen: Westdeutscher Verlag.
Schneider, Bernhard (1995): Personalbeschaffung: Eine vergleichende Betrachtung von Theorie und Praxis. Frankfurt a. M.: Lang (Europäische Hochschulschriften: Reihe 5, Volks- und Betriebswirtschaft 1794).
Sievers, Florian/Wozniak, Astrid (2001): Große Umfrage: Wo Studenten arbeiten wollen. In: FAZ hochschulanzeiger 53, 55-56.
Watson Wyatt (1999): The war for talented people. A Watson Wyatt research study.
Weigand, Edda (2000): The dialogic action game. In: Coulthard, Malcolm et al. (eds.): Dialogue Analysis VII: Working with dialogue. Tübingen: Niemeyer (Beiträge zur Dialogforschung 22), 1-18.
– (2001): Wissen und Meinen im Handlungsspiel. In: Wichter, Sigurd/Antos, Gerd (eds.): Wissenstransfer zwischen Experten und Laien: Umriss einer Transferwissenschaft. Frankfurt a. M.: Lang (Transferwissenschaften 1), 65-81.

Anamaría Harvey / Luisa Granato

Discussions in the media

1. Introduction

The object of this paper is to report on the results of a study on the contextual and interactional features of 'on air' radio interviews, conducted with the purpose of assessing the possible sociopragmatic effects of their linguistic realisations on rapport management.
    We have selected this media and this genre as the object of investigation for the following main reasons:
a)   radio broadcasting is still the most widespread (and sometimes the sole) source of information for a vast majority of the Chilean and Argentinean people, and thus an extremely important means of influencing public opinion in both our countries;
b)   radio interviews take place in the public forum; for this reason they constitute privileged samples of naturally occurring dialogue whose use for analytical purposes is not constrained for ethical reasons;
c)   from an analytical standpoint they allow the researcher to detect perspectives or viewpoints of both, the interviewer and the interviewee, on the topic or issue at hand, and also
d)   they have the advantage of being easily accessible and not difficult to collect.
In the first part of this presentation we will briefly outline the necessary theoretical and methodological framework and in the second part we will inform about results obtained; in so doing we will examine three prototypical cases and illustrate some of the resources deployed by interlocutors to enhance, maintain or reduce rapport as the exchanges proceed.

2. The theoretical framework

To examine the role of talk in social life in general and the features of radio interviews in particular it is necessary to have a theoretical framework of the social aspect of talk as well as a research paradigm. To conduct the study a socio-pragmatic perspective was adopted. Socio-pragmatic in the sense that we take into account features of the context to be able to assess the pragmatic effects of strategies, resources and lexico-grammatical choices made by participants on rapport management. The term rapport management is used by Spencer-Oatey (2000) to explain the way in which participants to a verbal encounter manage social relations. She states that this concept has the advantage of suggesting a balance between *self and other* which the concept of face does not do and, at the same time, it allows considerations about *sociality rights*. Her model seems to solve the problems arising from the discrepancies between Brown and Levinson's postulates in their Theory of Politeness (1987/1990), and the conceptualisations of authors who reject the idea of the universality of face. These authors hold that the concept is not tenable in other than the anglo-saxon culture, especially in what concerns the opposition between *positive and negative face and politeness*. In her framework of analysis, Spencer-Oatey separates face and sociality rights management as two components of rapport, that is, the handling of harmony and disharmony in verbal encounters. She defines face "as the positive social value a person claims for himself by the line others assume he has taken during a particular contact" (Spencer-Oatey 2000, 14), while sociality rights are related to the expectations interactants have of being entitled to a fair treatment and association with others.

The premise underlying this study is that rapport is co-constructed between parties to an interaction, and that rapport is detected through a careful consideration of contextual and interactional features.

3. Working methodology and analytical procedures

To conduct the study, a corpus of *on air* radio interviews at different levels of formality and on a variety of topics was collected in each of the participating countries. For this presentation we use ten randomly selected interviews on current events or issues, held by professionals in different broadcasting stations in Argentine and Chile. Interviewers and interviewees participating in these encounters are well-known journalists and public figures who exchange views and opinions on topics of general interest for their respective audiences.

Prior to an in-depth analysis, the samples were first transcribed and observed to detect regularities and differences at a macro-level and salient features were registered, compared and described. As an outcome of this stage we were able to identify three prototypical cases in the data: enhancement, maintenance and reduction of rapport management respectively. The second stage consisted in a thorough micro-analysis of the texts and results obtained allowed us to detect resources and identify those lexico-grammatical selections most commonly used by participants in each case.

4. Results and discussion

4.1 Overall features

The overall structure of the ten radio interviews that constitute the sample under analysis follows the same pattern, made up of an initiation, a development and a closing move. The interview proper is actually developed through a series of co-constructed episodes which may exhibit the same characteristics throughout or may depart from the tacit agreement reached between the interlocutors at the outset, as a consequence of the reactions the sort of utterances employed by either of them generate.

The interviews chosen for illustration exemplify 'pure' samples in the sense that all episodes in them exhibit the same features throughout. They represent three clear cut cases of very positive, very negative and middle point positions out of the possible stances that interactants may adopt, thus representing the benchmarks of a cline, as the following diagram exemplifies.

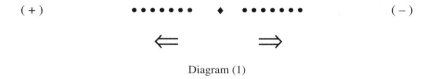

Diagram (1)

Evidently, and as the diagram intends to show, we have also found within the corpus intermediary cases which may take up different forms representing different degrees in the cline. They may either lean towards the positive or the negative poles or towards the intermediate point, without occupying extreme positions. We have found evidence of two distinct types in our data. On the one hand, some interviews are mostly developed in a neutral atmosphere but certain episodes exhibit characteristics that depart form the positions described and which should be placed nearer the extremes. On the other hand, there are cases where the whole encounter is held in such a way that it can be placed in an intermediate position, between very positive and neutral or between neutral and very negative.

The following table highlights and summarises the results of the macro-analysis of the three prototypical cases mentioned.

Interview	First impression	Interactants and their actions	Resulting effect
Case 1 (Clariá – Pelloni)	Very positive	– Appropriate cues and prompts are provided. – Enough time allowed for the production of complete contributions is given.	Sympathetic and collaborative atmosphere
Case 2 (Guiñazú – Cámpora)	Neutral	– Supportive attitude. – Realization of typical interview activities: Ellicitations followed by responses.	Pleasant, formal atmosphere
Case 3 (Clariá – Vani)	Very negative	– Production of negative statements is generated. – Challenging utterances are produced. – Frequent interruptions and overlaps are observed.	Confrontational atmosphere

Table (1) Radio interviews: the overall context

The second stage implied a further analysis at a greater level of delicacy to characterise each of the cases from an overall sociopragmatic perspective.

	CASE 1	CASE 2	CASE 3
COMMUNICATIVE EVENT	Resembles a friendly CONVERSTION	Corresponds to an INTERVIEW	Appears to be a DEBATE
SOCIO-LINGUISTIC VARIABLES	– Minor distance between interactants; – Both formal and functional symmetry	– Conventional distance between interactants; – Formal & functional asymmetry	– Major distance between interactants; – Formal asymmetry/ functional symmetry
DISCOURSIVE ROLES	Partners	Mediator/ Expert informant	Opponents
EFFECTS	Extremely positive	Neutral	Extremely negative
RAPPORT	Enhancement	Maintenance	Reduction

Table (2) Radio interviews: overall features and sociopragmatic effects

The three cases mentioned above may be characterised as communicative events in the following terms:

Case 1: Spontaneous, friendly conversation between equals who share the same perspective on a given topic, where expressions with elicitation function other than the 'question-answer format' are used.

Case 2: Prototypical media exchange, complying with norms and conventions normally associated with the genre: Participant *A* elicits information on a topic and Participant *B* responds.

Case 3: Confrontational exchange exhibiting the characteristics of a debate between opponents holding divergent views on a topic, where role distinction is neutralised.

A closer observation of the encounter reveals a clear difference in the distance between the participants in the three cases. In the first situation, the speakers are very close to one another and act as partners who mutually support each other's positions. They sound sympathetic, amicable and favour the exposition of positive viewpoints that are believed to be accepted as such by the audience. In this sort of encounters the image of both interactants is preserved. The result is a collaborative atmosphere where both participants comply with the conditions and respect their assigned roles enhancing the already existing rapport.

In the second case, the distance established is perhaps what in theory is expected from this kind of genre. The participants are co-operative but not equal partners to a conversation; the journalist is mostly a sympathetic listener acting as a mediator between the interviewee and the audience and does not take a stance on issues being discussed. She limits herself to act as a mediator since she recognises the authority of her interviewee on the topic being dealt with, either because he has the information, the status or the appropriate job. Such being the case, the interviewer produces an utterance with elicitation function and leaves the floor open for the response with the effect that, in many instances, the interviewee's answer resembles more a monologic contribution than a direct answer to a specific question. A pleasant but formal atmosphere is the consequence of this type of behaviour. This guarantees the maintenance of the rapport between the participants.

In the last interview the participants keep a major distance between themselves. Both seek to generate statements and reactions from the interlocutor, whose views are not shared and which, in some instances, are considered erroneous or seen as negative. There is constant challenge to discursive roles from both participants. In the case of the interviewee, for example, responses may range from non-conforming answers to blatant refusals to comply with the interviewer's request for information. The inevitable ensuing aggressive atmosphere reduces the rapport to a minimum.

4.2 Functional values of utterances and linguistic resources

In order to assess the functional values of utterances and linguistic resources utilised by participants a further detailed analysis of salient features at a micro-level was carried out.

Despite the differences highlighted, greetings and closings are always present and based on standard formulaic expressions. In the initiation of the communicative events under analyses, there are always greetings and a first request for information as well as closing remarks signalling the end of the event. But, the contextual characteristics created and the wording of elicitations and responses utilised inevitably modify the sort of rapport established. This may even change step by step as the conversation progresses in such a way that episodes within the whole are clearly identifiable.

An examination of the elicitation utterances reveals that the function is present as expected in the communicative genre under study, and also quite recurrent; in other words, it is possible to observe the same types repeated in all cases. However, the particular selection of linguistic realisations varies from case to case and serves to anticipate the position the interviewer takes in relation to the interviewee and to the matter at hand. One of the most salient lexical choices is found in the particular selection of terms of address which also contributes to signal the status, posture and the discursive role of the interactants, in the sense that they show how the interviewer places him/herself with respect to the interviewee and *vice versa*.

4.3 Strategies and resources

Greetings and terms of address, typical of all initiation moves in the genre, may be realised in different ways thus giving evidence of the first strategic decision made by the interviewer. The sort of ritualistic expression selected together with the accompanying response are the first indicators of the kind of relationship the interlocutors are building up, as the following examples from interviews conducted by the same journalist show.

Case 1:
    Interviewer: M.Clariá (journalist), Interviewee: Sister Pelloni
    The interview opens with the following words:

    MC: Buenos días. ¿Cómo está, hermana Pelloni?
        (Good morning. How are you, Sister Pelloni?)
    HP: Buenos días, Miguel. ¿Cómo está usted?
        (Good morning, Miguel. How are you?)

Conversely, the next interview follows an altogether different introductory pattern.

Discussions in the media

Case 3:
Interviewer: M. Clariá, Interviewee: Vani

MC: Que tenga usted buen día
(A good day to you)
SP: Buen día
(Good morning)
MC: Eh... Vani. Qué son las Brigadas Vani?
(¿Ehm... Vani. What are the Vani Brigades)

As we see, this is certainly an altogether atypical beginning where there is no apparent effort on either part to establish a good climate for the development of the interview. An impersonal and neutral greeting from the interviewer is answered in the same way by the interviewee. Usual complementary formulae normally utilised at this stage are absent and the intonation used by the speakers does not add any overtones of politeness. The journalist takes the floor again and starts with a filler whose function seems to be that of occupying the space which in other circumstances would have been taken up by utterances tending to reinforce social links, such as the use of titles or first names or the production of ritual questions typical of initiation movements. The question is simply introduced by the surname of the interlocutor, a public figure whose activities were very well known at the time of the interview. The role of the question which immediately follows was evidently not to seek information for the sake of the audience but rather to make the speaker publicly commit himself and recognise the kind of *illegal* political activities in which he was involved. This interpretation is further supported by the explicit justification included in the reply given: "[...] The brigades have just occupied an empty space [...]".

The use of questions by interviewers is considered to be a prototypical and constitutive feature of the genre. In this case we observe that this conventional pattern – the format *question-answer* – is often disrupted as the interviewee attempts to assume the interviewer's role, with a greater or lesser degree of success.

Pronominal usage has also resulted to be an interesting feature since it contributes to generate positive rapport and is quite common at the outset of the interviews. Terms corresponding to second person singular pronominals are common in elicitations when the interviewer seeks to make explicit the position his/her interlocutor has. Conversely, the use of first-person singular pronominals is a common feature of interviewees' responses whereas a high density third-person pronominals reflects distancing on the part of the interlocutors from the issues or persons under discussion, results which correlate with the views stated by Alber, O'Connel and Kowal for TV interviews (2002).

4.4 Topic development

Morphosyntactic, lexical and functional selections may give evidence of the possible views taken on the topic being dealt with.

Utterances with elicitation function not only bear upon the strategic decisions and intentions of the interviewer but also anticipate his/her views on the topic being dealt with.

Similarly, responses give clear indication of the interviewees' reactions to the request for information put forward by the journalist, as the following episode illustrates.

> INTERVIEWER: Buenos días Alcalde Lavín.
> (Good morning Major Lavín.)
> INTERVIEWEE: Que tal, como está.
> (Hello, how are you?)
> INTERVIEWER: Sr. Lavín cuál es la postura de su repartición con relación a ....
> (Mr Lavín what is the position of your department with respect to...)
> LAVÍN: Bueno, me parece que no hay cambios sustanciales.
> (Well, it seems to me that there are no substantial changes.)
> INTERVIEWER: Me quiere decir entonces Alcalde que las medidas propuestas son solo cosméticas?
> (Do you mean to say then Major that the measures proposed are only cosmetic?)
> LAVÍN: No...No... lo que quiero decir es que el gobierno....
> (No...No... what I mean is that the government...)

On the other hand, choice of the introductory verb of the response has also proved to be relevant and significant. Changes of verb and/or of mood give evidence of the three different types of rapport that have been foregrounded by our data; additionally answers beginning with a repeat verb show a greater degree of agreement between participants with respect to the matter at hand. In effect, data has shown that the selection of a different verb may imply that:

a) the interviewee is going to introduce a new insight and a different perspective to the topic, or add additional information without necessarily disagreeing with the interviewer;

b) change of verb and or mood may show reluctance or unwillingness to comply with the interviewer's request for information and give indication of the introduction of a new topic, or

c) change of verb may represent a blatant refusal to comply with the interviewer's request and thus a challenge to the topic proposed.

5. Conclusions

This study has permitted us to identify contextual and interactional features of radio interviews and to determine how and to what degree they bear upon the overall effect of the communicative event. It has also shown how these aspects of dialogue depend on the changing roles assumed by both the interviewer and the interviewee, that interactants may adopt different roles and postures, and that these strategic decisions bring about chain reactions affecting the rights and obligations of the interlocutors. The microanalysis has revealed the resources used and the lexico-grammatical choices made to enhance, maintain and reduce rapport in the communicative genre under study. Moreover, it has provided new evidence to further support the statement that spoken language is the overt form into which and from which covert thoughts unfold in interaction.

References

Alber, J./O'Connel, D./Kowal, S. (2002): Personal perspective in TV news interviews: In: Pragmatics. 22/3, 257-271.

Brown, P./Levinson, S. (1987; ^{2}1990): Politeness. Some universals in language usage. Cambridge: Cambridge University Press.

Spencer-Oatey, H. (ed.) (2000): Culturally speaking. Managing rapport through talk across cultures. London, New York: Continuum.

Kamila Karhanová

Rhetorical questions in polemical media dialogue

1. Introduction

The rhetorical question ranks among those figures of speech that are the most widely used: it is to be found in poetry, in the Bible and in ordinary conversation, in conjugal disputes or in political polemics. On the other hand, the rhetorical question – at least as far as I know – is not one of those figures of speech to which much attention is paid in literary theory or linguistics, it seems to be regarded as a banal phenomenon of little interest to researchers. Dealing in my dissertation with the issue of rhetorical questions in media dialogues, in particular those involving political argumentation, I find this phenomenon on the contrary to be very complex and by no means unproblematic. Of the many aspects which this subject includes I focus above all on the following issues: How can the participants in a dialogue recognise that an utterance *is* a rhetorical question? What reactions to such utterances are possible and which ones are actually selected by the participants? What are the functions and effects of rhetorical questions in this genre of dialogue?

2. Defining "rhetorical question"

To define 'rhetorical question', literature refers to its answer or, to be exact, to the hypothetical answer to a rhetorical question. For instance, Lausberg's *Handbuch der literarischen Rhetorik* (1960, p. 379, §767) says that a rhetorical question is a question to which no answer is expected:

> Die *interrogatio* ist der Ausdruck eines gemeinten Aussagesatzes als Frage, auf die keine Antwort erwartet wird, da die Antwort durch die Situation im Sinne der sprechenden Partei als evident angenommen wird.

Other definitions do not mention the speaker's expectations, merely observing – as a popular handbook *Persuading People. An Introduction to Rhetoric* by the Cockrofts (1992) does – that the answer to this question "*is by implication obvious*" (p. 157). Certain more detailed definitions, especially those in grammar books, specify the obviousness of the answer: a rhetorical question suggests or implies an emphatic contrary assertion. As regards this semantic aspect, I have found a more precise explanation in *Mluvnice angličtiny na pozadí češtiny* (*Grammar of English compared with Czech*) by L. Dušková. In the context of yes/no questions the author says:

> the rhetorical question is characterised by its inverse relation of positive and negative to the reality asserted or denied. A positive rhetorical question denies something emphatically, a negative rhetorical question asserts something emphatically. (p. 316)

As for wh-questions, the author goes on:

> The answer to a rhetorical wh-question is evident from the situation. An affirmative rhetorical question usually implies an answer with a negative universal quantifier (*Who could have known*? *Nobody could have known*.). A negative rhetorical question implies, more often than not, an answer with a positive universal quantifier. (p. 326)

Another constitutive feature of a rhetorical question is its function. Individual definitions differ as regards the emphasis they put on it: for some it is the main definitional feature, for others an additional characteristic. The functions typically attributed to a rhetorical question are: emphatic assertion, persuasion of the hearer, or an appeal to him by means of emotions. In short, it has an expressive function from the speaker's point of view and a persuasive function from that of the hearer. One of those who define a rhetorical question principally by its possible functions is the Roman rhetorician Quintilian. He starts his explanation in his *Institutio Oratoria* thus: "an interrogative becomes a figure of speech, then, if we resort to it not in order to learn something, but to assail our adversary" (p. 401). Then he lists other functions or effects of this figure, observing among others: "This figure has many nuances; after all, it will do as well for indignation [...] as for astonishment." Despite the fact that Quintilian's definition may sound less "scientific" compared with the modern definitions, I find his formulation about "assailing our adversary" to be very apt and directly applicable to analysis of the rhetorical question in the genre of polemics.

There are also definitions which identify the rhetorical question with any indirect speech act in the form of interrogative, hence, according to these definitions, even a polite request formulated as a question, such as "*Could you pass me the salt, please*?", is counted as a rhetorical question. This extension of the concept may be logical from some points of view, but it is unhelpful in an analysis of polemics.

Although I am not assuming that I can arrive at any strict definition of rhetorical question, because "this figure has many nuances", some interrogative forms used as an indirect speech act can – for the purposes of my analysis – be excluded from the very outset. Polite requests in the form of a question are one such type of indirect speech act, and formulae used in order to announce a piece of news in conversation, such as "*Did you know that Jim has got married?*" (meaning "*I'd like to tell you that Jim has got married, unless you know already*"), are another type that I shall ignore. The reason I would not subsume these types of utterances under the concept of the rhetorical question is, among others, the different attitude of the speaker to his/her audience in these types of speech act. Whereas requests or polite phrases are a means of toning down, or what has been called hedging, that is, the speaker is showing consideration for his/her partner, by using a rhetorical question the speaker is "assailing his adversary", as Quintilian puts it. This adversary may be either a present hearer, a direct participant in the debate in progress, or an absent, even merely potential opponent; but whether real or purely hypothetical, some sort of adversary is always implied by the rhetorical question.

Now, having run through what some authorities say, let us go back to the TV political debates to examine some exchanges that I have culled from them and consider to be rhetorical questions or at least, say, candidates to be considered such.

3. Rhetorical questions in televised political debates

3.1 "Was that just a rhetorical question?"

I will begin with one exchange from a Czech TV debate whose participants were negotiating whether an utterance was or was not a rhetorical question. The programme where this sequence took place was called *Arena*. It involved – as a rule – an anchorman, one main guest sitting apart on the "hot seat", several other guests standing at lecterns, who were to act as opponents of the main guest, and a small audience. Viewers were invited to participate in the programme via a telephone poll, voting yes or no to a question encapsulating the guest's main contention. The topic discussed in the programme in question was the possible introduction of positive discrimination in favour of the Roma in the Czech Republic, especially in the education system, and the main guest, Emil Ščuka, chairman of a Romany political party, was advocating this idea. At the beginning of the programme he was allotted three minutes in which to sum up his case. The conversation proceeded as follows (*A* stands for anchorman, *S* for Mr. Ščuka., *Au* for audience. The original Czech text is given first –

the lines marked C,[1] followed by an English translation,[2] marked E, on the following line. Non-relevant passages are omitted between slashes):

(1) Arena 1, Czech television, 7. 1. 1998

1.C	A:	/.../ nuže v tomto okamžiku máte tři minuty na to, abyste vysvětlil svůj názor na
1.E		*/.../ well at this moment you have three minutes to explain your opinion on*
2.C		pozitivní diskriminaci, <u>proč si</u> myslíte, že určité uplatnění, jistých prvků
2.E		*positive discrimination, <u>why</u> do you think that some application of certain elements of*
3.C		pozitivní diskriminace, by u nás v České republice mohlo mohlo být pozitivní? prosím,
3.E		*positive discrimination could be positive here in the Czech Republic? please,*
5.C	S:	/.../ a domnívám se, že <u>veřej</u>nost pak eh <u>přij</u>me i tuto výhodu za svou,
5.E		*/.../ and I believe that the public will then uh <u>accept</u> this advantage too as their own,*
6.C		protože bude vědět, že <u>jednou</u> se to společnosti vrátí. vzdělání, které investuje
6.E		*because they will know that <u>one day</u> it will be given back to society. the education they invest*
7.C		do nás, pak se může samozřejmě eh (.) pro celou společnost nějakým způsobem eh
7.E		*in us, afterwards can of course uh (.) for the whole of society somehow uh*
8.C		vyj- ( ) ozřejmit. takže <u>já</u> dávám spíše takovou otázku, myslíte si že, pokud budeme,
8.E		*ex- ( ) become apparent. so I would rather ask a question like this, do you think that, if we,*
9.C		investovat do vzdělání, pokud budeme mít zvýhodnění ve vzdělání, a tím pádem
9.E		*invest in education, if we are given some preferential treatment in education, and thereby*
10.C		i ve státní ((gong)) správě, že je to zvýhodnění jenom pro Romy? nebo je to
10.E		*also in the state ((stroke of the gong = the end of the allotted time)) administration, is it an*
11.C		zvýhodnění pro nás pro všechny? pro celou společnost.
11.E		*advantage only for the Roma? or is it an advantage for us all? for the whole of society.*
12.C	A:	..děkuji pane doktore, to byla jenom řečnická otázka? předpokládám. tady zaznívá
12.E		*thank you Doctor, was that just a rhetorical question? I suppose it was. I can hear*
13.C		takový [potlesk]
13.E		*sort of [applause here,]*
14.C	Au:	[((slabý potlesk))]

---

[1] The trancription conventions used in the extracts are following:
    ?   rising intonation
    .   falling intonation
    ,   continuing intonation
    :   lengthening of the previous syllable
    (.)   a very short, still audible pause
    (..)   a longer pause,
    (...)   a long pause
    vyj-   a cut-off of the prior word or syllable
    (toto byla jenom)   items enclosed within single parentheses are in doubt
    ( )   no words could be distinguished in the talk enclosed within single parentheses
    ((gong))   in double parentheses there is a comment by the transcriber
    <u>jednou</u>   underlining indicates emphasis
    [ ]   the onset and the ending of simultaneous talk of two speakers (overlap)
    =   subsequent utterance follows without an audible pause (latching on)
    /.../   omitted passage

[2] The English translations of the TV debates are only approximate. They are intended to imitate the structure of the Czech sentences, not to be idiomatic English equivalents.

14.E	[((*weak applause*))]
15.C A:	[trošku,] tak, děkuji. eh: ta otázka na které sme se dohodli pro televizní
15.E	[*a bit*] *so, thank you. uh: the question we have agreed upon for the television*
16.C	diváky do ankety samozřejmě platí, (toto byla jenom) řečnická otázka na
16.E	*viewers for the poll of course remains in force*, (*this was just*) *a rhetorical question as a*
17.C	závěr vašeho úvodního proslovu. nuže, vážení televizní diváci, pan doktor Emil Ščuka
17.E	*conclusion of your opening speech. well, dear television viewers, Dr. Emil Ščuka chairman*
18.C	předseda Rómské občanské iniciativy vás přesvědčoval, a bude nadále přesvědčovat o
18.E	*of the Romany Civic Initiative has been persuading you and will go on persuading that in*
18.C	tom, že v zájmu odstranění diskriminace je třeba Romy po určitou dobu, a: v určitých
18.E	*the interest of abolishing discrimination it is necessary to give preferential treatment to the*
19.C	situacích zvýhodňovat. ano, nula šest /.../ a my se do toho pustíme,
19.E	*Roma for a certain period and under certain circumstances. yes zero six /.../ and let's get on*
20.C	dámo a pánové, kdo prosím začne? paní senátorka?
20.E	*with it, madame and gentlemen, who will start, please*? (*Mme*) *Senator*?

After Ščuka had finished speaking (l. 11), the anchorman, in his subsequent turn, expressed a degree of uncertainty about the function or communicative force of the closing part of the guest's speech: "*was that just a rhetorical question?*" (l. 12). This reaction shows that there was an ambiguity here and that the linguistic form had not been sufficient to distinguish a rhetorical question from a genuine one, or from an utterance with some other communicative force. What, then, led the anchorman to conclude eventually (l. 16-17): "*this was just a rhetorical question as a conclusion of your opening speech*"?

Taking into consideration what we know about the inverted polarity of a rhetorical question and its implied answer we could compare the closing utterance of Ščuka's speech with the intent of his preceding argumentation and ask whether there was an obvious answer. But the anchorman either did not do this or – if he did – he did not find it sufficient to ascertain whether the question had been genuine or merely rhetorical. A plausible explanation for this exchange may be sought – taking inspiration in the methods of Conversation Analysis – in its sequential context and in the overall structure of the debate. In his study *On questions and ambiguities in conversation* (1984) E. A. Schegloff treats the issue of the role linguistic forms and sequential features play in the recognition of an utterance as a question. According to Schegloff, a question form is not heard as a question "by virtue of the question form, but by virtue of the relevance of finding a question there if one can" (p. 46). Linguistic form is said to have merely a constraint-meeting power, not an action-determining power – a question form has the question function because its position in the structure of a dialogue allows for this interpretation.

Now, let us look at what the anchorman considers to be the relevant context for understanding Mr. Ščuka's utterance. The alternative to a rhetorical question, which the anchorman mentions explicitly in lines 15 and 16, is not just any genuine question, but a quite specific one – "*the question for the TV viewers we have agreed upon*". Thus having assured himself that the guest had not broken their previous agreement, he goes on to announce the wording of the "right question" for the viewers and to give them the phone numbers to vote on. Eventually, he invites the opponents to discuss the contention, using the phrase "*let's get on with it*". This phrase constitutes a borderline between the two parts of the programme: it closes the introductory part and opens the discussion proper. The introductory part consists of the several actions that the anchorman is to carry out: a brief explanation of the point at issue, an introduction of the main guest and his opponents, welcoming the studio audience, asking the main guest to sum up his viewpoint, and announcing the question on which the television audience is invited to vote. As the guest is delivering the utterance in lines 5-11, the last task left for the anchorman to perform is to announce the question for the viewers before he opens the discussion proper. In trying to disambiguate the communicative function of his partner's utterance he does not seem to focus on whether the answer to it is obvious or not. Instead, he follows the script of the programme for whose realisation he is responsible and expects that the other participants are willing to co-operate. He is focussing on his future action – announcing the question for the viewers – and accordingly, at the first moment, he understands his guest's words "*I would rather ask a question*" as related to this question, taking it as the guest's alternative to the question proposed previously. But he immediately rejects this possibility of changing what had been prearranged as not an action fit to occur at this juncture. The contextual feature relevant for identifying an utterance as "*just a rhetorical question*" is the position of the ambiguous utterance in the sequential structure of the dialogue – it simply appears at a point where the anchorman cannot allow any real questioning.

3.2 "Who wants to oppose me?"

The exchange from the previous example also seems to confirm those definitions, which claim that no answer is expected after a rhetorical question. In labelling the guest's preceding utterance as "*just a rhetorical question*" the anchorman neither answers it nor gives the floor to any of the guests' opponents to answer it, as would accord with his role as moderator. Nor is any comment made as to any emotive assertion of the kind said by some definitions to accompany rhetorical questions. So, judging by this example, we might conclude that a rhetorical question is not only a question, which does not require an answer, but that it is, in addition, an assertion which does not require any comment, any response to its content. But, when we move to another example from the same debate, an exchange that occurred in its middle part, during the discussion proper, the situation is different.

(2)   Arena 1, Czech television, 7. 1. 1998
      31.C S: =[takže tady] v podstatě by se mohla stanovit eh kvóta v opačném eh s:
      31.E   =[*so here*] *in essence a quota could be set uh in the opposite uh s: sense*
      32.C   smyslu slova, jako v podstatě mít nanejvýš pět procent rómských dětí ve

32.E	*of the word, like in essence having at most five per cent of Roma children in*
33.C	zvláštních školách. protože eh: kdo mně chce oponovat? eh pak eh: se
33.E	*special schools. because uh: who wants to oppose me? uh then uh: do you think*
34.C	domníváte, že teda my máme eh nutnost tam mít víc dětí? že naše děti ( )
34.E	*that thus there is uh a necessity for us to have more children there? that our children ( )*
35.C R:	= samozřejmě, protože ty děti mají, mají (v: eh:) ty ty maj tak špatnou průpravu
35.E	= *of course, because the children have, have (v: uh) they they have such a bad grounding*
36.C	předškolní, nechodí do mateřské školy, velmi zřídka. to prostředí v romských
36.E	*pre-school, they do not go to nursery school, very seldom the background in Roma*
37.C	rodinách je velmi často, ne-neříkám že u vás, ale velmi často je takové, že to
37.E	*families is very often, I don't don't say that in your case, but very often it is the case*
38.C	dítě nedostane do ruky tužku.
38.E	*that a child doesn't get a pencil in his hand.*

When speaker R, one of the opponents, enters the dialogue at l. 35, it might look – superficially and at first sight – like a seamless exchange, an answer following a question. The initial *of course* seems to be a signal of an affirmative response to the preceding question. The only disruptive element here is the fact that speaker S (Mr. Ščuka again) obviously had not completed his utterance in l. 34 – "*that our children*" is not a complete sentence; instead, speaker R took the floor. Taking into account the course of the argumentation that both precedes and follows this exchange, it becomes obvious that in effect speaker R is contradicting the assertions of speaker S, that is, the assertions made by Ščuka's two subsequent rhetorical questions: "*Who wants to oppose me?*" and "*Do you think that thus there is a necessity for us to have more children there?*" These questions imply answers (according to the description in Dušková's Grammar): "*Nobody dares (to) oppose me*" and "*There is no necessity to have more Roma than non-Roma children in so-called special schools*".[3] But these are not the answers that speaker R gives. Instead, giving a seemingly affirmative answer to the second of the two preceding questions, he in effect contradicts the negative assertion of the implied answer. In other words, he takes his partner's rhetorical question literally, as a genuine one, to challenge the assertion implied by this question. This example reveals the inherently ambiguous nature of rhetorical questions. As a consequence of this ambiguity the literal interpretation of any rhetorical question remains available to the participants. This literal interpretation may be unwitting, but – as in the case of this exchange – it may also be exploited for a particular rhetorical strategy in the handling of a rhetorical question, which is not mentioned in reference books and which I would call "challenging a rhetorical question".

Nevertheless, this is not the typical, expected reaction to a rhetorical question and the next example may help us to explain why. It comes from another televised debate of the same format, the same speaker S arguing about the same topic, namely Roma children in

---

[3] There is a net of so called "special schools" in the Czech republic originally meant for mentally retarded children. In fact, most of the pupils attending these schools are Roma children.

special schools. (S stands for Mr. Sčuka, M for Mr. Macek, a politician from the *Civic Democratic Party*, then the political party in government.)

(3) Arena 2, Czech television, 19. 5. 1999
    41.C S: devěd let o nic jiného od revoluce neusilujeme, jenom aby
    41.E   *nine years for nothing else since the revolution we have been*
    42.C zvláštní školy byly zrušené. nebo si myslíte? že sedumdesát procent našich dětí
    42.E *striving but that the special schools be closed down. or do you think? that seventy per*
    43.C mentálně postižených a imbecilů? že tam opravdu patří? nebo je to jenom jazyková
    43.E *cent of our children are really mentally retarded and imbeciles? that they really do belong*
    44.C bariéra a sociální hendikep? /.../
    44.E *there? or is it just a language barrier and a social handicap? /.../*
    45.C M: =[já s vámi (...)]] s velkou většinou toho co ste teď řekl zcela souhlasím,
    45.E =*[I with you (...)] with the vast majority of what you have said now I quite agree,*
    46.C až na to zrušení vlá-zvláštních škol, myslím si že zvláštní školy mají své místo
    46.E *except for the closing down of the pe-special schools, I think that special schools have their*
    47.C pro děti mentálně hendikepované, které /.../ ale souhlasím zcela s vámi
    47.E *place for mentally handicapped children who /.../ but I do agree with you, and it would*
    48.C a byl by to také biologický nesmysl, kdyby sedumdesát procent romských dětí m: patřilo
    48.E *be also a biological nonsense, if seventy per cent of Roma children did so belong in special*
    49.C do: tedy zvláštních škol. je: pravdou jistě je to co říkáte, že to je otázka sociálního prostředí
    49.E *schools. it is true certainly that which you say, that it is a question of social environment*

As we can see from lines 42-44, Mr. Sčuka is again putting his case in the form of a chain of questions: "*or do you think? that seventy per cent of our children are really mentally retarded and imbeciles? that they really do belong there? or is it just a language barrier and a social handicap?*" What is different here is the other participant's response: speaker M assents to the preceding utterance of speaker S. Or rather, he agrees with the negation of the propositions of the formal questions: if they were true, it would be a "biological nonsense". Of the examples I have dealt with so far this one perhaps corresponds most closely to the classical definitions of a rhetorical question: What the speaker puts in the form of questions is not understood as a question requiring an answer, but as an assertion requiring an assent, the meaning of this assertion being the negation of the literal meaning of these question forms. Speaker M expresses this agreement, but only partially, going on speaking in order to elaborate his view on the issue; it is more a concession than approval. The concession by speaker M: "*it would be a biological nonsense*" helps us to understand why Mr Sčuka had repeatedly formulated his views on special schools in the form of rhetorical questions. Asking "*Who wants to oppose me?*" in extract 2, speaker S is suggesting that his subsequent statement is based on presuppositions which nobody dares question: to say that most Roma children have to attend schools for the mentally retarded is tantamount to overt racism, which is unthinkable in this programme. So, challenging a rhetorical question may be tantamount to challenging presupposed shared knowledge and values, which the speaker, using the form of a question, is actually taking for granted.

Rhetorical questions in polemical media dialogue 211

3.3 "Not to be worthy of a reply"

Before I finish I would like to mention one more strategy for handling a rhetorical question in dialogue, or, in effect, two subtypes. My next example is not drawn from a TV debate, but from fiction. This is not to suggest that I am going to confuse examples from authentic communication within a specific polemical genre with literature. But, when reading fiction one often encounters dialogical situations that are in a way prototypical and may be instructive for understanding the phenomenon under investigation in other genres.

The dialogue in extract 4 comes from Dostoyevsky's novel *The village of Stepanchikovo and its inhabitants*. It takes place in the mansion of a local squire and his nearby village, the main character, Foma Fomich, being a sort of parasite who, pretending to be an unappreciated intellectual, abuses the squire's kindness and naivety. By emotional blackmail and hysterical scenes he takes control of the whole house and village. The extract describes one scene between him and the squire, who is referred to as "uncle", since he is the uncle of the narrator.

(4) "Who exactly were you to begin with?" he once enquired [...].
"What sort of person were you before I arrived? But I have kindled a spark of the divine fire in you, and it will glow in your soul forever. Have I kindled a divine spark in you or not? Answer me: have I, or have I not, kindled a spark in you?"
If the truth were known, Foma Fomich did not know himself why it was that he had asked such a question. [...]. Uncle's silence offended him and he had to insist on an immediate answer.
Uncle hesitated, hummed and hawed, and did not know what to say.
"May I remind you that I'm still waiting for a reply," continued Foma Fomich in offended tones.
"Mais répondez donc, Yegorushka!" the General's Lady chimed in, [...].
"I'm asking you: have you got this spark in you or not?" repeated Foma in a patronizing tone [...].
"Good heavens, I don't know, Foma," my uncle replied at last in despair [...].
"Very well! It follows that I'm not even worthy of a reply – is that what you wanted to say? [...]."

(Dostoyevsky, *The village of Stephanchikovo*, 40-41)

Foma Fomich repeatedly asks and varies the question "*Have I kindled a divine spark in you or not?*". By the definitions quoted above this is a rhetorical question, since the implied answer is both obvious and undoubtedly very emotive; the uncle takes it as such instinctively, not knowing what to answer. Nevertheless, Foma repeatedly insists that the uncle should answer. In the end he takes offence at not receiving an answer. So, if we accept that Foma's question was rhetorical, we have here another way of treating a rhetorical question in dialogue – and one which the literature does not mention: a speaker insists on his partner's voicing the obvious implied answer.

The last example, now again from a TV political debate, is not quite the same as that from Dostoyevsky, but both dialogues have something in common and one throws light on the other. (VK stands for Václav Klaus, then Czech Prime Minister, TH for Tomáš Halík.)

(5) V pravé poledne ("*At high noon*"), Czech television, 9. 7. 2000

1C VK: ( ) já hlavně bych prosil každého aby nemluvil za žádnou občanskou společnost.
1E ( ) *I above all I would ask everybody not to speak on behalf of any civil society.*
2C mluvte za sebe:. tomáš halík.
2E *speak on your own behalf, Tomáš Halík*
3C TH: (za občanskou společnost já to nikdy) -
3E (*on behalf of a civil society I never did it*) -
4C VK: mluvte za sebe plus mluvte za to své jedno sdružení které je někde posazeno v tom
4E *speak on your own behalf plus on behalf of the one association of yours which has its*
5C spektru názorovém,-
5E *position somewhere in the spectrum of views,-*
6C TH: [řekl sem tady že mluvím za občanskou společnost?]
6E [*have I said here that I am speaking on behalf of civil society*]
7C VK: [mluvme nepokoušejme se]
7E [*let's speak let's not try*]
8C TH: já mám na to názor, jako vy na to máte názor.
8E *I have my opinion on it, as well as you have your opinion on it.*
9C VK: nepokoušejme se nikdo ukrást si tu občanskou společnost,
9E *let's none of us try to steal the civil society for ourselves*
10C TH: ale to přece nikdo nedělá, v jakém, v kterém momentě sem si snažil tady ukrást
10E *but – come on – nobody is doing that, at what moment, at which moment did I try*
11C občanskou společnost? ( )
11E *here to steal civil society for myself?* ( )
12C VK: a pan pan pan předseda falbr.
12E *and mister mister mister chairman falbr.*

In this exchange, an answer to a question is sought repeatedly: "*have I said here that I am speaking on behalf of civil society*" (l. 6) and "*at what moment, at which moment did I try here to steal the civil society for myself?*" (l. 10) and the expected answer does not come. Instead, speaker VK addresses another participant, *chairman Falbr* (l. 12). If we took the questions in lines 6 and 10 as being rhetorical, this dialogue and that from Dostoyevsky would seem to be of the same type. What speaks in favour of this interpretation is the obviousness of the implied answers: speaker TH suggests: "*I have never tried to steal the civil society*." On the other hand, there is also something that does not accord with this interpretation: these would-be rhetorical questions follow the other partner's assertions which contradict its implied answers (ll. 4, 5, 7, 9). I think, therefore, that these questions allow for two kinds of answer: one is that described above as the implied answer to a rhetorical question, the other is giving evidence for prior contrary assertions. The first possibility would mean that speaker VK withdraws his assertions, making it tantamount to a sort of apology. But, speaker VK neither gives such evidence for his assertions, nor does he assent to the implied answers to the questions of his partner; he just ignores these questions completely. To use Foma Fomich's terms, speaker TH is "*not worthy of a reply*". This example shows that taking a question as a rhetorical one may entail different actions and may have different consequences: an obvious implied answer may be given as a signal of assent or concession either aloud or tacitly, but silence may also mean just ignoring the other partner's utterance. It facilitates a specific polemical strategy: to ignore one's partner in debate, avoid answering a question by taking a genuine question as a rhetorical one.

4. Conclusion

To sum up, a rhetorical question is an utterance of ambiguous nature and as a consequence its literal interpretation remains available to the speakers. It allows for various ways in which the participants might deal with it in the dialogue. The five examples we have examined suggest six possibilities: 1) a rhetorical question remains unrecognised and is thus unwittingly treated as a genuine question; 2) it is recognised, but ignored because it is seen as not requiring any response; 3) a recognised rhetorical question is followed by a concession; 4) a sufficient manifestation of the expected concession is not given by the partner and the speaker urges it; 5) a recognised rhetorical question is challenged, being deliberately treated literally in order to oppose the partner's assertions; 6) a genuine question is treated as a rhetorical one, being left unanswered and ignored so that the addressee can avoid having to give an unpleasant answer or make an unwelcome assertion.

References

Cockroft, Robert/Cockroft, Susan M. (1994): Persuading people. An introduction to rhetoric. London, Basingstoke: Macmillan.
Dostoyevsky, Fyodor (1983): The village of Stephanchikovo and its inhabitants. Transl. by Avsey, Ignat. London: Angel Books.
Dušková, Libuše (1994): Mluvnice současné angličtiny na pozadí češtiny [English grammar in comparison with Czech]. Praha: Academia.
Lausberg, Heinrich (1960): Handbuch der literarischen Rhetorik (Eine Grundlegung der Literaturwissenschaft). München: Hueber.
Quintilianus, Marcus Fabius (1985): Základy rétoriky [Institutio Oratoria]. Transl. by Bahník, Václav. Praha: Odeon.
Schegloff, Emanuel A. (1984): On some questions and ambiguities in conversation. In: Atkinson, Maxwell J./Heritage, John (eds.): Structures of social action. Studies in conversation analysis. Cambridge: Cambridge University Press, 28-52.

Adriana Bolívar

The president and the media in Venezuelan political dialogue

1. Introduction

Venezuelan political dialogue has gone through important changes since its first democratic government in 1958. For over forty years, every five years, only two major parties (Social Democrats and Christian Democrats) took turns at governing. This situation changed in 1998 when, as a reaction against the failure of these two traditional parties, Hugo Chávez Frías was elected president with the support of the party he himself founded (*Movimiento Quinta República*, MVR), and the votes of the people who saw in him some hope to correct the errors of the past: corruption, bad administrations, authoritarianism. Venezuelans gave their trust to him despite the fact that he had attempted a *coup* against the Social Democracy of Carlos Andrés Pérez in 1992. There was hope Chávez would take the country out of the deep economic and social crisis in which it had been left by previous governments. The high level of popularity he enjoyed immediately after the elections allowed his government to dissolve Congress, change the Constitution, change the name of the country (from *Venezuela* to *República Bolivariana de Venezuela*, Bolivarian Republic of Venezuela), and approve a number of measures that have given him control of the National Assembly, as well as of most Institutions. He reached power promoting a "democratic revolution" which, in his own words, has now become an "armed revolution" (Chávez 2003).

In this process, the media have had an important role, first to ease Chávez's way to power (Bolívar/Kohn 1999) and later to attack his policies, his "personalism" and his "authoritarianism". Radio stations, television channels, and newspapers have taken sides with the opposition, which includes a wide variety of organizations, Social Democrats, Christian Democrats, a sector of the Socialist party, and various organizations called *Sociedad Civil* (Civil Society). The government has taken hold of the National State Television Channel and uses it almost exclusively for the "revolution's" purposes. The President has been accused of instigating violence in his speeches, which are frequently followed by physical attacks on his opponents. Editorials with titles that allude to the consequences of his words are common, as in: *Verbobomba* ("*Bombverb*") (*Tal Cual*, 25th February 2003, 3 front page). Also, headlines call attention to his aggressive language and the legitimation of violence: *El lenguaje del Presidente ordena y legitima la violencia* (The President´s language orders and legitimates violence) (*El Nacional*, 2nd March 2003, front page). The participation of pro-government groups called *Círculos Bolivarianos* (Bolivarian Circles), created by the President himself, have been asked repeatedly "to defend the revolution", with the result that opponents' protests have been attacked with stones, sticks, guns and tear gas grenades. In 2002 more than 200 journalists were attacked and several newspapers as well as television channels (29) received some kind of aggression, from damage to equipment to bomb explosions (*El Nacional*, 3rd January 2003, p. A-1-2). Terrorist attacks have added to the violent scene. The building where the Commission for Negotiations and Agreement had its meetings was recently blasted. Ironically, this Commission is alternatively called the Commission for Dialogue by the government. The President has lost the popularity he initially enjoyed and democracy is now in danger of becoming a dictatorship, although, for some, Venezuela is already a "constitutional dictatorship" (Subero 2003).

In this context of violent political confrontation, *Aló Presidente*, Chávez's radio and television program, has had an important role. There is no record in Venezuelan history of such a program led by a president of the Republic. *Aló Presidente*, created in order to establish direct contact with the people and also to compete with the private media, is highly interactive and may last as long as seven hours. The opening words of the first program focus on its explicit purpose:

(1) For the first time in Venezuela a President of the Republic conducts his own program of opinion and popular participation with the only interest of listening to the people's claims. Venezuela talks directly with the head of government Hugo Rafael Chávez Frías. Welcome to the National Radio of Venezuela and all the country's radios that in this moment join the transmission".

(*Radio Nacional, Aló 01*, May 29, 199; my translation, A.B.)

Although the president now controls the State Television Channel, his program, his speeches, his public appearances, etc. frequently have to be transmitted by all radio and television channels *en cadena nacional* (national broadcast). This has been harshly criticized as power abuse and even fined, but he justifies this behaviour by arguing that private radio and television channels have been in the hands of the rich to the detriment of excluded groups for too long. The aggressive language he uses in his programs has partly contributed to extreme polarization and ingovernability (Bolívar 2001b, 2002; Montero 2003; Bolívar/Erlich/Chumaceiro 2003).

The permanent confrontation and violence associated with verbal aggression coming mainly from *Aló Presidente*, Chavez' close contact with Fidel Castro, his defense of Sadam Hussein's regime, and his reported association with Colombian *guerrillas*, do not help to give the impression that Venezuela's government is either peaceful or fully democratic. It is then relevant to examine the President's program with more attention, both as a type of political text and as a new style of politics in Venezuela.

In what follows I shall examine the features of *Aló Presidente* as a new genre, and will show how this genre changes in the dynamics of the political confrontation. To do so I shall adopt a critical discourse analysis perspective (Fairclough 1989, 1992; Bolívar 2001a) because *Aló Presidente* was born out of the political struggle for power and is itself a site for political confrontation. In a first approximation, I will rely on the ethnography of communication (Hymes 1974) to characterize the program as a communicative event. In order to define it in terms of genre and text type I will mainly follow the framework offered by systemic functional linguistics (Eggins 1994). While I am aware that studying genres implies describing goal-oriented and purposeful interactions in cultural and situational contexts considering their formal characteristics with respect to schematic structure, internal constituents, and register variables, I favour the view that "a genre implies not only a particular text type, but also particular processes of producing, distributing and consuming texts" (Fairclough 1992, 126).

2. The corpus[1]

At the time of writing this paper 142 programs had been issued. However, because they were too long and difficult to obtain, we concentrated our efforts on 60, which amounted to a total of 2.122.330 words. As it was important to consider how the program varied, it was agreed that we would examine in more detail a sequence of programs taking into account the length and the relevance of the political events covered. It was likely that the longer ones would have most of the constituent elements. Also, it could be anticipated that a particularly conflictive event might cause changes in the structure. So, we focused on number 100, the longest at the beginning of the year 2002, which took place before April 11th, when the country went through a very tense and dramatic time.

number	date	place	n. of words	moderator
100	17-03-02	National Park	52.576	yes
101	07-04-02	Miraflores	30.967	no
102	28-04-02	La Casona	21.429	no
103	05-05-02	Miraflores	23.278	yes
104	12-05-02	Fuerte Tiuna	25.687	yes

Table 1: *Aló Presidente* before and after 11th of April 2002

---

[1] I would like to express my gratitude to Estrella Camejo for her valuable help in the preparation and analysis of the corpus.

The description of the program was done in two stages. First we focused on *Aló Presidente* as a communicative event and did the analysis using the categories offered by Hymes' (1974). The acronym SPEAKING proved useful to understand the genre from a cultural angle. Then we looked for the genre/register/language relationship (Eggins 1994) and applied formal and functional criteria to discover the schematic structure and its constituents. The interpretation and explanation of the *raîson d' etre* of the genre and its dynamics has to be explained in terms of the knowledge about the Venezuelan social, economic, and political context (Madriz 2002; Hernández 2003; Bolívar 2001c, 2003).

3. The results

3.1 *Aló Presidente* as a communicative event

One of the main features of *Aló Presidente* is that the physical setting changes for every program, from the most important room in *Miraflores* to the poorest *barrio* (shanty town) in Caracas. As observed in the study of 60 programs, only some are broadcast from the presidential palace (*Miraflores*, only 13 out of 60) because they tend to move around the country and cover Bolivarian schools, airports, slum areas, historical places, islands, national parks, army headquarters, etc. The setting extends beyond the frontiers of Venezuela to include Guatemala, República Dominicana, the Vatican, Russia. The scene is carefully designed and adjusted to the setting and the situation. The President wears outfits that symbolically bring him closer to his followers such as sport shirts, jackets with the national flag colours, his parachuter's uniform, a red beret, varieties of hats, formal suits when necessary. In each setting he surrounds himself with national and/or religious symbols (for example, Simón Bolívar's portraits or images of Jesus Christ) and makes good use of the landscape when the program is outdoors. He also makes a point of drinking Venezuelan coffee in front of the cameras.

The participants in this program are varied and numerous. First, we find the participants in the program setting: the president himself, the whole or part of the Cabinet, special guests, international press journalists, governors and majors supporting the government, members of the *Movimiento Quinta República* party, technical assistants, etc. The guests may be national and/or international and there is no age limit, children are often received, they bring presents, songs and stories. These participants either stay in the setting with the president all the time, or come and go. Secondly, some participants join the program by phone, either at a national or international level. Thirdly, some participants join by microwave transmissions from mobile units in the city of Caracas. Fourth, some participate in videos which are varied as they may include replays of television programs, interviews, reports, and comments. The recognized ends of the program are mainly to talk with the people and/or give the people an opportunity to speak up their problems. The president and his guests in the program engage in conversations on various topics, particularly "the process", that is, the social and political changes advanced by the government. Depending on the occasion, the length of telephone conversations varies. These are often interrupted by narratives of personal experience by the President (his childhood, his life in the military academy, his experiences abroad, his comments on various things, etc.). Another purpose of *Aló Presidente* is to report on the national agenda (what the president and the government have done), to discuss national and international events, to comment on the events of the week, to make announcements of economic measures and other decisions such as new appointments and destitutions. Petitions from the people and their evaluations of events also find room in the program. The final aim seems to be to strengthen national and regional identities and cultures in the light of Bolivarian ideals, inspired by Simón Bolívar, the maximum leader of Independence in early XIXth century.

The speech acts are extremely varied and range in degree of politeness from very informal and affectionate with visitors and friends to highly threatening and insulting with opponents. They include greetings, which run all along the text, not just at the beginning of the program, as the presidents greets the participants when they arrive and also as he spots them in the public, or when he mentions somebody not present (he sends greetings). Congratulations are common and so are exhortations, appeals and insults to his opponents.

The key is mainly friendly but varies according to the situation. The president classifies the general mood as "spontaneous" (*Aló* 100). This spontaneity expresses itself in highly informal conversations, jokes, folk songs, improvisations of poems and songs. Also, in forms of address that indicate a close and intimate contact such as *hermano* (to men) and *mi amor*, my love, *mi vida*, my life, (to women and children). His manner changes when he addresses the opponents, either persons or nations. The opposition is addressed as *cúpulas podridas* (rotten cupules), *ilegítimos* (illegitimate), *escuálidos* (squalids), *oligarcas* (oligarchs), *traidores* (traitors), *neoliberales* (neoliberals), *fascistas* (fascists), *golpistas* (putchists), *conspiradores* (conspirators). The media are *mentirosos* (liers), *basura* (rubbish), *manipuladores* (manipulators), *terroristas* (terrorists) (See *Aló* 101 and also editorial of *Tal Cual*, 14th February 2003, front page).

While the channel is spoken, written texts are often present, mainly the new Constitution (approved by referendum in December 1999) whose reading the president permanently recommends. We also find the major works and letters of Simón Bolívar and extracts from famous novels and poems. Economic reports by the ministers, short stories, letters, emails are included.

The norms are those recognized by Venezuelan speakers from different regions in terms of varieties of Spanish and general rules of behaviour. However, the President often breaks the rules of "decorum". He often says things that irritate the media and shows little tact in his humorous comments. He is harshly criticized for this attitude (see for example *El Nacional*, Editorial *Ya Basta* ("Enough is enough"), 16th January 2001, p. A-6).

The program displays similarities with talk shows at some points when there are conversations and songs that may be entertaining for some. It also shares some features with news reports when the President presents the government's view on events. But it is, above all, a program whose aim is to spread the word of the "revolution" and to legitimize it. It is also a very expensive political text due to the changes of location and because it is on the air longer than any other radio or television program (Socorro 2003). It is not easy to label it as one class of text, partly because its aim is explicitly political and partly because of the great variety of genres that it contains. It is truly intertextual and interdiscursive and, in spite of its length and changes of setting and participants, it is possible to identify its generic structure, as we shall see in the next section.

3.2 *Aló Presidente* as text

Aló Presidente number 100 presented a good example of the sequence that the program generally follows. The elements identified in Table 2 below may all appear in one episode, roughly in that order. The announcement of the program by an announcer may be optional and the moderator may also be optional. The national agenda always goes first, although it may be preceded by a reminder or description of the location of the program. Each of the elements identified in Table 2 may in turn include a variety of other elements: comments by the president (obligatory) after every segment; narrations of personal experience of the president (obligatory) at any time in the sequence, songs by the president and other participants (optional), jokes (optional), announcements, preferably in the middle or end (obligatory). Table 2 gives an idea of what goes on in a step by step description of the program.

Aló Presidente 100: 52.676 words. Date: 17-03-02

1. Announcement of the program *Aló Presidente 100* (*Oficina Central de Información*).
2. Presentation of video (1) on first *Aló* Presidente (29-05-1999). This includes the presentation by the radio speaker, the President's greeting and the first telephone call to the program.
3. The President's greetings corresponding to *Aló Presidente 100*.
4. Conversation (1) between President Chávez and Vice-president Diosdado Cabello.
5. Telephone call (1) Haydée González, who made the first call to the first *Aló* in 1999.
6. Conversation (2) between president Chávez and vicepresident Diosdado Cabello.
7. Greetings of the President to the members of the Executive Cabinet accompanying him in the program.

8   Conversation (3) between president Chávez and Gastón Parra Luzardo, president of PDVSA (The national oil company).
9   Greetings of the president to a group of people attached to the government, to journalists of the international press, and some members of Bolivarian Circles of Galipán, also present in the program.
10 Presentation of video (2) *Misión cumplida* (*Mission accomplished*) by the moderator of the program.
11 Conversation (4) between president Chávez and Deputy Juan Barreto. The vicepresidente Diosdado Cabello intervenes.
12 Telephone call (2). 72 year old lady who previously phoned *Aló* n° 5 (27-06-99). Her daughter, Teresa, and a child also participate.
13 Telephone call (3). A Pemon princess who phoned during *Aló* n° 38 (16-04-00). Elena Gil (Pemon princess) sings a song.
14 Conversation (5) between Juan Barreto and president Chávez.
15 Telephone call (4). Salvador Perdomo from Mérida.
16 Microwave transmission from *Cota mil* (Motorway). Three women, two men and two children greet and congratulate the President.
17 Greetings from the president to children who are bringing flowers from Galipán.
18 Conversation (6) between Juan Barreto, president Chávez, Diosdado Cabello and Roberto Ruiz (moderator).
19 Microwave transmission from Petare. President talks with Stella Coluccio about the drums that Major José Vicente Rangel Avalos is playing (to celebrate the anniversary of *Aló Presidente*).
20 Telephone call (5). Richard Hidalgo from Caracas.
21 Telephone call (6). Barreto from Maracaibo.
22 Conversation (7) between Diosdado Cabello and president Chávez.
23 Video (2) from Ministry of Energy and Mines about oil prices.
24 Conversation (8) between president Chávez and the Minister of Energy and Mines, Alvaro Silva Calderón.
25 Microwave transmission from Petare. Conversation between Major Rangel Avalos and president Chávez.
26 Participation of the *soberano* (sovereign) introduced by Roberto Ruiz. Rafael Mendible speaks ("el soberano").
27 Conversation (9) between Parra Luzardo, president Chávez, Diosdado Cabello, Juan Barreto. Also participate Argenis Rodríguez and Jesús Villanueva, executives of PDVSA while Parras Luzardo was president of the corporation.
28 Telephone call (7). Alí Rodríguez Araque, Secretary General of OPEP from Vienna. 29 Microwave transmission from Nueva Esparta. President Chávez talks with the Governor Alexis Navarro Rojas, and a General (Gaviria). The conversation ends with a song *El chivato de la playa*, from Margarita (the Island).
30 Conversation (10) between José Vicente Rancel, presidente Chávez and Diosdado Cabello.
31 Video (3) on the dollar weekly changes after the economic measures of the government in 2002.
32 Conversation (11) between president Chávez and Francisco Usón Ramírez.
33 Conversation (12) between president Chávez, a boy called José Gabriel, a girl called Liseth, Diosdado Cabello and Juan Barreto.
34 Telephone call (8). President Portillo from Guatemala. Remembering *Aló Presidente* done from Guatemala.
35 Conversation (13) between Diosdado Cabello and president Chávez.
36 Video (4). Recapitulation of the one hundred *Aló Presidente*. Roberto Ruiz mentions all the places from where *Aló Presidente* has been broadcast.
37 Telephone call (9). Hipólito Mejías, president of República Dominicana, remembering *Aló Presidente* n° 54 (11-03-01) broadcast from Santo Domingo.

38 Video (5). Colombian public attorney apologizes to a Venezuelan pilot for having accused him of transporting arms into Colombian territory.
39 Comments of president Chávez on the video.
40 Video (6) where president Chávez is singing with Fidel Castro.
41 Telephone call (10). Fidel Castro from Cuba.
42 Conversation (14) with Liseth Rodríguez, who thanks FUS (Fondo Único Social) and the president for transplant for her 4-year-old son.
43 Telephone call (11) from Puerto La Cruz, Rafael Méndez.
44 Telephone call (12). Marlene Alfonso. Diosdado Cabello presents it as a call from "El Soberano".
45 Conversation (15) between president Chávez and navy captain Morales Márquez.
46 Conversation (16) between president Chávez, Diosdado Cabello and Luis Reyes Reyes.
47 Video (7) on the opinion of *el soberano* (the sovereign) on *Aló presidente*.
48 Comments by President Chávez.
49 Video (8). Luis Mariano Rivera, singer and revolutionary poet.
50 Closing of the program. The president says: "This has been a historic program. Thank you from Galipán, from Caracas, to Venezuela and the world".

Table 2: Schematic structure of *Aló Presidente* 100

In this program there were 16 different conversations, 12 phone calls, 8 videos, and several microwave transmissions. The mood was festive and aimed at displaying the strength of the government. The president sings, other participants sing. In Chávez's words:

(2) There have been expressions of joy all over the country, because this is a program of the people, a program with no precedent in the history of communication in Venezuela. A program where truths are told, a program respectful of ethics, a program that attends to needs and petitions. A program that informs the people on the management of the revolution. A program where we do political and economic analysis ... to you the owners of this revolution ...

(*Aló* 100, my translation, A.B.)

It is also reiterated that the program was created to confront the private media, as seen at the beginning of this program in his conversation with Juan Barreto, a deputy of the National Assembly:

(3) PRESIDENTE CHÁVEZ: yes, we were just starting the process of the political revolution, the first phase that was the political phase, ... and then we had the typical problem, one of the so many problems, well ... the media..
JUAN BARRETO: the competition of the media wouldn't let us work
PRESIDENT CHÁVEZ: (yes) the media, misleading information, "that dictatorship is coming, that communism is coming, that Human Rights negotiation is coming, that Chávez is going to impose a 20 years government, etc."... well ... and all this was born ...

(*Aló* 100, my translation, A.B.)

The happy mood of *Aló* 100 made the comments about the national media seem very mild. The President even congratulated two tabloids for publishing the news about the rating of the program. The president only has complaints against the international media, as there were members of the international press in the program:

(4) The European country that has treated the Venezuelan people and its revolution the worst through its media is called Spain. The Spanish media have spread lies and rubbish as other media in any other European country and this is a truth as big as the sun. This is why I insist on inviting the media to reflection and I am very glad that they are here, well, representatives of the Spanish press. We love Spain very much, its people, its institutions, their example, we are friends of the King, don Juan Carlos, of his President José María Aznar, etc.

(*Aló* 100, my translation, A.B.)

Things were quite different in *Aló* 101 when the attacks on the national media were frontal, together with attacks on PDVSA executives (*Petróleos de Venezuela*, Venezuela´s Oil Company) and CTV workers (*Confederación de Trabajadores de Venezuela*, Venezuela´s Workers Union) who called to a national strike. The tone is challenging. He refers to *Aló* as "the best program in the world, we have no competition" and celebrates that the program is *en cadena* and actually competing with *Globovisión* (one of the television channels leading the opposition).While the president greets the international press, he attacks the Venezuelan media (all supporting the strike). The expression *medios de comunicación* (media) was used 30 times with reference to the "tyranny of the media"; some of the epithets used were: "lies" (30 times), "manipulation", "subversive", "terrorists", "sowers of discord", "the voices of the rotten", and others.

In *Aló* 101 the President is angry with the strikers and angry with the media. The National Agenda is broken into three parts, there are only two videos and 4 telephone calls. One of these is from a journalist who supports the government and belongs to a Bolivarian Circle and another from a PDVSA worker who is not on strike. There was no contact with the people by phone and only two conversations in the setting. In the announcements section, seven PDVSA executives were removed after being insulted as PDVagos (*PDvaga bonds*), *subversive*, *saboteurs*, *the privileged*. Chávez assumes the role of referee and denounces:

(5) These elites have crossed the line, they have began to cross the line, then I announce the following: I announce the destitution of the following persons who have been removed from their posts, ENOUGH IS ENOUGH, the following persons: Eddy Ramírez, Managing Director of Palmaven until today. You are OUT! You had been given the responsibility of managing a corporation as important as Palmaven, a PDVSA member. Palmaven belongs to all the Venezuelans, so Mr. Eddy Ramírez, you are OUT, gentleman.

(*Aló* 101, my translation, A.B.)

In this *Aló* the leader exerts his maximum power. It is no surprise that the explicit pronoun *Yo* (I) is used *120* times, *mentira* (lie) *19*, *verdad* (truth) 23, to refer to his truth. He does not sing this time. He challenges the private media and goes *en cadena* so the whole country has to listen to his words and see him:

(6) We are *en cadena nacional*, I think, this is a very interesting point. We have decided to transmit this program in national radio and television broadcast because this is a vital theme for all Venezuelans and I am going to celebrate with a little coffee that they are bringing me, national *cadena* with coffee, Rafael (in the public) let's have a coffee? man? to celebrate this *cadena* OK? I love *cadenas* OK? Hugo *Cadenas* Chávez you can call me. I don't care. I accept that you call me Hugo *Cadenas*.

(*Aló* 101, my translation, A.B.)

Alo 102, the first program after his absence of power for 48 hours in the April events, opens with a short editorial on rectification and tolerance followed by the president's comment and greeting. No national agenda. No conversations with other participants. One telephone call from a 72 year old woman who declares herself *Bolivariana* and another from a man whose shop was looted and who is offered a credit to restart his business. Two videos, mainly to deny accusations against the president (who presumably ordered a military plan to repress the protesters that were asking for his resignation, and called Bolivarian Circles to defend the revolution "with whatever they had at hand"). Three important announcements were made, a 20% salary increase, the creation of a National Dialogue Committee, and the appointment of a new vice-president of the Republic. While this program was shorter than 101, and mainly devoted to appeals to dialogue, we found 37 mentions to the media. In this program the president contrasts the information and opinions collected by the *Aló* team with the information provided by private media. He appeals for a dialogue without lies and he says:

(7) We cannot get together to talk and tell lies. No. The Bolivarian Circles are not those armed bodies that some media or some sectors have described for several months. Bolivarian Circles are organizatios of social participation and this is indicated in the Constitution, they are fundamental elements, there will be many more, circles of neighbours, circles for sports, circles of friends, etc.

(*Aló* 102, my translation, A.B.)

While shorter than 101 and supposedly in a mood for peace and dialogue, the use of the pronoun *Yo* (I) goes up to 182 in *Aló* 102. *Aló* 103 and 104 show a return to the regular structure of *Aló Presidente*. However, this apparent "normality" hides the action that runs parallel in the world of the opposition, where thousands of opponents in the streets reject the "dialogue" proposed by the government. The president frequently ignores the events that take place while he is talking, such as the big *Firmazo* (the big Signing), when 3.200.000 signatures asking for a referendum were collected while he was in *Aló* 137 (2nd February 2003). Although this program lasted more than six hours, the president did not refer to this event once (*El Nacional*, 3rd February 2003, A-6), thus excluding from the dialogue those who do not follow him.

4. Conclusions

In the Venezuelan political dialogue, *Aló Presidente* has become a new genre with two major effects. On the one hand it encourages group cohesion as mainly party supporters have access to the program. On the other, it strengthens division as it attacks those who do not agree with the course given to the democracy. It may be argued that the media should not have taken a political role against the government, but it is hard to criticize the newspapers and television channels that have kept Venezuelans alert to the concentration of power in only one person. More than 18.000 PDVSA executives, technicians and workers have been fired by the government so far in retaliation to the strike. A bill to control "content" is being discussed by the National Assembly. *Aló Presidente* has become more and more aggressive and violence increases.

We have no doubt that the problem goes beyond the search for "dialogue" and moves into the world of political interests in which personalities, social and economic variables are in the center of it all. Nations have shown their concern for the president's "irritating rhetoric" (e.g. USA Department of State, *El Nacional*, 25th February, 2003, A-1), and the Venezuelan media as well as opposition protesters have reacted with a larger variety of insults and offenses to the president's verbal agression (Bolívar 2001b), but it is Hugo Chávez, chosen by vote in 1999, who has the responsibility of maintaining the democratic dialogue where all Venezuelans have the right to participate. The hope remains that both the president and the private media may soon accept that true dialogue starts by listening to the other and working together for the well being of all, particularly those who suffer the consequences of the confrontation.

References

Bolívar, Adriana (2001a): Changes in Venezuelan political dialogue: the role of advertising during electoral campaigns. In: Discourse and Society 12/1, 23-46.
– (2001b): El insulto como estrategia en el diálogo político venezolano. In: Oralia. 4, 47-73.
– (2002): Violencia verbal, violencia física y polarización en el diálogo político venezolano. In: Molero de Cabeza, Lourdes/Franco, Antonio (eds.): El discurso político en las ciencias humanas y sociales. Caracas: Fonacit, 125-136.
– (2003): La descortesía como estrategia política en la democracia venezolana. In: Bravo, Diana (ed.): Actas del primer coloquio del programa EDICE. Edición electrónica: www.primercoloquio. edice.org/Actas/actas.htm.
Bolívar, Adriana/Erlich, Frances de/Chumaceiro, Irma (2003): Divergencia, confrontación y atenuación en el diálogo político. In: Bolívar, Adriana (ed.): Revista Iberoamericana de Discurso y Sociedad. Monográfico: Discurso y Democracia en Venezuela. Barcelona: Gedisa, 121-151.

Bolívar, Adriana/Kohn, Carlos (1999): Diálogo y participación ¿Cuál Diálogo? ¿Cuál participación? In: Bolívar, Adriana/Kohn, Carlos (eds.): El discurso político venezolano. Un estudio multidisciplinario. Caracas: Editorial Tropykos y FHE, 103-115.

Chávez, Hugo (2003): Discurso en el Día de la Victoria Heroica. Acto de cierre del Encuentro Mundial de Solidaridad con la Revolución Bolivariana. 13 de abril de 2003 desde la Avenida Bolívar en Caracas. www.Globovision.com [16th april 2003].

Eggins, Suzanne (1994): An introduction to systemic functional linguistics. London: Pinter Publishers.

Fairclough, Norman (1989): Language and power. London: Longman.

Fairclough, Norman (1992): Discourse and social change. London: Polity Press.

Hernández, Daniel (2003): Populismo, neoliberalismo y bolivarianismo en el discurso político venezolano. In: Bolívar, Adriana (ed.): Revista Iberoamericana de Discurso y Sociedad. Monográfico: Discurso y Democracia en Venezuela. Barcelona: Gedisa, 11-36.

Hymes, Dell (1974): Models of the interaction of language and social life. In: Gumperz, John/Hymes, Dell (eds.): Directions in Sociolinguistics. The ethnography of communication, New York: Holt, Rinehart and Winston, 35-71.

Madriz, María Fernanda (2002): La noción de pueblo. In: Revista de la Asociación Latinoamericana de Estudios del Discurso 2/1, 69-92.

Montero, Maritza (2003): La retórica amenazante y crisis de gobernabilidad en Venezuela. In: Bolívar, Adriana (ed.): Revista Iberoamericana de Discurso y Sociedad. Monográfico: Discurso y Democracia en Venezuela. Barcelona: Gedisa, 37-56.

Socorro, Milagros (2003): Chávez nos cuesta entre 10 y 12 millones de bolívares diarios. In: El Nacional, 13 de abril, A-5.

Subero, Carlos (2003): Dictadura Constitucional. In: El Universal, 10 de febrero, 1-4.

Margareta Magda

Zur argumentativen Funktion der Gesprächsformeln im öffentlichen Dialog (am Beispiel der rumänischen Massenmedien)

1. Einleitung

In der vorliegenden Arbeit werden Aspekte des kommunikativen Verhaltens, insbesondere des persuasiven kommunikativen Verhaltens, am Beispiel des rumänischen öffentlichen Dialogs dargestellt. Dabei wird die Auffassung vertreten, dass jedem pragmatischen Sprachtypus bestimmte argumentative bzw. persuasive Merkmale zuzuordnen sind (vgl. Manu-Magda 1996).[1]

Nachfolgend wird auf die persuasive Funktion bestimmter Gestaltungsarten von gesprächseinleitenden Sprechakten, die im sozialen Dialog vorkommen, eingegangen. Ferner soll auf die persuasive Funktion bestimmter Gestaltungsarten von Anreden, die in den hier untersuchten Texten vorkommen, hingewiesen werden.

Quellen der hier exemplarisch wiedergegebenen Belege sind rumänische über die Massenmedien vermittelte Texte.

Es wird hier davon ausgegangen, dass die Argumentation eine Erscheinung der Kommunikation darstellt (Gilbert 1995, 127). Letztere stellt einen komplexen Akt dar, der den kulturellen und subkulturellen Symbolismus, die sozialen Aktanten und den lokalen Kontext integriert. Dies bedeutet, dass jedes Argument akzeptabel, geeignet oder nützlich sein muss, wenn es innerhalb einer Personengruppe unter bestimmten räumlichen und zeitlichen Bedingungen zur Anwendung kommt, oder aber es muss inakzeptabel sein, wenn diese Bedingungen nicht ganz erfüllt sind. Das Gespräch zwischen Menschen, die verschiedenen Kulturen angehören, weist eine Vielzahl von Organisationsstrukturen der Rechtfertigung auf. Diese Muster sind zum Teil mit kulturellen Werten und Einstellungen verbunden.

Sprachen sind generell nach der Vorliebe ihrer Teilhaber für deklarative (direkte) oder nicht-deklarative (indirekte) gesprächseinleitende Verhaltensweisen in unterschiedlicher Weise charakterisiert worden (in ihrer dialogischen Hypostase als explizit oder nicht-explizit bezeichnet).

---

[1] Das konstante und konventionelle Merkmal der Verbindung zwischen einer bestimmten lautlichen Sequenz und dem Kontext, ebenso wie die spezifischen Strategien zur Äußerung der pragmatischen Bedeutungen in einer beliebigen Sprache ermöglichen die Erfassung des *pragmatischen Typus* der betreffenden Sprache.

Ferner gibt es Unterschiede zwischen den einzelnen Sprachen je nachdem, ob ihre Teilhaber ein bestimmtes *persuasives Verhalten* in verschiedenen *rhetorischen Situationen* bevorzugen. Dieses Verhalten kann *explizit oder implizit* sein, sofern die Kommunikationsabsicht im Text ausgedrückt wird oder nicht (d.h. vermutet wird); es kann *rational oder emotional* sein je nach den objektiven oder subjektiven Argumenten der Gesprächspartner bei der Verteidigung des eigenen Standpunkts; es kann ferner *offensiv oder defensiv* sein je nach der Initiative des Sprechers während der Kommunikation; es kann schließlich mehr oder weniger *standardisiert* sein je nachdem, ob die Sprecher zu *kulturell spezifischen argumentativen Mustern* greifen oder nicht.

Die Einleitung eines Textes ist (ebenso wie der Schluss) eine »privilegierte rhetorische Stelle« (Zafiu 2001, 48). In ihrer dialogischen Form unterscheiden sich Sprachen auch nach der Neigung ihrer Sprecher zur Spitzen- oder Endstellung der Hauptinformation im Text unter Anwendung von spezifischen Mitteln, mit denen *argumentative Bedeutungen* ausgedrückt werden.

Sprachliche Elemente, die ihrem Wesen nach keine explizite thesenunterstützende Funktion erfüllen oder bei denen generell keine argumentative Funktion vermutet wird, bekommen häufig eine *argumentative Dimension*, und zwar unabhängig von der Absicht des Sprechers oder sogar von der logischen Gliederung der Aussage. Dies ist der Fall bei den gesprächseinleitenden Formeln, die von einer Sprache zur anderen variieren und für das kommunikative Verhalten der Sprecher der einzelnen Sprachen eine »diagnostische« Funktion besitzen.

In der vorliegenden Arbeit wird von der Annahme ausgegangen, dass die Art und Weise, in der die verbale Initiative im Gespräch wahrgenommen wird, aufschlussreich ist für die typologische Bestimmung der Sprachvarianten unter Berücksichtigung des jeweiligen Forschungsparameters. In der rumänischen Sprache (insbesondere in der südrumänischen Variante) lässt sich ein argumentatives Schema feststellen, das sich aus einem *expliziten*, *emotionalen*, *offensiven* persuasiven Verhalten ableitet. Dabei wird die Argumentation oft mittels einer Reihe von sprachlichen Elementen ausgeführt, die *semantisch vage* gekennzeichnet sind und damit der Äußerung eher ein Merkmal der *Ambiguität* als der Eindeutigkeit verleihen, so dass der Sprecher seinem Gesprächspartner die Aufgabe überlässt, den Sinn der argumentativen Vorgehensweise zu erfassen.

Zu bemerken ist die Orientiertheit der rumänischen Sprache an den Personen, die an der Kommunikationssituation beteiligt sind, zum Unterschied etwa zur deutschen Sprache, die typologisch durch Orientiertheit an Handlung und Kommunikationskontext gekennzeichnet ist (s. hierzu Thun 1979). Aus diesem Grund ist die rumänische Sprache sehr reich an sprachlichen Mitteln und Formen, die zum Initiieren von kommunikativen Beziehungen zwischen Menschen beziehungsweise zur expliziten Gestaltung der sozialen Kontakte mithilfe der Sprache dienen. Von diesen Mitteln, die stark konventionalisiert sind, sind hier das

System der Appellmittel, das Pronominalsystem, der Vokativ und die Interjektionen mit hortativer Funktion zu erwähnen. Hinzu kommt noch eine Klasse von Kontaktformeln, deren Funktion darin besteht, den Schock des offensiven Verhaltens des Sprechers zu mildern, etwa durch: *nu te supăra* [*sei (mir) nicht böse, nimm es mir nicht übel*]; *fii amabil* [*sei so nett*]; *fii drăguț* [*sei so lieb*]; *fii bun* [*sei so gut*] etc.

Im Vergleich zum Deutschen kommen in den rumänischen Äußerungen zahlreiche Wörter (Appellwörter) vor, die eine *Herausforderung* des Sprechers für dessen Dialogpartner zum Ausdruck bringen. Im Rumänischen gibt es ein interessantes Paradigma von appellativen Kurzwörtern, die dazu bestimmt sind, den bereits angeknüpften sprachlichen Kontakt mit dem Gesprächspartner zu erneuern, zum Beispiel dann, *wenn es sich um etwas Wichtiges handelt, worauf also mit großer Aufmerksamkeit geachtet werden muss*, oder wenn die Aufmerksamkeit des Gesprächspartners nachlässt. Solche Wörter haben folglich über ihre Appellfunktion hinaus auch eine *Betonung*sfunktion. Außerdem können sie auch eine zusätzliche Bedeutung der Bewunderung oder der Missbilligung erhalten.[2]

Rumänische Sprecher messen der Beharrlichkeit eine große Überzeugungskraft bei. Rhetorisch wird die Insistenz am häufigsten durch Wiederholungen oder durch eine spezifische Intonation der Kontaktpartikeln wiedergegeben.

Eng verbunden mit diesem typologischen Merkmal sind die grammatischen Ausdrucksformen des Vokativs im Rumänischen, ferner die besondere Neigung zum Gebrauch von Wörtern mit hypokoristischem Anredewert (*dragă, iubito, iubitule*), die in der Kommunikation produktiver sind als ihre deutschen Äquivalente (*mein Lieber, meine Liebe*).

In diesem Zusammenhang kann man noch feststellen, dass die Kategorie des Unpersönlichen vorzugsweise mithilfe der pronominalen Kurzform der zweiten Person Singular ausgedrückt wird (*nu-ți poți închipui* [*man kann sich nicht vorstellen*]) (vgl. Thun 1979, 200f.). Dies hat im Laufe der Zeit zur Stärkung der allgemeinen Bedeutung der zweiten Person Singular und sogar zu deren Grammatikalisierung in der Form *domnule*, bzw. als synkopische Variante *domle*, geführt (ursprünglich lediglich als protokollarische Anredeformel verwendet und nachträglich in *Merkmal der Orientiertheit des Sprechers an seinem Gesprächspartner* umgewandelt).

Dieses ganze besonders gut entwickelte System der Kontaktelemente im Rumänischen dient nicht nur zur Erfüllung der phatischen Funktion der Sprache, sondern es unterstützt auch die Verwirklichung der persuasiven Funktion der Sprache. Ein Beispiel: Während für

---

2   Schema der Appellpartikeln im Rumänischen (zit. nach Rusu 1959, 248, ergänzt von Thun 1979, 60) [unübersetzbar]: *mă* (m. f.) [Sg. Pl. --- *tu* --- *măi* (m. f.) ([m.f.] *bă/băi* --- *bre* --- (Sg. Pl.) *fa, fă, făi* (f. [Sg. Pl.]).
    Das Schema muss wegen der strukturellen und funktionalen Änderungen, die im Lauf der Zeit bei deren Positionierung während der Kommunikation eintreten, noch durchgesehen und ergänzt werden.

die rumänischen Sprecher, insbesondere für diejenigen im Süden des Landes, die *ungehemmte emotionale Selbstbehauptung* charakteristisch ist, pflegen die Rumäniendeutschen kulturelle Werte wie vor allem die Distanz und die Zurückhaltung gegenüber dem Gesprächspartner (vgl. Magda 2003). Dieses allgemein gültige typologische Merkmal des rumänischen sprachlichen Verhaltens ist heutzutage immer mehr und in übertriebener Form in Texten der Massenmedien, selbstverständlich vorwiegend in den gesprochenen Medien, anzutreffen. Dabei ist es oft schwierig, verbale Aggressivität und Höflichkeit voneinander abzugrenzen.

Dass der aktuelle journalistische Stil zahlreiche Elemente der mündlichen Ausdrucksweise übernimmt und volkstümliche oder salopp umgangssprachliche Formen schriftlich fixiert, ist eine Tatsache, auf die bereits wiederholt und banalisierend hingewiesen wurde; der mündliche Charakter ist eine der wichtigsten Innovationen, die bei uns in diesem Register nach 1989 sichtbar wurden. Dieses Phänomen stellt keinen Einzelfall dar; vielmehr verfolgen die Medien in vielen anderen modernen Kulturen eine solche linguistische Strategie, die zweifelsohne ihre Vorteile hat: Zugänglichkeit, Herausbildung eines Gefühls der Vertrautheit und der Komplizenschaft beim Publikum, Expressivität, Kompensation inhaltlicher Banalität durch Einführung von lexikalischen Überraschungen. Zu den spezifischen (und umstrittenen) Merkmalen der rumänischen Journalistik gehört jedenfalls eine äußerst starke Orientierung an der Mündlichkeit, die oft zum stilistischen Manierismus oder zur Vagheit der Ausdrucksweise, manchmal auch zur Vulgarität verleitet, ebenso wie die Tendenz zur Nichtanpassung des Stils an Thema und Situation; dies gilt auch für seriöse Pressebeiträge, die Informationen vermitteln oder politische Analysen pflegen. Die Mündlichkeit manifestiert sich sowohl auf der orthoepischen Ebene (unter Aufzeichnung des phonetischen Akzentes, der dialektalen oder ungepflegten Aussprache) als auch auf lexikalischer, syntaktischer und pragmatischer Ebene (vgl. Zafiu 2000).

Die Haupteigenschaft der rumänischen medialen Texte der Gegenwart ist also deren informelle, ungezwungene Ausdrucksweise, die gerade auch von Persönlichkeiten der »hochrangigen« Sphäre des politischen und/oder kulturellen Lebens (den sogenannten VIPs) verwendet wird. Hierarchische Unterschiede zwischen Gesprächspartnern werden in bestimmten (soziokulturellen und politischen) formellen Kommunikationskontexten bewusst verwischt, indem protokollarische Anredeformen absichtlich weggelassen werden (deren Markierung im Text durch verbale und pronominale Anredeformen, durch Grußformeln und Vorstellungsritual, durch gesprächseinleitende Formen und die appellative Art und Weise während des Dialogs erfolgt). Ziel dieser soziolinguistischen Nivellierung (d. h. der Durchsetzung des Egalitarismus) ist es, in die Intimsphäre der sozialen Akteure virtuell einzudringen, sich Anspruch auf deren Beurteilung anzumaßen, Sympathie oder Antipathie bei den Massen zu bewirken, Gegner durch Verachtung zu vernichten.

Der vorliegende Beitrag setzt sich nicht zum Ziel, eine Übersicht über die im derzeitigen rumänischen politischen Diskurs anzutreffenden Merkmale der informellen Sprache zu präsentieren. Es wurden hier hauptsächlich diejenigen Elemente ausgewählt, die kommunikativ für den *pragmatischen Typus der rumänischen Sprache* spezifisch sind (vgl. Manu-Magda 1996): die Art und Weise, wie die verbale Initiative im Gespräch wahrgenommen wird (zu erwähnen ist hier etwa die Vorliebe für den »exklamatorischen« Stil zu Beginn des Gesprächs); die Tatsache, dass rumänische Sprecher eher am Gesprächspartner und weniger an der Kommunikationssituation orientiert sind (worauf z.B. die Präferenz für *Interjektionen* und *hypokoristische Anredeformen* zurückzuführen ist).

Nachfolgend sollen die bisherigen Ausführungen an einem rhetorischen Sonderfall exemplifiziert werden. Es handelt sich um eine TV-Talk-Show, genauer gesagt, um Fragmente aus zwei Tucă-Shows vom 17. und 18. März 2003, in denen der »Krieg im Irak« thematisiert wurde. Außer dem Moderator Marius Tucă (T)[3] treten in beiden TV-Sendungen bekannte Intellektuelle des aktuellen rumänischen politischen und kulturellen Lebens auf:

Erste Sendung: Florin Constantiniu (FC), Historiker; Emil Hurezeanu (EH), Journalist; Octavian Paler (OP), Schriftsteller; Cristian Pârvulescu (CP), Politologe.

Zweite Sendung: Mircea Dinescu (MD), Schriftsteller; Cornel Nistorescu (CN), Chefredakteur der Tageszeitung »Evenimentul Zilei«; Alin Teodorescu (AT), Direktor des Meinungsforschungsinstituts.

Die hier analysierten Texte lassen sich zunächst einmal generell durch den stilistischen Kontrast charakterisieren, der bei der Verwendung von Ausdrücken des mündlichen Registers einerseits in einem durch eine Amts- und Gelehrtensprache dominierten Kontext und andererseits im Verhältnis zum Diskussionsthema sichtbar wird. Die übermäßige Verwendung von familiären Ausdrucksweisen verlagert den Schwerpunkt von der Information zur sprachlichen Expression, wobei der Text inkonsistent wirkt (s. Zafiu 2001, 51).

---

[3] Mircea Vasilescu hat dieser umstrittenen Gestalt der rumänischen Medien nach der Wende einen Zeitschriftenaufsatz in *Dilema* vom 6.-12. Dezember 2002 gewidmet, in dem Marius Tucă folgendermaßen beschrieben wird:
»Mit Hosenträgern und Mikrophon à la Larry King [...] ist Marius Tucă zu einer populären Gestalt geworden und hat den ›Anspruch auf einen Namen‹ erworben, der sonst den Stars vorbehalten ist: [...] Marius Tucă hinterlässt bei vielen TV-Zuschauern den Eindruck, dass er ›einer von ihnen‹ sei, ein Gefühl der Vertrautheit als Grundlage der Mechanismen zur Identifizierung des Publikums mit den modernen Helden des TV-Monitors. ›Marius-Tucă-Show‹ beinhaltet in spezifischer Weise eine Seite der Transitionsgeschichte, wo geschrieben steht, wie schwer wir gelernt haben, den Dialog miteinander zu führen, wie schwer es ist zu moderieren oder ›sich moderieren zu lassen‹«.

2. Äußerungsmittel für den Impuls zur Gesprächsführung

Festzuhalten ist, dass die Sprecher immer wieder zu den oben genannten Formen des adressierten Diskurses greifen, die für die Wahrnehmungsart der gesprächseinleitenden Initiative (etwa die offensive oder defensive Einstellung) und für die einzelsprachlichen Äußerungsmittel der *Gesprächsführung* kennzeichnend sind (so wie sich etwa bei den Rumänen und Lateinern im Allgemeinen ein stark dialogischer Impuls beobachten lässt.)

Die große Anzahl solcher Elemente verleiht der Äußerung ein erhöhtes Maß an *Subjektivität, die vor allem durch Emotionalität manifestiert wird*: Die Autoren können sich nur mühsam beherrschen beim Äußern der eigenen Aufregung, Sympathie und Antipathie, und es gelingt ihnen nur selten, das Gleichgewicht der Professionalität, den neutralen informativen Ton zu wahren. Die Persönlichkeit jedes einzelnen Sprechers ist hypertrophiert, jeder Sprecher ist verlockt, Urteile zu fällen, Lehren zu erteilen und daran zu glauben, dass seine Meinung von größtem Interesse ist für seine potentiellen Gesprächspartner (Zafiu 2001, 41).

> Fragmente aus der Tucă-Show vom 17. März 2003 (alle Beispiele wurden so textgetreu wie möglich ins Deutsche übersetzt):
>
> CN: *Domle* (mein Herr/meine Herren/Mensch), alle Schriftsteller waren gegen den Krieg!
>
> MD: Lass mich meine Meinung sagen, lass mich gegen den Krieg sein! Ich hab dir etwas gesagt, was dich eigentlich beeindrucken sollte, und zwar dass ich mir Filme anschaue über ... von Discovery, über ... den ersten Weltkrieg, den zweiten Krieg, und ich sehe, dass dort Bomben fallen, und ich fragte mich, »*Domle*/ Mensch, was haben die denn gemacht, *domle*/ Mensch, wie so ist man so weit gekommen?« [...]
>
> CN: Ja. Was glaubst du, warum protestiert die rumänische Gesellschaft nicht?
>
> MD: Die rumänische Gesellschaft schläft leider seit einigen Jahren, die Zivilgesellschaft schläft! Tut mir leid, dass ich's sagen muss: bei uns ist's /*chestia asta*/ nun mal so, dass man guten Eindruck macht, /*dă bine*/ wenn man pro Amerika ist; so wie alle Parteibeamten, alle Stasi-Leute für die Amerikaner sind, da muss man natürlich mitmachen, das macht guten Eindruck, /*dă bine*/, denn sonst wäre man wie einer von Vadims Leuten! Geht mich nicht an, *bre* [unübersetzbar]! Lass mich sagen, was ich davon halte! /*dă bine*/ Was hat man vom guten Eindruck gehabt, als der ... der pfiffige Kerl von der NATO anrüchige /*făcea mânării*/ Geschäfte in Rumänien gemacht hat ..., er hat gesagt »*Domle*/ mein Herr, die von der NATO wollen jetzt die Geschichte mit der Stasi nicht mehr wissen /›*Domle*, pă NATO nu-l mai interesează? chestia cu securitatea*‹ /...«. Wie war sein Name? ... Sag mal, ... der, der Geschäfte gemacht hat mit ...
>
> CN: Wenn du zahlst, sag ich dir, wie er heißt.
>
> MD: *Măi* [unübersetzbar]! /*Măi*! Eu spun o chestie foarte serioasă! Dă bine, mă! Dă ... refacerea imaginii*/ Ich red jetzt von seriösen Dingen! Macht guten Eindruck, *mă* [unübersetzbar]! Es heißt Wiederherstellung des Image ... . Egal, ob man bei der Stasi war, ob man Parteibeamter war, [den Hochschulabschluss] in Moskau gemacht hat, man soll ja auf der Seite der Amerikaner sein: »Wir sind für die Amerikaner!« /»*Vezi-ţi, domle, de bătătura ta, băi*«/ *Domle*/ Mensch, kümmere du dich, um deine Sachen, *băi* [unübersetzbar]! Rumänien hätte das bleiben können, worauf wir so stolz sind, und zwar eine Latein-Insel in einem slawischen Meer, wir hätten eine saubere Insel bleiben können, damit die nach Rumänien kommen und ihre Wunden lecken! ...[...]

Zur argumentativen Funktion der Gesprächsformeln 233

T: *Domnule/* mein Herr, wie hätte sich Rumänien benehmen müssen, was meinen Sie? [...]
MD: Rumänien hätte unterstützen sollen, hätte sagen sollen »*Domle/* meine Herrschaften, wir wollen in die NATO, wir mögen die Amerikaner sehr, aber wir wollen nicht ..., wir sind zu klein, als dass wir uns in diese Geschichte /*chestie*/ einmischen könnten ...«.
T: Aber wir haben uns nicht eingemischt, *domle/* mein Herr! ...
MD: Doch! ... Wenn man Militärstützpunkte vergibt, eigene Müllmänner, Gasriecher dorthin verschickt ... achtzig sind unsereiner achtzig ... . Hab doch gleich gesagt, ich will nicht, dass in zwei Wochen ... Gott behüte! Die werden doch Fragen stellen ... »*Domnle/* he du, aus welchem Land kommst du denn?« »Aus Rumänien, Caracal.« »Was willst du denn eigentlich hier bei uns, *bă* [unübersetzbar]? Wer hat dich denn hierher geschickt?« »Tucă hat mich geschickt, geschickt hat mich Nistorescu und Iliescu (!) [...]
AT: Hört auf, *bă*! ...
MD: Bei Caragiale heißt es: /»Ce să caute neamțu în Bulgaria?« »Ce cautǎ, *bă*, românu în Irak, *băi*?!«/ »Was soll der Deutsche in Bulgarien?« »Was soll, *bă*, der Rumäne im Irak, *băi*?!«

3. Klischees der Mobilisierung und Demobilisierung (*hai* und *stai*)

Bei der Feststellung des persuasiven Typus stellt sich auch die Frage nach den linguistischen Kriterien zur Abgrenzung und hierarchischen Gliederung der *signifikanten rhetorischen Episoden*. An dieser Stelle soll kurz auf die Funktion von *hai* und *stai* hingewiesen werden, die im Rumänischen den Wert von Interjektionen haben.

Im Text werden zahlreiche Interjektionen verwendet, die die Äußerung eines Wunsches oder des Willens wiedergeben: *hai*, *haide*.

Fragmente aus der Tucă -Show vom 17. März 2003:

a) *hai*

MD: [...] wenn die Amerikaner zu den Zeiten von Ceaușescu gekommen wären und gesagt hätten »*Domle/ Leute, seht mal*, ihr habt einen Diktator. Wir werden heute das Wohnviertel ›Primăverii‹, ›Casa Poporului‹ (das Volkshaus), die Brücke über der ..., die Brücken über der Dâmbovița bombardieren, so, seid ihr damit einverstanden?« Ich hab ja auch Domizilarrest gehabt. Nur wenn ich blöd gewesen wär, hätt ich's mir gefallen lassen. Nein, stimmt nicht, ich wär glücklich auf die Straße gegangen: »*Hai/ Komm*, wir wollen sehen, wie die Amerikaner uns bombardieren! *Hai/ Komm*, wir sollen sie empfangen!«
T: Sagen Sie, was Sie glauben! [...]
AT: Ich sag ja, was ich glaube. *Haideți/ Lasst mich euch sagen*, was ich glaube: ...[...]
T: *Haide ... haide/* wir wollen weiter reden über die Involvierung Rumäniens in den Krieg und nicht nur darüber nach einer Werbungspause.
[Werbung]
T: Herr Nistorescu, *haideți/* bitte, Sie sind nicht dazu gekommen, Ihren Gedanken auszuformulieren.

Nach Graur/Avram/Vasiliu (1966, II, 426) »sind diese dem Imperativ bedeutungsähnlich, und diejenigen mit Anredefunktion sind dem Vokativ bedeutungsähnlich; sie weisen Merkmale des Vokativs und des Imperativs wie folgt auf: sie können im Satz isoliert vorkommen, sie werden mit einer eigenartigen Intonation ausgesprochen und sind zweckdienlich, wenn jemand angesprochen werden soll; deshalb können diese Interjektionen einen Vokativ oder einen Imperativ begleiten«; die gleichen Erscheinungen lassen sich in südrumänischen Dialekttexten beobachten. Im Kontext haben die angeführten Aussagen verschiedene Nuancen (s. hierzu die Definition in Coteanu/Mareş 1996, s.v.). Unter Umständen fügen diese Interjektionen der Kommunikation eine emotionale Nuance hinzu, die bedeutungsundifferenziert und dazu bestimmt ist, die Zustimmung des Sprechers zum Gesagten auszudrücken und damit eine Behauptung, eine Verneinung oder eine Frage zu betonen oder zu verstärken (s. GA 1966, II, 425).

Wegen der großen Anzahl und Häufigkeit dieser Äußerungen wirken die jeweiligen Redebeiträge fast »aufrührerisch« und hinterlassen (in übertriebener Weise) den Eindruck, dass jeden Augenblick Ereignisse von grundlegender Bedeutung stattfinden.

Die exzessiv mobilisierende Rolle von *hai* beeinflusste jedoch auch die Entwicklung eines anderen, am Gegenpol befindlichen Elements desselben linguistischen Felds, mit dem die Funktion Tempoverlust bzw. Demobilisierung aktualisiert wird. Damit ist das Wort *stai* gemeint, das im Imperativ auch die Funktion einer Interjektion erfüllt: *Opreşte!* [*Halt!*] *Aşteaptă!* [*Warte!*]; (in Fügungen) *Stai să-ţi spun* (sau *să vezi*) = *lasă-mă să-ţi spun, ai răbdare, aşteaptă.* [*Warte, bitte, ich will's dir sagen, lass mich erzählen, lass mich (weiter) sprechen, Moment (mal), Augenblick (mal)*].

    Fragmente aus der Tucă-Show vom 17. März 2003:
    b) *stai*
    T: *Domule/ mein Herr*, wir müssen in die NATO!
    MD: *Stai puţin!/Augenblick mal!* Militärstützpunkte in Constanţa ...
    [...]
    CN: Nun, es ist mir nicht gelungen, den Vortrag des Militärstrategen Mircea Dinescu (!) zu unterbrechen ... Nach seiner Analyse also sieht's ja umgekehrt aus, man sollte eher für Bagdad sein.
    MD: *Stai măi/ Halt, măi*, ich bin nicht für, ich will nicht ... Saddam loben. Ich mein ja nur, dass die blöd sind ... die amerikanischen Führer. Das ist alles. [...]

Zum Unterschied vom temporeduzierenden Merkmal, das durch den Einsatz bestimmter Interjektionen der nordrumänischen Mundarten Äußerungen einverleibt wird (etwa durch *no, apăi, no apăi, eh, ehei*), wird durch *stai* eine plötzliche Demobilisierung zum Ausdruck gebracht und damit der kontinuierlichen Bewegung in von *hai* beeinflussten und geprägten Äußerungen entgegengewirkt. Das Aufeinanderfolgen von *hai* – *stai* nimmt für die Versprachlichung der minimalen syntagmatischen Interaktion im Rumänischen (Aktion-Reaktion) eine pragmatisch wichtige Position ein.

4. Äußerungsmittel der Verspottung, der Verachtung oder der Abschwächung des offensiven Schocks

Außer den oben genannten stark konventionalisierten Ausdrucksmitteln (Appellmittel, Pronominalsystem, Vokativ, Interjektionen mit hortativer Funktion) gibt es eine Klasse von Kontaktformeln, deren Funktion darin besteht, den Schock des offensiven Verhaltens des Sprechers zu mildern, etwa durch: *nu te supăra* [*sei (mir) nicht böse, nimm es mir nicht übel*]; *fii amabil* [*sei so nett*]; *fii drăguț* [*sei so lieb*]; *fii bun* [*sei so gut*] etc.

> Fragmente aus der Tucă-Show vom 18. März 2003:
> T: Wie hätten denn eigentlich sieben Verwirrte bloß kontrollieren können, ... ob der Irak biologische und Massenvernichtungswaffen hat? /*Haideți să fim serioși*!/ *Lassen wir doch den Spaß bei Seite*!
> FC: Herr Tucă, *entschuldigen Sie*, ich nehme an, ich bin ein ernster Mann, sonst hätten Sie mich nicht hierher eingeladen! [...]
> EH: Ja, Herr Professor, Sie reden immer von Legalität, und Herr Paler geht von konkreten Bezugspunkten aus, was anderes haben wir ja nicht.
> FC: Das ist, /*dacă vreți*/ *wenn Sie die Dinge so sehen*, die These von Titulescu. [...]
> FC: Aus humanitärer Sicht, /*dacă vreți*/ *wenn Sie die Dinge so sehen*, kann ich Ihren Standpunkt durchaus verstehen, aber als Historiker, der sich die Frage nach der Entwicklung des weltweiten Beziehungssystems stellt, nein, nein. [...]
> FC: Nun ja, das Gleiche haben wir auch jetzt.
> EH: Die Gegenwart ist doch anders!
> FC: /*Nu vă supărați*/ *Seien sie (mir) nicht böse*!
> OP: Das stimmt nicht, stimmt nicht ganz!
> FC: Derzeit wird die Welt ausschließlich von den Vereinigten Staaten dominiert ... [...]. Die Vereinigten Staaten konnten ja so viele andere Diktaturen hinnhemen!

Darüber hinaus gibt es aber auch zahlreiche Ausdrucksmittel (etwa Formen der informellen oder salopp umgangssprachlichen Ausdrucksweise), mit denen Spott und Verachtung geäußert werden als Mittel der emotionalen Argumentation, die den Gesprächspartner dazu bringen soll, eine bestimmte Handlung auszuführen oder nicht oder aber einem bestimmten Standpunkt, der gerade durch den Sprecher vertreten wird, zuzustimmen (*Ete Gogu*, *mânca-v-ar tata*, *haideți să fim serioși*, *cu unu cu altu*, *că-i mai dai că-i mai iei*) .

> Fragmente aus der Tucă-Show vom 17. März 2003:
> MD: Wir hätten eine Volksabstimmung machen müssen.
> CN: *Ete Gogu*!/ Hört euch 'n Gescheiten an!
> MD: Doch, doch!
> CN: *Ete Gogu*!/ Hör euch 'n Gescheiten an!
> MD: Also, *băi*, der Iliescu will sein Image verbessern, das Image eines Menschen, der in Moskau studiert hat, verstehst du, der Russisch gesprochen hat, und er spricht's auch jetzt noch, und er ist für die Amerikaner! Und die machen ihm ein sehr gutes Image auf meine und deine Kosten und auf Kosten unsrer Kinder! [...]

AT: Wir wollten in die NATO, die wollten uns aber nicht haben, *domle/* mein Herr, schon seit sieben, acht Jahren fordern wir sie hartnäckig auf, »*primiți-ne băi, mânca-v-ar tata!«,/* »*nehmt uns bitte an, băi, wir haben euch ja so wahnsinnig lieb!«*, und dann gab's noch die Geschichten, /*chestiile alea/* von denen ja auch Mircea erzählt hat, /*cu unu cu altu, că-i mai dai că-i mai iei și-așa mai departe/* dass man auch noch verhandeln musste über die Bedingungen, dass man noch etwas versprach und dafür noch etwas kriegen sollte usw. Und sie haben uns angenommen.

5. Schlussfolgerung

Der Überschuss an Sprachhandlungen und Sprechakten im rumänischen Diskurs kann in gewissem Maße auch als eine Reaktion gegenüber dem »betonsprachlichen« Totalitarismus, als eine Reaktion auf den dadurch entstandenen Leerraum verstanden werden, bei dem die Subjektivität immer geringer wurde und schließlich durch den Einsatz von unpersönlichen Konstruktionen und in Ermangelung der Bezugnahme auf die erlebte Gegenwart völlig beseitigt wurde. Die derzeit üppigen Kontaktformen sprachlichen Verhaltens lassen sich hingegen als *kontinuierliche Suche nach dem Empfänger der mitgeteilten Botschaft* interpretieren (»Wiederfinden des Individuellen und Neuauftritt des *Ich*, das unter eindeutig bestimmten Bedingungen in einem bestimmten Kontext mit einem *realen Messageempfänger* spricht«, Zafiu 2001, 42).

Literatur

Coteanu, Ion/Mareș, Lucreția (Hgg.) (1996): Dicționarul explicativ al imbii române (DEX). București: Univers Enciclopedic.
Gilbert, Michael A. (1995): Argument and arguers. In: Teaching Philosophy 18/2, 125-138.
Graur, Alexandru/Avram, Mioara/Vasiliu, Laura (Hgg.) (1966): Gramatica limbii române (GA). Bd. I-II. București: Editura Academiei RSR.
Holtus, Günter/Metzeltin, Michael/Schmitt, Christian (Hgg.) (1989): Lexikon der Romanischen Linguistik (LRL). Tübingen: Niemeyer.
Magda, Margareta (2003): Dialog in mehrsprachigen Gebieten: Das Beispiel Siebenbürgens, Rumänien. Vortrag auf dem 1. Kongress der IGDD, Marburg, 5.-8. März 2003.
Manu-Magda, Margareta (1996): Unele trăsături ale tipului pragmatic românesc. In: Balkanarchiv. Beiheft. Veitshochheim bei Würzburg: Lehmann, 327-337.
Rusu, Valeriu (1959): Formules d'interpellation en roumain. In: Revue roumaine de linguistique IV/2, 243-253.

– (1964): Notă despre »fă« şi »mă« în limba română. In: Studii şi cercetări lingvistice XV/6, 759-761.
Thun, Harald (1979): Die Existimatoren des Deutschen und ihre rumänischen Äquivalente. In: Beiträge zur deutsch-rumänischen Grammatik I, Bukarest: Universitätsverlag, 193-206.
– (1989): Rumänisch: Partikelforschung. In: Holtus, Günter/Metzeltin, Michael/Schmitt, Christian (Hgg.) (1989): Lexikon der Romanischen Linguistik (LRL). Tübingen: Niemeyer, 55-62.
Vasilescu, Mircea (2002): Tucă. In: Dilema, 508, 6.-12. Dezember, www.ziare.com
Zafiu, Rodica (2000): Şturlubatic. In: România literară 3, www.ziare.com
– (2001): Diversitate stilistică în româna actuală. Bucureşti: Editura Universităţii din Bucureşti.

Diana Ghido

Fragmentation in talk shows

Fragmentation is often said to be characteristic of spoken language. Cresti (2000) defines fragmentation as a relation between information units and intonation units, resulting in some pragmaphonetic phenomena: overlappings, interruptions, repetitions, false starts, word-truncation, hesitations a.s.o. In this paper, we will study the way in which such phenomena are reflected in media discourse, that usually exhibits a higher degree of discourse planning. Talk shows, in particular, have been described as "host controlled, participant shaped, audience evaluated speech events" (Ilie 2001, 209). The heterogeneous nature of talk shows has been the very reason why we have chosen them for our analysis, because it allows a certain flexibility inside this media genre. Their variety is even more interesting when approached from the perspective of their ever changing rules, especially when some hosts willingly reveal the rules of 'making a talk show' (in a sort of meta-talk show).

1. Corpus

The corpus consists of Romanian TV programs,[1] selected in accordance with the definition of talk shows proposed by Ilie (2001, 210-211). While gathering the corpus, we followed three steps: a) taking notes based on audio recordings of talk shows from 1998-1999 to obtain some guidelines for the hypothetically relevant pragmalinguistic aspects; b) compiling a new 20 talk show corpus of video recordings, and c) selecting 10 talk shows as a 'core corpus' for the analysis of talk show fragmentation.

The core corpus is presented in Table 1, which highlights some extralinguistic parameters describing talk shows as media products. Our corpus design aims at showing variation in relation to a number of parameters: a) the target audience – see the TV channels and broadcasting data: weekday shows (4) vs. weekend shows (6), morning / noon / evening / night shows, time span: from 30' to 90', b) live (5) vs. prerecorded shows (5), c) a general

---

[1] We have included some programs with two participants (see TS3, TS4, and TS6) because, aside from the number of participants, they have more features of a talk show than of a news interview.

characterization of their position on the information – entertainment scale, d) the number of guests: from 1 to 9, and e) the studio audience.

In our talk shows, the dialogue mostly takes place in public settings, but also in private settings or both public and private settings within same show.

	Talk Show	TV Chan.	Broadcasting				General topic	Parts (different dialogues)	No. Guests	Studio audience
			Times/ week	Hour day	Time span	Live				
TS 1	Teo	Pro TV	5	17:45	90'	yes	entertain.	5	1+1+4 +1+2	yes
TS 2	*Salut! Big Brother* ('Hello' Big Brother!')	PRIMA	5	23:30	60'	yes	entertain.	2	2+4	no
TS 3	*Uite cine mă întreabă* ('Look who's asking me questions')	PRIMA	1	22:30	30'	no	entertain.	1	1	yes
TS 4	*Seara bună!* ('Good evening!')	TVR 1	3	22:00	60'	no	infotain.	1	1	yes
TS 5	*Parte de carte* ('A share of books')	Pro TV	1	Sun 11:00	60'	no	culture	1	2	no
TS 6	*Istorie polemică* ('Polemical history')	TVR 1	1	Sat 13:15	60'	yes	science (history)	1	1	no
TS 7	*România mea* ('My Romania')	Antena 1	1	Sat 16:00	60'	no	science (history)	1	1	–
TS 8	*Profeții despre trecut* ('Prophecies about the past')	Pro TV	1	Sun 12:00	60'	no	soc.-pol.	1	1 (perm. guest)	no
TS 9	*Ultima ediție* ('The last edition')	TVR 1	1	Sun 13:00	60'	yes	soc.-pol.	2	4+5	no
TS 10	Marius Tucă Show	Antena 1	4	22:30	60'	yes	soc.-pol.	2	2+1	no

A talk show can be made up of two or more distinct parts, each with a different topic and different guests.

All the above mentioned elements have a certain influence on the development of the verbal interaction. Some of them are reflected in the "talk-related restrictions" (Ilie 2001, 222), i.e. time restrictions and turn-taking restrictions, others are correlated with adapting one's discourse to more than one kind of receiver: the host, the other participants, the studio audience, and the viewers.

A very important distinction is, in our opinion, *live* vs. *prerecorded* shows. The commercial break may not even be announced in prerecorded shows because it is actually inserted later, while in live programs it is sometimes clear that during that break there have been discussions between the participants and therefore some of the controversial subjects announced at the beginning of the show are approached differently after the break.

The general topic of the show proved to have a considerable influence on the degree of cooperation / conflict between the participants; for instance, approaching social and political issues is often connected with verbal conflict, while the culture shows in our corpus are characterized by a higher degree of cooperation between the participants and, therefore, less instances of expressing disagreement, less overlappings or interruptions, less other-corrections, etc.

2. Aims and method

The aims of this study are: a) to establish an inventory of elements deriving from the institutional nature of talk shows and which may influence the verbal interaction (as it is produced or perceived) and b) to analyze the way these elements surface as fragmentation in talk shows. As Ilie stated, the semi-institutional nature of talk shows "is largely based on embedding conversational discourse into institutional discourse" (2001, 224).

The analysis is based on a CA approach, trying to discover more general patterns from a number of observations based on our corpus. In studying fragmentation, we have considered two basic units: the show and the verbal interaction (with notes on turns, utterances, intonation units, etc). Our assumption has been that, on the one hand, a considerable part of the elements causing fragmentation in the verbal interaction are connected to the institutional features of talk shows, on the other, the heterogeneous parts which make up a TV show are integrated (usually, by the show host) into the verbal interaction.

We have tried to gather some extralinguistic information that may be significant for the analysis of the show as a whole. As Mey stated, "conversationalists are placed under the obligation to operate contextually", and by context he refers to "the entirety of societally relevant circumstances that surround the production of language" (2000, 134).

The choice for a corpus of video recordings is due to the fact that it has been often said and proved (Levinson 1983, Moeschler/Reboul 1994) that speech acts can be accomplished by means of units other than speech units, that is non-linguistic units: laughter, gesture, silence, etc. Therefore, some discursive phenomena cannot be interpreted merely on the basis of audio recordings, since the participants have had access to visual information and decoded the other's message based on mimicry and body language. Moreover, the TV show itself is meant to be seen, not just heard by the public. Nonverbal communication is very well represented, especially in entertainment shows. Talking about taboos (which is still quite frequent in entertainment shows) is often related to employing nonverbal means of conveying information. Using the videos, we have recovered a lot of nonverbal information together with some additional visual information, the so-called "grammar of television" (Chandler 1994), for example, camera techniques or graphics displayed on the TV screen.

The limitations of our method are linked with the very way a talk show is recorded and perceived: as a media product, an end product, without showing all the constituents and the process behind it (the production team, the studio interaction with the audience, reading from a teleprompter, all the information transmitted to the moderator, in the earpiece, or to the studio audience, on a stage screen). The nonverbal component, however, is still only partially available for a linguistic analysis. In general, the camera focuses on one participant at a time: sometimes we even hear the voice of one person and see the face of another.

3. An inventory of elements causing fragmentation

Given the two main units considered, the show and the verbal interaction, we have distinguished two categories of elements triggering fragmentation: external vs. internal to the show, the latter class including elements which belong to the verbal interaction as such as well as those which do not.

3.1 Elements external to the show

In Table 2 we present a number of aspects connected to the institutional nature of talk shows and which influence the verbal interaction between the host and the guest(s). The fact that, ultimately, these kinds of shows are not instances of casual conversation is obvious in the in-

Fragmentation in talk shows 243

sertion of commercial breaks or news flashes (a short presentation of the most important events commented in the coming news bulletin). The table includes some data about the number of such insertions and their total duration, which results in the fragmentation of the verbal interaction. Ilie analyzes these breaks in terms of an "embedded and mixed interdiscursivity between conversational and institutional discourse" (Ilie 2001, 224). In live shows, the non-standardized prefaces of commercial breaks can be stated in different tones, even under different pretexts, inducing the viewers various attitudes. The break may even be disguised as a time-out for the host, to prepare his or her speech, as the host Teo does in TS1, seemingly because one of her guests misunderstood her question:

Talk Show		Time span	Commercial Break		Footage		Viewer's call			Footage/Reportage		Music	
			No. occ.	Total dur.	No. occ.	Total dur.	No. occ.	Total dur.	Quiz	No. occ.	Total dur.	Studio music band	Singers as guests
TS 1	Teo	90'	3	12'	1	2'	–	–	–	–	–	no	4 occ. (11')
TS 2	Salut! Big Brother	60'	2	12'	–	–	3	7'	1	11	31'	no	–
TS 3	Uite cine mă intreabă	30'	2	12'	–	–	–	–	–	–	–	no	–
TS 4	Seara bună!	60'	1	6'30"	–	–	–	–	–	–	–	yes	–
TS 5	Parte de carte	60'	1	3'30"	–	–	–	–	–	1	2'	no	–
TS 6	Istorie polemică	60'	–	–	–	–	–	–	–	–	–	no	–
TS 7	România mea	60'	1	30"	–	–	–	–	–	–	–	no	–
TS 8	Profeții despre trecut	60'	2	2'	–	–	–	–	–	7	5'30"	no	–
TS 9	Ultima ediție	60'	–	–	–	–	–	–	–	3	5'30"	no	–
TS	Marius Tucă Show	60'	2	8'	–	–	–	–	–	1	5'	no	–

H: *I think we'd better come back after a few moments, so that we try and formulate complete, complex and unambiguous questions.*

The same hostess pretends to insert a commercial break to allow the viewers to call their friends and relatives and let them know that some singer is going to perform in the show immediately after the break:

H: *Ladies and gentlemen, get ready, call everybody, your friends, your neighbors, because you're going to listen to that song. However, we'll have a short break to give you the time to make your calls.*

All these pretexts seem to soften the impact of the institutional constraints on the entertainment facet of the show; the negative reaction toward the commercial break is presumably diminished when the hostess takes it as a duty (and not having a break would be a serious mistake on her part):

H: *My dear viewers, I'd like you to give me – if you could – a length. A length and a felt-tip pen for me to write in big letters, 'Andreea, please, don't talk in my earphone during applause because I CAN'T HEAR YOU.' She says, 'will you please', she says, 'introduce Adrian,' and then 'blah blah blah blah'. As a rule, this indicates a break. Now, you know something? Whether it's true or not this time, we'll have one, just in case.*

The news flash, which we found in only one of the programs from the core corpus, was inserted immediately after the commercials, so the host didn't need to explicitly introduce this news slot in the show. However, the larger corpus would suggest that the serious and often negative tone and content of news flashes is usually ignored by entertainment show hosts.

3.2 Elements internal to the show

Aside from the institutional management of the program imposed by the TV channel, there are other elements which we consider internal to the show, as opposed to the above-mentioned ones, because: a) they can be the host's choice and they have an argumentative function (such as footages) and/or b) they belong to the entertainment component (viewer's call for quizzes, singers invited to perform during the show, etc) or c) they belong to the verbal interaction as such (interruption, false start, word truncation, hesitation, etc).

Regarding the pragmaphonetic fragmentation phenomena at the linguistic and discursive level, we will present only those examples which are closely connected with media talk. The intonation unit is truncated in false starts, which sometimes occur because of the speaker's sudden realization of the difference of background information between the host and the guest, on the one hand, and the guest and the audience, on the other. Shows, especially entertainment shows, are preceded by a discussion between the host and the guest. Therefore, during the show, the questions are very specific and the context is familiar to the show host. Yet, on more than one occasion, the guest had the impulse of 'plunging into' the answer, and then stopped to make a general presentation of the context for the audience. Other false starts are caused by the extra rules which are imposed on the speakers during a TV show, those regarding media taboos (the speakers must not utter the name of any brands, products, other TV channels, etc).

An interesting fact is that Romanian talk shows are characterized by a high degree of media intertextuality.[2] In almost half of the extended corpus of 20 talk shows, we encountered a show host from another program as a guest.[3] This has a great influence on the role distribution, which tends to become symmetrical instead of asymmetrical roles (Ilie 2001) between host and guests. This results in a series of overlappings and interruptions while competing for the role of the controller; such guests initiate more often questions for the host or for the other guests.

Another element specific to TV (and radio) verbal interaction is an initial pause (which may be misinterpreted as hesitation) occurring due to the media of communication (using the telephone while the whole verbal interaction is broadcast on TV): sometimes guests from the same show are not co-present, and they interact via satellite transmissions which cause a delay in viewers' perception of a turn, especially within an adjacency pair.

There are some uncontrollable variables that might hint at the underlying structure of talk shows as media products, at the virtually permanent communication between the producing team.

One of these elements is the teleprompter, which prevents us as viewers from knowing for certain which parts are read and which are spoken. In TS5, for example, the host reads from the teleprompter a pretty long fragment from the book discussed in the show. We know for a fact that it is a quotation because the exact same fragment has been read before in some footage. If we compare the host's reading and speaking, we have to admit that it is approximately same speed, while false starts or word truncation are not frequent in his spontaneous

---

[2] Chandler (1994) discusses television intertextuality: "Intertextuality refers to the relationships between different elements of a medium (like formats or participants) and links with other media. One aspect of intertextuality is that program participants who are known to the audience from other programs bring about images of other contexts which effect the audience perception of their current role."

[3] A lot of data and suggestions about the making of a show have been offered by the talk shows themselves. TS3, for example, presents a guest who is a more experienced show host than the current host; the host and the guest actually get to talk about contract issues, how to treat the show guests when they do not obey the rules of media discourse or try to take over the control, how to 'read' the studio audience, interpret their reactions a.s.o.
In TS1, the host is known to the public for bringing in front of the camera her studio team, for addressing her backstage colleagues during the show, etc which reveals interesting 'bits' of the underlying studio communication.

speech, so it would normally be difficult for a viewer to distinguish reading from spontaneous speech. In most of the cases, we believe that the opening and the closing parts are read from the teleprompter (except for TS6 and, maybe, TS1). TS3, the show with the 10-year-old host, has offered us most interesting information about studio communication. When the boy asks his guest a question (who is actually a much more experienced show host than himself) and he is not able to read fluently what is written on the teleprompter, the guest reads the question herself loudly. Also, at the end of the show, the young host is probably told in the earpiece to read the closing part form the teleprompter, he looks puzzled, and then we can hear the guest whispering to him: *The teleprompter...* The supposition that all of his questions are written on the prompter is enforced by the fact that he feels the need to preface an unplanned question:

> H: *Now here's a question from me. Er... er... er You er... So now you're working for B1TV till September. And in autumn you are going to start to work for Antena 1. Again, right?*
> G: *Right.*
> H: *So they have forgiven you.* [...]

The reportages included in the shows (especially in those with social or political topics) end in "non-standard questions" (Ilie 1999) and are meant to trigger a debate. However, their insertion is more or less flexible, always requested by the host. In TS10 we have an example of an unpredictable moment of insertion (even for the host, note the false start), where the moderator offers the reportage like a coffee to a guest, just to make her feel more comfortable:

> H: *And you came to Bucharest,*
> G: *Yes.*
> H: *where you have worked before – but you are rather nervous, I must tell you this. What should I say to you to help relax a bit? Would you like us to show the recording of your performance today at the Government? Do you think that would help?*
> G: (laughs) *No, no.* (laughs)
> H: *That's an interesting tape.* (to his guest and the audience) *Let's watch it.* (to his colleagues in the studio) *The tape, please! The tape, please! The tape, please!*

An interesting type of fragmentation occurs as an inherent ingredient of talk shows as media products, although it does not affect the verbal interaction in the studio, but our perception of it, from the standpoint of the viewer. Most of our examples belong to a category of visual elements and techniques: identification labels for each of the participants involved in the show, topic labels, information boxes placed 'over' the images of the participants, but also the whole television 'grammar'.[4] We consider that these elements contribute to a sort of me-

---

4 Close-ups in TS10 and TS9, medium shots in TS1, long shots TS7, TS4, TS3, etc. Also, a low angle of shot is often employed in TS7, a technique which, according to Chandler (1994) gives

dia discourse fragmentation, as opposed to the face-to-face conversation, because it requires the viewers to divide their attention for short periods of time. On the one hand, during face-to-face communication we can monitor our interlocutor throughout the interaction and this kind of additional information is neither possible, nor, indeed, necessary. On the other hand, the visual fragmentation on the screen acts as a means of achieving a different kind of unity, providing an extralinguistic context.

The labels with the names, profession, etc are displayed for a fixed number of seconds (always 10" in TS4, 7" in TS7, 4" in TS9, etc) or for a variable time span (like in TS1). These identifying labels usually occur on the screen when that participant first begins to speak, or at the beginning of each of his turns. Sometimes, labels are shown precisely because of what is being said (as in TS1 or TS9), occurring even in the middle of a sentence. This happens, for example, when an ex-Secretary of Finance condemns the system as if he had never been a part of it, while the label reminds the viewers of his past status. In TS1, one of the guests is told that the name of her job is so pompous that it is almost impossible to articulate or remember, and after that the name of her job is posted for almost 20". The labels tend to be more extensive in political shows, for example, than in entertainment shows (when they may only mention the first name of the guest).

In live shows, the turn-taking system has a great influence on the camera shifts from the close-up of one participant to a two-shot (a shot of two people together) or a split screen (if the participants who are shown are not co-present, but 'brought together' by means of satellite transmission). The address forms used by the host have the extra role of signaling to the cameraman that the interlocutor is going to change, and he has to change focus, too. In the next example, we have signaled the persons on the screen between brackets (only H and G3 are co-present):

> G1: *And if the data requires that whole ensembles should remain untouched, they will remain so, because otherwise there will be NO approval from the Ministry of Culture. In other words –*
> H: **Thank you very much, sir.** (images form the studio: H and G3) *Mr. Piso, are you satisfied with this answer? Briefly,* (H and G2) *because I also want to speak to Mr. Dumitrascu.*
> G2: *I'm not clear about the galleries. These galleries –*
> H: *What about the galleries?*
> G2: *It is the galleries that we must protect by all means. But a representative of Gold Corporation stated in November that there would be only one gallery left* (only G2) *and even that is still to be found. But I don't think this solves the problem. It is the galleries that we must protect by all means. And not even-*
> H: *You mean the Roman galleries,* (H and G2) *is that right?*
> G2: *Yes, and not even that one will be preserved properly since every day will be tens of tons of dynamite fired there, will it? If it crushes-*
> H: *All right. On the phone we have Gabriel Dumitrascu* [...]

the impression of an overwhelming importance of the character. Indeed, the guest in TS7 is presented as a hero because he was a dissident during communism.

4. Conclusions and perspectives

Talk shows exhibit some particular types of fragmentation at the linguistic and discursive levels due to the superposed economic / institutional requirements (from inserting breaks to interrupting everybody because an unexpected, but important guest is on the phone for a short while etc), to the media embedded in TV broadcasting (the participants are not always co-present), to the negotiation of power relations etc. The elements causing fragmentation can be show external (commercial breaks, news flashes) or show internal. In the latter case, these elements (labels, subtitles, sound, etc) can overlap with the verbal interaction, being 'added' to it, or can actually interrupt it (reportages, telephone calls, etc).

For a future analysis, we believe that it would be useful for the linguist to attend some shows, at least as a part of the studio audience. Also, the tapes from the studio would be preferable to the show *broadcast* as an end product.

References

Cresti, Emmanuela (2000): Corpus di italiano parlato. Vol. I, II, Firenze: Accademia della Crusca.
Chandler, Daniel (1994): The 'Grammar' of Television and Film. http://www.aber.ac.uk/media/Documents/short/gramtv.html.
Ilie, Cornelia (1999): Question-response argumentation in talk shows. In: Journal of Pragmatics 31, 975-999.
– (2001): Semi-institutional discourse: The case of talk shows. In: Journal of Pragmatics 33, 209-254.
Levinson, Stephen C. (1983): Pragmatics. Cambridge: Cambridge University Press.
Mey, Jacob (2001): Pragmatics. Oxford: Blackwell Publishers.
Moeschler, Jacques/Reboul, Anne (1994): Dictionnaire Encyclopédique de Pragmatique. Paris: Editions du Seuil.

Laurenția Dascălu Jinga

Other-correction in TV talk shows

1. The typical format of other-corrections

A successful other-correction is typically based on a three-turn format *xyy* (Jefferson 1983, 60):
I   Speaker A produces an error (*x*)
II Speaker B offers the correct variant (*y*)
III Speaker A accepts this variant, usually by repeating it (*y*); for instance:

(1) CP: *Noi am titrat în ziarul Adevărul de astăzi cu privire la interzicerea absenței presei și observatorilor interni la numărătoarea voturilor.*
    OA: *Accesului.*
    CP: *Accesului.*

   [CP: We've published in today's newspaper "Adevărul" something about the interdiction of the press absence and of the internal observers at the vote counting.
    OA: Of the access.
    CP: Of the access.]

This triple sequence, which we have called "metalinguistic triad of repair" (Dascălu Jinga, 2003) has very rare exceptions:
– when the corrected person ratifies the new term by a mere confirmation, without repeating it;
– when the correction is made without the third phase (the acceptation by the corrected speaker).

The relation between the three parts of the basic structure is quite asymmetrical (Dascălu Jinga 2002b, 88-89). After the first turn (containing the error), the interlocutor can decide to correct it or not; hence, the second part is optional. In exchange, the second and the third phases are much more strongly connected to each other. We can use here Schegloff's (1972) "conditional relevance" concept to define this relation: "by conditional relevance of one item on another we mean: given the first, the second is expectable" (364). In our case, the second turn (of the corrector) is conditionally relevant on the third one (of the corrected speaker); in other words, the sequence made up by these two turns has a certain internal unity, as once launched the interlocutor's turn, it necessarily triggers some reaction on the part of the corrected speaker. The momentary break or the "conversation clock stopping" caused by an other-correction can be overcome only by putting an end to the crisis moment, which has been provoked paradoxically not by the error itself, but by the interlocutor's decision of correcting it (Dascălu Jinga 2002b, 125).

2. Reactions to an other-correction

The verbal reactions made by the speakers during a conversation have been thoroughly investigated; the analysts paid much attention to the "classic" cases, such as the possible responses to a question, an offer, a compliment, an order and so on (see for instance, Stati 1990, 91-113), whereas the reactions to an other-correction have been rather neglected. For this reason, in our present contribution we shall focus on this very kind of reactions, analyzing the speakers' behavior during the repair procedures in TV talk shows.[1]

The reactions to an other-correction can be classified following the three criteria proposed by Stati (1990, 93) for the verbal reactions in general:
– according to the criterion of the relation between the speakers, there can be *cooperative* reactions (of acceptance) and *conflictual* ones (of reject);
– according to the criterion of conformity to the partner's expectations, there can be *congruent* and *incongruent* reactions;
– according to the criterion of observance of the rules of pragmatic functions concatenation, there can be *coherent*, *incoherent* and *non-coherent* reactions.

2.1 Cooperative, congruent, and coherent reactions

The triadic structure *xyy* is actually based on a cooperative, congruent, and coherent reaction of the corrected speaker. This kind of behavior can have slightly different variations:

2.1.1 Simple acceptation, by repeating the term proposed by the corrector, as in example (1); the repetition can be preceded occasionally by a specific marker, such as *sau* 'or':

(2) SB: *acuma intervine ŞI legea asta a regiunilor /î* [...] */ î:: subdezvoltate*↑
     LM: *Defavorizate*.

---

[1] The investigation relies on a TV corpus of 15 political talk shows (amounting to some 13 hours), recorded from 5 Romanian TV channels between July 1996 – April 1999. The total number of participants was 49; out of them, 42 (i.e. 85.7 %) were journalists or publicists.

Other-correction in TV talk shows 251

SB: *sau defavorizate↑ care creează un cadru legal . . cu foarte mari avantaje↓ stimulente date întreprinzătorilor↑ [...] .*

[SB: now also intervenes this law of the regions [...] underdeveloped//
LM: Underfavoured.
SB: or underfavoured, which creates a legal frame with great advantages, incentives offered to the investors [...]] .

2.1.2 Strong acceptation, made by various devices:

– repetition of the correct term with phonetic emphasis:

(3) SB: *Generalu Lupu a spus că [...] zice↓ "prefectu"↑ //*
MT: <u>SubpreFECtu</u>↓ *da.*
SB: *că <u>subpreFECtu</u> a fost acela care a ordonat.*

[SB: The general Lupu said that [...] says 'the prefect' //
MT: The VICEprefect, yes.
SB: that the VICEprefect was the one who commanded.]

– repetition of the correct term with lexical emphasis:

(4) NM: *Cred că <u>asta</u> ar fi fost spre câştigu tuturor şi-n primu rând al acestor oameni <u>care</u> ne ascultă [...] şi <u>care</u> <u>ne vor vota</u> [...] pentru că <u>ASta</u> este de fapt important.*
 [ ]
OA: <u>Ne vor vota sau nu.</u>
NM: <u>Ne vor vota sau nu</u>↓ *evident.*

[NM: I think this would have been for the benefit of all and especially for these people who are listening to us [...] and who will vote us [...] because THIS is actually important.
OA: Will vote us or not.
NM: Will vote us or not, obviously.]

– double repetition of the correct term, possibly phonetic and/or lexical emphasis added:

(5) CP: *S-a revenit asupra acestei măsuri↑ care cum să vă spun↓ era o invitaţie pe faţă↓ nu↑. la <u>măsluirea</u> alegerilor. Era o //*
SB: *La <u>camuFLArea măsluirii</u>.*
CP: *<u>camuflarea</u>↓ exact↓ <u>camuflarea măsluirii</u>.*

[CP: They reconsidered this measure, which, how can I say, was an overt invitation, wasn't it, to gerrymandering. It was an //
SB: To HIDE gerrymandering.
CP: to hide, exactly, to hide gerrymandering.]

– repetition of the correct term with excuses:

(6) HP: *Atunci când judecăm că România este o parabolă↑ [...]*
IS: *<u>paragină</u>.*
HP: *<u>paragină</u>↑ iertaţi-mă↓ . . . ./ă trebuie să ne-ntrebăm dacă <u>paragina</u> <u>este</u> de-acuma↑ este EXclusiv în cei cinzeci de ani↑ sau <u>este</u> mai VEche.*

[HP: When we take Romania as a parabola [...]
IS: a ruin.

HP: a ruin, I'm sorry, we have to wonder if the ruin is from now, is exclusively from the (last) fifty years, or is an earlier one.]

– a combination of some of these devices; for instance, double repetition, phonetic emphasis, and excuses:

(7) AU: *Prima care care mi-a sărit în ochi [...] era o ştire în care se vorbea despre un cadou făcut congresmanului Vunderberg↓ o minge de fotbal <u>cu dedicaţii</u> //*
    CP: *Nu↓ <u>Clinton</u> chiar.*
    AU: *lui <u>Clinton</u>↓ pardon↓ <u>CLINton</u>↓ cu dedicaţii din partea fotbaliştilor români.*
    [AU: The first which struck my eye was a news about a present offered to the congressman Vunderberg, a soccer ball with dedications //
    CP: No, (to) Clinton himself.
    AU: to Clinton, sorry, CLINton, with dedications from the Romanian soccer players.]

2.1.3 A more cooperative reaction of the corrected speaker is admitting explicitly that he made a mistake:

(8) CP: *Vaclav Havel <u>a spus</u>↑ Ţară MEMbră <u>NAto</u>↓ ... care trebuia să sărbătoREAScă intrarea-n nato↓ <u>la nivelu înTREgii Iugoslavii</u>↑ <u>a spus</u>↓ "Nu↑" aTÂT <u>a spus</u>↓ "Nu mai sărbătorim nimic↑ pentru că nu mai avem ce sărbători." Ăsta a fost //*
    MT: *NU <u>la nivelu întregii IugoSLAvii</u>↑ la nivelu întregii /î: CEhia.*
    CP: *Am spus <u>Iugoslavia</u>↓ da.*
    [CP: Vaclav Havel said, a NATO MEMber COUNtry, which was about celebrating its entrance in NATO, at the level of the whole Yugoslavia, said, 'No', that was all he said, 'We will not celebrate anything, because we have no more reasons to celebrate.' This was //
    MT: NOT at the level of the whole YugoSLAvia, at the level of whole CZECH (republic)
    CP: I said Yugoslavia, yes.]

2.2 Cooperative, congruent, and non-coherent reactions

When the basic triadic structure is not achieved as such, the corrected speaker produces a "dispreferred" (Schegloff /Jefferson /Sacks 1977) or a "marked" (Levinson 1983, 307) reaction.

If his attitude remains within the limits of a cooperative behavior, after a short negotiation, in a side-sequence (Jefferson 1972), he will accept the new term, which proves that the crisis moment has been solved before becoming conflictual. According to Stati (1990, 96), we can say that this is a *non-coherent* type of reaction, that is, one which is formally incoherent, but is followed by an adequate reaction; in other words, the right reaction was only delayed, "after a momentary obstruction and a useful and, thereby, cooperative interruption" (Stati 1990, 113).

– Sometimes, if the corrected speaker is amazed or incredulous about his making an error, the triadic format is accordingly extended:

(9) ST: *Deci intelectualii de marcă↓ între care fusese și Radu Popescu↓ care pledase în procesul Anei Pauker din anii treizeci. Deci //*
AP: *Radu Olteanu↓ Radu Olteanu.*
ST: *Radu Olteanu↓ așa. Am spus altfel?*
VA: *Popescu.*
ST: *Radu Olteanu.*

[ST: Therefore the important intellectuals, among which was Radu Popescu too, who had pleaded in Ana Pauker's trial in the thirties. Therefore //
AP: Radu Olteanu, Radu Olteanu.
ST: Radu Olteanu, yes. Did I say otherwise?
VA: Popescu.
ST: Radu Olteanu.]

– Other times, the speaker accepts unwillingly the variant proposed by the interlocutor, as in the following example, where a long side-sequence of negotiation arises, due to both participants' uncertainty about the exact date of a given event:

(10) MD: *În obzeșunu↑ [...] șefu de post a descoperit lista agenților caghebe* [K.G.B.] *din România.* [...]
MT: *Da' în obzeșinouă↓ NU în obzeșunu.*
MD: *În ob- în /î::*
MT: *obzeșnouă ↓ obzeșunu?*
MD: *În obzeșUnu↓ eu am înțeles.*
MT: *Da↓ mă rog.*
MD: *Deci era încă ⊥ Sau BIne↓ obzeșinouă.*

[MD: In eighty one a policeman discovered the list of the K.G.B. agents in Romania.
MT: But it was in eighty-nine, not in eighty-one.
MD: in eig- in ...
MT: eighty-nine, eighty-one?
MD: In eighty-one, I understood.
MT: Yes, well.
MD: So it was still... Or, well, eighty-nine.]

2.3 Non-cooperative, incongruent, and incoherent reactions

In the cases when the attitude of the corrected speaker is not maintained within the limits of a cooperative behavior, there are two situations, as revealed in the corpus.

2.3.1 The speaker ignores the variant proposed by his interlocutor, because he did not hear or grasp it; the transgression of the "normal" succession of the repair phases is an involuntary one.

– If the corrector does not insist, a failed correction results:

(11) SB: *A. N.↑ de câteva ori a subliniat în ultima vreme↑ . . că politica de alianţe a <u>pedesereu-
lui</u>* [P.D.S.R.-ului] *a ajuns într-o FUNdătură↑ . . . că alianţa cu pemere↑* [P.M.R.] *pen-
tru <u>pedesere</u> înseamnă <u>ruptura</u>↓*
[ ]
MT: *pereme* [P.R.M.]
SB: *<u>ruptura</u> de occident.*

[SB: Recently A.N. underlined for several times that the alliance policy of P.D.S.R. has led up a
blind alley, that the alliance with P.M.R. means for P.D.S.R. a break
MT: P.R.M.
SB: a break with the West.]

– If the corrector insists to obtain a successful repair, his procedure is repeated and the sequence takes the form of a multiple correction:

(12) BT: *Cine-i <u>deţinutul politic</u>.*
LM: *<u>Deţinutul politic</u> este deputatul pedesere* [P.D.S.R.] *despre care vorbea B. P.↑ //*
DA: *<u>peneţecede</u>.* [P.N.Ţ.C.D.]
LM: *<u>care-l sprijină pe</u>*
[
DA: *Dacă nu vă deranjează↓ e <u>peneţeceDE</u>.*
LM: *<u>peneţecede</u>↓ <u>care-l sprijină pe</u> directorul de la Aro Câmpulung↑* [...] .

[BT: Who is the political prisoner?
LM: The political prisoner is the P.D.S.R. deputy B.P. was speaking of //
DA: P.N.Ţ.C.D.
LM: who is supporting
DA: If you don't mind it is P.N.Ţ.C.D.
LM: P.N.Ţ.C.D. which is supporting the manager of Aro Câmpulung Company [...]] .

2.3.2 The current speaker does not accept the variant proposed by the interlocutor, adopting a negative attitude towards it. This is a typical conflictual or "dispreferred" situation, and, from the interlocutor's point of view, an incongruent one. Instead of cooperating for urgently solving the crisis moment, the corrected speaker insists in maintaining his own variant, although it is considered erroneous or inappropriate by the interlocutor and it is signalled as such.

Levinson (1983, 307) remarks that "in essence preferred seconds are unmarked – they occur as structurally simpler turns, in contrast, dispreferred seconds are marked by various kinds of structural complexity". He mentions (334-335), as typical features of dispreferred reactions: various elements of *delay* (pauses, introductory particles, inserts), *prefaces* (expressions of disagreement preceded by agreement signals, excuses, hesitations), *accounts* of why the preferred second cannot be performed, or *declination* components (typical indirect or mitigated).

– The corrected speaker may not accept the corrector's variant and defend his opinion, sometimes even by correcting in his turn the interlocutor, in an argumentative sequence. In the following example, we can see a *preface* (a disagreement preceded by an agreement), then, an *explanation*, so that the third turn actually contains a correction of the correction:

(13) MD: *N-au făcut nimic. Și nu acuma↓ după / î: șase ani↑ //*
VA: *După patru.*
MD: *după patru ani↑ după șase ani↓ că au trecut șase ani de când sânt ăștia.*
[MD: They have done nothing. And not only now, after six years //
VA: After four.
MD: after four years, after six years, as six years passed since these ones have been (in power).]

– The current speaker may not accept the variant proposed by the interlocutor and produce some arguments against it, in a contradiction turn; in Romanian talk shows the contradiction is often made not very tactfully, as a response to an unmitigated form of other-correction:

(14) SB: *A constituit un act categoric↑ / î:: RĂsunător↑ de izolare a singurului partid .. care a participat la instiGArea↓ .. marșului minerilor↓ a singurului partid care se situează pe o //*
LM: *Haideți să NU spunem "instigarea"↓ că minerii N-AU avut nevoie de instigare↓ ei o duceau .. sufciENT de greu ca să //*
            [
SB: *Scrisoarea scrisoarea scumpule↓ scrisoarea lui V. T. către mineri duce la instiGArea lor.*
[SB: It was a clear, SOnorous act of isolation of the only party which participated in the instiGAtion of the miners' march, of the only party which is placed on a //
LM: Let's NOT say "instigate", as the miners did NOT need instigation, they lived sufficiently hard to //
SB: The letter, the letter, dear, the letter of V.T. to the miners led to their instigation.]

– The corrected speaker may not accept the variant proposed by the interlocutor and may not accept to be corrected either, as his irritated reaction and the conflictual exchange prove:

(15) IC: *Nu s-a respectat o trea- cum să spun↓ o negustorie [...]*
MT: *Un "protocol politic" spuneți.*
IC: *Eu îi zic "negustorie"↓ nu te supăra [...] udemereu [U.D.M.R.-ul] a constatat că nu se respecta afacerea. Și dacă nu se respecta↑ //*
MT: *Domle ↓ ori "negustorie"↑ ori "afacere".*
IC: *"Negustorie" sau "afacere" M. T.↓ HAI să terminăm.*
[IC: A th-, how to say, a trade hadn't been observed [...]
MT: The correct term is (litterally: say) 'a political protocol' procedure.
IC: I call it 'business', if you don't mind. [...] U.D.M.R. found that the trade was not observed. And if it was not observed //
MT: Sir, or 'trade' or 'business'.
IC: 'Trade' or 'business' M. T., LET'S finish with it.]

As one can see, taking into account the general intuition that the dialogue can not be continued without solving the moment of crisis triggered by an other-correction, the corrected speaker reproaches to the corrector the excessive delaying of the moment of turning back to the main topic. Levinson (1983) remarks that "the participants are constrained to utilize the expected procedures not (or not only) because failure to do so would yield incoherent discourses, but because if they don't, they find themselves accountable for specific inferences that their behavior will have generated" (321, footnote 16) [my emphasis (L.D.J.)].

3. Discussion

As any intervention developed in a public space, TV talk shows are characterized by a certain degree of formality; besides, the participants in our corpus are all representing a category of speakers with a high instruction and education level. Consequently the great majority of the repair strategies are based on cooperative, congruent, and coherent reactions (as the examples in 2.1), which testifies an affable, polite and cooperative attitude.

How could the other examples be explained, those of non-cooperative reactions? Ilie (2001) convincingly describes the TV talk shows as a mixed discourse type, "oscillating between the poles of conversation and institutional discourse" (219), which she calles a "semi-institutional discourse". According to her, talk shows can be seen to display "deviations from conversational and institutional norms to varying degrees, by combining spontaneous and purposeful talk, non-institutional and institutional roles, non-controlled and host-controlled talk, interlocutor-oriented, message-oriented, and multiple audience-oriented talk" (249).

As the institutional side of the talk shows is concerned, an important factor to be considered refers to the specific roles of the participants: the guests have to answer the questions asked by the show host, which gives him a dominant role. In addition, he has the task of controlling the discussion, not only by deciding its topic, but also by watching over the veracity of the information spread, over the maintaining of an ethic level of the debate, and, not in the least, over the correctness of the expression. Therefore the professionalism of a host imposes him, among other tasks, correcting the others. In this sense, his repair strategies pertain to the institutional side of the talk show. In many of our examples (1, 2, 3, 4, 6, 8) the corrections are made by the host and are accepted by the corrected guests; in some cases, the new term is ratified only after a side-sequence of clarification (10), or after a repeated repair procedure (12).

Concerning the conversational side of the talk shows, Ilie (2001, 227) remarks that "the authority of the show host is not absolute; the show guests themselves may also initiate a turn without necessarily being prompted by the host". This explains the occurrence of the corrections made by the guests, who feel free to correct the show host, to ignore one of his repair interventions (11), or even to reject it (13, 14, 15).

As for the negative reactions to an other-correction, it is worth noting that all our examples of non-cooperative reactions contain responses to unmitigated ("unmodulated" or "aggravated") other-corrections (Dascălu Jinga in press), which induces in the corrected speaker a tensional state of mind, rather favoring a non-cooperative attitude.

A final remark: maybe not incidentally, all our examples of non-cooperative, incongruent, and incoherent reactions (2.3) are due to participants who were journalists or publicists. Speaking about the interview, Walter (1991, 259) points out that "les professeurs d'écoles de journalisme conseillent effectivement aujourd'hui d'être 'plutôt offensif et impertinent que complaisant' ". As 85.7 % of the participants in our corpus have worked in mass media, it is not surprising that their reactions were to a great extent of a conflictual type, which means that, in spite of their different roles (host as dominant vs guests as dominated), they knew sufficiently well "the rules of the game", for their participation to be no longer "un combat à armes inégales" (ibidem), and to have great chances in the battle for their public image.

Transcribing conventions

Essentially based on Jefferson's (1978) and slightly adapted for a more proper notation of prosodic aspects (Dascălu Jinga 2002a, 30-43):

text text	repeated items underscored
text ⊥	incomplete or abandoned construction ("false start")
/ text	non-phonemic hesitation ("filled pause")
. . . .	silent pause (number of dots indicates extent)
TEXT	prominence (pitch and/or intensity)
.	terminal falling intonation contour
↓	non terminal falling intonation contour
?	terminal rising intonation contour
↑	non terminal rising intonation contour
text::	final syllable lengthening (number of colons indicates extent)
[ ]	overlapping of (parts of) utterances
text-	self-interruption
//	interruption (made by interlocutor)
" "	quotation

References

Dascălu Jinga, Laurenția (2002a): Corpus de română vorbită (CORV). Eșantioane. București: Oscar Print.
– (2002b): Corectare și autocorectare în conversația spontană. București: Editura Academiei Române.
– (2003): Metadiscursive triads. In: Bondi, M./Stati, S. (eds.): Dialogue Analysis 2000. Selected Papers from the IADA Anniversary Conference, Bologna 2000. Tübingen: Niemeyer, 163-172.
– (in press): Modulated and unmodulated other-corrections in TV talk shows. In: Revue Roumaine de Linguistique.
Ilie, Cornelia (2001): Semi-institutional discourse: The case of talk shows. In: Journal of Pragmatics 33, 209-254.
Jefferson, Gail (1972): Side sequences. In: Sudnow, D. (ed.): Studies in social interaction. New York: Free Press, 294-338.
– (1978): Explanation of transcript notation. In: Schenkein, J. (ed.): Studies in the organization of conversational interaction. New York, San Francisco, London: Academic Press, XI-XVI.
– (1983): On exposed and embedded correction in conversation. In: Studium Linguistik 14, 58-68.
Levinson, Stephen C. (1983): Pragmatics. Cambridge: Cambridge University Press.
Schegloff, Emanuel A. (1972): Sequencing in conversational openings. In: Gumperz, J.J./Hymes, D. (eds.): Directions in sociolinguistics. The ethnography of communication. New York: Holt, Rinehart and Winston, 346-380.
Schegloff, Emanuel A./Jefferson, Gail/Sacks, Harvey (1977): The preference for self-correction in the organization of repair in conversation. In: Language 53, 361-382.
Stati, Sorin (1990): Le transphrastique. Paris: Presses Universitaires Françaises.
Walter, Henriette (1991): L'interview, ou le Regne des Conventions. In: Stati, S./Weigand, E./Hundsnurscher, F. (eds.): Dialoganalyse III. Referate der 3. Arbeitstagung. Bologna 1990. Teil 2, Tübingen: Niemeyer, 253-260.

Claudia Bubel

"I'm on total ovary overload": The linguistic representation of women in *Sex and the City*

1. Introduction

In this paper I will investigate how all-female talk is represented in popular culture. I draw on a corpus of transcriptions of the US-American sitcom *Sex and the City,* which centres around conversations between four female friends. The success of this sitcom runs contrary to the social stigmatisation all-female talk has suffered. I will first of all discuss this negative evaluation of women's talk, linking it to anti-dialogue dicta in the film industry. Secondly, I will give a brief background on *Sex and the City* in order to contextualise my data. The main part of the paper is based on a detailed sequential analysis of an excerpt from the TV series. It attempts to show in how far the representation of all-female talk in *Sex in the City* corresponds to the findings of language and gender studies that talk is central to the establishment and maintenance of female friendships, and that conversation amongst female friends is a crucial locus of the creation of feminine identities. This has implications for the status of sitcom dialogue.

2. *A woman's tongue is only three inches long, but it can kill a man six feet high* and *Silence is golden*

Society's devaluation of all-female talk has been a starting point for feminist linguistic research, which challenges folk linguistic stereotypes, for instance that women talk excessively (Eckert/McConnell-Ginet 2003, 114ff.; Holmes 1998). Johnson and Aries (1983, 354) argue that "folk wisdom has long denigrated women's talk as 'idle chatter', 'yackedy yack', 'hen cackling', 'gabbing', and 'gossip'", thus placing women "in the position of having nothing better to do with their time than talk and of having nothing important to talk about." Yet, Jones (1980, 245) states, in spite of its alleged triviality women's talk is at the same time considered a threat and women have been prevented from interacting with each other for fear of gossip and its subversive power. This claim has been supported by Harrison's study of the friendships of married middle-class women (1998). She reports that one of the rituals of the female friends' meetings was to begin by exchanging stories "of how they had all 'managed to escape'" in spite of their husbands' attempts to prevent them from doing so (1998, 98).

The question as to the origin of this negative attitude towards female speech has to my knowledge not been sufficiently explored. Proverbs such as *Silence is golden*, or *Talk is cheap* allow for the interpretation that the ambivalent attitude towards women's speech is only part of a tendency to devaluate and distrust language in general. Though Holmes (1998, 49) and Giles et al. (1992, 219) argue that talk is highly appreciated in western cultures, the proverbial view mirrors a certain wariness towards language. De Caro (1987, 27) concludes that American proverbs reflect a "deep suspicion of speech because it may conflict with a strongly held value of the culture, the desire to get things done". Norrick (1997, 282) also lists "language versus action" and "take care with language" as typical themes of proverbs on speech. However, one can also reason that these negative clichés about speech have their origin in the fact that speech is associated with women whereas action is connected with men, thus again reflecting society's denigration of women. Kozloff (2000) establishes exactly this link to account for negative attitudes towards speech in the film industry. She argues that "dialogue has been continually discredited and undervalued in film because it is associated with femininity" (Kozloff 2000, 13). Indeed, screenwriting courses and manuals are rife with anti-dialogue dicta and waste no time and space on illustrating how to write good dialogue. In Hollywood movies, we encounter the taciturn Western hero, who believes in action instead of talk, and diametrically opposed to this ideal, the garrulous screwball heroine who does not let her interlocutor get a word in edgewise, all the while babbling on incoherently. Consequently, speech is trivialised, and genres which are built around talk like soap operas and sitcoms are considered inferior. Not surprisingly, soap operas and sitcoms are "women-targeted genres" (Brunsdon et al. 1997, 1). The complex interrelations between language, gender and screenwriting outlined so far render women-targeted TV genres an interesting field of research. In the following I will focus on a US-American sitcom to challenge the stereotype of the triviality of screen dialogue.

3. *Sex and the City*

Sex and the City premiered on the pay TV channel HBO in June 1998 and has drawn record ratings for the five seasons shown so far. The series is loosely based on Candace Bushnell's column in the *New York Observer*, which was turned into a best-selling book in 1997. The sitcom centres around the dysfunctional romantic lives of Bushnell's fictional alter ego, columnist Carrie Bradshaw, and her three thirty-something friends: PR executive Samantha Jones, corporate lawyer Miranda Hobbes, and art gallerist Charlotte York. This set-up fits nicely into the new television genre identified by Marshall/Werndley (2002, 49) as "'thirty-something' drama or modern 'comedies of sexual manners'", which is concerned with "the lifestyles, interpersonal relationships, careers and rites of passage anxieties of middle-class young professionals."

Roughly 20% of the broadcasting time in an episode of *Sex and the City* consists of all-female conversation. We listen in to the talk of the four friends in various locations, mostly in public places. The dialogue introduces the episode's theme, which is also the theme of Carrie's weekly newspaper column, e.g. "To be in a couple, do you have to put your single self on a shelf?" (Episode 62). It also serves to characterise the four women by displaying their opinions on a theme. Apart from that, the dialogue provides narrative causality by relating the women's experiences. Often conversational storytelling functions as an anchor for flashbacks, and the audience then travels back into the conversationalists' presence for the resolution and evaluation of the story. Finally, the dialogue of the four friends provides one of the main sources of the sitcoms' humour and is rife with witty repartee and sarcastic remarks like Samantha's "It's slim pickings out there. You can't swing a Fendi purse without knocking over five losers" (Episode 25).

Given my focus on the linguistic representation of the female friends through this dialogue, it is relevant to explore how the dialogue comes into existence. Sitcom dialogue is highly scripted and differs from natural conversation in many aspects, for example in its speed of delivery. Yet, screenwriters base their dialogue on their own intuitions about and expectations of how conversation works. These intuitions stem from first-hand experiences and from listening in on other's conversations. Cindy Chupack, one of the writers for *Sex and the City*, explains: "Every restaurant you go to seems like a possible set, and you overhear great conversations, and you can't help getting ideas because they are all around you" (HBO 2003). Certainly, the directors and the actors also have an influence on the fabric of the talk; the latter basing their performance of the scripted lines on their knowledge of how conversations between female friends sound. As the sequence analysed in the following section was also scripted and directed by women (Minsky/Seidelman 1998), it is to be expected that features characterising naturally occurring all-female conversation will show.

4. The talk of female friends – Creating feminine identities and maintaining friendships

The discursive turn (Weatherall 2002) in the social sciences, which led to a constructionist view of gender, has spawned new research on how feminine identities are negotiated through talk in "communities of practice" (Eckert/McConnell-Ginet 1992). One type of CofP which is replete with such discursive negotiations of gender identities is the circle of female friends (Coates 2000). Research on women's friendships has demonstrated that talk is a central element of these relationships, which functions not only as a way of mediating gender identities but also as an essential tool in the development and maintenance of these relationships (amongst others Harrison 1998; O'Connor 1992; Johnson/Aries 1983). Since friendships are defined as voluntary relationships in which "participants treat each other as equals and adhere to an ethic of reciprocity" (Coates 1997, 247), linguistic strategies deployed to achieve these two conditions are key to how women do being friends. Coates lists the following strategies: self-disclosure, especially through the telling of stories, hedging, questions, repetition, jointly-constructed utterances, interruptions, overlapping speech, and joking or teasing (1996, 263ff.).

In the following, I will investigate how the women's friendships in *Sex in the City* are constructed through their dialogue and how feminine identities are created in their talk. The fact that the four women are friends is established in the TV series through their frequent interactions, especially through their having meals together, which also presents the friendship circle as a surrogate family. Apart from eating together, they share various other activities like having their nails done at beauty parlours, playing cards, or strolling across a flea market. All of these joint activities, however, are dominated by their talk. For example when the women are shown watching TV together, the audience does not learn which programme or movie; the focus is on the conversation they are having. Thus, the centrality of talk in women's friendships is clearly demonstrated in the sitcom.

I will now take a close look at one instance of their verbal communication to demonstrate, firstly, the occurrence of features that Coates (1996) considers constitutive of female friendship talk and, secondly, the negotiation of feminine identities in the women's conversations. In the following excerpt Carrie and Miranda are shopping for a pregnancy test for Carrie, and Carrie is wondering whether she would make a good mother.

SC_10.9
1   C: I'm on total ovary overload. which kind do I get?
2   M: here. this one's on sale. half off.
3   C: sweetie, I just spent three hundred and ninety five dollars on a pair of open-toed Guccis last week. this is not the place to be frugal.

4	M:	all right. ((mumbling))
5	C:	wha- what about this one?
6	M:	oh First Response. I remember First Response. I had a very reassuring moment once with First Response. .hhh hhh here's hoping.
7	C:	hh {walking towards the cash desk} what if I am?
8	M:	(2.0) if you am you am.
9	C:	hh I don't think, I'd be very good at this. I mean .. am I maternal?
10	M:	(1.0) um ... ye-
11	C:	you know, when I was a little girl, I left my favourite baby doll out in the rain for four days. her face peeled off. that can't be good.
12	M:	yeah but I mean if you-
13	C:	I shaved my Barbie's head when I was mad at her.
14	M:	(1.0) when I was little, I took a rubber band, and put it around my dog Pepper's snout. (2.0) what?
15	C:	god. h {walking on then stopping again} can you picture it? us .. with (1.0)
16	M:	kids?
17	C:	(2.0) babies.
18	M:	hhh I'll probably end up with five. hhh

In this short excerpt we find various linguistic patterns which Coates (1996) has shown to be typical of women actively doing friendship through talk. First of all, there is humour at the beginning and the end of the sequence, which apart from providing entertainment also serves interpersonal goals. Carrie's first utterance "I'm on total ovary overload" (turn 1) creates humour through the unexpected combination of the terms *ovary*, which is part of the gynaecological register and the term *overload*, which is predominantly used in technical contexts (cf. Raskin 1985). This contrast between a female body part and the technical associations evoked by the word *overload* is accentuated through the alliteration. The humorous key facilitates the actual function of Carrie's utterance, namely to signal that she is in trouble and needs Miranda's help. At the end of the sequence we find a self-mocking remark by Miranda: "I'll probably end up with five." (turn 18). The mocking shows in her tone of voice as well as in the contrast of the utterance content with the foregoing theme of the conversation, namely the two of them not being fit for motherhood. In line with Norrick's research on conversational humour, this humorous attack on the self serves "to reiterate group opinion" (1993, 79), in this case the notion that motherhood is not something to strive for.

The second linguistic pattern which has a share in the discoursal construction of friendship is self-disclosure. Carrie's humorous statement "I'm on total ovary overload" (turn 1) signals that she is in trouble. In turn 6, Miranda reveals that she has been through the same kind of trouble: "I remember First Response. I had a very reassuring moment once with First Response." This can be considered a reciprocal self-disclosure, i.e. a mutual revelation of sensitive personal information, which has been shown to be a key way of doing friendship (amongst others Johnson/Aries 1983; Coates 1996; Harrison 1998). The disclosure renders Miranda vulnerable, but the vulnerability is contained through the fact that Carrie is now in the same situation. Likewise, Carrie needs not worry about her own vulnerability.

An even more striking example of mutual self-disclosure in this sequence is the mirroring storytelling (turns 11-14). Carrie's story consists of a general frame "when I was a little girl" followed by two narrative clauses "I left my favourite baby doll out in the rain for four days" and "her face peeled off" (cf. Norrick 2000). The main action is then succeeded by an evaluation, "that can't be good.", which in Norrick's terms "bids to win the audience over to a particular point of view" (2000, 116), in this case Carrie's being unfit to have children. Miranda reacts to Carrie's story with partial agreement "yeah but I mean if you-", which typically initiates a dispreferred turn in terms of the CA concept of preference organisation (Pomerantz 1984). Carrie, however, does not allow for any disagreement and goes on reasoning that she is not fit for motherhood. Her turn: "I shaved my Barbie's head when I was mad at her." (13) is almost a continuation of her minimal story about neglecting her doll. The general frame of the doll story still holds: this happened when she was a little girl. We are given one more narrative clause, "I shaved my Barbie's head", and a narrow frame (Norrick 2000): "when I was mad at her." Miranda then orients to the story-telling frame and aligns with her friend through a response story which matches Carrie's narrative (turn 14). Like Carrie's, it is a minimal story and the general frame is almost the same: "when I was little". It also consists of two narrative clauses: "I took a rubber band, and put it around my dog Pepper's snout." and depicts Miranda as being just as irresponsible as Carrie. The thematic and structural parallelism of the two stories creates rapport. Miranda's story shows that she understands Carrie. As Sacks phrases it, a relevant second story signals 'My mind is with you' (1995, 257). Miranda communicates that if Carrie considers herself to have a character flaw, she shares this flaw. Such mirroring self-disclosure stories are a typical strategy for doing friendship between women (Coates 1996, 264).

A third linguistic pattern which has been shown to create solidarity and thus fosters friendship is repetition (Tannen 1989, 51; Coates 1996, 266). This occurs in turn 8, when Miranda replies to Carrie's question "what if I am" (turn 7) with the tautological statement "if you am you am." The repetition of the first person singular verb form "am" from Carrie's question results in a grammatically incorrect sequence; the interpersonal function thus even overrides the grammatical rule of subject-verb concord.

Connection and solidarity is also created on the floor-constructional level. Carrie interrupts Miranda twice: In turn 11, she keeps Miranda from answering her "am I maternal?" and in turn 13, she does not wait for Miranda to finish her response to Carrie's initial minimal story, but continues illustrating her point. While interruptions generally are considered disruptive in conversation (cf. James/Clarke 1993), this specific instance shows that they can also create high involvement (Tannen 1994), because Miranda neither protests about Carrie taking over the floor nor does she try to maintain it. Coates (1996, 141) argues that this is a sign of a collaborative floor, in which case "the idea of 'seize the floor' becomes redundant because the floor is already occupied by all speakers." The interruption in this case carries "a metamessage of interpersonal rapport" (James/Clarke 1993, 240).

Carrie's interruption in turn 11, however, can also be interpreted as indicating that her interrogative clause "am I maternal?" (turn 9) is not meant to elicit information but is a rhetorical question, so that no extended answer is necessary. Rhetorical questions also occur frequently in Coates's data of naturally occurring conversation between women friends to express "truths, which assert the group's world view and check that consensus still exists" (1996, 188). This interpretation is sustained by the fact that Carrie prefaces the yes/no-question with a hedge: "I mean .. am I maternal?". Hedges are generally considered as expressions of caution about the proposition expressed in the utterance (amongst others Coates 1996, 154). In this case, Carrie displays doubts about being maternal.

A further means of the establishment of a collaborative floor is the joint construction of utterances, which also occurs in this sequence of talk. Carrie's incomplete utterance "can you picture it? us .. with" (turn 15) is finished by Miranda with the word *kids* in question intonation. This requires that Miranda has closely followed what Carrie is saying at all linguistic levels so that on the grammatical level, she knows a noun phrase is missing, and on the lexical level, she anticipates the meaning of this noun phrase from the context of the foregoing discourse. Even on the level of intonation Miranda's "kids?" fits Carrie's unfinished utterance. In the next turn, which follows after a two-second pause, Carrie herself contributes the word "babies", as a more precise completion to her utterance, which, however, confirms Miranda's utterance in so far as *baby* is a hyponym of *kids*.

Only one linguistic device on Coates's list (1996), namely overlapping talk, hardly ever occurs in my data, presumably because this feature interferes with the convention that dialogue on screen should be audible and clear. However, aside from the linguistic tools which Coates (1996) has shown to be instrumental in women's doing friendship, there is also another linguistic tool in my data which can be interpreted as creating solidarity, namely the usage of endearment terms like Carrie's "sweetie" in turn 3, used to introduce a dispreferred answer (Pomerantz 1984).

I now turn to the second major function of female talk which is well documented in the literature on language and gender (e.g. Coates 1996; 2000): the negotiation of female identities and thus the "performing of gender" in the sense of Butler (1990). Cameron (1997) argues that the fact that analysts are able to extract features typical of female talk is due to the existence of "a more general discourse of gender difference" which conversationalists also tap into to perform certain gender identities (p. 48). This means that all the features described above are also used by conversationalists to do traditional female identities. Apart from that there are more explicit ways of doing gender, starting off with Carrie's remark "I'm on total ovary overload" in turn 1, with which she presents herself as a woman who is subject to biological predetermination. The humorous key of the utterance, however, indicates ambiguity towards this destiny. This ambiguity is negotiated in the following discourse through to Miranda's final, self-mocking utterance "I'll probably end up with five." Apart from humour there are other strategies to mediate feminine identities. It is noticeable that neither Carrie nor Miranda ever use the word *pregnant*. In turn 7, Carrie poses the elliptical question "what if I am" and Miranda answers "if you am you am" (turn 8). The two women construct the concept of pregnancy as taboo. Contrary to the dominant discourse of pregnancy being a desirable part of womanhood, they consider it anathema. Likewise, the mirroring stories display the women as unfit for motherhood. Carrie presents herself as someone who behaves irresponsibly towards those in her care (turn 11,13) and Miranda even tops Carrie's story by admitting to irresponsibility towards a living being, her dog (turn 14). These mirroring stories are reminiscent of a study by Cook-Gumperz on little girls' interactional accomplishment of gender (2001), showing how girls reject the image of the nurturing mother and adopt an oppositional stance, for example when talking about boiling babies until their skins fall off while they are playing with dolls. Coates (2000) provides data of naturally occurring conversation between adult women with a similar tenor, namely expressing negative attitudes towards children. This kind of talk clearly challenges the dominant discourses of femininity which incorporate the image of the nurturing mother, and make it a typical topic of women's "backstage talk" (Coates 2000). In Goffman's theatre metaphor, backstage talk (as opposed to frontstage talk) is where a performer "can relax, he [sic] can drop his front, forgo speaking his lines, and step out of character" (Goffman 1971, 115). In the above example of all-female talk Carrie and Miranda drop their fronts, disclosing socially stigmatised behaviour and thus perform femininities which are not in line with frontstage norms, though such dominant norms still creep in as can be seen in Carrie's uneasy response to Miranda's story in turn 15.

5. Conclusion

In this paper, I have demonstrated that the representation of all-female talk in popular culture can be very close to naturally occurring conversation between women friends. Carrie and Miranda's dialogue is full of language patterns which linguists have shown to be typical in this context like a collaborative floor, humour, reciprocal story-telling and repetition. The talk of the two female friends on screen fulfils important interpersonal and identity functions for Carrie and Miranda, which also makes their characters and their relationship appear coherent to the audience. This clearly challenges the notion that excessive talk on the screen is trivial: talk is not cheap, neither in real life nor on TV. Consequently, genres which contain a great amount of dialogue like sitcoms or soap operas should not be labelled inferior.

Considering that the sequence analysed in this paper was scripted, directed and acted by women, it is not surprising that it appears to epitomize all-female talk. However, most of the episodes of *Sex and the City* are written by men (Season 1: 8 out of 12), and one wonders in how far this fact influences the dialogue and with it the feminine identities and relationships created. Future research, therefore, needs to compare dialogue scripted and directed by men and women to determine in how far they diverge.

Appendix: Transcription conventions

She's out.	Period shows falling tone in the preceding element.
Oh yeah?	Question mark shows rising tone in the preceding element.
nine, ten	Comma indicates a level, continuing intonation.
(2.0)	Numbers in parentheses indicate timed pauses.
	If the duration of the pauses is not crucial and not timed:
..	A truncated ellipsis is used to indicate pauses of one-half second or less.
...	An ellipsis is used to indicate a pause of more than a half-second.
.h	Inhalations are denoted with a period, followed by a small h. Longer inhalations are depicted with multiple hs as in .hhhh
h	Exhalations are denoted with a small h (without a preceding period). A longer exhalation is denoted by multiple hs.
((whispering))	Aspects of the utterance, such as whispers, coughing, and laughter, are indicated with double parentheses.
{drinking}	Other relevant aspects seen on screen are indicated with braces.

Adapted from Dressler/Kreuz (2000).

References

Butler, Judith (1990): Gender trouble – Feminism and the subversion of identity. London: Routledge.
Brunsdon, Charlotte et al. (eds.) (1997): Feminist television criticism. Oxford: Clarendon.
Cameron, Deborah (1997): Performing gender identity – Young men's talk and the construction of heterosexual masculinity. In: Johnson, Sally/Meinhof, Ulrike (eds.): Language and masculinity. Oxford: Blackwell, 47-64.

Coates, Jennifer (1996): Women talk. Oxford: Blackwell.
– (1997): Women's friendships, women's talk. In: Wodak, Ruth (ed.): Gender and talk. London: Sage, 245-262.
– (2000): Small talk and subversion – Female speakers backstage. In: Coupland, Justine (ed.): Small talk. Harlow: Pearson. 241-263.
Cook-Gumperz, Jenny (2001): Girls' oppositional stances – The interactional accomplishment of gender in nursery school and family life. In: Kotthoff, Helga/Baron, Bettina (eds.): Gender in interaction. Amsterdam: Benjamins, 21-49.
de Caro, Frank A. (1987): Talk is cheap – The nature of speech according to American proverbs. In: Proverbium 4, 17-37.
Dressler, Richard A./Kreuz, Roger J. (2000): Transcribing oral discourse – A survey and model system. In: Discourse Processes 29, 25-36.
Eckert, Penelope/McConnell-Ginet, Sally (1992): Think practically and look locally – Language and gender as community-based practice. In: Annual Review of Anthropology 21, 461-490.
– (2003): Language and gender. Cambridge: Cambridge University Press.
Giles, Howard et al. (1992): 'Talk is cheap...' but 'My word is my bond' – Beliefs about talk. In: Bolton, Kingsley/Kwok, Helen (eds.): Sociolinguistics today. London: Routledge, 218-243.
Goffman, Erving (1971): The presentation of self in everyday life. Harmondsworth: Penguin.
Harrison, Kaeren (1998): Rich friendships, affluent friends – Middle-class practices of friendship. In: Adams, Rebecca/Allen, Graham (eds.): Placing friendships in context. Cambridge: Cambridge University Press, 92-116.
HBO (2003): Sex and the City – The official webpage. at: http://www.hbo.com/city/
Holmes, Janet (1998): Women talk too much. In: Bauer, Laurie/Trudgill, Peter (eds.): Language myths. London: Penguin, 41-49.
James, Deborah/Clarke, Sandra (1993): Women, men, and interruptions. In: Tannen, Deborah (ed.): Gender and conversational interaction. Oxford: Oxford University Press, 231-280.
Johnson, Fern, L./Aries, Elizabeth J. (1983): The talk of women friends. In: Women's Studies International Forum 6, 353-361.
Jones, Deborah (1980): Gossip – Notes on women's oral culture. In: Women's Studies International Quarterly 3, 193-198.
Kozloff, Sarah (2000): Overhearing film dialogue. Berkley: University of California Press.
Marshall, Jill/Werndley Angela (2002): The language of television. London: Routledge.
Minsky, Terri/Seidelman, Susan (1998): Sex and the city – The baby shower. HBO.
Norrick, Neal R. (1993): Conversational joking. Bloomington: Indiana University Press.
– (1997): "Speech is silver" – On the proverbial view of language. In: Proverbium 14, 277-287.
– (2000): Conversational narrative. Amsterdam: Benjamins.
O'Connor, Pat (1992): Friendships between women. New York: The Guildford Press.
Pomerantz, Anita (1984): Agreeing and disagreeing with assessment – Some features of preferred/dispreferred turn-shapes. In: Atkinson, John M./Heritage, John (eds.): Structures of social action. Cambridge: Cambridge University Press, 57-101.
Raskin, Victor (1985): Semantic mechanisms of humor. Dordrecht: Reidel.
Sacks, Harvey (1992): Lectures on conversation, Vol. 2, ed. by Jefferson, Gail. Oxford: Blackwell.
Tannen, Deborah (1989): Talking voices. Cambridge: Cambridge University Press.
– (1994): Interpreting interruption in conversation. In: Tannen, Deborah (ed.): Gender and discourse. Oxford: Oxford University Press, 53-83.
Weatherall, Ann (2002): Gender, language and discourse. London: Routledge.

Gerhard Pisek

The translation of comic dialogue for film and television

1. Introduction

In his article *The English Dubbing Text*, Rowe (1960, 120) comes to the following conclusion regarding the translation of humor:

> [...] the intensity of the audience reaction to a comic line is far more important than any literary fidelity to the original sense. A funny line is intended to get a laugh. If it fails to do so when translated into the foreign tongue, then the translation has failed, whatever its literary excellence or fidelity to the original.

In this paper I want to focus on comic lines and dialogues in which humorous effects depend on the language itself, i.e. puns and other types of wordplay. These can either occur as purely verbal phenomena or be supported visually by the action on the screen. In other words, in all the examples discussed below, wit is indeed "the prisoner of its own language" (Rowe 1960, 120). In addition, however, wit can also be the prisoner of the image, and if this is the case, translators are faced with the double challenge of having to deal with both linguistic and visual restraints.

2. The translation of wordplay

It is not my aim to present a comprehensive analysis and typology of all instances of wordplay and their translations[1] in the corpus chosen (*Annie Hall*, a film by Woody Allen, and several episodes of the British TV series *Fawlty Towers*).

Instead, typical examples shall illustrate some of the basic problems dubbers and subtitlers are faced with in connection with wordplay.

The terms 'wordplay' and 'pun' will be used interchangeably, both referring to the fact that specific structural characteristics of a language make it possible to achieve semantic and

---

[1] This is, for example, done by Heibert (1993), who analyzes 735 examples of wordplay in James Joyce's *Ulysses* and their translations into German, French, Italian, Spanish and Portuguese.

pragmatic effects that can be employed for various rhetorical purposes.[2] As regards the translation of wordplay, there is often talk of its basic untranslatability, or at least of its reaching the limits of translatability (Macheiner 1995, Koller 1983). This is the result of a purely source-language oriented approach with emphasis on the isolated pun as the unit of translation. If we, however, adopt a more target-language oriented approach that also considers the function of the pun within the text and the function of the text in general, various translation strategies are at our disposal. Heibert (1993) lists 20 of them, not even taking into consideration the various combinations translators often resort to, as pointed out by Delabastita (1994, 239).

3. Dubbing or subtitling?

Subtitling is preferred in smaller European speech communities (e.g. the Scandinavian countries, the Netherlands, Portugal), whereas dubbing dominates in large markets like Germany, Italy or France.[3] When a film is dubbed, a soundtrack with the voices of actors speaking a translation of the original dialogue is added, creating the illusion for the viewers that the actors on the screen are actually speaking in their own, i.e. the viewers', language. Subtitling, in contrast, preserves the original dialogues by adding a written translation that appears at the bottom of the screen; subtitles usually consist of two rows of text, each about 35 characters in length.[4]

Arguments over dubbing vs. subtitling have been going on ever since the two methods were first practiced in the 1930s (Pruys 1997, 148), and even today staunch supporters of either method can be found. Advocates of subtitling claim, for example, that it is more honest than dubbing because it "is an *overt* type of translation, retaining the original version, thus laying itself bare to criticism from everybody with the slightest knowledge of the source language" (Gottlieb 1994, 102). In dubbing, on the other hand, the original text is not present, making it, of course, more difficult to criticize the translation.

If we accept the basic honesty of subtitles, we also have to be aware that such honesty can have its drawbacks: subtitles disturb the visual experience and distract the audience be-

---

[2] When a distinction is made between 'pun' and 'wordplay', the former is usually described as "a play *on* words" (*Oxford Companion to the English Language*), whereas the latter comprises all kinds of playing "*with* the sound, spelling, form, grammar, and many other aspects of words" (*Oxford Companion to the English Language*) and thus includes puns.

[3] Cf. Herbst (1994, 18-23).

[4] For a detailed discussion of the two methods, see Herbst (1994) or Pisek (1994).

cause it is forced to divide its attention between the images and the text that continuously flashes on and off (Vöge 1977, 120). In addition, subtitles have also been criticized for being reminiscent of telegrams (Mounin 1967) and for bringing about a certain loss of information.[5] On the other hand, subtitles have the advantage of allowing the audience to hear the voices of the original actors and actresses, which may contribute greatly to the overall aesthetic experience of enjoying a film.

This element is, of course, lost in dubbing, where specially trained actors speak the target language dialogues. Dubbing has also been criticized for disturbing the identity between gesture and speech (Balázs 1949), the argument being that, say, passionate Italian body language does not agree with the cool English way of saying 'I love you'. Some critics oppose dubbing for phonetic reasons, an argument that is easy to support with carefully chosen isolated words but not as valid when longer segments of speech are dealt with and factors like camera angle, lighting etc. are taken into consideration (cf. Goris 1993, Herbst 1994, Müller 1982, Pisek 1994).

There are also economic reasons that determine the choice between dubbing and subtitling. Since dubbing is about 15 times as expensive as subtitling (Gottlieb 1994), it seems only logical that the cheaper method should be employed in the smaller, less lucrative markets.

3.1 *Annie Hall* and *Fawlty Towers*

As mentioned above, for the dubbing examples Woody Allen's 1977 comedy *Annie Hall* (German title: *Der Stadtneurotiker*) was chosen. The subtitled examples are from *Fawlty Towers*, "a funny British television program about a hotel called Fawlty Towers, and its owner, Basil Fawlty, played by John Cleese. In the hotel, things often go wrong and the people who work there, esp. Basil Fawlty, often behave in strange ways" (*Longman Dictionary of English Language and Culture*).

In the case of Woody Allen it is worth noting that 'literary' translations of many of his scripts into German have also been published. This means that identical source texts – the original scripts – were translated for two different media – book and film –, making it possible to observe how a particular medium can influence the translations produced for it. Unfortunately, such comparisons cannot be made in the case of *Fawlty Towers*, where no other German-language versions apart from the subtitles are available.

---

[5] This view is not held by Gottlieb, for whom "the only loss implied in a condensation is the loss of redundant oral language features" (1992, 167).

4. Wordplay and dubbing

In the first example from *Annie Hall*, Alvy Singer, a successful comedy writer, is strolling along a street together with his friend Rob. At first the two can hardly be seen in the distance, but then they come closer and closer to the camera, move past and finally disappear off-screen. All the time they can be heard talking. Alvy is extremely sensitive about being Jewish and complains to his friend that several people have been making allusions to his ethnic background.

> ROB: Alvy, you're a total paranoid.
> ALVY: Wh- How am I a paran-? Well, I pick up on those kind o' things. You know, I was having lunch with some guys from NBC, so I said ... uh, 'Did you eat yet or what?' and Tom Christie said, 'No, didchoo?' Not did you, didchoo eat? Jew? No, not did you eat, but jew eat? Jew. You get it? Jew eat?
>
> (Allen 1982, 9f.)[6]

The phonetic similarity between *(did)choo eat* and *Jew eat* helps Alvy to prove his point. The fact that word boundaries are ignored is typical of such puns involving distant or allusive homophony, which are so easy to produce in English because of its tendency "to link words together to form a single stream of sound, a single phonological word" (Chiario 1992, 35).

Both the German dubbing version and the literary translation manage to convey Alvy's paranoia.

> ALVY: Was, wieso bin ich para-? Mir fallen nur solche Dinge auf. Neulich war ich mit 'n paar Leuten von NBC zum Essen verabredet. Ich sagte, kommt Kinder, ich lad' euch alle ein. Darauf sagt Tom Christie: 'Also jut.' Nicht 'also gut,' sondern 'also jut.' Verstehst du, nicht 'gut,' sondern 'jut. Jud.'[7]

> ALVY: Wieso – ich bin verfolgungswahnsinnig? Nein, sowas fällt mir einfach auf. Hör mal, ich hab neulich mit Leuten vom NBC geluncht, da hab ich äh zu einem gesagt: 'Haben Sie schon gegessen?' Und Tom Christie hat gesagt: 'Nein, noch nicht, wars jut?' Nicht 'gut', sondern 'jut'. Also 'Jud'! Nicht 'wars gut', sondern 'jut'! Klar? 'Wars Essen Jud?'
>
> (Allen 1981, 18)

In both translations the same solution can be found: a pronunciation of the German adjective *gut* is chosen that is usually associated with the dialect spoken in Berlin, where the *g* in *gut* is pronounced like the *j* in *Jude*; when omitting the final *e* in *Jude*, as is often done when this word is used in a derogatory fashion, the result is a combination of sounds that is almost

---

[6] The spelling follows *Four Films of Woody Allen*, which contains the scripts to *Annie Hall, Interiors, Manhattan* and *Stardust Memories*.
[7] My transcript of the dubbed dialogue.

identical with the Berlin pronunciation of the adjective *gut*, which is also a semantically clever choice because it can be incorporated into almost any given context.

In another scene in *Annie Hall*, a flashback shows Alvy speaking in an auditorium during the 1956 presidential election campaign for Adlai Stevenson, the Democratic opponent of the Republican candidate and incumbent president, Dwight D. Eisenhower.

> ALVY: I ... interestingly had, uh, dated ... a woman in the Eisenhower Administration ... briefly ... and, uh, it was ironic to me 'cause uh ... tsch ... 'cause I was trying to, u-u-uh, do to her what Eisenhower has been doing to the country for the last eight years.
>
> (Allen 1982, 21)

The audience responds with roaring laughter because it is able to complete mentally what is left unsaid; this strategy is typical of off-color spoonerisms, where the taboo part of the utterance has to be supplied by the recipient through transposition of initial word sounds.

In this example, however, the audience has to find a polysemous verb that can describe both activities alluded to by Alvy. Two solutions come to mind: *to fuck* ('have sexual intercourse; damage, ruin sthg.') and *to screw* ('have sexual intercourse; cheat').

The two German translations fail to convey the double entendre. Although the viewers and readers do get faithful renderings of what is said by Alvy, they are bound to fail in their attempts to fill the gap of what is left unsaid because there are no German verbs that combine the different meanings in a similar fashion.

> ALVY: Ich äh, ich hab neulich ein Mädchen kennengelernt, das äh, das in der Eisenhower-Administration beschäftigt war. Und äh, das kam mir irgendwie komisch vor ... weil ich mit ihr das, das gleiche versucht habe zu machen, was Eisenhower mit dem Land gemacht hat ... in den letzten acht Jahren.
>
> (transcript)

> ALVY: Ich – das wird sie vielleicht interessieren – hatte da ein Rendezvous mit einer Frau aus der Eisenhower-Administration, sie war kurze Zeit ... und äh mir schien, das Ironische war, daß – naja – ich im Sinn hatte, das gleiche mit ihr zu tun, was Eisenhower mit dem Land gemacht hat, all die letzten acht Jahre.
>
> (Allen 1981, 33)

The fact that a comic element gets lost in the translation is underlined by the laughter of the audience that can, of course, also be heard in the dubbed film version. This means that the viewers will have the feeling of being deprived of or missing something, or just be amazed at such a reaction to those lines that are not funny at all in German.

Since Alvy is barely visible when he makes this joke, it would have been possible for the dubbers to replace it with a totally different one in the target language; such a pragmatic and functional approach would preserve the dynamic process of the text better than a faithful but interactionally poor translation.

In the literary translation, we are simply told that the audience responds with laughter, which is, of course, just as puzzling as hearing the actual laughing sounds in the dubbed version.

Sometimes, however, a functional approach does not work, either; this is, for example, the case when a pun is not just dependent on the source language but also on the situational context like material objects that are clearly visible.

In another flashback, we see young Alvy at a family gathering, standing next to an elderly man called Joey Nichols.

> JOEY: Joey Nichols. (Laughing) See, Nichols. See, Nichols! (*Joey shows young Alvy his cuff links and tie pin, which are made from nickels, as Alvy stands with hands on hips, unconcerned. Joey then slaps his hand to his forehead and puts a nickel on his forehead*) Yuh see, nickels! You can always remember my name, just think of Joey Five Cents. (*Laughing*) That's me. Joey Five Cents! (*Joey grabs Alvy's cheeks and pinches them*).

(Allen 1982, 74)

The pun is based on the homophony of the man's last name (*Nichols*) and the plural form of the American term for the five-cent coin (*nickels*); it is visually supported by all the nickels the man proudly displays. This close link between verbal and visual elements means that replacing the untranslatable wordplay by a functionally equivalent one from the target language is impossible because what is seen on the screen cannot, of course, be manipulated by the dubber. In the German film version the viewers get a semantically faithful rendering of the English text that does not, however, make much sense since there is no connection between *Nickel* and *Fünf-Cent*.

> JOEY: Joey Nichols. Siehst du, Nickels. Hier auch Nickels. Hähähä.Nickel. So kannst du dir immer meinen Namen merken. Denk nur einfach an Joe Fünf-Cent. Hähähä. Das bin ich. Joe Fünf-Cent. Hähähä.

(transcript)

The literary translation is almost identical. There is, however, one essential difference: the first mention of *Nickel* is accompanied by a footnote informing the reader that there is an untranslatable wordplay based on the identical pronunciation of *Nichols* and *nickels*, the latter being five-cent coins. This editorial technique of presenting a target language explanation is also mentioned by Heibert (1993) as one of the methods translators sometimes resort to, although it obviously disturbs the stylistic and aesthetic identity of the text.

> JOEY: Joey Nichols. Schau mal, Nickel. Und hier, 'Nickel'. Lauter Nickel, siehst du. So kannst du dir meinen Namen merken, du brauchst bloß an Joey Fünf-Cents zu denken, das bin dann ich: Joey Fünf-Cents.

(Allen 1981, 112)

Faced with the choice between a translation that makes no sense, on the one hand, and a translation that resorts to an explanatory footnote, on the other, most readers will probably prefer the latter – even if this means putting up with the disruptions mentioned above. In dubbing, any explanations are obviously out of the question if the instance of wordplay is as dependent on visual aspects as in the *Nichols-nickels* example. If this is not the case, a pun can be compensated for by finding a target language solution that fulfils the same function, especially when the purpose of the original pun is "merely to raise laughter" (Newmark 1988, 217), as in the case of jokes that are not related to the action in any other way. Chiario (1992, 95) suggests this solution specifically for comic plays or films, where "it is often preferable to replace a 'difficult' joke with a totally different one in the target language, which, while bearing no relation to the source joke, is, however, obviously a joke in the target version."[8]

This strategy can be observed in the translation of the following pun, which comes from a third-rate comedian Alvy meets at the beginning of his career.

> COMEDIAN: Hey, I just got back from Canada, you know, they speak a lotta French up there. The only way to remember Jeanne d'Arc means the light's out in the bathroom.
>
> (Allen 1982, 53)

In the dubbing version, this intentionally bad pun – based on the homophony of a slightly incorrect pronunciation of *Jeanne d'Arc* and *john* (bathroom) *dark* – is replaced with an equally bad one in German.

> KOMIKER: Hey, ich war mal eben oben in Kanada. Die moderne französische Küche hat viele Vorteile ... die brauchen gar keine Pille in dem Land. Da nehmen die Frauen einfach den Rock vor.
>
> (transcript)

Since the only function of this joke is to illustrate what a pathetic comedian this man is, the solution with *Rock vor* (which sounds almost like the German pronunciation of the French cheese *Roquefort*) can be said to be perfectly adequate.

The literary translation also succeeds in preserving the function of the pun; in addition, it manages to abuse the name of the French national heroine for this purpose – as is done in the source text.

> KOMIKER: Hey, ich komm grad von Kanada rüber, und sie wissen, dort wird ziemlich französisch parliert. Also zur Heiligen Johanna fällt mir immer nur der Hintern meiner Alten ein: Schann d'Arsch.
>
> (Allen 1981, 79)

---

[8] Levy (1969, 104) offers the same solution for literary translations, emphasizing that in certain situations it is more important to preserve the type of wordplay rather than the meaning of the individual words of the source language.

5. Wordplay and subtitling

As mentioned above, when audiovisual material is subtitled, the original voices are preserved, which means that a viewer who understands the source language to some extent will not have to rely on the subtitles alone to be able to follow the dialogues. For viewers not familiar with the foreign language at all, watching a subtitled film can still be a pleasurable experience because they might be able to enjoy just the images or, in the case of *Fawlty Towers*, laugh about the many slapstick elements that work perfectly without any words at all. But what about verbal humor that is entirely dependent on the source language? Is it possible to make people laugh with subtitled translations of puns, or at least give them an idea of why canned laughter can be heard in the background as a reaction to something a character has just said? The following passages illustrate how difficult a task this can be.

In the first example, Basil Fawlty sees Manuel, the Spanish waiter, who is just serving breakfast.

> FAWLTY: Manuel, there is too much butter on those trays.[9]
> MANUEL: Que?
> FAWLTY: There is too much butter on those trays.
> MANUEL: No, no, Senor. Not 'on those trays.' No, sir. Uno, dos, tres. Uno, dos, tres.

When he repeats the sentence, Fawlty points in rapid succession at the three trays, creating the impression that he is indeed counting them. The waiter, whose imperfect command of the English language is often exploited for humorous effects, falls victim to the far-fetched phonetic similarity between the three English words and the Spanish terms for 1, 2 and 3. This bilingual pun is rendered in the German subtitles by first introducing the English word *tray* in parentheses after the literal translation of Fawlty's first sentence, and then by using it instead of its German equivalent when he repeats the statement.

> FAWLTY: Manuel ... da ist zuviel Butter auf den Tabletts. (Trays)
>   Da ist zuviel Butter auf diesen 'Trays'.
> MANUEL: Nein, Sir, man sagt 'uno, dos, tres'.

Only the last part of the pun is preserved on the textual level. However, the fact that Fawlty clearly seems to be counting the trays makes Manuel's response at least comprehensible.

Another misunderstanding between Fawlty and Manuel occurs when Fawlty wants to know where his wife is.

> FAWLTY: Where's Sybil?
> MANUEL: Que?

---

[9] All the examples quoted in the following discussion have been transcribed.

FAWLTY: Where's Sybil?
MANUEL: Where's the bill?
FAWLTY: I own the place. I don't pay bills. Where's my wife?

For the Spanish waiter, whose English is heavily accented, the name of Fawlty's wife and *the bill* are phonologically so similar because he mispronounces the definite article as /zi:/. In the German version, the content of this exchange is faithfully reproduced on the semantic level, but it remains totally unclear why Fawlty is misunderstood by Manuel since in German *Sybil* and *die Rechnung* are, of course, not even distantly homophonous. Therefore those viewers who have to depend on the subtitles can only attribute the waiter's reaction to his generally poor command of English. This is what they get:

FAWLTY: Wo ist Sybil?
MANUEL: Wo ist die Rechnung?
FAWLTY: Ich bin der Besitzer. Ich bezahle keine Rechnungen! Wo ist meine Frau?

Sometimes the dubbers are lucky and wordplay based on sound similarity can be reproduced to some extent in the target language, as can be seen in the following example.

FAWLTY: Go and get me a hammer.
MANUEL: A hammer?
FAWLTY: Hammer.
MANUEL: Hammer? ... oh, hamah sandwich.
FAWLTY: Oh, do I have to go through this every time? Look, a hammer.
MANUEL: My hamster?
FAWLTY: No, no, not your hamster. How can I knock a nail in with your hamster?

In the subtitles, the first pun (*hammer – hamah sandwich*) is simply left out, creating the impression that Manuel just does not understand what is said to him, whereas the second can be reproduced on a one-to-one basis because semantically and phonologically the German words *Hammer* and *Hamster* are perfect mirror images of the respective English counterparts. This is due to the fact that *hammer* and *Hammer* are both, of course, of Germanic orgin and that *hamster* was even taken over into English from German *Hamster*.

FAWLTY: Holen Sie mir einen Hammer! – – – Jedesmal dasselbe! Einen Hammer!
MANUEL: Meinen Hamster?
FAWLTY: Ich kann doch mit einem Hamster keinen Nagel einschlagen!

As seen in connection with the example involving *nickels* and *Nichols* from *Annie Hall*, some puns depend on visual effects, creating an unsurmountable obstacle for the translator. In a scene from *Fawlty Towers*, this can also be observed.

Two elderly couples who do not know each other are waiting in the hotel bar shortly before dinner. They are Colonel and Mrs. Hall and Mr. and Mrs. Twitchen.

> FAWLTY: Oh, Colonel. Ah. Colonel and Mrs. Hall. May I introduce Mr and Mrs. T – – Have you met?

He does not finish the name because Colonel Hall has a nervous twitch, and at the very moment Fawlty wants to say *Twitchen*, the Colonel's head jerks uncontrollably and Fawlty, to his great horror, realizes that it would be most impolite to pronounce this name that is almost homophonous with the *ing*-form of the verb that describes Colonel Hall's affliction (*twitching*). The whole humor that follows this embarrassing moment is built on Fawlty's refusal to utter this name; therefore it is not possible for him to introduce the two couples appropriately although they insist repeatedly that he do so. He pretends not to understand what they want from him and ultimately even feigns unconsciousness.

The German subtitles fail to reveal Fawlty's dilemma. Although the fact that he refuses to act properly in this situation does get across to the viewers, they never learn the reason for his strange behavior because an important element is lost in the translation, namely a pun that depends on the combination of verbal and visual effects.

> FAWLTY: Gut. Oberst, Frau Hall. Darf ich vorstellen, Herr und Frau … Sie kennen sich schon?

6. Conclusion

Summing up the observations made above, it can be said that wordplay in audiovisual texts is not a priori untranslatable; it can, however, be impossible to translate when it is integrated into the visual context.

When this is the case, dubbing translators may be forced to produce a translation that can only be seen as a compromise between word and image, whereas their literary counterparts, who are free to focus on the verbal aspects alone, have considerably more strategies at their disposal, like adding information within the text or using explanatory footnotes. That this advantage is, unfortunately, not always realized can be seen in the example of the implicit pun involving President Eisenhower. As with other instances of wordplay, the necessary information could have been added in a footnote. The dubbing translation of the same pun is equally unsatisfactory, especially when one considers the fact that this cannot be blamed on any visual restraints. Although footnotes or similar explanatory additions are obviously out of the question, lighting and the camera angle would have made it possible to adopt a purely functional approach, like inventing a totally new political joke for this specific context.

As other examples – such as the translations of the pun based on *Jeanne d'Arc* – show, such a functional approach may yield satisfactory solutions, i.e. solutions that enable the target language audience to enjoy a film even if the semantic meaning of the original lines cannot always be preserved.

Translating comic dialogue for subtitles is an even more challenging task. Most instances of wordplay are lost because of the special restrictions posed by this type of translation. The fact that the original dialogue can always be heard by the target-language audience makes it impossible, for example, to completely abandon the semantic meaning of a funny line and try to find a functionally appropriate solution instead. One must always bear in mind, however, that it is not words alone that make people laugh when watching comedy programs like *Fawlty Towers*. For the creation of humorous effects, what can be seen on the screen is at least just as important as – or even more important than – what can be read at the bottom of the screen. And if this combination of visual and verbal elements succeeds in entertaining the target-language audience, also the translation can be said to have succeeded.

References

Allen, Woody (1981): Der Stadtneurotiker. Transl. by Henscheid, Eckhard/Rahm, Sieglinde. Zürich: Diogenes.
– (1982): Four films of Woody Allen. New York: Random House.
Balázs, Bela (1949): Der Film. Wesen und Werden einer neuen Kunst. Wien: Globus.
Chiario, Delia (1992): The language of jokes. London: Routledge.
Danan, Martine (1991): Dubbing as an expression of nationalism. In: Meta 36/4, 606-614.
Delabastita, Dirk (1994): Focus on the pun: Wordplay as a special problem in translation studies. In: Target 6/2, 223-243.
Goris, Olivier (1993): The question of French dubbing: Towards a frame for systematic investigation. In: Target 5/2, 169-190.
Gottlieb, Henrik (1992): Subtitling – a new university discipline. In: Dollerup, Cay/Loddegaard, Annette (eds.): Teaching translation and interpreting. Amsterdam: Benjamins, 161-170.
– (1994): Subtitling: diagonal translation. In: Perspectives: Studies in Translatology 1, 101-123.
Heibert, Frank (1993): Das Wortspiel als Stilmittel und seine Übersetzung. Tübingen: Narr.
Herbst, Thomas (1994): Linguistische Aspekte der Synchronisation von Fernsehserien. Tübingen: Niemeyer.
Koller, Werner (1983): Einführung in die Übersetzungswissenschaft. Heidelberg: Quelle & Meyer (UTB 819).
Levy, Jirí (1969): Die literarische Übersetzung. Frankfurt a. M.: Athenäum.
Longman Dictionary of English Language and Culture (1992). Burnt Mill: Longman.
McArthur, Tom (ed.) (1992): Oxford companion to the English language. Oxford: Oxford University Press.
Macheiner, Judith (1995): Übersetzen. Frankfurt a. M.: Eichborn.
Mounin, Georges (1967): Die Übersetzung. Geschichte. Theorie. Anwendung. München: Nymphenburger.
Müller, J.-Dietmar (1982): Die Übertragung fremdsprachigen Filmmaterials ins Deutsche. Diss. Univ. Regensburg.

Newmark, Peter (1988): A textbook of translation. Hemel Hempstead: Prentice Hall.
Pisek, Gerhard (1994): Die große Illusion. Probleme und Möglichkeiten der Filmsynchronisation. Trier: WVT.
Pruys, Guido Mark (1997): Die Rhetorik der Filmsynchronisation. Tübingen: Narr.
Rowe, Thomas (1960): The English dubbing text. In: Babel 6/3, 116-120.
Völge, Hans (1977): The translation of films: Sub-titling versus dubbing. In: Babel 2/3, 120-125.

Hélène Labbe / Michel Marcoccia

Tradition épistolaire et médias numériques: du billet au courrier électronique

Introduction

De nombreux travaux sur le courrier électronique sont d'inspiration comparatiste. Ainsi, pour définir les spécificités du courrier électronique, de nombreux chercheurs procèdent par comparaison avec des genres de dialogues préexistants. On considère généralement que le courrier électronique se situe entre trois usages: la conversation en face à face, la correspondance traditionnelle et la correspondance d'entreprise (Orlikowski/Yates 1994). Le dialogue par courrier électronique serait, selon ces hypothèses, une pratique de communication déterminée par les normes et les conventions de l'échange oral ou de la lettre (Danet 1998, Ivanova 1999). Nous présenterons dans cet article l'intérêt mais aussi les limites de ces deux comparaisons.

Notre hypothèse se place toujours dans cette optique comparatiste mais varie du point de vue de l'objet à partir duquel s'établit la comparaison. Selon nous, le courrier électronique est un genre de dialogue qui s'inscrit dans une tradition épistolaire particulière, celle des formes brèves, et plus particulièrement du billet.[1]

En d'autres termes, le courrier électronique s'inscrit dans la continuité d'un genre, le dialogue épistolaire de forme brève (Haroche-Bouzinac 2000), dans lequel on trouve le billet mais aussi la carte postale, le pneumatique, le télégramme, et, dans une certaine mesure, la note de service ou le fax. On verra ainsi les points communs entre billet et courrier électronique, en s'appuyant à la fois sur des exemples et sur la littérature existant sur le sujet. Notre approche combinera l'analyse conversationnelle (pour examiner les composantes de base des interactions épistolaires en ligne) et les recherches en littérature (pour identifier les caractéristiques des billets, particulièrement au XIXe siècle). En conséquence, les exemples qui étayeront notre analyse constituent un corpus hétérogène puisque nous comparerons des billets d'écrivains[2] à des courriers électroniques envoyés sur nos propres messageries pro-

---

[1] On peut noter que cette relation entre billet et courrier électronique est déjà évoquée, mais de manière très rapide, par Haroche-Bouzinac (2000, 51).
[2] Les exemples utilisés dans cet article sont extraits de la correspondance de Charles Baudelaire (deux tomes, édités par C. Pichois et J. Ziegler, en 1973, aux éditions Gallimard – collection La

fessionnelles (par des étudiants ou des collègues). De notre point de vue, l'apparente incongruité de ce rapprochement renforce notre hypothèse car elle met en évidence la détermination des messages par leurs supports, plus que par leurs auteurs.

1. Le courrier électronique et le dialogue en face à face

De manière générale, on admet que la communication médiatisée par ordinateur est une forme de communication hybride, qui relève à la fois de la communication écrite et de la communication orale, qu'elle soit en face à face ou téléphonique (Baron 1998): le code utilisé est l'écrit, mais les échanges de messages entrent dans une structure dialogale permise par la rapidité de la rédaction et de la transmission des messages. Comparée aux autres formes de communication écrite, la communication numérique favorise la production de messages brefs, des «écrits spontanés naïfs» (Cusin-Berche 1999) au style marqué par l'oralité[3] et par la présence de procédés de représentation du non verbal (Marcoccia 2000a, 2000b). Selon cette approche, comparer la communication médiatisée par ordinateur à la conversation orale est utile pour comprendre les spécificités du courrier électronique.

Pourtant, sur de nombreux aspects, le courrier électronique n'a rien à voir avec le face à face. En effet, les courriers électroniques sont écrits «sous contraintes»: la supposée oralité de ces écrits se combine à la rigidité de leur organisation formelle, souvent négligée par les analystes. Lorsqu'on rédige un message numérique, cet écrit doit correspondre à un format très spécifique, contraint par le dispositif technique (Marcoccia 2003a). Le cadre participatif des échanges médiatisés par ordinateur est aussi spécifique (Marcoccia 2004b). La médiation technique nécessaire pour l'envoi d'un message introduit une hiérarchisation possible de l'instance de production des messages, à la fois technique, sociale et humaine. De plus, un courrier électronique peut être envoyé en hiérarchisant les destinataires de manière assez formelle, par le procédé de la copie, par exemple.

Enfin, le point le plus important relève du bon sens: la communication médiatisée par ordinateur implique une forme de dématérialisation de l'échange impliquant l'anonymat partiel ou total des participants. En bref, si la comparaison avec le face à face peut avoir un intérêt heuristique, elle n'a pas de réelle vertu descriptive.

Pléiade) et de Gustave Flaubert (quatre tomes, édités par J. Bruneau, en 1973, aux éditions Gallimard – collection La Pléiade). Les références des exemples qui ne sont pas extraits de ce corpus sont explicitement mentionnées dans notre article.

3   De nombreux travaux portent sur ce point: on peut citer Yates (1996) pour l'anglais, Anis (2000) pour le français.

2. Le courrier électronique et la lettre

L'autre comparaison couramment établie est instaurée entre le courrier électronique et la lettre. Quelques travaux rapprochent de manière assez logique le courrier électronique de la relation épistolaire d'ordre privé (Mélançon 1996, Ivanova 1999, Yates 2000) ou professionnel (Orlikowski/Yates 1994). Cette comparaison présente cependant elle aussi quelques limites.

Tout d'abord, on peut constater des différences du point de vue de la structure des messages. Ainsi, le courrier électronique est, au moins de manière conventionnelle, un message bref, ce qui n'est pas le cas de la lettre. Par ailleurs, contrairement à la lettre, le courrier électronique comporte généralement pas ou peu de formules d'adresse. Plusieurs échanges par jour amènent à considérer les messages électroniques comme les répliques d'un dialogue continu et non pas comme des messages indépendants dont chacun posséderait sa propre unité structurelle. Le courrier électronique privilégie le morcellement de la chaîne d'échanges sur les grands textes structurés.

Du point de vue de la matérialité du support, le courrier électronique possède des caractéristiques qui le distinguent nettement de la lettre. Comme le souligne Mélançon (1996, 13-19), la dimension matérielle est un élément important de la lettre: le papier, la taille de l'enveloppe, les petits rituels pour décacheter les enveloppes, etc. On peut cependant noter que diverses fonctions des logiciels de messagerie semblent reposer sur des métaphores des actions concrètes de la correspondance traditionnelle: poster une lettre, ouvrir son courrier, le conserver ou le jeter à la corbeille, etc.

Si l'on compare les échanges médiatisés par courrier électronique et les interactions épistolaires (Kerbrat-Orecchioni 1998), on peut noter d'autres différences du point de vue de la mise en scène de l'échange. La lettre est un acte de communication qui repose sur une mise en scène des composantes de l'échange: le destinataire et le cadre spatio-temporel. Dans la lettre, la date et l'indication du lieu font partie des procédés destinés à créer un effet de réalité. Aussi, il est courant que les épistoliers oublient de dater leurs envois ou les datent de manière fantaisiste. La situation est toute différente dans le courrier électronique, où la date, le nom du participant et le lieu d'émission sont des données objectives, fournies par le système dans le péritexte du message.

Par ailleurs, le délai entre la rédaction du message et sa lecture est différent pour la lettre et le courrier électronique: le discours épistolaire traditionnel se caractérise par un ensemble de décalages qui constituent ce que Haroche-Bouzinac (1995a, 77-80) appelle la «temporalité épistolaire». Il est projeté dans l'avenir au moment de l'écriture et au passé au moment de la lecture. C'est un discours différé, qui s'efforce d'imiter un discours en temps réel. Par rapport aux décalages de la correspondance traditionnelle, le courrier électronique est en mesure d'assurer un dialogue quasiment en temps réel. Cette caractéristique régit aussi bien la forme que le fond du message, surtout au niveau de l'ouverture et de la clôture du courrier électronique. Ainsi, la supposition d'une réception immédiate fait que le présent de la narration correspond à peu près au présent de la lecture.

Au-delà de ces différences, le courrier électronique et la lettre présentent un point commun remarquable: il s'agit dans les deux cas d'écrits pour lesquels il existe des conventions. Les manuels de l'épistolaire ont fleuri jusqu'au XIXe siècle. D'une manière comparable, l'apparition du courrier électronique a été accompagnée d'une production importante de textes et d'ouvrages recommandant comment bien utiliser sa messagerie: le style des écrits médiatisés par ordinateur est défini de manière normative, par exemple du point de vue des règles de courtoisie de la nétiquette (Marcoccia 1998).

3. Le courrier électronique et le billet

3.1 Définition du billet

En France, le courrier électronique est venu vraisemblablement occuper le créneau qui était celui du fax, lui même ayant pris la place du télégramme ou du pneumatique. Observant cette généalogie, on peut identifier un genre: le dialogue épistolaire de forme brève, dont l'ancêtre est le billet. A partir de cette observation, on peut soulever l'hypothèse suivante: le courrier électronique n'est-il pas une nouvelle forme (numérique) du billet? Les divers travaux sur la forme épistolaire brève (Haroche-Bouzinac 1995a, 1995b; Fisher 1998; Bray 2000; Gruffat 2001) s'accordent pour donner du billet la définition suivante: le billet est un message bref dans son écriture, son contenu et sa forme. Il est apparu au XVIIe siècle lorsque les épistoliers ont éprouvé le besoin de se dispenser des formules de politesse conventionnelles. Tout en étant plus familier que la lettre, le billet conserve une expression soignée. C'est souvent pour l'épistolier l'occasion de briller par une remarque spirituelle ou un bon mot. Mais le billet peut être aussi écrit dans l'urgence et avoir une fonction strictement informative. Le billet remplit de multiples fonctions: billet de spectacle, billet doux, billet de logement, etc.

Un tour d'horizon de la littérature sur le billet permet de mettre en évidence divers paramètres à partir desquels peut s'établir la comparaison avec le courrier électronique.

3.2 Un message bref

Avant tout autre critère, c'est la brièveté qui distingue le billet de la lettre (Gruffat 2001, 39). C'est dans la concision et l'économie de moyens que s'exerce la virtuosité des auteurs de billets (Haroche-Bouzinac 2000, 49). Pour autant, cette brièveté est mesurée et ne doit pas favoriser la confusion. Comme le soulignent les manuels d'art épistolaire de l'époque classique, «il faut rechercher la brièveté, mais éviter l'extrême concision» (Bray 2000, 56). C'est aussi une caractéristique du courrier électronique: les messages sont brefs mais clairs, comme si le principe d'économie constituait un impératif (Anis 2000). La brièveté fait même partie des recommandations proposées dans les textes normatifs sur la communication par messagerie (par exemple, Angell/Heslop 1994).

3.3 Un style peu formel

Selon Fisher (1998), la pratique du billet a correspondu à une contestation des conventions dites bourgeoises relevant du savoir-vivre traditionnel. Par exemple, les écrivains du XIXe siècle peuvent se permettre entre eux de s'écarter de l'éloquence et des convenances épistolaires. Si ces libertés s'expriment aussi parfois dans des lettres, elles se radicalisent dans la pratique du billet, qui permet de prendre ses distances à l'égard de l'étiquette et des formules de politesse traditionnelles (Bray 2000, 59). Néanmoins, la suspension des convenances est également un signe de reconnaissance entre pairs: elle appartient aux us et coutumes d'une communauté d'artistes. Ainsi, le billet sera souvent désinvolte, comme le montre l'exemple suivant:

(1) Baudelaire demande à un directeur de théâtre, qu'il ne connaît pas particulièrement, de lui offrir deux places pour un spectacle:
Cher Monsieur, vous êtes trop aimable pour me refuser 2 bonnes places pour l'Eternel Schamyl

On dit aussi du courrier électronique qu'il est informel (Baron 1998). Les règles de politesse qui sont normalement respectées en face à face sont parfois suspendues:

(2) Une étudiante envoie un message à son enseignant, sans aucune formule de politesse, ni de remerciements:
Bonjour
Je suis étudiante en dea OSS et en dernière année de cycle ingénieur GSI à l'utt. J'ai donc suivi l'enseignement SI10 en tc01 au semestre automne 1998. Concernant le module d'initiation méthodologique à la recherche (IMR), je n'ai pu assister à toute la journée de conférence que vous nous aviez organisée. J'étais présente le matin mais pour des raisons personnelles j'ai du m'absenter l'après-midi. Sachant qu'une session de rattrapage est organisée le 30 avril et que je ne fais pas mon stage à l'utt (et pas dans l'aube non plus!), est-il possible que vous nous proposiez une alternative permettant de valider le module sans suivre la session du 30 avril?

Il faut toutefois indiquer que le caractère informel des billets et des courriers électroniques est sans doute en rapport avec le fait que l'on sélectionne son destinataire. L'échange de billets se fonde sur une implicite communauté d'esprits entre correspondants vis-à-vis des conventions épistolaires et, plus largement, des usages imposés par la société. Lorsque le destinataire n'est pas un familier, le billet peut retrouver le caractère formel d'une lettre (3). On observe aussi ce phénomène pour le courrier électronique (4).

(3) Billet envoyé par Barbey d'Aurevilly à Baudelaire (premier échange épistolaire):

Monsieur,
J'ai l'habitude d'être chez moi de 11 heures à midi, tous les jours, excepté le mardi et le dimanche. Je serai heureux de vous y recevoir.
Agréez, Monsieur, l'expression de mes sentiments distingués

(Exemple cité par Fisher 1998)

(4) Message envoyé par un étudiant à un enseignant:[4]

Bonjour, Monsieur
J'aimerai bien fixer un rendez-vous avec vous pour que vous me donner votre avis sur un CV que j'ai écrit. Je vous prie d'agréer, Monsieur l'expression de mes salutations les plus distinguées.

Même si le billet et le courrier électronique sont des écrits peu formels, il faut admettre que cette caractéristique stylistique s'accompagne d'un relâchement plus général dans le courrier électronique (fautes d'orthographe, tournures argotiques, abréviations, etc.), ce qui n'est évidemment pas le cas dans les billets d'écrivains. Mais, sur ce point, c'est sans doute plus la nature des scripteurs que le moyen d'expression qui est déterminant.

3.4 Des jeux stylistiques et graphiques

Tout en étant des écrits peu formels, les billets et les courriers électroniques sont des supports privilégiés pour des jeux sur le code, que ce soit d'un point de vue stylistique ou purement graphique. On trouve par exemple des billets rimés.

(5) Extrait de billet envoyé par Baudelaire à Auguste Poulet-Malassis, en avril 1865, pour s'excuser de ne pas visiter un ami à Namur:

Puisque vous allez vers la ville
Qui bien qu'un fort mur l'encastrât
Défraya la verve servile
Du fameux poète Castrat,
Puisque vous allez en vacances
Goûter un plaisir recherché

---

4   Les exemples sont reproduits tels quels.

*Usez toutes vos éloquences
Mon bien cher Coco-Malperché*

De la même manière, de nombreux travaux ont montré que la dimension ludique et poétique (au sens de Jakobson) caractérisait le courrier électronique. On trouve ainsi, mais de manière exceptionnelle, des courriers électroniques rimés:

(6)   Extrait d'un courrier électronique:
       *Et comment va ce cher Antoine?
       Je lui fais un salut idoine* […].

Les jeux sur le langage des courriers électroniques ne sont généralement pas les mêmes que ceux qui sont présents dans les billets mais on peut observer que les scripteurs assignent une finalité comparable aux deux formes. Ainsi, on trouve dans les courriers électroniques des utilisations ludiques et créatives des abréviations:

(7)   Extrait d'un courrier électronique:
       *LOL:-)
       > Mise à jour ratée: page recherche disparue !!!!! Je recommence …*
       (LOL signifie: Laughing Out Loud – Mort de rire)

Parmi les jeux sur le langage présents dans le billet et dans les courriers électroniques, on trouve de nombreux jeux graphiques: soulignements, majuscules, gros caractères, etc.

(8)   Billet envoyé par Baudelaire à Alphonse de Calonne, éditeur, le 28 avril 1860 (extrait):
       *Cher Monsieur,
       Je suis désolé de vous faire observer pour la dixième fois qu'<u>on ne retouche pas MES vers</u>.
       Veuillez les supprimer.* […].
       *Mille compliments.
       CH. BAUDELAIRE*

(9)   Extrait d'un courrier électronique:
       Voilà en gros. Avec ça, tu ne peux PAS te tromper, ça tiendra forcément debout si tu as ton IDEE au départ.

Dans le courrier électronique comme dans le billet, ces procédés permettent assez souvent de simuler des données non verbales, et de renseigner le lecteur sur l'état d'esprit du scripteur au moment de la production de son message (Marcoccia 2000b).

3.5 Une visée informative et pratique

Le contenu et la forme des billets sont déterminés en partie par le contexte socio-historique de leur production. Les billets répondent aux exigences de certaines situations de communication: la discrétion, la rapidité ou la quotidienneté des échanges (Charrier-Vozel 2000, 68). On peut penser que la pratique du billet est adaptée au mode de vie de ceux qui les écrivent au XIXe siècle: vie occupée, souvent agitée, parfois harassante. Aussi, le billet a souvent une fonction informative et pratique: apporter ou demander des services ou des renseignements, prendre et annuler des rendez-vous, lancer une invitation, s'excuser d'un contretemps, accompagner une pièce jointe (cadeaux, poèmes, documents). Sur ce dernier point, on ne peut que souligner la proximité avec le courrier électronique, qui n'est souvent qu'un texte d'accompagnement d'un fichier plus volumineux envoyé en document attaché. Le billet peut être parfois un véritable outil de logistique, accompagnant la réception d'un objet (Fraisse 2000, 97) ou permettant la bonne organisation des déplacements de son auteur. Plus qu'une réponse écrite, c'est souvent une action qu'il requiert de son destinataire:

(10) Billet envoyé par Flaubert à l'imprimeur de la revue *L'Artiste*, date inconnue:
8h du soir, jeudi. Faire attention à mettre en petit texte les 5 premières lignes

(11) Billet envoyé par Flaubert à Michel Lévy, son éditeur, le 10 janvier 1857:
Samedi, 11h du soir. Je crois qu'il ne serait pas mal que vous disiez que l'on imprime sur une seule colonne...

On trouve des courriers électroniques aux fonctions équivalentes, particulièrement dans les organisations:

(12) Extrait d'un courrier électronique:
Les services qui possèdent trop d'enveloppes pour le courrier interne, peuvent-ils en remettre dans le local du courrier comme d'habitude?

3.6 Une visée relationnelle

Le billet, comme le courrier électronique, permet aussi d'entretenir son réseau de relations. Au sujet des multiples billets de Mallarmé, Kaufmann (1986, 392) rappelle leur valeur de carte de visite, de poignée de main.

(13) Billet envoyé par Flaubert à Théophile Gautier, le 2 décembre 1856:
Mardi
Souviens-toi, ô maître et ami, que c'est demain, mercredi, que tu dînes chez
GVE FLAUBERT, 42, boulevard du Temple

De manière proche, le courrier électronique peut être utilisé pour accomplir des rituels de sociabilité (vœux, remerciements, etc.). Par exemple, un courrier électronique envoyé à la fin de l'année: «*je vous souhaite une très bonne année, avec plein d'énergie, et beaucoup de bonnes choses encore…*».

3.7 Un écrit en relation avec d'autres écrits

Le billet est parfois une écriture d'appoint. Il se positionne en effet souvent par rapport à une lettre, en l'annonçant ou en la reprenant. Ainsi, on peut observer des cas où l'épistolier s'excuse de manière presque paradoxale d'écrire un simple billet et laisse entendre qu'il écrira plus longuement par la suite.

(14) Billet de Baudelaire, envoyé à sa mère le 13 novembre 1861 (extrait):
Je t'écrirai longuement demain.
Tu me rends bien malheureux en supposant toujours que je ne t'aime pas.
Je t'embrasse. CB

Un billet peut aussi être envoyé après une lettre pour en atténuer le ton, la commenter, etc.

(15) Billet de Baudelaire, envoyé à sa mère, le 4 août 1860 (extrait):
Si je t'écris aujourd'hui, c'est uniquement pour te dire, pour te répéter combien je suis inquiet sur l'effet que ma lettre va produire sur toi […].

On trouve des procédés comparables avec le courrier électronique, parfois utilisé pour annoncer ou organiser un échange par un autre moyen. Par exemple, un message se conclut par «*Merci quand même, je vous téléphonerai d'ici le 7, à bientôt*».

3.8 Un écrit qui manifeste la séquentialité

Le billet permet parfois de manifester explicitement l'échange dans lequel il s'inscrit. En effet, les correspondants répondaient parfois sur le billet qui leur avait été envoyé.

(16) Billet envoyé par Baudelaire à Edmond Duranty, écrivain, le 11 octobre 1860:
Mon cher Duranty, il m'est impossible de prendre rendez-vous avec vous pour cette affaire avant le 16. Je suis plein de tourments. CB

Baudelaire écrit ce billet sur le billet même par lequel Duranty, le même jour à 5h, lui demandait, pour le lendemain matin 9h, un entretien au sujet de la biographie du poète qu'il devait écrire et qu'on lui réclamait. Baudelaire ira même jusqu'à découper et coller certains passages de lettres pour ne pas avoir à les recopier dans les billets en réponse. Même exceptionnel, ce procédé ne peut être que rapproché de celui de la citation automatique: lorsqu'on répond à un courrier électronique, le dispositif insère automatiquement une citation de ce message dans sa réponse (Marcoccia 2004a).

(17) Extrait de courrier électronique:
Quelle est la salle? A tout à l'heure.
XX a écrit:
> Bonjour,
> C'est d'accord pour moi le Jeudi 20 a 10h30.

Conclusion

Cet article rend compte d'un travail de recherche qui est encore dans une phase exploratoire. En effet, les comparaisons qui étayent notre hypothèse doivent être analysées afin de vérifier si les points communs entre billet et courrier électronique renvoient à des raisons communes, ou ne sont que de pures coïncidences de forme. Quelques pistes d'analyse peuvent être explorées. Tout d'abord, le billet a incarné la crise de la sociabilité bourgeoise au XIXe siècle. De la même façon, le succès du courrier électronique symbolise peut être la manière dont les relations sociales sont redéfinies, particulièrement dans les organisations. En d'autres termes, les conventions traditionnelles de la correspondance administrative ne correspondent plus à la manière dont se vivent les relations sociales au travail. Par ailleurs, l'apparition du billet est lié à l'évolution des services postaux. Schématiquement, la pratique du billet correspond au moment où, à Paris, il devient possible d'avoir plusieurs échanges de lettres dans la même journée. Ainsi, comme pour le courrier électronique, on peut faire l'hypothèse que, dès lors qu'il est possible de mener plusieurs tours de parole par l'écrit, il y aura une préférence pour la brièveté des messages et leur mise en séquence. Enfin, le sentiment d'appartenir à une communauté d'écriture est aussi un facteur permettant d'expliquer la proximité entre le billet et le courrier électronique, au-delà de l'anachronisme apparent de ce rapprochement.

Références

Angell, David/Heslop, Brent (1994): The elements of e-mail style: communicate effectively via electronic mail. New York: Addison-Wesley.

Anis, Jacques (2000): L'écrit des conversations électroniques de l'Internet. In: Le Français Aujourd'hui 129, 59-69.

Baron, Naomi S. (1998): Letters by phone or speech by other means: the linguistics of email. In: Language & Communication 18, 133-170.

Bray, Bernard (2000): Recherchez la brièveté, évitez l'extrême concision: théorie et pratique de la lettre et du billet à l'époque classique. In: Revue de l'AIRE – Recherches sur l'épistolaire 25-26, 52-64.

Charrier-Vozel, Marianne (2000): Les billets de Beaumarchais le libertin. In: Revue de l'AIRE – Recherches sur l'épistolaire 25-26, 65-76.

Cusin-Berche, Fabienne (1999): Courriel et genre discursif. In: Anis, J. (éd.): Internet, communication et langue française. Paris: Hermes, 31-54.

Danet, Brenda (1998): Computer-mediated communication. In: Bouissac, P. (éd.): Encyclopedia of semiotics. Oxford: Oxford University Press. http://atar.mscc.huji.ac.il/~msdanet/cmc1.htm

Fisher, Martine (1998): De la pratique du billet: Baudelaire et ses correspondants. In: Mélançon, B. (éd.): Penser par lettre. Actes du colloque d'Azay-le-Ferron (mai 1997). Montréal: Fides, 75-88.

Fraisse, Luc (2000): Typologie de la lettre brève dans la correspondance de Proust. In: Revue de l'AIRE – Recherches sur l'épistolaire 25-26, 85-101.

Gruffat, Sabine (2001): L'épistolaire. Paris: Ellipses.

Haroche-Bouzinac, Geneviève (1995a): L'épistolaire. Paris: Hachette.

– (1995b): Billets font conversation. De la théorie à la pratique: l'exemple de Voltaire. In: Bray, B./Stosetzki, C. (éds.): Art de la lettre, art de la conversation à l'époque classique en France. Paris: Klincksieck, 341-354.

– (2000): Une esthétique de la brièveté. In: Revue de l'AIRE – Recherches sur l'épistolaire 25-26, 49-51.

Ivanova, Nadia (1999): Courrier électronique: renaissance du genre épistolaire. http://izuminka.free.fr/mailomanie/expose1.html

Kaufmann, Vincent (1986): Relation épistolaire. In: Poétique 68, 387-404.

Kerbrat-Orecchioni, Catherine (1998): L'interaction épistolaire. In: Siess, J. (éd.): La lettre, entre réel et fiction. Paris: Sedes, 15-36.

Marcoccia, Michel (1998): La Normalisation des comportements communicatifs sur Internet: étude sociopragmatique de la Netiquette. In: Guéguen, N./Tobin, L. (éds.): Communication, société et internet. Paris: L'Harmattan, 15-32.

– (2000a): Les Smileys: une représentation iconique des émotions dans la communication médiatisée par ordinateur. In: Plantin, C./Doury, M./Traverso, V. (éds.): Les émotions dans les interactions communicatives. Lyon: ARCI – Presses Universitaires de Lyon, 249-263.

– (2000b): La représentation du non verbal dans la communication écrite médiatisée par ordinateur. In: Communication & Organisation 18, 265-274.

– (2003a): Parler politique dans un forum de discussion. In: Langage & Société 104, 9-55.

– (2004a): La citation automatique dans les messageries électroniques. In: Lopez-Muñoz, J-M./Marnette, S./Rosier, L. (éds.): Le discours rapporté dans tous ses états. Paris: L'Harmattan, 467-478.

– (2004b): On-line polylogues: conversation structure and participation framework in internet newsgroups. In: Journal of Pragmatics 36/1, 115-145.

Mélançon, Benoît (1996): Sévigné@Internet. Fides: Montréal.

Orlikowski, Wanda J./Yates, JoAnne (1994): Genre repertoire: the structuring of communicative practices in organizations. In: Administrative Science Quarterly 39/4, 542-574.
Yates, Simeon J. (1996): Oral and written linguistic aspects of computer conferencing: A corpus based study. In: Herring, S. C. (éd.): Computer-mediated communication. Linguistic, social and cross-cultural perspectives. Amsterdam, Philadelphia: Benjamins, 29-46.
– (2000): Computer-mediated communication – The future of the letter? In: Barton, D./Hall, N. (éds.): Letter writing as a social practice. Amsterdam: Benjamins, 233-251.

Hassan Atifi

Les usages conversationnels dans les dialogues électroniques entre Marocains

Introduction

Pour préserver la qualité des échanges fondés sur les règles élémentaires du savoir-vivre, mais aussi sur des considérations techniques censées optimiser l'utilisation du réseau, certains pionniers d'Internet ont élaboré un code de «savoir communiquer» (Marcoccia 1998, 2000). En proposant un «bon usage», la Nétiquette définit des règles globales, transculturelles et universelles censées être valables pour les internautes du village planétaire. Concrètement, cet idéal conversationnel universaliste repose, dans une certaine mesure, sur la valorisation de quatre comportements relativement centraux dans *l'ethos* communicationnel nord-américain: la recherche du consensus (opposée à l'acceptation du conflit), la maîtrise des émotions (opposée aux cultures plus expressives), la concision des messages (opposée aux cultures volubiles), la préférence pour la parole indirecte (opposée à la parole directe tolérée dans certaines cultures...) (Blum-Kulka/House/Kasper 1989, Orecchioni 1994).

Dans cet article nous décrirons comment des internautes marocains s'approprient ces règles globales pour mettre en évidence des particularismes langagiers en décalage, en rupture, voire en contradiction avec les règles communicatives normatives de la nétiquette. Ces observations nous permettront de jeter les premières bases descriptives des cyber-pratiques langagières émergentes d'une communauté peu étudiée: les Marocains en ligne.[1] Ce travail s'inscrit dans le cadre des recherches qui traitent de l'impact de l'Internet sur les pratiques communicationnelles selon les pays. Nous tentons de répondre à la question suivante: Internet favorise-t-il la standardisation ou la variation culturelle?

Le survol de la littérature sur la communication médiatisée par ordinateur permet d'opposer schématiquement deux thèses principales. Certains auteurs, surtout en France, considèrent qu'en standardisant les façons de communiquer, par le biais par exemple de la nétiquette, l'Internet contribue à la diffusion et à l'universalisation des pratiques culturelles nord-américaines. Ces chercheurs s'insurgent d'une certaine manière contre le dispositif lui-même, coupable d'être un instrument de plus, entre les mains de la puissance américaine

---

[1] Voir cependant un travail à dominante linguistique de Berjaoui (2001) centré sur la question de l'orthographe et de l'écriture de l'alphabet arabe marocain dans les *chats*.

(Flichy 2001), de l'uniformisation et de l'homogénéisation (Mattelart 2000) et d'un nouveau «colonialisme» culturel (Wolton/Jay 2000). D'autres auteurs contestent la validité de cette thèse. Ils réfutent l'idée d'une standardisation culturelle en montrant au contraire que, dans les usages, l'Internet reproduit quelques caractéristiques des différentes cultures observées. Il s'agit essentiellement de travaux empiriques sur les modalités d'appropriation des règles globales par des communautés culturelles diverses: l'Amérique latine (Nocera 1998), les Amérindiens (Baird 1998), la Thaïlande (Hongladarom 1998), la diaspora arabe du Moyen-Orient (Anderson 1997), les Indiens (Nitra 1997), la France (Marcoccia 1998, 2000).[2]

1. Corpus et méthodologie

Malgré sa nouveauté, la faiblesse de sa diffusion et de sa pénétration au Maroc, Internet suscite un engouement réel chez les Marocains, surtout chez les jeunes très férus de ce nouveau média de communication. Certes, en janvier 2001, le taux de connexion était seulement de 0.36 pour mille habitants. En comparaison, selon les chiffres de l'Association des Fournisseurs d'Accès et de Services Internet (AFA), on comptait, à peu près la même période en France, 5.968.000 comptes d'accès individuels à Internet ouverts au 31 mars 2001. Ce qui fait un taux de connexion de presque 100 pour mille habitants.[3] Mais comme les abonnés marocains se partagent les abonnements, cela peut représenter une connexion pour mille habitants (Vermeren 2002). Il faut aussi tenir compte du développement extraordinaire des cybercafés – point de connexion privilégié des internautes marocains –, et du succès des forums de discussion chez les internautes marocains de l'étranger.[4]

Notre méthodologie inspirée par le relativisme culturel, se méfie des approches spéculatives ou expérimentales et privilégie une démarche empirique basée sur la description des pratiques langagières authentiques. Cette approche empirique et ethnographique relève de la pragmatique de la communication dans son acception anglo-saxonne notamment ethnographique (Hymes 1972). Elle participe de l'objectif global poursuivi par tous ces chercheurs qui tentent d'établir un tableau comparatif des pratiques communicatives culturelles. L'observation et l'analyse portent sur une centaine de messages envoyés à divers forums de discussion accessibles à partir du *club.maroc.net*, important fournisseur privé au Maroc.[5]

---

2 Pour le Maroc, voir aussi Atifi (2003).
3 http://www.afa-france.com/html/action.
4 Deuxième enquête en ligne sur les internautes marocains, www.iecmarketing.com [février 2000].
5 Il existe d'autres fournisseurs comme Menara (généraliste de Maroc Télécom) et Wanadoo.net.ma (généraliste et filiale de France Télécom au Maroc).

Les usages conversationnels dans les dialogues electroniques   295

L'internaute intéressé par les forums de discussion est invité à participer à la rubrique «Maroc conférences: joignez la discussion».

Dans ce cas, il est dirigé vers le site albarid.net,[6] dont la page d'accueil lui propose de choisir entre *albarid.forums* ou *albarid.chat*. L'internaute a le choix entre 6 grands thèmes divisés en 18 forums ou sous-thèmes. Nous allons détailler les 6 thèmes en donnant pour chacun les différents sous-thèmes ainsi que le nombre des messages:[7] 1 Media & Special Events: *Aujourd'hui* (19 481), *festivals & evenements* (55); 2 Culture & Society: *Cuisine* (100), *associations* (28), *art & musique* (73), *religion* (2059), *history & traditions* (58); 3 Commerce & Business Opportunities: *Buisness opportunities* (66), *investir & entreprendre au Maroc* (23); 4 Education, Sciences & Technologies: *Nouvelles technologies* (26), *recherche* (112), *education* (144); 5 Sport, Loisirs & Tourisme: *Blagues et charades* (88), *sports* (66), *travel & tourism* (81), *loisirs* (1744); 6 En face: *Dirham.com* (498), *Morocco* (585).

Nous procédons en deux phases. Dans une première phase, le corpus est soumis à une lecture régulière, pour voir tous les phénomènes pertinents qui «sautent aux yeux». Cette première approche, que certains chercheurs qualifient d'observation-balayage (Goodwin/ Goodwin 1989), a permis une observation suivie et régulière de seize forums. Dans une deuxième phase, nous avons décidé de focaliser notre attention sur le forum «aujourd'hui» le plus important des forums. Sa large audience et sa richesse thématique – actualité quotidienne, sociale et politique – en font un cas largement représentatif des usages des forums de discussion des Marocains.[8]

Toute référence aux «Marocains» renvoie à des observations générales récurrentes reflétant sans doute des tendances moyennes partagées par la majorité des participants indépendamment du lieu de connexion de l'internaute (le Maroc ou l'étranger) et sans tenir compte des variables intra-culturelles telles que identité sexuelle, statut socioprofessionnel et origine géographique. De plus, nos analyses sont relatives au seul domaine observé, des discussions électroniques dans les forums de discussion sociétaux. Elles portent sur des phénomènes langagiers récurrents, routiniers et significatifs. Concrètement, nous nous intéressons aux thèmes discutés, aux participants, à la longueur des messages, aux ouvertures, aux clôtures, aux termes d'adresse et aux fonctionnements de certains rituels langagiers comme les salutations et les vœux… Les quelques exemples cités dans cet article le sont à titre d'illustration de notre démarche d'observation-description.[9]

---

6   A l'adresse: http://poste.albarid.net/email/scripts/loginuser.pl.
7   Les termes d'origine, y compris les fautes d'orthographe en anglais ou en français ont été conservés; les sous-thèmes sont indiqués en italiques et le nombre des messages postés figure entre parenthèses.
8   Cette analyse est basée, en partie, sur notre propre connaissance de la langue et de la culture arabo-marocaine.
9   Voir Atifi (2003) pour une présentation plus détaillée de l'ensemble des résultats de cette recherche.

Les premiers résultats de montrent que les usages des utilisateurs marocains de forums de discussion sont éloignés de ce que les règles globales du «bon usage» prévoient. Ils soulignent surtout une adaptation locale des règles globales. Surtout, au-delà de la simple question du respect ou du non-respect de la Nétiquette on assiste à l'émergence d'une communauté en ligne – entre les Marocains du Maroc et ceux de l'étranger – fortement impliquée dans sa culture d'origine. Ainsi, de très nombreux rituels communicatifs et conversationnels propres à la culture marocaine subsistent dans les dialogues en ligne entre Marocains:

2. Une communauté émergente: la persistance identitaire

2.1 Les thèmes

Grâce à Internet, tout Marocain – même celui qui se trouve éloigné géographiquement – peut établir, maintenir ou consolider le lien communautaire avec les autres Marocains. Les internautes marocains, surtout les résidents à l'étranger, utilisent les forums de discussion pour parler du pays d'origine. Beaucoup se sentent concernés par l'avenir du pays, son image et son développement. Une des questions les plus débattues est le problème du retour définitif au Maroc. Cet intérêt pour le pays d'origine est à rapprocher, d'une certaine manière, de certains comportements similaires observés chez de nombreuses communautés expatriées comme par exemple les Irlandais (Church 1996).

Le dispositif permet à chacun de s'impliquer dans sa communauté d'appartenance et de vivre pleinement sa «marocanité» en se connectant à un forum de discussion pour y chercher des réponses à toutes les questions (sérieuses ou futiles) qui l'intéressent: Comment téléphoner moins cher au Maroc?, Que penser du début de règne du nouveau Roi?, Faut-il rentrer et s'installer définitivement au Maroc?, Comment aider le Maroc à se développer?, Faut-il épouser une étrangère ou une Marocaine?, Pourquoi le Maroc n'arrive-t-il pas à organiser la coupe du Monde de football?, Que penser de la polygamie?, Que penser de l'expérience démocratique marocaine?, Faut-il séparer la religion de l'Etat?, Faut-il un entraîneur national ou étranger pour l'équipe de foot marocaine?, etc.

2.2 Les salutations

Les pratiques langagières des Marocains confirment l'étude de Desjeux (2001) sur l'anthropologie des communautés étrangères à Paris sauf sur un point particulier: on apprend, dans cette étude, que les internautes d'origine sénégalaise, par exemple, ont purement et simplement abandonné le protocole.[10] Dans leur pays, impossible pourtant d'échanger une information avant plusieurs instants de conversation! On s'enquiert d'abord de la santé de son interlocuteur et de sa famille. Même chose au téléphone! Mais avec la messagerie électronique, la pratique a évolué, les internautes sénégalais abandonnent les formulations successives de «comment ça va?» et modifient ainsi les traditions.

Les internautes marocains ne semblent pas encore prêts à sacrifier ces moments phatiques dans leurs discussions électroniques. Seuls quelques rares messages font l'économie de ces moments. A la différence même des forums français où les internautes peuvent sauter l'étape des salutations pour entrer tout de suite dans le vif du sujet, sur les forums marocains, les salutations sont nombreuses, chaleureuses, et privilégient le groupe plutôt que l'individu. Elles semblent une étape nécessaire à l'ouverture des discussions. Cette dimension relationnelle (phatique) très présente est renforcée par l'importance du tutoiement. Dans la majorité des messages, cette préférence pour le «tu», même dans les messages écrits en français, est une caractéristique intéressante des usages langagiers des internautes marocains.

Nous avons fait l'inventaire des principaux termes d'adresse et des formules utilisés pour saluer les participants aux forums. On peut citer, à titre d'exemple: *Marocains*, *Chers compatriotes*, *Frères et sœurs*, *Tous*, *Brothers and sisters* ... En ce qui concerne les salutations elles-mêmes, on retrouve, par exemple, dans la séquence d'ouverture les formulations suivantes en arabe: *Salam* [Paix], *assalamo 3ala mani itaba3a alhoda* [Paix sur tous ceux qui suivent le droit chemin], *Salamou alaikoum* [Paix à tous], *Salam Alaykom Wa Rahmato Lahi Taala Wa Barakatoh* [Paix et miséricorde de Dieux à tous], *Salam el har* [Paix chaleureuse].

2.3 Les ouvertures et clôtures

La dimension identitaire religieuse musulmane propre aux rituels langagiers marocains est donc bien présente dans les messages des forums de discussion marocains, notamment dans les ouvertures et les clôtures. Contrairement, par exemple, aux internautes français très sou-

---

10 Voir «La diaspora dans le miroir du réseau. Anthropologie des communautés étrangères à Paris», *Libération en ligne* du 24 mai 2001.

vent influencés par les usages de la correspondance électronique anglo-saxonne dont ils calquent les rituels, réduisant les ouvertures et les clôtures à un strict minimum («salut», «cordialement», «A+»...) les Marocains produisent des ouvertures et des clôtures assez développées, qui correspondent à des rituels langagiers très précis, dont certains ont une origine religieuse bien marquée. Le dispositif technique n'annule pas tous ces rituels langagiers. Par exemple, dans certaines ouvertures, on trouve le rituel classique qui consiste à saluer tous les gens co-présents dans une situation de communication, même lorsqu'on produit un message adressé à une personne en particulier:

(1) *Abouhafce2000 from Albarid, Posted 9-15-2000 00:06*
     assalamo aalukom [Paix à tous]
     pour mokayada, tout d'abord je te dis bienvenue parmi nous, c'est pas grave si ton francais n'est pas parfait c'est pas grave le mien aussi n'est pas vraiment impeccable c'est normal c'est pas notre langue maternelle...

(News.Albarid.net: forum «aujourd'hui»)

Le fonctionnement des clôtures des échanges est un autre exemple de particularisme. On trouve dans certains messages la combinaison d'une invocation divine à une formule de salutation pour prendre congé de son interlocuteur: ‹*Que dieu nous aide et au revoir!*›; ‹*Que Dieu guide nos pas vers le droit chemin*›; ‹*Puisse Dieu nous sauver et guider nos pas vers le droit chemin et nous sauver de l'enfer*›...

2.4 Des messages écrits en arabe

De nombreux internautes marocains écrivent leurs messages en arabe (y compris à partir d'un clavier «latin» qui n'a pas d'équivalents graphiques pour tous les phonèmes arabes). L'utilisation de l'arabe – attendue de la part d'internautes marocains – implique donc un ajustement du dispositif technique. Aussi ce fait montre-t-il une possible résistance de la part des internautes marocains à la prétendue homogénéisation linguistique, qui découlerait d'un usage exclusif des langues étrangères aux dépens des langues nationales. En réalité, l'analyse des forums marocains montre qu'une langue locale peut coexister avec une langue véhiculaire et son usage se développer sur la toile. Ainsi les internautes marocains utilisent-ils beaucoup de proverbes ou des locutions en arabe pour agrémenter leur discours. On retrouve, par ailleurs, énormément de vœux. Toutes les occasions sont bonnes pour entretenir la dimension relationnelle en souhaitant: un bon Ramadan, le nouvel an musulman, l'Aid el Fitr [la fin du Ramadan], la fête du Sacrifice.

3. Des usages en décalage avec les préconisations normatives

3.1 Des messages trop longs, inappropriés

De manière générale, les messages adressés aux forums marocains contiennent de nombreuses violations des règles du «bon usage». Parmi les premiers exemples de violation de ces règles du «bon usage», les messages envoyés sont régulièrement «trop longs». Par exemple, un message (trop long à reproduire) est composé de 85 paragraphes et 104 lignes de texte! On note aussi des entorses à la règle de pertinence avec des messages qui se trompent de forum ou qui sont hors sujet, comme cet internaute qui s'interroge sur une année de règne du nouveau roi dans un forum consacré à la cuisine!

(2) *Comment jugez-vous l'expérience d'une année de regne du nouveau Roi du Maroc?*

(Club.maroc.net: forum «cuisine»)

Ces messages trop longs ou inappropriés montrent déjà comment les modalités d'appropriation par les internautes marocains des règles du «bon usage» sont en décalage avec les préconisations normatives. La volubilité propre au style communicatif marocain semble justifier que les règles de pertinence et de concision ne soient pas respectées.

3.2 Des messages conflictuels et fortement polémiques

De la même manière, dans les forums marocains beaucoup de messages sont conflictuels. Ces messages sont surtout beaucoup plus «agressifs» (injurieux, infamants) que ce que la Nétiquette tolère. Ils prennent la forme d'insultes comme dans l'exemple suivant:

(3) *delcaprio from Albarid*
looser!!!! Posted 9-13-2000 19:31 Hey! Pourquoi tu ne te cherche pas un travail au lieu de poster des ‹messages stupides› fhal wajhak! est-ce que tu es bete de demander aux gens comment etre une bonne personne? Oula rassek khawi, ma aarafti ma tkteb! [tu n'a rien dans la tête (ta tête est vide), tu ne sais pas quoi écrire!]

(News.Albarid.net: forum «aujourd'hui»)

Parfois, ces violences sont de vraies attaques personnelles et peuvent même s'accompagner de menaces physiques. La violence apparente de nombreux messages envoyés sur les forums marocains peut être mise en relation avec le fait que l'ethos communicationnel marocain, très expressif, ne refuse pas forcément la discussion animée et les joutes verbales conflictuelles. Surtout, il implique des formes d'expression assez directes et sans doute assez éloignées de la valorisation du consensus. Elle doit aussi être mise en relation avec le statut de la liberté d'expression dans un contexte politique en transition.[11] Sur le réseau qui n'est pas censuré,[12] les Marocains abordent certains thèmes nationaux de politique ou de société très conflictuels. Internet permet donc de réintroduire dans l'espace public tous ces thèmes – la monarchie, l'intégrité territoriale, la question berbère, la religion, le colonialisme, l'identité marocaine, l'histoire du Maroc… – qui sont peu ou pas assez débattus par les média classiques (télévision, radio, presse). Ces thèmes divisent les internautes en donnant lieu à des échanges passionnés, très vifs et très agressifs.

3.3 Des messages plurilingues

Dans certains messages, on note l'importance du plurilinguisme et du code-switching, entre l'arabe, l'anglais et le français. Ceci représente une sorte de violation d'une autre règle qui consiste à «utiliser la langue du forum», ce que préconise, par exemple, explicitement le fournisseur d'accès AOL ou les modérateurs des forums du journal français *Libération*. Par contre, nous n'avons trouvé aucune préconisation sur la langue à utiliser dans les forums marocains. L'interface du forum est bilingue (anglais et français) alors que la langue dominante des forums est le français! D'autre part, l'origine géographique et linguistique des internautes marocains qui résident à l'étranger est très variée: Europe, Amérique du Nord, Canada… Même si la majorité des messages sont en français, les autres langues sont présentes: l'anglais, l'arabe marocain, l'espagnol, et dans une moindre mesure le berbère.

Manifestement, les internautes marocains sont plurilingues ce qui est assez représentatif de la situation linguistique au Maroc, pays plurilingue à cause de sa géographie et de son histoire (Bentahila 1983). La langue officielle est l'arabe. Cependant, la majorité des Marocains vit une situation de diglossie (coexistence de l'arabe classique avec sa version dialectale) ou de bilinguisme voire de plurilinguisme avec le français, l'espagnol ou le berbère. Certains internautes marocains, même parfois ceux de l'étranger, peuvent écrire entièrement leur message en arabe marocain. Mais on constate que l'arabe marocain est surtout utilisé dans les ouvertures, les clôtures et les formules rituelles comme les salutations, les vœux et les proverbes. Dans l'exemple suivants, en plus du code-switching (français, arabe, anglais), l'ouverture et la clôture sont en arabe alors que le corps du message est en français et en anglais (4):

---

[11] Le Maroc est, durant cette période, en pleine alternance consensuelle avec pour la première fois l'arrivée au pouvoir d'une nouvelle majorité formée d'une coalition des socialistes et de leurs alliés, dirigée par le Premier ministre A. Youssoufi.

[12] Dans son rapport sur «l'Internet au Moyen-Orient et en Afrique du Nord» l'association non gouvernementale Human Rights Watch confirme que le gouvernement marocain ne censure pas Internet et ne limite pas son accès, cf. *The Internet in the Mideast and North Africa*, http://www.hrw.org/advocacy/internet/mena/morocco.htm.

(4) *Felicitation a M6 pour son marriage!!!*
News.Albarid.net: forum «aujourd'hui»
mesmoudi from Albarid, Posted 7-15-2002 04:27
mabrook wallah itammam bekheer [*félicitations et que Dieu fasse que tout se passe* (*se termine*) *bien*]*..!zaghertou! mabrook! and a flower from heaven named al maghreb to it's king MO-HAMED ASSADISS!* THIS FLOWER REPRESENT NORTH AND SOUTH OF AL MAGHREB! *SALAM & MABROOK!* [Paix & félicitations]

4. Conclusion

Dans l'usage des forums de discussion, on retrouve donc différents traits du style communicatif de la communauté émergente des Marocains du Maroc et de l'étranger. Ces traits concernent essentiellement le fonctionnement des dialogues (ouverture, clôtures, salutations, termes d'adresse…), leur contenu (thèmes de discussion, intérêt pour le pays d'origine, forte persistance identitaire religieuse…) et leur mode polémique.

En décalage avec l'idéal communicationnel et la standardisation des comportements normalement impliqués par la Nétiquette, ces dialogues électroniques laissent transparaître des variations langagières, culturelles et communautaires propres aux Marocains. Les pratiques langagières sont fortement ancrées dans la culture marocaine, et, en plus, elles sont partagées par des internautes qui peuvent être géographiquement très dispersés.

On a d'un côté des règles globales de comportement supposées universelles et de l'autre des modalités singulières d'appropriation de ces règles. Ainsi, la communication dans les forums marocains semble plus marquée par l'écart, la différence, et l'hétérogénéité que par la standardisation. Ces résultats empiriques vont aussi à l'encontre de l'idée d'un déterminisme technique, puisque les variables culturelles semblent être plus fortes et influencent plus les usagers que les seuls dispositifs techniques.

En définitive, ce travail montre les limites d'une approche en terme de globalisation-homogénéisation. Les usages d'Internet permettent, en réalité, une émergence communautaire, qui se traduit par un réel intérêt pour son pays d'origine, une forte implication dans sa culture locale, même lorsqu'on en est éloigné géographiquement. De ce point de vue, l'émergence, la permanence et la reconnaissance des langues locales, des communautés identitaires des cyberpratiques culturelles représentent une vraie limite à l'universalisme supposé du cyberespace.

Références

Anderson Jon W. (1997): Cybernauts of the arab diaspora: Electronic mediation in transnational cultural identities. In: Couch-Stone Symposium «Postmodern culture, global capitalism and democratic action», University of Maryland, 10-12 April 1997. http://www.bsos.umd.edu/ CSS97/papers/ anderson.html.

Atifi, Hassan (2003): La variation culturelle dans les communications en ligne: analyse ethnographique des forums de discussion marocains. In: Fraenkel, B./Marcoccia, M. (éds.): Langage & Société, numéro spécial «Les écrits médiatisés par ordinateur» 104, Juin, 57-82.

Bachmann, Christian/Lindenfeld, Jacqueline/Simonin, Jacky (1981): Langage et communications sociales. Paris: Hatier-Crédif.

Baird, Ellen (1998): Ain't gotta do nothin but be brown and die. In: Computer-Mediated Communication Magazine 5/7. http://www.december.com/cmc/mag/1998/jul/baird.html.

Bentahila, Abdelâli (1983): Language attitudes among arabic-french bilinguals in Morocco. Clevedon: Derrick Sharp.

Berjaoui, Nasser (2001): Aspects of the Moroccan Arabic orthography with preliminary insights from the Moroccan computer-mediated communication. In: Beißwenger, M. (éd.): Chat-Kommunikation. Sprache, Interaktion, Sozialität & Identität in synchroner computervermittelter Kommunikation. Perspektiven auf ein interdisziplinäres Forschungsfeld. Stuttgart 2001, 431-465. http://www.chat-kommunikation.de.

Blum-Kulka, Shoshana/House, Juliane/Kasper, Gabriele (1989): Cross-cultural pragmatics: Requests and apologies. Norwood: Ablex.

Boukous, Ahmed (1977): Langage et culture populaires au Maroc. Essai de sociolinguistique. Thèse de 3ème cycle. Université de Paris V.

– (1985): Bilinguisme, diglossie et domination symbolique. In: Langages 61: Du bilinguisme. Paris: Denoël, 39-54.

Brown, Penelope/Levinson, Stephen (1987): Politeness. Some universals in language use. Cambridge: Cambridge University Press.

Church, Sue (1996): Expatriate keeps in touch via the web. In: Computer-Mediated Communication Magazine 3/8. http://www.december.com/cmc/mag/1996/aug/church.html.

Desjeux, Dominique (2001): La diaspora dans le miroir du réseau. Anthropologie des communautés étrangères à Paris. In: Libération en ligne, 24 mai 2001.

Flichy, Patrice (2001): L'imaginaire d'internet. Paris: La Découverte.

Goffman, Erving (1974 [1967]): Les rites d'interaction. Paris: Minuit.

Goodwin, Charles/Goodwin, Marjorie (1989): Travaux en analyse de la conversation. (Propos recueillis par Lacoste, M./Dannequin, C.). In: Langage et Société 48, 81-102.

Grice, H. Paul. (1979 [1975]): Logique et conversation. In: Communications 30, 57-72.

Hambridge, Sally (1995): Netiquette guidelines, traduction française «Les règles de la netiquette». http://www.sri.ucl.ac.be/SRI/rfc1855.fr.html.

Heaton, Lorna (1998): Preserving communication context: Virtual workplace and interpersonal space in Japanese CSCW. In: EJC/REC – Electronic Journal of Communication/La Revue Electronique de Communication 8/3-4.

Hongladarom, Soraj (1998): Global culture, local cultures and the Internet: The Thai example. In: EJC/REC – Electronic Journal of Communication/La Revue Electronique de Communication 8/3-4.

Hymes, Dell H. (1972): Models of the interaction of language and social life. In: Gumperz J./Hymes, D.H. (éds.): Directions in sociolinguistics. The ethnography of communication. New York: Holt, Rinehart & Winston, 35-71.

Kerbrat-Orecchioni, Catherine (1994): Les interactions verbales, tome III. Paris: Armand Colin.
McLaughlin M./Osborne, K./Smith, C.B. (1995): Standards of conduct in usenet. In: Jones, S. G. (éd.): Cybersociety. Computer-mediated communication and community. Thousand Oaks: Sage Publications, 90-111.
Marcoccia, Michel (1998): La normalisation des comportements communicatifs sur Internet: étude sociopragmatique de la Nétiquette. In: Guégen, N./Tobin, L. (éds.): Communication, société et Internet. Paris: L'Harmattan, 15-32.
– (2000): La sociabilité sur Internet: réflexions sur une «révolution informationnelle». In : Bourg, D./ Besnier, J.-M. (éds.): Peut-on encore croire au progrès? Paris: Presses Universitaires de France, 229-247.
Mattelart, Arman (2000 [1997]): La nouvelle idéologie globalitaire. In: Cordelier, S. (éd.): La mondialisation au-delà des mythes. Textes revus et mis à jour. Paris: La Découverte (collection Essais), 81-92.
Nitra, A. (1997): Diasporic websites: ingroup and outgroup discourse. In: Critical Studies in Mass Communication 14/2, 158-161.
Nocera, Abdelnour Jose Luis (1998): Virtual environments as spaces of symbolic construction and cultural identity: Latin American virtual communities. In Ess, C./Sudweeks, F. (éds.) Cultural attitudes towards technology and communication. CATAC' 98. London, England: University of Sydney, 149-151.
Rinaldi, Arlene (1995): The net: user guidelines and netiquette. http://www.fau.edu/netiquette/net.
Seongcheol, Kim (1998): Cultural imperialism on the Internet. In: The Edge: The E-Journal of Intercultural Relations 1-4. http://www.hart-li.com/biz/theedge/.
Shea, Virginia (1994): Netiquette. San Francisco: Albion Books.
Vermeren, Pierre (2002): Le Maroc en transition. Paris: La Découverte.
Wolton, Dominique/Olivier, Jay (2000): Internet. Petit manuel de survie. Paris: Flammarion.

Stefania Stame

Marques pragmatiques et marques de l'oral dans le dialogue par courrier électronique

1. Introduction

Avec Internet, l'usage du courrier électronique est de plus en plus répandu dans le monde, un phénomène qui augmente progressivement selon une logique en quelque sorte circulaire. Pour ainsi dire, son épanouissement est à la fois un effet et une cause du processus de mondialisation. Nous ne nous occuperons ici que du courrier électronique par rapport à la dimension dialogique qui lui est propre, sans considérer d'autres types de communication télématique également très répandus, tels que les *chats* ou les forums.

Tout comme dans un dialogue épistolaire, dans les échanges par courrier électronique les participants ne partagent pas les mêmes coordonnées spatio-temporelles. En outre, les deux types de messages – courrier traditionnel et courrier électronique – sont caractérisés par la forme écrite. Cependant, il est possible de relever dans les messages par e-mail des traits, ou bien des marques, proches de la forme discursive et linguistique de l'échange oral, tels qu'un style informel et fragmenté, des énoncés très courts (et aussi des holophrases), des fautes de grammaire, des fautes d'orthographe qui ne seraient pas si bien tolérés par les mêmes interlocuteurs dans la forme épistolaire traditionnelle. D'autres caractères de ce genre sont également: des usages familiers, argotiques ou de jargons; des mots ou des phrases entières abrégées, tout comme dans les SMS ou dans les notes sténographiques qu'on prend pendant une conférence. Il y a aussi l'emploi des *emoticons*, des *smileys*, voire des icônes qui devraient avoir une fonction métacommunicative, fonction qui, dans le dialogue oral en face-à-face, peut être accomplie par le comportement non verbal (tel que le regard ou le sourire) ou, au téléphone, par les composantes suprasegmentales et les particules phatiques. Dans notre corpus, toutefois, il est très rare de trouver ce genre d'icônes.

Cependant il y a des usages du courrier électronique qui se présentent comme très proches de ceux du courrier traditionnel; notre corpus contient, par ailleurs, une vaste gamme d'usages tout à fait innovatifs qui semble s'en éloigner considérablement. Ce sont justement ces usages les plus nouveaux que notre analyse a privilégiés, ceux qui, à notre avis, se proposent en quelque sorte de profiter des avantages offerts par l'intermédiaire électronique et de les exploiter.

L'un des caractères distinctifs de l'échange par e-mail porte sur le rythme des tours, potentiellement plus rapide par rapport au rythme de l'alternance des répliques des correspondances épistolaires traditionnelles. En principe, l'envoi d'un message électronique peut arriver à son/ses destinataire/s en une seule seconde. C'est peut-être à cause de cette vitesse des expéditions qu'on a souvent tendance à avoir un sentiment de simultanéité qui rapproche l'échange par courrier électronique de l'oral (Violi/Coppock 1999). On dirait que, même quand il y a des écarts temporels assez éloignés entre les différents envois, le temps – le *maintenant* – de celui qui envoie le message est assumé comme le *maintenant* de celui qui répond (et vice versa): c'est-à-dire que c'est comme s'il s'agissait de deux espaces d'énonciation assumés par les locuteurs comme très proches, voire superposés ou coïncidents, dans le micro-univers de l'échange, ou mieux d'un seul espace d'énonciation partagé par les deux locuteurs.

Cette perception (ou selon d'autres optiques cette *représentation* ou, encore, cette *simulation*) par rapport aux coordonnées temporelles de l'énonciation est souvent renforcée par la présence de plusieurs messages, envoyés à des dates différentes, à l'intérieur d'un même message. On reviendra plus tard sur cet aspect distinctif de l'e-mail. L'on pourrait objecter qu'il n'est pas rare de repérer cette sorte d'illusion de co-présence lors d'autres genres de dialogue qui se déroulent grâce à quelque médiation interposée entre les locuteurs. Là où l'écart concerne la dimension de l'espace, mais non celle du temps, comme dans les conversations téléphoniques, nous avons parfois observé l'usage d'expressions déictiques employées ‹comme si› les locuteurs partageaient la même location spatiale. Dans les échanges par courrier traditionnel, où à l'écart spatial entre les deux locuteurs est censé s'ajouter un écart temporel beaucoup plus évident que celui de l'e-mail, cette optique ‹égocentrique› semble plus rare; alors qu'il n'est pas rare de remarquer une sorte de simulation de partage des coordonnées spatio-temporelles dans l'usage de certaines formules, par exemple, dans les salutations finales («je t'embrasse»).

2. La recherche

2.1 Le corpus

Comme il est bien reconnu, il y a une masse de courrier électronique échangé à tout instant, et partout dans le monde, qui circule entre la plus grande variété de correspondants; des correspondants qui sont différents entre eux par rapport à la langue qu'ils parlent, ou qu'ils emploient en l'empruntant à d'autres langues, différents par rapport à une énorme quantité de variantes individuelles et subculturelles, sociologiques ou anthropologiques. Toute cette variété rend tout à fait impossible la constitution d'un corpus qui soit vraiment représentatif du genre discursif e-mail.

Notre tentative ne concerne qu'un corpus constitué de messages envoyés, et surtout reçus, personnellement, et d'autres échanges de messages que des amis, des collègues et des étudiants ont mis gracieusement à notre disposition. Il s'agit de 200 messages environ, datés entre début 2002 et 2003, trop peu nombreux pour constituer un répertoire ou une typologie exhaustive, mais peut-être assez consistants pour proposer une hypothèse concernant le repérage de quelques-uns des aspects spécifiques du fonctionnement dialogique de ce type nouveau de correspondance. Notre but est donc de cerner des ‹constantes› qui aillent, en quelque sorte, au delà du folklore ou de l'originalité des choix linguistiques ou de registre particuliers à l'intérieur des énoncés examinables.

2.2 L'hypothèse

L'usage des formes déictiques dans la correspondance traditionnelle se limite, pour ainsi dire, à signaler la présence d'un «je/tu» à l'intérieur de l'énoncé, de façon plus ou moins conventionnalisée. Cependant il y a d'autres marques dans le courrier électronique, relevant de l'organisation même du message et de l'échange, qui mettent en relief la dimension de la déixis. Ce sont des marques qui signalent et mettent en place, à nos yeux, les coordonnées déictiques de ce type de dialogue: c'est-à-dire le niveau de l'*énonciation*. Dans notre hypothèse, la fonction déictique de ce genre de marques doit être d'abord recherchée dans le «pré-texte» qui encadre les messages et, ensuite, dans l'enchâssement de ces éléments pré-textuels à l'intérieur des différentes séquences dialogiques. C'est pourquoi nous proposons d'abord d'analyser le message électronique à partir des éléments qui en constituent le format, le cadre ‹formel›:

a) l'*usager* (De:)
b) la *date* (Envoyé:)
c) le *destinataire* (À:)
d) l'*objet* (Objet:)

Nous privilégions ici l'analyse des ‹rôles›, ou mieux, des fonctions métadiscursives et dialogiques de deux de ces éléments, que nous considérons dans cette optique comme des variables indépendantes expérimentales: l'*usager* et l'*objet*.

3. L'usager

L'*expéditeur*, ainsi que le *destinataire*, peuvent être indiqués par le prénom et le nom de famille du titulaire, auxquels l'*usager* peut ajouter ou non des titres, tout comme dans le papier à en-tête de la correspondance épistolaire institutionnelle. Mais le seul nom ou le seul prénom peut bien suffire. Cela dépend du type de courrier (amical ou formel). Plusieurs personnes utilisent des *servers* différents selon le type différent de courrier et de destinataire, où ils affichent des noms d'usager différents. À la place du nom on a droit aussi à des ‹noms de plume›, des *nicknames* (tels que zorro79, lamu77, a-cat, pulcina, lupoalberto, tarzan ou Tarzan, mais la minuscule est considérée comme beaucoup plus pratique). Ces noms correspondent en général à la première partie de l'adresse électronique (par exemple, lamu77@katamail.com). D'après notre corpus, nous avons remarqué qu'en Italie, auprès des jeunes, ces surnoms sont souvent empruntés aux héros des dessins animés. Il s'agit vraisemblablement d'un souvenir nostalgique qui renvoie aux passions enfantines des expéditeurs, mais qui semble avoir aussi un but d'‹affiliation›, c'est-à-dire la fonction de signaler aux destinataires le partage d'une même subculture.

Comme nous l'avons déjà souligné, dans le courrier traditionnel, ainsi que dans les échanges électroniques, les locuteurs n'occupent pas le même espace. Ainsi, privés de leur présence physique, de leur nature corporelle, ces expéditeurs pourraient bien, à loisir, cacher ou déguiser leur propre identité, jusqu'à leur identité de genre. Dans le courrier traditionnel, cela correspondrait à une signature falsifiée ou à l'omission de la signature, comme dans les lettres anonymes – choix qui seraient considérés comme une sorte d'anomalie. En revanche, il est assez fréquent et admis dans la communication télématique que les locuteurs se représentent seulement par leurs noms de plume. Même si ce phénomène est beaucoup plus courant – voire normal – dans les *chats*, il peut se présenter aussi dans le courrier électronique (entre usagers qui se connaissent personnellement ou qui ne se connaissent pas). Dans certains cas, ces *nicknames* suffisent largement à signaler l'identité de l'expéditeur à ses destinataires, sans la révéler davantage, car l'univers de cette interaction se limite au niveau de la communication électronique. Cela ne peut qu'avoir des conséquences sur le plan de la coopération et de l'engagement dialogique et, aussi, sur le plan psychologique, en ce qui concerne la définition de l'intersubjectivité dans ce type d'échange.

En outre, par rapport à la question de l'identité de l'envoyeur du message, nous avons remarqué que dans beaucoup de messages électroniques ne figure aucune signature. Il s'agit, en général, de messages amicaux ou même de messages de travail sans un caractère formel. Ce manque de signature pourrait s'expliquer par le fait que l'envoyeur est en même temps l'usager – le seul usager titulaire – d'une adresse électronique: l'expéditeur s'introduit directement chez l'autre avec une identité qui correspond à son adresse électronique. En d'autres termes, le locuteur *est son adresse électronique*, «je» est une adresse électronique. Dans cette optique, le fait de signer son propre message peut apparaître comme superflu, redondant: un peu comme un usager qui voudrait signer sa propre communication après une conversation au téléphone, ou même *à la fin* d'un message enregistré dans un répondeur (où l'on est censé communiquer, *dès le début*, ses propres coordonnées personnelles: le nom, la date, l'heure de l'appel).

Ce processus à la fois de présentation et de représentation de l'identité de l'expéditeur est exactement le contraire des modalités employées et exigées dans le courrier traditionnel. Même dans les lettres sur papier à en-tête, le «je» présenté par le locuteur n'acquiert une véritable identité que par sa signature; une signature qui est un nom, une troisième personne, qui représente un «je», première personne (Benveniste 1966; Lejeune 1980). Il faut aussi ajouter que seule une signature manuscrite est de droit une véritable signature: le nom qui renvoie directement à la main du sujet qui l'a tracé dans toute sa matérialité. C'est justement ce caractère immédiat, unique, de la signature qui sans doute renforce la continuité, et donc l'identité, entre la troisième personne – le nom du signataire – et la première personne «je», le signataire. Une signature imprimée n'est pas une signature. Une signature reproduite dans une télécopie n'est pas une vraie signature, elle n'est pas valable légalement.

À propos de cette question de la signature, je voudrais ajouter qu'il y a aussi un type de courrier où le seul apport qui rend l'envoi ‹valable› en tant que message est la signature. Il ne s'agit pas, ici, d'une correspondance ayant une valeur institutionnelle, mais d'un type de message considéré comme très peu formel, en quelque sorte ‹futile›. Nous parlons de l'envoi des cartes postales qui, du moins dans la culture italienne, autorise l'expéditeur à rédiger un texte qui peut se borner à la seule signature. C'est la carte elle-même, en soi et pour soi, par sa reproduction photographique ou par son illustration qui constitue le pré-texte ou le para-texte, transformé en texte (des salutations).

4. L'objet

Plusieurs *objets*, dans notre corpus, mettent en lumière le sujet principal de façon presque institutionnelle (par exemple: «renseignements stage», «BASTA!», «incontro lunedì», «Salzburg», «anniversaire Julie»).

L'*objet* a la fonction métacommunicative de mettre en relief le contenu principal du message. Il crée une cohérence entre un thème particulier et les contenus des énoncés du message. Ensuite, dans les répliques éventuelles, il souligne un lien de co-référence entre ce sujet et les énoncés présents dans la réponse. En d'autres termes, l'objet a donc la fonction de mettre en place un terrain commun grâce auquel inférer tout ce qui est implicite, lacunaire, imprécis dans le texte des messages. Quand le nom de l'objet correspond effectivement au *topic* principal, on peut même retrouver le mot qui constitue l'objet répété par-ci par-là dans la structure superficielle du texte du message. En tout cas, même là où le renvoi à l'objet dans le texte est réalisé par des reformulations qui n'en mantienent qu'une représentation sémantique générale, l'objet fonctionne selon un mécanisme de type anaphorique (Stame/Lorenzetti 1993).

Notre corpus propose aussi des objets dont la co-référence sémantique par rapport au contenu du message est beaucoup moins évidente que celle des exemples mentionnés plus haut. Il s'agit parfois d'objets qu'on pourrait définir comme «créatifs», visant surtout à mettre en lumière l'originalité de celui qui les a inventés. Quand des objets tels que «sifflements de merle», «ta ta ta» ou des calembours, se rattachent au contenu d'un message prétendu, dans sa globalité, créatif, nous avons envisagé une sorte de cohérence implicite, entre le texte et son objet, concernant le niveau stylistique. Mais souvent il n'est pas donné de retrouver un sens ni un lien implicite de cohérence entre les objets et le contenu du message, même au niveau stylistique. Sans doute cet objet mystérieux se réfère à un présupposé qui ne peut être partagé que par les seuls correspondants. Dans ce cas-ci, la principale et véritable référence de l'objet est la complicité entre les locuteurs et sa fonction est surtout de type relationnel.

Il arrive aussi que l'espace réservé à l'objet reste vide, que l'objet manque. Ou bien que l'*objet*, après différents tours de courrier, où le sujet du dialogue a plusieurs fois changé, devienne périmé: «Re: Re: Re: Merry Christmas» arboré par un message daté le 3 avril. Les usagers qui choisissent un objet «RE:» périmé se servent d'un vieux message par distraction ou par paresse: pour ne pas en entamer un à zéro, pour ne pas être obligés à rechercher l'adresse du destinataire. Le temps et les tours passent, les interlocuteurs ne sont pas intéressés à changer leurs objets, ils ne les ‹voient› même plus, ils les oublient. Donc, si d'une part l'objet a une fonction d'ancrage extra-textuel visant à la construction d'une référence commune selon un mécanisme de type anaphore/déictique, d'autre part, son emploi distrait rend nulle cette fonction. Pas de problème: il ne faut pas attacher trop d'importance aux règles d'emploi de l'intermédiaire électronique, y compris celle de signaler l'objet du courrier. L'infraction à la règle du jeu est déjà comprise dans le jeu même de l'échange et, surtout, elle peut être compensée par d'autres procédés visant à remplir ce vide. L'un des principaux dispositifs ayant pour but de mettre en évidence la co-référence (ou la continuité référentielle) est la co-présence de différents envois dans un même message.

5. L'alternance des tours

Dans l'échange épistolaire il n'est pas très difficile de comprendre le contenu de la lettre d'un seul des deux correspondants: il n'est pas nécessaire de lire la lettre de l'autre. Celui qui répond repropose anaphoriquement, reformule, une bonne partie des contenus de la lettre de l'autre, ou bien il indique des éléments suffisants à reconstuire ces contenus. Dans le cas du courrier électronique, répétitions et reprises ne sont pas nécessaires: celui qui écrit n'a pas besoin de s'efforcer d'expliciter une référence par rapport aux informations présentes dans le message de l'autre. Cette fonction de reconstruction du texte et du contexte est confiée à la présence matérielle des messages précédents, à côté du message actuel (ils le suivent ou le précèdent dans le texte), signalée par les marques graphiques « > » ou « >> ». À l'oral, on oublie parfois des mots prononcés par l'autre, dans l'e-mail tout reste dans une mémoire, *scripta manent* (à moins qu'on ne décide de les effacer ... ou de les manipuler!).

Dans une optique dialogique, l'organisation textuelle d'un message électronique contenant d'autres messages met en place la représentation d'un système de tours conversationnels enchaînés: c'est l'instrument technologique même qui permet dans ce cas cette simulation/mise en scène. Nous renonçons, ici, à montrer un exemple de ce type de message multiple, à séquences enchaînées, car il prendrait trop d'espace. D'ailleurs, croyons-nous, sa structure est bien familière à la plupart des lecteurs.

Le mécanisme de l'alternance des tours dialogiques est mise en évidence de façon bien plus marquée là où les correspondants intercalent leurs énoncés *à l'intérieur* des énoncés constituant le texte du courrier déjà envoyé par l'interlocuteur. Nous observons ainsi différents tours de parole: des énoncés interrompus par d'autres énoncés-tours ajoutés ou bien enchâssés (des réponses, des commentaires). Dans l'extrait qui suit, l'alternance est mise en scène par une structure à tours enchâssés:

> Come va? E' da molto tempo che non ci sentiamo e spero che tutto, lavoro e vita privata procedano bene. ABBASTANZA, A PARTE CHE SI LAVORA TROPPO ANCHE SE SONO LE VACANZE APPENA FINITE Dopo aver lungamente riflettuto, ho atteso fino a settembre SEMBRA GIA' DICEMBRE per rivolgermi a te per consigli circa la pubblicazione in una rivista italiana di un articolo di una giovane collega ricercatrice LYZA WKEY? Si tratta di un lavoro sull'interazione medico-paziente. INTERESSANTE Ti chiedo scusa del disturbo. MI FA MOLTO PIACERE INVECE RIPRENDERE CONTATTO CON TE ED AVERE L'OCCASIONE DI PARLARE DI PUBBLICAZIONI CHE CI INTERESSINO, ma non è facile trovare delle buone riviste che si occupino di comunicazione e di linguaggio da un punto di vista psicologico e pragmatico Ho pensato che forse la vostra rivista poteva essere una buona possibilità e che un tuo consiglio sarebbe stato prezioso. MANDAMI IL LAVORO, DOVRO' PERO SOTTOPORLO' AI REFEREES: E' SEMPRE PREVISTA UNA VALUTAZIONE ANONIMA DA PARTE DI DUE REFEREES. E POI ANDREBBE COMUNQUE TRADOTTO IN INGLESE Ti auguro

una buona ripresa e ti ringrazio fin d'ora del tuo interessamento. SE MI DAI IL TUO INDIRIZZO DI CASA AVREI PIACERE DI INVIARTI UN NUMERO DELLA RIVISTA CON LE NORME.
Con affetto, Pia CON AFFETTO ANCH'IO, A PRESTO

Dans cet exemple, le deuxième correspondant exploite l'un des avantages du système, il choisit les points précis où insérer ses phrases afin de commenter ou de donner une réponse à certaines questions proposées par le premier correspondant. Ce procédé lui permet d'économiser à la fois son temps et ses forces, qui seraient nettement plus considérables s'il devait écrire et organiser un texte tout nouveau. Le message qui en résulte est une sorte de co-construction d'un dialogue. Le choix actif concernant les points d'insertion, pourrait être considéré comme une mise en scène de la négociation pour la prise du tour de parole.

Comme nous l'avons déjà remarqué, c'est l'intermédiaire électronique qui se charge de métacommuniquer sur les différents tours du dialogue, par rapport à l'ordre de leur parution temporelle: il met en évidence la date de chaque message et il les range en juxtaposant aux séquences des phrases des chevrons simples ou doubles, c'est-à-dire les signes « > » ou « >> ». Les correspondants, de leur côté, peuvent, s'ils le veulent, marquer davantage leur propre contribution en modifiant les caractères typographiques, comme dans l'extrait que nous venons de montrer, et/ou leurs couleurs.

6. Conclusion

En guise de conclusion, encore quelques mots au sujet de la négociation. Nous avons suggéré plus haut que la structure à tours enchâssés pourrait en quelque sorte représenter une stratégie de négociation de la prise du tour de parole. Toutefois, en principe, de véritables stratégies de négociation ne semblent pas s'appliquer à ce système de dialogue, où le locuteur ne risque jamais d'être interrompu ou de couper la parole à l'autre. Si la correspondance épistolaire, avec ses traces de l'oral dans l'écrit, est un type discursif «hybride» (Blanche-Benveniste 1997), le courrier électronique est un hybride à la puissance deux qui, malgré tout, n'est jamais en mesure de s'émanciper des contraintes relevant de l'écrit; et qui, d'autre part, n'à même pas toujours intérêt à y renoncer complètement.

Quant au courrier adressé à plusieurs destinataires secondaires, on a pu observer des tentatives d'insertion de ces derniers dans le dialogue. En général, le résultat n'est pas la mise en scène d'une conversation, mais une fragmentation du dialogue en plusieurs pièces détachées (où l'on a souvent du mal à cerner des micro-dialogues isolés). Plus souvent, les destinataires indirects jouent un rôle d' «écouteurs» (à la Goffman) ou de «témoins».

Il faut peut-être reconnaître que le choix le plus actif à la disposition du locuteur électronique, à propos de la négociation, est celui de ne pas coopérer en se refusant à répondre aux messages.

Une réponse manquée, ou un retard, propose toujours à l'autre des inférences ou des ‹implicatures› concernant le sens de ce ‹silence›. Cela, d'ailleurs, arrive dans tous les types de dialogues, à l'oral comme à l'écrit. Dans le cas du courrier électronique, ces inférences sont moins ‹forcées›, plus faibles par rapport au dialogue oral en face-à-face, où une petite pause peut se charger de plusieurs sens par rapport au contexte de l'interaction; mais elles semblent plus fortes – et même constituer des d' «insubordinations» – par rapport à l'écrit du courrier traditionnel. Cet aspect attesterait, en quelque sorte, que le courrier électronique représente dans le vécu subjectif des participants une forme de communication plus proche du dialogue en face-à-face. Parmi les options fournies par les systèmes de courrier électronique, est aussi prévu un dispositif automatique, une sorte de «message vide», ayant une fonction d'accusé de réception. La présence d'un tel dispositif, qui exclut la possibilité d'une non-réponse causée par un dysfonctionnement, peut, dans certaines circonstances, donnier lieu à l'élaboration d'inférences plus fortes en cas de non-réponse.

Références

Benveniste, Émile (1966): Problèmes de linguistique générale. Paris: Gallimard.
Blanche-Benveniste, Claire (1997): Approches de la langue parlée en français. Paris: Ophrys.
Goffman, Erving (1981): Forms of talk. Philadelphia: University of Pennsylvania Press.
Lejeune, Philippe (1980): Je est un autre. L'autobiographie de la littérature aux médias. Paris: Seuil.
Stame, Stefania/Lorenzetti, Roberta (1993): The anaphoric reference: Theoretical and research frameworks. In: International Journal of Psycholinguistics 9, 95-103.
Violi, Patrizia/Coppock, Patrick J. (1999): Conversazioni telematiche. In: Galatolo, R./Pallotti, G. (éds.): La conversazione. Introduzione allo studio dell'interazione verbale. Milano: Raffaello Cortina, 319-364.

Amelia Manuti / Michela Cortini / Giuseppe Mininni

Job on line: The diatextual rhetoric of e-recruitment

0. Introduction

A dialogical approach to the analysis of mediated interaction allows for the pointing out of at least two axes of pertinence: the dialogue *with* the media and the dialogue *within* the media. This distinction originates from a dialogical conception of human communication (Weigand 1999; 2000). Thus, *dialogue* could be meant both as a general format of the communicative practices of sense making and as a specific discursive genre. The implicit dialogism of every verbal interaction is then enriched by a very special dynamics as the negotiation of meaning is not immediate (as by face to face communication) but rather mediated by the potentialities of such a communicative technology. The participants of the communicative event do not simply communicate with each other but in some sense – although sometimes even unconsciously – they communicate with the medium by estimating its opportunities and limits and thus by validating its symbolic claim.

As Bachtin (1973) magisterially highlighted (literary) writing has an heteroglossic relevance and a very rich poliphonic texture. This contribution then aims at investigating some of the dialogical dynamics which operate within computer mediated communication. Finally, although the argumentative context analysed (job offer and demand) may seem problematic at first sight as it emphasizes a power dimension more than a solidarity one, the choice is justified both by the relevance for the lives of people and the potential broadening granted to the theoretical comprehension of the resources of dialogicity.

1. The construction of a new meaning of working

Working life was subjected to radical changes over the last decades of the 20th century. Economic changes, technological innovation, industrial restructuring and accelerated global competition have proved to be crucial factors influencing the labour market and the nature of human work activity. In this light, work flexibility has become a key word for organizations, a necessary condition for the survival of national labour markets in a fast moving world of global competition, which forces modern workers to be able to adapt to changing circumstances and to be prepared for multiple careers (Reilly 1998; Peiro et al. 2002). As a result, these radical changes in the labour market rapidly reshape the meaning of work and the strategies people use to cope with this increasing work and job flexibility demands.

Moreover, though organizations see and depict flexibility as an opportunity for workers, who by this are able to "use" flexibility to better plan their daily working and leisure activities, most workers are forced to become flexible, thus with relevant psychological implications. Therefore, from an organizational perspective, flexibility supports many companies in adapting to the demands of a changing environment, but unfortunately from an individual point of view, although some may view flexibility positively, many negative consequences are evident and dominate the psychological literature (Sverke/Hellgren 2002).

In this light, there is a significant gap between the organizational and the individual perspective on new work opportunities and modalities, resulting in a general restructuring of the traditional social representation of work. The notion of a secure and stable workplace, which was a myth in most western societies in the past, has gradually been replaced by that of flexible and atypical work. Careers are then no longer seen as linear but rather as a mosaic of experiences, which obviously influences the construction of professional identity.

2. Internet as a dialogic tool for online work socialization and recruitment practices

The changing meaning of working and the consequent restructuring of its importance in life (Meaning of Working Team 1987) signs of the times, contribute to reshape traditional work socialization processes, meant as a preparatory stage which introduce career starters or long lasting unemployed to the world of work.

During these anticipatory stages people generally plan their careers, look for training opportunities and organize a set of beliefs about the importance of work in their life, thus wondering about the position they will have in the world of work (Meaning of working Team 1987). Thus, the Internet becomes a privileged medium for workers to keep informed about job opportunities and new working modalities.

In this light, the e-recruitment web sites, that is those sites which select curricula online by trying to match the organizational demands with the individual offers, seem to adhere to the model of interactive and functionalist communication (Rodger/Thorson 2000). These sites could rightly be labelled as a public service, since they try to fulfil specific objectives by offering several ad hoc services. A potential candidate as well as a company who is looking for a specific professional profile could 'use' the Internet, driven by a research motivation, which is a serious and highly goal oriented.

Moreover, some e-recruitment web sites aim to fulfil the need for communication of some candidates, who 'use' the forum discussion as a means to both keep informed about recent developments of the labour market (serious motive) and simply to exchange points of view and experiences about work (playful motive) thus creating a sort of virtual community. That is why these web sites are so structured as to better suit all the needs and demands of potential interlocutors.

The Internet then becomes an ideal bridge, which mediates between workers and labour market, a sort of mirror which dialogically reflects and connects market demands with individual desires. In this context, CMC with its most evident features, such as immediacy and easy accessibility, grants advantages both to the organization and to the candidates: the former being able to select the ideal professional profile more cheaply and rapidly, while the latter are easily and comfortably in touch with the labour market directly from home. By this the e-recruitment web sites introduce themselves as the ideal link between job offer and demand.

3. The study

The corpus of data is made up of 10 web sites (*stepstone, jobpilot, jobonline, talentmanager, cliccalavoro, cercalavoro, bancalavoro, carriera24, monster, click4talent*) dedicated to e-recruitment, that is online work selection, assessment and training practices. The analysis was oriented towards two different but parallel aims. On the one hand, the focus is on the self presentation rhetorical strategies used by the web sites to introduce themselves to the Internet users, as an online customer service, oriented toward the match between job offers and demand. On the other hand, the focus is on the positioning strategies displayed by the participants to the newsgroup discussion about new working modalities and contract typologies.

The objective is to investigate whether the social theme of job flexibility is differently constructed through discourse in these two different forms of communication (web sites versus newsgroup forum discussion), whether the specific features of the Internet influence the negotiation of meaning and whether the peculiarities of this new media highlight the gap between the image of work presented by the sites and that conveyed by concrete experiences within the newsgroup discussion.

To this purpose, the data have been investigated by adopting the theoretical and methodological format of the diatext (Mininni 1992; 2000), since it allows to better catch the relationship between interlocutors, text and context, by recalling the dialectics and the dialogics of the construction of sense which is realized through communicative events. The articulation of some pragmatic indices such as *intentionality, rhetoricity, cognitive and emotional modality*, allows for the comprehension of the sense/identity nexus which emerges spontaneously from each kind of text.

3.1 The web sites

According to the taxonomy proposed by Morris and Ogan (1996) the web site is a form of Computer Mediated Communication (CMC) which is characterized by a *one to many asynchronous relationship*. Generally a web site could be conceived as a virtual and interactive catalogue which, in a window shows the users several services and products. Usually the structure and content organization of the web pages follows a similar scheme which in turn tries to fulfil the users' objectives. There is generally a menu which presents the contents of the web sites and the different types of services offered to the Internauts. In this case the organization of the e-recruitment web sites reflects the dual nature of this type of web sites that is a service for both the organization and the workers. That is why we find different concepts of navigation in almost every site, which do mark the different motives of the users.

Thus the focus of our investigation is on the home pages and on some of the links (*Who we are and what we do*) which generally introduce the site to its virtual interlocutors, striking its values, goals and objectives to better foster and establish an affiliation relationship.

To this purpose, to create a sort of regular interaction, these descriptions make use of peculiar discursive strategies, which aim at constructing and conveying the most credible image of the site's manager often in contrast with its competitors. The manager is in fact central to these pages, although he is in a sense 'invisible' to the web users, since generally the name of the site could conceal a local company, a successful multinational or a non profit organization. As a result famous names or successful promotional campaigns are used as a warrant of loyalty, trust and success to improve the credibility of web sites whose users are supposed to become as famous and successful as the sites suggest.

(1) Monster.it is part of the Monster network, leader of the online recruitment and division of TMP worldwide, the greatest international counselling company, which recruits and assesses human resources

(Monster.it)

Moreover, this management impressions' strategy, which explicitly aims at gaining credibility, is often supported by further links, which guide the web users through a sort of interactive tour of the archives, where photos, interviews and newspaper articles about the site and its successful reputation are presented as evidence of its credibility and reliability (*What they say about us*).

On the other hand, while credibility seems to be a common strategy for introducing themselves to the Internauts, the e-recruitment web sites follow different discursive routes to confront with their competitors (*intentionality index*). It should not be forgotten that the modern and interactive kind of recruitment modality originates from the USA. Hence, most of these sites are the Italian partners of huge multinational companies which have their seat in the States. As a result, both in content, structure and communicative style they mirror a foreign worldview and representation of the world of work. It is not surprising, then, that some web sites (e.g. Monster, Stepstone, Jobpilot) construct their public image by counting on those names and world known reputations which are quoted as a warrant for the candidates and for the companies who choose them. On the other hand, other e-recruitment web sites (Jobonline, Cliccalavoro, Cercalavoro), which are younger and smaller economic realities, stake their credibility on this differentiation. Their smaller dimension could be of value for both the candidates and the companies, since it is better oriented toward the local labour market.

(2) Our editorial staff has been driven by a double intuition: on the one hand the consciousness that a strategic localization process of the Italian labour market could be the only opportunity to face a global concurrence while on the other they supported the belief that differently from traditional mass media within the interactive domain offers actually lead job demands.

(Jobonline)

Hence, the first macro-difference between the e-recruitment web sites is concerns their *local versus global* origins, thus with obvious implications for the contents conveyed. These global e-recruitment web sites in fact do account for a labour market which doesn't actually resemble the Italian economic and social reality. This is mostly evident in the discursive construction of flexible working modalities.

Flexibility is presented as an opportunity for both the company and the candidate to improve knowledge, to earn higher wages and to be more competitive and dynamic on the market. The chance to change job whenever desired, to find the job we have always dreamt of, or rather the our lifelong job, seems at least ironic in such a local context, characterized by high unemployment rates and huge occupational differences between the North and the South. Moreover, these sites give no space to the workers, who are not allowed to reply, whilst the web sites which we defined local, through the forum, give them the chance to express their opinions and also contradict a social representation of the world of work which actually doesn't resemble to the reality of experience (*rhetoricity and modality indices*).

(3) Temporary work is an optimal opportunity for those who are looking for the first job, as it gives them the opportunity to choose the occupation which best suits his needs and aspirations.

(Jobpilot)

Another difference concerns the ideal interlocutor they are appealing to. Then, it is possible to distinguish between *organization-* and *individual-oriented* web site typology. Some web sites in fact explicitly declare themselves to be a service for the working companies, which are often defined as organizational partners. However, the individual-oriented websites define themselves as virtual career centres, focused on the socialization and training needs of different types of future workers.

As a result, a different representation of the workers also emerges, which further marks the distinction between the two typologies of e-recruitment web sites. The *organization-oriented* web sites seem to consider the candidates merely as human capital, which could be turned into profit by the organizational partners. On the other hand, the *individual-oriented* typology, which present itself as a service for the candidates often defines the latter as human resources, thus underlining competence and potential which should be considered not merely as professional.

3.2 The newsgroup forum discussion

The newsgroup forum discussion is a very peculiar form of CMC, being *many to many* and asynchronous (Morris/Ogan 1996). The interlocutors are invited to exchange e-mails about a theme of discussion which could either be proposed by the web site or by the participants to the forum thus creating a sort of communicative thread.

This form of communication is potentially dialogical in nature since both kind of messages, the one which is addressed to a specific interlocutor and the other which, by contrast, is meant as a message for the unknown community, are both conative and phatic, that is concretely willing to position the self and the other waiting for a reply and for the debate to begin. By communicating, the participants to the newsgroup create, and identify with, a sort of virtual community, which shares norms, jargon, routines and meanings, thus revealing that although distant in space and time and without physical cues the form of communication which develops is socially embedded (*modality and rhetoricity indices*).

In this case, the corpus of data is thus made up of respectively 25 and 38 messages sent to the forum of two e-recruitment web sites Bancalavoro and Cliccalavoro. Actually, only 2 of the 10 web sites analysed present a discussion forum about new working modalities and atypical contracts. The theme of the two newsgroup discussions is similar although they differ in discursive construction.

The Bancalavoro forum opens with the following question:

(4) Atypical Contracts: opportunity or swindle? With new contract typologies (part time, temporary jobs, etc) it has become easier to enter the labour market, but what is at stake? Few warrants, low wages and sometimes few investments on professional training.

The Cliccalavoro forum, on the contrary, begins with the question:

(5) Stable workplace or flexibility? Is the myth of a stable workplace still valid in the 3th millenium? What is better: a secure workplace or an higher wage and the challenge to learn new professions, being always ready to change job? What do you think about this?

They both begin with a rhetorical question to stimulate discussion and the positioning process. Thus the possible communicative positions are already signalled by the dichotomic opposition which marks two different social interpretative repertoires about job flexibility (opportunity or swindle? Stable workplace or flexibility?). Although they use different strategies, both forums hint at the potential opportunities that flexibility offers. The first forum, in fact, makes an assumption about the new working modalities focusing on the opportunity granted by flexibility to career starters, thus taking for granted that the latter agree with this position. The second half of the assumption on the contrary is centred on the other face of the coin, thus underlining what flexibility could actually mean. Moreover, the term 'swindle' is a very informal word, typically used by young people, as to refer to events and situations, which although apparently positive, actually turn negative, thus causing disappointment. So the choice of this peculiar term to label flexibility implicitly explains the evolution of atypical working modalities, which although apparently advantageous could easily turn into a strategic tool for the employees and a swindle for the employers.

The second forum also underlines the dual nature of flexibility thus clearly inviting potential interlocutors to take part in the discussion (*What do you think about this*?). Nevertheless, in this case the negative aspects of atypical work are hidden behind the positive ones which are discursively highlighted. The economical security of stable work is thus compared with a higher wage and the challenge of continuous learning and self-improvement. This rhetorical strategy implies that work flexibility is always exclusively a synonym for economical advantages for workers, thus omitting the psychological implications of its composite features (temporal, geographical, functional, contractual, etc.), which are differently experienced by each of them. The social theme of work flexibility is thus reduced to a mere question of work personality: economic and professional stability versus risk and work adaptability. Hence while the first forum is opened with a more tempered remark about the changing of the labour market, the communicative thread of the second forum sounds rather like a provocation, which is artfully constructed by the pressing rhetorical questions and aims at stimulating the discussion. Although with slight differences, the discussion emerging from the two forums accounts for evident discursive positions (*intentionality index*) which can be distinguished into 4 broad categories, each with his/her personal and social features: the pro-flexibility, the undecided, the system deniers, the undeceived.

There are actually few *pro-flexibility* positions. As the label suggests, they obviously support new flexible work modalities by underlining the opportunities granted to workers with regard to time and competence. Paradoxically, most of these optimistic interlocutors do not mention any personal experience with atypical work, thus suggesting that they actually don't know much about the concrete flex-working situation and simply mirror shared interpretative repertoires. Hence, the positive features of flexibility highlighted by these interlocutors recall those used by the sites while describing the advantages of the new working modalities.

(6) We are entering a new era where technological development is involving almost everybody. I think that thanks to the Internet a new way of considering work is developing. New work opportunities are offered to the candidate, provided that the shows mental flexibility and availability in accepting the new working relationships.

(Ok to Flexibility – Edo- Forum of Cliccalavoro)

Nevertheless, other pro-flexibility supporters, who do make reference to their experience, stress that flexible working modalities could be a valid alternative while waiting for a stable job. In this sense, they support flexibility only in part as job stability still remains a goal.

(7) Hi, I am a Architecture student and I am 25 years old. I worked part time in a call centre with a temporary contract for three months. I think that this could be an optimal solution for students, as it allows one to work while studying. My wage was not so high, but for a student it could be ok. Of course if it would be my "real" job I would definitely not be satisfied [...].

(Alessandra 75 – Forum of Bancalavoro)

The *undecided* group is characterized by an ambiguous attitude toward flexibility. The expressed doubts do not concern the core of flexibility as a working philosophy but rather the social application modalities which are, in practice, often influenced by the limits of the Italian labour market. As a result these messages often sound socially engaged, as they concretely invite the participants to the forum to react to the social system which should better represent all social classes with their needs.

(8) I believe in work flexibility as I think that it pushes toward continuous professional improvement. It is important to understand and to specify the application modalities of work flexibility: when it is a choice, then it is experienced with optimism and enthusiasm. But when it is imposed by a tyrannical employee or by the critical situation of the labour market (as in the South of Italy) then the worker undergo a sort of blackmail which is seldom accompanied by a large profits [...].

(...it depends...sabrina – Forum of Cliccalavoro)

This group is characterized by a polemic attitude toward work flexibility which is artfully used as a pretext to criticize the social system as a whole, and in particular the Italian one. The people in this group talk like 'modern prophets' who are able to show the way to social redemption as they feel smarter than the others, whom they even ridicule. Nonetheless their messages do not make any reference to the concrete situation or to their personal experiences.

(9) We should thank: the politicians (right and left wing), the trade unions who allow these situations go on and on and then we should thank ourselves too as we accept everything and live on thoughtlessly until we miss the bread...we should behave like our French cousins: something doesn't work? Everything is stopped!

(Massimo – Forum of Bancalavoro)

The *undeceived* group is the most numerous. It includes both people who have personally experienced flexibility but with negative results and those who a-priori express a contrary point of view as they are convinced that flexibility could not be a solution to unemployment. Anyway, in contrast with the previous category, the undeceived people feel they are part of the system, and although the tone is very often ironic it is used to strengthen the identification with the other interlocutors.

(10) I feel half a worker. I have no rights with this kind of contract. I would like to attend an English course but I can't as I am busy all day long and for the employment agency I am unemployed. How can I change this situation? By the way I work 8 hours a day for 1.200.000 Italian Lire. It is not right!

(Vanessa – Forum of Bancalavoro)

The four discursive categories make use of different rhetorical strategies. As for the argumentation, the four interlocutionary profiles use different arguments to support their positions, which could be thought of as a continuum between *collective and individual* argumentation strategy. This should be considered in relation to the references that the messages make to personal experiences ("Hi I am Alessandra I have worked in a company for 7 years. One morning they fired me without notice. After two months I succeeded in having what I was due but how fatiguing it was!" Alessandra – Forum of Bancalavoro) more than to more social points of view, that is arguments which are socially constructed, conveyed and shared, for example by mass media or more generally by social talk ("Atypical contracts are both an opportunity to collect work experiences and a swindle as time goes by and nothing is secure"– Katia – Forum of Bancalavoro).

The communicative format of the forum discussion allows for a more problematic than assertive discursive construction in relation to the pro or contra positions as the ones who support flexibility display an *assertive* communicative style ("personally I am pro-flexibility" or "I believe in flexibility") while the undecided, the undeceived and the system deniers have a more *problematic* communicative style. The latter often make use of rhetorical questions which have different functions in relation to the three groups.

Hence, by the system deniers' rhetorical questions sound like a provocation, where the tone is ironic and attempts at creating and maintaining the discussion ("Can someone tell me where's the planet where a job is so easy to find?"). On the other hand, for the undecided interlocutors these questions are actually a request for information about flexibility ("Should the wage of occasional collaboration be declared within the income declaration?"). Finally, for the undeceived group, rhetorical questions are a means to express inner dilemmas which are finally spoken loud ("The question is not flexibility or stable work but how to find job after at 45 years of age. Too young for the retirement and too old for work, what should I do?").

Dialogicity is an evident peculiarity of this communicative format. The discursive thread is produced by the exchange of questions and replies which could be both addressed to a specific interlocutor or to everyone. Choosing a forum on work flexibility among several different newsgroup is already a positioning strategy which reveal the personal interest of the interlocutor or perhaps his/her willingness to share information and opinions with a virtual community which may have had similar experiences. This dialogicity, then, emerges in the use of plural form 'we', mostly used to define themselves as members of a particular group of workers, and in other specific communicative strategies, such as the use of capital letters and inverted commas which presume that a community of interpreters is able to understand and share meanings without further explanation. Although with different shadings in the discursive positions (pro or contra flexibility) the participants of the forum share a personal interest in the theme and therefore move in a sort of microcosm which identifies them. In this light, the newsgroup forum is more than a virtual board where messages are stuck: it is a live community whose substance is discussion. Then, although it's an asynchronous communicative format it could be seen as more similar to a conversation since messages are often addressed to a specific interlocutor thus creating a dyadic relationship which is but parallel to the forum (i.e. "reply to Joe" "I agree with you" etc.).

4. Concluding remarks

The self description of our time as 'the society of knowledge and communication' makes reference to the dynamics of dialogue, thus characterizing the 'attempts towards meaning' which are central to human existence. Therefore, the promotion of any dialogic potentiality is a very relevant interpretative category within the analysis of the rapid development and social spreading of new media. Then, computer mediated communication contexts offer both new relational modalities and meeting chances to individuals and to groups, since they highlight routes of co-construction of meaning which once were totally unbelievable. Moreover, dialogicity is a constitutive trait of human experience about the world not simply because it pervades the pragmatic dimension (what people actually do), but also because it shapes the cognitive dimension (how people think about themselves and about the social reality). Nonetheless, these dimensions are strictly linked to each other as underlined by the analysis of the meaning that work plays for the construction of self and social identity (Manuti 2003). Actually, the representation of the working praxis which best suits the 'society of knowledge and communication' passes trough the key word of "flexibility". Hence, the modalities though which flexibility actually circulates within social textuality is nourished by the myth of free, efficient and concrete dialogue both between 'social parts' and between individuals and organizations. In line with a Critical Discourse Analysis perspective, the diatextual analysis of some discoursive practices within the virtual communication domain (Mininni 2002) – WEB sites and newsgroups discussions about the new working modalities – shows that the model of flexible work could be justified by referring to the dynamic and versatile nature of dialogue, only after having highlighted the radical differences that the enunciators attribute to themselves and to the others regarding both for cognitive control skills and social influence. Then, the concept of 'flexible work' becomes an ideological instrument strategically used to stiffen the power relationships within the global community, as an unspoken tension of power, which hides itself behind the culture of dialogue.

References

Bakhtin, M. (^{2}1973): Problems of Dostoevsky's poetics. Transl. by Roetsel, R.W. Ann Arbor, Mich.: Ann Arbor.
Manuti, A. (2003): Il significato del Lavoro nella costruzione dell'identità personale e sociale. Tesi di dottorato in Psicologia della Comunicazione. Università degli studi di Bari.
Meaning of Working Team (1987): The meaning of working. London: Academic Press.
Mininni, G. (1992): Diatesti. Psicosemiotica del discorso sociale. Napoli: Liguori.
– (2000): Psicologia del parlare comune. Bologna: Grasso.
– (2002): Virtuale.com. La parola spiazzata. Napoli: Idelson Gnocchi.
Morris, M./Ogan, C. (1996): The Internet as a mass medium. In: Journal of communication 46/1, 12-23.
Peiro, J.M./Garcia Montalvo, J./Gracia, F. (2002): How do young people cope with job flexibility? Demographic and psychological antecedents of the resistance to accept a job with non-preferred flexibility features. In: Applied Psychology: An International Review 51/1, 43-66.
Reilly, P.A. (1998): Balancing flexibility: meeting the interests of employer and employee. In: European Journal of Work and Organizational Psychology 7/1, 7-22.
Rodgers, S./Thorson E. (2000): The interactive advertising model: How users perceive and process on line ads. In: Journal of Interactive Advertising 1/1, 23-32.
Sverke, M./Hellgren, J. (2002): The nature of job insecurity: Understanding employment uncertainty on the brink of the new millennium. In: Applied Psychology: An International Review 51/1, 23-42.
Weigand, E. (1999): Rhetoric and argumentation in dialogic perspective. In: Rigotti, E. (ed.): Rhetoric and argumentation. Tübingen: Niemeyer, 53-69.
– (2000): The dialogic action game. In: Coulthard, M. (ed.): Dialogue analysis VII. Working with dialogue. Tübingen: Niemeyer, 1-18.

The e-recruitment web sites:
www.stepstone.it; www.jobpilot.it; www.jobonline.it; www.talentmanger.it; www.cliccalavoro.it; www.cercalavoro.it; www.bancalavoro.it; www.ccarriera24.it; www.monster.it; www.click4talent.it

Ana I. Moreno

Perceiving coherence and text structure: Which cohesive ties are really textual?

1. Introduction

According to most models of cohesion in English, cohesive items play an important role in perceiving texts as unified and meaningful. These models attempt to account for the explicit linguistic devices used in texts to signal relations between sentences (cf. Halliday/Hasan 1976). However, to date the exact role of the different kinds of cohesive devices in the perception of text coherence and relevance remains unclear. On the one hand, cohesive devices are not all that matters in order to account for coherence, since there are many coherence relations between text fragments that are implicit. And, as is commonly acknowledged, what is crucial for text comprehension is being able to interpret the coherence relations between text fragments, whether they are explicit or implicit.

On the other hand, in most of these models texts seem to have been approached as products rather than processes, while ordinary users of the language are more likely to approach texts as processes. That is, readers do not need to wait until they have finished reading the whole written product to try and make sense of the text. Competent readers will attempt to make sense of the discourse from the very moment the reading process begins, and – if motivation and interest endures – may continue doing so at every stage in the reading process. In other words, accomplished readers will attempt to retrieve discourse meaning as they come across subsequent textual units in their search for relevance.

The present paper claims that a better understanding of this role in ordinary language processing should at least be based on the analysis of all possible textual mechanisms, whether explicit or inferred, when the discourse is approached as process rather than as product. The aims of the present study are: a) to identify which textual mechanisms of a given text play a crucial role in helping the reader to perceive text relevance and, therefore, coherence in the process of reading; b) to compare these mechanisms with those identified on approaching the text-as-product in order to determine which features distinguish one group from the other. In particular, the present study will focus on the scope of the tie.

2. Assumptions about coherence and relevance

A text can be qualified as coherent when it is perceived as unified and meaningful to a particular reader. If coherence at a given point in a text is understood as a relation between linguistic units (Blakemore 1987, 111), then being able to perceive the relevance of a text segment at that point in the reading process may contribute to perceiving the text as coherent at that point. A sentence will be said to be relevant if it conveys relevant information, and relevance will be defined in terms of a relationship between propositions (cf. Blakemore 1987, 111; Sperber/Wilson 1986). Two utterances may be connected in coherent discourse in either of two ways:

(1) Either in virtue of the fact that the interpretation of the first may include propositions used in establishing the relevance of the second. This type has been called relevance (dependent on the interpretation) of content, as shown in the following example taken from the text found in the appendix:

> (39) In my day, I was expected to annotate scripts to explain my marks to the chief examiner. (40) Remove *that requirement*, and the examining process will only appear to be more open, while in fact retaining an almost smug inscrutability.

In this example, it is clear that there is one segment in the second sentence, *that requirement*, whose interpretation is affected by the interpretation of another segment of previous discourse. In other words, we can say that in order to establish part of the content of the second proposition, an essential task to establish the relevance of the current unit, we need to use the propositional meaning created by the interpretation of the previous sentence: i.e. the requirement that in her day, the author was expected to annotate scripts to explain her marks to the chief examiner.

(2) Or in virtue of the fact that a proposition conveyed by one is affected by the interpretation of the other (Blakemore 1987, 122). This type has been called relevance (dependent on the interpretation) of relational function, as can be seen in the following example:

> (19) Conscientious marking is a killer. (20) And examiners never did work in an irresponsible vacuum – (21) the chief examiner always loomed over one's shoulder, checking, commenting, re-marking if necessary. (22) *At least*, I think that's what he did.

Let us focus our attention on coherence unit (22), which becomes the current unit of interpretation or *text of the moment*. On trying to establish its relevance as a whole (not simply one element in it – as in relevance of content), the reader needs to do some extra inferential work to interpret the discourse function (i.e. an implicit import) of the whole of a previous discourse unit in relation to the discourse function of the whole of the current discourse unit. In this particular case, (22) is interpreted functionally as a correction of a statement of fact previously made. What is then interpreted is a *relational proposition* (cf. Mann/Thompson 1986) of *statement-correction* that helps to perceive the relevance of coherence unit (22) in relation to previous discourse.

In either case we might say that the relevance of the current coherent unit is somehow dependent on the interpretation of another one.

3. Design of the empirical research

3.1 Research strategy

The present study attempted to establish a comparison between the cohesive mechanisms identified when approaching the same text in two different ways: 1) the discourse-as-process; and 2) the text-as-product.

1) The first approach attempted to analyse the textual mechanisms, whether explicit or implicit, identified by a group of readers as crucial in perceiving connections between successive coherence units of a given text that contribute to establishing the relevance of each new coherence unit in the process of reading (see section 4).

2) The second approach attempted to analyse the explicit cohesive devices identified by the researcher as playing a role in establishing connections of all kinds between the different coherence units of the same text analysed as product, that is, going back and forward as much as necessary in the search for these ties (see section 5).

3.2 Corpus

These two ways of approaching a text were applied to the same comment article from *Guardian Unlimited*. This article represents typical dialogic written text and was chosen for its length and the relevance of its topic to the participants' learning situation. A segmented version is shown in the appendix and the full reference to this text is in the bibliography section below (Moriarty 1999).

The text, made up of 56 sentences, was split into 60 constituent coherence units. As can be deduced, in most cases, the minimal unit of coherence corresponded with the orthographic sentence, or the clause complex (Downing/Locke 1992), enclosed by a full stop.

However, based on Sinclair's (1993) conclusions about this issue, a few variations were introduced (cf. Moreno 2003). The same division of the text into its coherence units was used for both approaches of the text, as product and as process.

It should be noticed that the text elements presented in parentheses preceded by an asterisk in the segmented text (cf. appendix) were not part of the original text but are meant to represent the type of connection inferred by the participants between text fragments (see section 4.2).

4. Discourse-as-process approach

4.1 Participants

The participants used in the discourse-as-process approach were the discourse community of Spanish advanced learners of English taking a degree in English at the University of León. First of all a pilot study was carried out with five participants. Then the final study was performed with 25. The study sought to capture the coherence pattern of the text as perceived by the majority of the group of individuals in their communicative role as readers of the same text, abstracting away from the particular appreciation of any individual participant (including the researcher herself).

4.2 Procedure

In order to gather the necessary data from looking at the discourse-as-process the following procedure was used.

First, the participants were required to read the above-mentioned text carefully. To control for the factor of purpose of reading (cf. Moreno 2003), they were said that they would have to produce a written summary later on. They were provided with a glossary with the most predictably difficult items. Then, they were asked to do a number of interpretation tasks in the form of a written test at each point in the reading process (see test below). Next, a round of discussions was opened to contrast the different interpretations, first in groups of five individuals, then open-class. A consensus on the most likely interpretation at each stage of the text was arrived at.

Perceiving coherence and text structure

4.3 Test

(1) Nineteen ninety-nine was the year we dipped a toe in the water:
A) Can you perceive any connection between coherence unit (1) and its co-text?   Yes _ No _
F) Does coherence unit (1) lead you to expect something specific in the following text? Yes _ No _
G) If this connection is explicit, circle and write down (the) prospective signal(s) that make(s) it explicit:_____

(2) and you know what?
A) Can you perceive any connection between coherence unit (2) and its co-text?   Yes _ No _
B) If you perceive an explicit connection with previous text, circle and write down the retrospective signal(s) that make(s) it explicit: _____
C) If you perceive an implicit connection, provide a signal/text fragment to make it explicit: _____
D) In relation to which part of previous text can you perceive this connection, whether implicit or explicit?
   A _ (a word)   B _ (a phrase)   C _ (a clause)   D _ (a sentence)   E _ (a larger unit)
E) In which sentence(s) is that part of previous text?   N° _____
F) Does coherence unit (2) lead you to expect something specific in the following text? Yes _ No _
G) If this connection is explicit, circle and write down (the) prospective signal(s) that make(s) it explicit:_____
H) Does coherence unit (2) satisfy a prospection created in previous text?   Yes _ No _
I) If so, in which coherence unit was the prospection created?   N° _____

Table 1. Sample Test Items (1 to 2)

4.4 Method of Analysis

Once the data had been gathered following the procedure mentioned in section 4.3, the data were arranged and classified according to the following criteria and categories:

Explicitness of connection:
    Explicit
    Implicit or inferred (I)
Phoric direction (cf. Moreno 2003; Sinclair 1993):
    Retrospection or encapsulation (E)
    Prospection (P)
    Fulfilment or satisfaction of prospection (S)
Coherence mechanisms and subtypes (cf. Moreno 2003; Sinclair 1993):
    Relevance of content: deictic act/discourse act
    Relevance of relational function: logical act
    Relevance of wording: wording act
Types and subtypes of cohesive tie (cf. Halliday/Hasan 1976; Moreno 2003):

Reference item: personal, demonstrative, comparative
Lexical item: repetition, synonym, hyponym, superordinate, general word, related word, opposite
Reference phrase: reference + lexical combinations
Reference clause: same meaning, similar meaning, inferred meaning, opposite meaning
Ellipsis: nominal, post-modifier, subject + operator, predicator, comparative clause, other clause type
Substitution: nominal, verbal, clausal
Conjunction: additive, causal, adversative, temporal
Punctuation: question mark, colon

Scope of the tie (cf. Moreno 2003; Sinclair 1993):
Point-to-point cohesion: a word, a phrase, a clause
Textual cohesion: a clause, a sentence, a larger unit
(Encapsulation = Retrospective textual cohesion)

5. Text-as-product approach

Looking at the text-as-product meant using a method whereby the researcher approached the whole text as a finished product in an attempt to identify all kinds of cohesive ties that play a role in establishing connections between a text fragment and another one beyond sentence boundaries. In order to make this and future comparisons possible, the analysis of these devices was carried out following Halliday/Hasan's (1976) classification of cohesive ties: lexical cohesion (repetition, synonyms, opposites, related words), substitution and ellipsis, reference (just endophoric) and conjunction. The analysis also considered the scope of the tie in each case.

6. Results

6.1 Results from the discourse-as-process approach

As can be seen in table 2 below, in most current units there was at least one encapsulating mechanism (54.7%), whether explicit (34%), inferred (1.7%), or both (19%). Prospection always occurred (5%) in combination with some encapsulating device, whether explicit

(1.7%), inferred (3.4%) or both (3.4%). Twelve coherence units in the text fulfilled a prospection (20.33%).

A common feature to all of these mechanisms is that they refer to discourse meaning derived from entire sentences, larger fragments of text, or certain simple clauses linked paratactically by a colon, a dash, or a comma or dash followed by some cohesive device (see column 5 in table 3 below).

Very few cases of point-to-point cohesion, that is, items referring to individual words, phrases or clauses, whether explicit (1.7 %), inferred (1.7%), or both (1.7 %) were identified when looking at the text in the process of reading. In any case, these did not seem to account for relevance by themselves. There was always a more powerful mechanism to account for coherence at that point.

Coherence mechanism	N	%	Number of coherence unit
Inferred encapsulation	19	32.2	12, 13, 14, 17, 18, 19, 21, 25, 27, 35, 36, 38, 39, 42, 43, 44, 52, 53, 56
Encapsulation	14	23.7	5, 6, 8, 15, 16, 20, 22, 32, 34, 37, 40, 41, 51, 57
Encapsulation + Inferred E.	8	13.6	24, 26, 31, 33, 45, 46, 54, 55
Encapsulation + Inferred E. + Inferred point-to-point cohesion	1	1.7	23
Encapsulation + Prospection	1	1.7	2
Encapsulation + Inferred E. + Prospection	2	3.4	28, 58
Inferred E. + Prospection	2	3.4	7, 47
Fulfilment of prospection	4	6.8	3, 29, 49, 50
Fulfilment of prospection + Encapsulation	4	6.8	4, 11, 30, 48
Fulfilment of prospection + Inferred E.	2	3.4	9, 10
Fulfilment of prospection + Point-to-point cohesion	1	1.7	59
Fulfilment of prospection + Encapsulation + Inferred point-to-point cohesion + Point-to-point cohesion	1	1.7	60
Total	59	100,0	

Table 2. Major coherence mechanisms affecting each coherence unit

The percentage of inferred encapsulations that account for coherence on their own was relatively high (32.2%). After the group discussion it was possible to arrive at a consensus on most cases without much difficulty. This suggests the existence of a standard of coherence shared by this discourse community that goes beyond the presence or absence of explicit signals.

A smaller number of inferred encapsulations (25.5%) were perceived in combination with other types of coherence mechanism. This might be interpreted as the participants' need to reinforce relevance in order to make better sense of the text at that point in the interpretation of the discourse.

6.2 Results from the text-as-product approach

As well as the previously mentioned coherence mechanisms – identified on reading the discourse-as-process –, there are many cases of point-to-point cohesion in the text that can be easily identified when approaching the text-as-product. Due to obvious space limitations, these mechanisms have only been underlined in the segmented text (cf. appendix).

A common feature that characterises all of these ties is that they effect a tenuous connection between isolated constituents of sentences such as words and phrases or, occasionally, clauses.

7. Conclusions

In all cases, the textual mechanisms identified or inferred by the participants deal only with discourse meaning derived from entire sentences, larger fragments of text, or certain simple clauses linked paratactically by a colon, a dash, or a comma or dash followed by some cohesive device.

If we agreed to consider as textual those elements that contribute to the perception of text coherence and, therefore, text structure, the point-to-point cohesive items underlined in the appendix cannot be regarded as such (i.e. textual in nature) because they were not essential to account for the relevance of each successive coherence unit (at least to this group of readers). They can only be said to contribute to creating superficial cohesion.

Several recommendations may arise from the present study. Teaching materials in reading comprehension should place a greater emphasis on raising students' awareness of and training students in identifying: a) textual cohesive mechanisms, i.e. encapsulating and prospecting mechanisms that establish connections across sentence boundaries and scope over fragments of text larger than the sentence or, occasionally, the clause; b) implicit connections between text fragments.

References

Blakemore, D. (1987): Semantic constraints on relevance. Oxford: Blackwell.
Downing, A./Locke, P. (1992): A university course in English grammar. Hertfordshire: Prentice Hall International.
Halliday, M.A.K./Hasan, R. (1976): Cohesion in English. London: Longman.
Mann, W.C./Thompson, S.A. (1986): Relational propositions in discourse. In: Discourse processes 9, 57-90.
Moreno, A.I. (2003): The role of cohesive devices as textual constraints on relevance: A discourse-as-process view. In: International Journal of English Studies. Discourse Analysis Today 3/1, 111-165.
Moriarty, H. (1999): Exam scripts pilot gets top marks for effort. In: Guardian Unlimited. EducationGuardian.co.uk © Guardian Newspapers Limited 2002.
http://education.guardian.co.uk/old/schools/story/0,10044,106551,00.html
Sinclair, J.M. (1993): Written discourse structure. In: Sinclair, J.M./Hoey, M./Fox, G. (eds.): Techniques of description: Spoken and written discourse. Festschrift for Malcolm Coulthard. London: Routledge, 6-31.
Sperber, D./Wilson, D. (1986): Relevance: Communication and cognition. Oxford: Blackwell.

Appendix: segmented text

Exam scripts pilot gets top marks for effort
The verdict on returning examination papers to students? Fairly good, room for improvement
HilaryMoriarty
Tuesday November 23, 1999
The Guardian

(1) Nineteen ninety-nine was the year we dipped a toe in the water:
(2) **and** you know **what**? <
(3) [The sharks didn't bite,
(4) **and the water** wasn't freezing.]
(5) **The water** was the great scary ocean of returning examination papers to candidates.
(6) This year saw the pilot scheme, with three different models for GCSE and at A level, for **the** copying and **return** of all **scripts** in 10 syllabuses, allowing centres to decide how to release the copied scripts **to candidates**.
(7) The Qualifications and Curriculum Authority has carried out **an** interim **evaluation** * (of **the pilot scheme**). <
(8) "How was **it** for you?"
(9) [The great news * (**about the pilot scheme**) is that there seems to be general approval for the principle of returning the scripts.
(10) * (**In other words**) The earth may not have moved, but the world didn't come to a standstill either.

(11) **It** was OK.]
(12) * (**In fact**) Not surprisingly, most of the people involved * (in **the pilot scheme**) felt that returning the scripts made the examination system more transparent and examiners more accountable.
(13) * (**because**) Sometimes you don't need to tell people to work better, you just tell them there's an audience for what they produce.
(14) * (**In other words**) Knowing that whatever was done to the papers would be seen in the outside world must have been salutary.
(15) **This is not to say that** examiners were sloppy before.
(16) Would I say **such a thing**? (= I would not say such a thing)
(17) * (**because**) I examined for years:
(18) * (**examining** was) the most gruelling job in the world, requiring painstaking effort and concentration to sustain standards justly for 300 scripts in three weeks.
(19) * (**In other words**) Conscientious marking is a killer.
(20) * (**And = but**) **And** examiners never did work in an irresponsible vacuum –
(21) * (**because**) the chief examiner always loomed over one's shoulder, checking, commenting, remarking if necessary.
(22) **At least**, I think **that**'s what **he did**.
(23) * (**Anyway**) Even if **he did**n't, the fear that **he would** was a great deterrent to misdemeanour.
(24) **But** how much simpl**er** and **more** thorough * (**than the chief examiner looming over one's shoulder...**) is the returning of marked scripts to the original writers.
(25) (**Returning the marked scripts... is**) Real accountability.
(26) **The irony** * (**of the pilot scheme**) is, of course, that * (**in spite of**) **having been offered their scripts**, most of the candidates didn't want them.
(27) * (**As a matter of fact**) Staff in the centres reported the percentage of students "very interested" in viewing the scripts as about 12%, with a further 27% only "fairly interested".
(28) **The reasons** * (**why most of the students did not want to view the scripts**) are obvious: <
(29) [if you did well, you really don't care about the papers –
(30) **and that** goes for doing well unexpectedly, as well as having the satisfaction of achieving just what you expected.]
(31) * (**By contrast**) **Interest in the papers is generated** by doing badly,
(32) * (**and = but; then = that**) **and then** only if **it** surprises you.
(33) * (**because**) **If you partied all year, or had a personal crisis**, then you will have done badly but you won't need to see the papers to see why.
(34) The interim report indicates **also** that pupils needed teachers to decode what they saw –
(35) * (**this** is) small wonder, if the rumours are right and examiners were virtually forbidden to write on the scripts for fear of litigation from insulted students.
(36) * (**because**) Without some sort of written explanatory commentary, candidates might well find the scripts "more meaningful when interpreted by their teacher".
(37) **Actually**, if the pilot scheme is judged successful and more scripts are returned in the future, **this** is an area where practice must be improved.
(38) * (**because**) Particularly in arts subjects, where marking is notoriously subjective, the examiner's commentary is vital evidence.

Perceiving coherence and text structure

(39) * (**In fact**) In my day, I was expected to annotate scripts to explain my marks to the chief examiner.

(40) Remove **that requirement**, and the examining process will only appear to be more open, while in fact retaining an almost smug inscrutability.

(41) * (**If = While**) **If candidates didn't care about the scripts**, 71% of staff cared a great deal:

(42) * (**As a matter of fact**) 82% * agreed that access to the scripts would help with teaching the syllabus in the coming year.

(43) (**Of course = this** is natural) Well of course.

(44) * (**because**) Knowing exactly where the last candidates got it wrong is the best learning tool a teacher can have to improve performance next year.

(45) * (**However**) **Better than knowing what they got** is knowing why they got it.

(46) * (**So**) If any government wants to conjure up massive whole school improvement, **this** is the magic wand.

(47) There will be logistical **problems** * (**with the process of returning the scripts to candidates**): <

(48) [returning all scripts will mean 13.5m papers whizzing through the postal system, **for instance**.

(49) Photocopying scripts sounds horrendous even to a convinced "pro-returner" like me.

(50) Proper scrutiny of the papers in school will take time, possibly precious holiday time.]

(51) **And if the big learners here are teachers, not pupils**, should they be returned at all? * (= with all these problems, it looks as if they should not be returned at all)

(52) * (**However**) The answer (to **this question**) is yes (**they should be returned**).

(53) * (**because**) I believe now, as I believed last year when I wrote one of the first articles calling for this move towards long-overdue transparency and accountability, and as the authorities hold in New Zealand, that **it** is simply the right thing to do.

(54) * (**And**) **The right thing** overrides **logistical problems**.

(55) **Pupil neglect of the papers** is beside **the point**. * (= is not relevant to **the question**)

(56) * (**because**) A few * will be very interested indeed,

(57) **and that**'s enough.

(58) * (**It** is) A bit **like** voting, really: <

(59) [lots of people don't care about **that either**,

(60) **but** for those * (people) who **do** * (**care**) , **it**'s one of the markers of a civilised world.]

Liana Pop

De l'*acte* aux *activités*: *les séquences*

Je prends ici en considération un type d'unités discursives intuitivement appelées *séquences*, dont certaines sont insuffisamment prises en considération par l'analyse du discours. Je pense notamment à des phénomènes comme *faire des compliments*, *donner des explications*, *faire des hypothèses*, *faire une digression*, *se plaindre*, etc., qui sont des *activités*, et non de simples *actes*, et sont perçues comme des *unités* à l'intérieur des discours. En raison de leur statut trop flou pour l'exigence de rigueur des catégories scientifiques (par opposition aux catégories naturelles), leur définition/délimitation a généralement posé problème. Mon intention ici est de faire reconnaître cette catégorie comme pertinente pour l'analyse du discours. Dans un premier temps je vais en repérer quelques traces dans des textes littéraires, des discours médiatiques ou didactiques (v. 1 et 2 ci-dessous) et je tenterai, dans un deuxième temps, de définir et/ou de décrire ces catégories essentiellement «naturelles» de discours (v. 3).

1. Catégorisation naturelle dans le discours: actes, activités, genres…

Rappelons ici que les langues catégorisent naturellement les actes par des verbes et des noms comme *féliciter/félicitation*, *demander/demande*, *refuser/refus*, *ordonner/ordre*, *promettre/promesse*, etc., et que les locuteurs reconnaissent, comme produits de leur discours, plusieurs types de textes, auxquels ils donnent des noms comme *récit*, *lettre*, *article*, *dispute*, etc. Une autre catégorie d'expressions semble désigner des activités discursives courantes, se constituant en parties distinctes dans les discours; pour celles-ci, les locuteurs utilisent des verbes ou locutions verbales comme *raconter*, *expliquer*, *faire des remarques*, *faire des hypothèses*, *faire une digression*, *faire une confidence*, etc.

Ces parties perçues comme distinctes dans le discours sont souvent désignées sous le nom passe-partout de *séquence*, catégorie qui s'est avérée difficile à définir en linguistique, car elle semble correspondre à une catégorie trop vague, peut-être pré-scientifique, et a par conséquent reçu des définitions très variables (cf. 3.2 ci-après). Ont fait l'objet de descriptions linguistiques plus poussées les séquences appelées *récit*, *explication*, *description*, car elles correspondent de façon plus évidente a) à des parties distinctes à l'intérieur de textes écrits, ou b) à des textes pris globalement.

Par contre, en ce qui concerne des catégories moins nettes comme *faire une digression*, *faire des confidences*, *faire des remarques*, *faire des hypothèses*, *dire des bêtises*, etc., les descriptions sont à ce jour presque inexistantes.[1]

Je vais repérer ci-dessous, à travers des fragments de discours littéraires ou médiatiques, les traces linguistiques de plusieurs de ces activités verbales, pour appuyer l'idée que l'étude de ces phénomènes est pleinement justifiée, qu'une définition doit être tentée pour ce que l'on dit être une *séquence* en général, et des descriptions particulières pour quelques types distincts de ces «ensembles d'actes».

2. Les noms des séquences: un problème de catégorisation

Plusieurs appellations courantes témoignent, comme pour les actes, de l'existence d'unités de communication naturelles du type *activité*, si par «activité» on entend, d'après le Petit Robert: l'«ensemble des actes coordonnés ou des travaux de l'être humain; fraction spéciale de cet ensemble».

En effet, les expressions désignant ces activités attestent l'existence:
(i) d'entités perçues compositionnellement comme plus ou moins homogènes, car les noms qui les désignent contiennent souvent, à côté d'un verbe-support, un substantif déverbal au pluriel, indiquant la répétition d'actes identiques: *promesses*, *suggestions*, *affirmations*, *arguments*, *explications*, *hypothèses*, *commentaires*, *propositions*, *injures*, *lamentations*, *bêtises*, *indications*, *prescriptions*, *conseils*, *confidences*... (v. 2.1 ci-dessous);
(ii) d'entités perçues globalement comme faisant «un tout» avec d'autres actes voisins; à preuve, leurs noms constitués de verbes désignant plus que des actes isolés, avec, dans leur sémantisme, un sème [processuel]. De tels verbes sont: *raconter*, *décrire*, *argumenter*, *expliquer*, *citer*, *analyser*, *se plaindre*, *plaisanter*, etc., recouvrant non pas des actes, mais une activité en cours (v. 2.2 ci-dessous).[2]

---

[1] Notons que lors des dernières Conférences IADA, la perspective sur *les séquences comme activités insérées dans d'autres types de discours* commence à s'imposer (cf. Pop (à paraître) pour la *séquence argumentative*, Kerbrat-Orecchioni (dans ces volumes) pour la *confidence*, et Galatolo, Fasulo/Zucchermaglio et Traverso (présentations à la conférence à Salzburg) pour les *séquences narratives*). Ces études confortent l'idée d'une catégorie *séquence-activité* comme objet d'étude en analyse du discours.

[2] Effectivement, à chaque fois qu'on dit: *je raconte, je décris, j'argumente, je me plains*, etc., c'est un *processus* qui est désigné et non un *acte* pris à part.

(iii) d'entités perçues globalement comme faisant «un tout» par opposition à d'autres parties d'un discours; le prouvent certains noms de séquences – substantifs dénommant des activités: *introduction*, *résumé*, *récit*, *description*, *argumentation*, *plainte*, *apologie*, *digression*, *plaisanterie* (v. 2.3 ci-dessous).

2.1 Locutions indiquant des séquences «en série»

Les dictionnaires et la langue de tous les jours attestent des expressions verbales constituées d'un verbe-support, sémantiquement appauvri (du type *faire*, *exprimer*, *émettre*, *apporter*, *donner*, *lancer*, *avancer*, etc.) + un nom déverbal, souvent au pluriel. Ces locutions, incluant un nom d'acte au pluriel (du type *faire des remarques*) semblent prouver que les locuteurs perçoivent ces unités comme *suites d'actes* et mettent en évidence, pour la définition de la séquence, cette pluralité d'actes «en série homogène». Comme on peut le voir ci-dessous, de telles locutions métadiscursives existent bien en français (fr), en anglais (an) et en roumain (ro), et d'autres langues en possèdent sûrement aussi:

> Faire fr: *faire des promesses, des suggestions, des compliments, des affirmations, des remarques, des commentaires, des prescriptions, ses excuses, des reproches, des hypothèses*; an: *to make a promise, make a suggestion, make compliments, make statements, make remarks/observations, make comments, make prescriptions, make an apology, to reproach sb for sth*; ro: *a face promisiuni, sugestii, complimente, afirmaţii, remarci/observaţii, comentarii, reproşuri, ipoteze*
> Dire fr: *dire des bêtises, des conneries, des mensonges*; an: *talk nonsense/crap, tell lies*; ro: *a spune prostii/măgării, minciuni, enormităţi*
> Exprimer fr: *exprimer des condoléances, des opinions, des regrets*; an: *express condolences/regret, give an opinion*; ro: *a exprima condoleanţe, felicitări, opinii, regrete*
> Apporter fr: *apporter des preuves, des nouvelles, des arguments, des accusations*; an: *give evidence, make an argument, bring charges*; ro: *a aduce dovezi/probe, veşti, argumente, acuzaţii*
> Donner fr: *donner des nouvelles, des informations, des renseignements, des explications, des indications, des conseils*; an: *to bring news, give explanations, give instructions, give advice*; ro: *a da informaţii, veşti, explicaţii, indicaţii, sfaturi*
> Avancer fr: *avancer des propositions, des hypothèses*; an: *to put forward a hypothesis*; ro: *a avansa propuneri, ipoteze*
> Lancer fr: *lancer des hypothèses, des accusations*; an: *make suggestions, to put forward a hypothesis, press charges*; ro: *a lansa ipoteze, acuzaţii*
> Se perdre fr: *se perdre en explications*; an: *get carried away*; ro: *a se pierde în explicaţii*

Une suite d'actes est illustrée par l'exemple (1) où, pour *faire des remarques* (au pluriel), le locuteur explicite à chaque fois le passage d'un(e) remarque/constat vers l'autre. Si un seul acte s'avère insuffisant pour l'effet perlocutoire voulu, les locuteurs l'«étoffent», en en ajoutant d'autres (cf. la séquence explicative en (6a) ci-dessous).

Les exemples ne manquent pas dans les discours, et dans les quelques-uns que nous donnons de (1) à (7), l'activité en train de s'effectuer est:

a) ou nommée explicitement: *faire des remarques*, en (1); *faire des reproches*, en (2); *faire des hypothèses*, en (3); *s'excuser*, en (4); *donner/apporter des nouvelles*, en (5); *donner des explications*, en (6);
b) ou exprimée métaphoriquement: *fouiller* pour *faire des hypothèses*, en (3b);
c) ou seulement «indiquée» par des marqueurs implicites, tel *c'est*, pour *les explications*, en (6b):[3]

(1) FAIRE DES REMARQUES
    C: […] on va corriger les comptes-rendus/ que je vais vous rendre/ […] [le professeur rend les papiers aux étudiants] Mi- Mândruţ Renata/ Andreea/ Ioana xxx/ […]
    E: (toussement)
    C: encore malade/
    E: oui\
    C: bon\ […] alors\ euh: QUELQUES REMARQUES euh générales/ sur euh […] sur vos travaux/ avant de-- de proposer une euh une correction/ euh […] D'ABORD donc\ je vous rappelle le compte-rendu c'est un exercice d'objectivité/ et donc encore une fois-- il s'agit de-- rendre compte-- des idées euh de: du texte/ sans s- apporter de d'informations personnelles\ je sais plus qui/ a euh: plus ou moins euh je sais pas j- vous ai rendu à quelqu'un xxx/\ […] DEUX-IÈME: DEUXIÈME CONSTAT / avant de faire ce: compte rendu/ on avait vraiment travaillé un texte/ c'est-à-dire qu'on avait essayé de décortiquer un peu euh le: le fonctionnement euh des idées/ l'ar- les articulations et caetera/ euh donc ce travail euh qui a été fait en amont/ il ne doit pas accos- il doit ressortir d'une manière voilée/ euh dans le compte-rendu\ c'est-à-dire que euh-- certaines mm: ont souligné-- l'auteur développe une argumentation/ des choses comme ça/ donc ça-- c'est c'est davantage un constat […] oui\ AUTRE: AUTRE CON-STAT n'oubliez pas\ dans un compte-rendu de toujours commencer par présenter l'idée générale/ hein/ l'idée euh directrice […] QUOI D'AU:TRE/ […] j'crois que c'était-- c'est tout euh pour euh les CONSTATS DE GÉNÉRALITÉ

                                                                                                          (Corpus Pop)

(2) FAIRE DES REPROCHES/REPROCHER
    ELLE: De toute façon tu t'endors tout de suite, tu tombes comme une masse. À chaque fois, c'est pareil; avoue, le grand air te réussit.
    LUI: Oui, je suis fatigué, j'ai le droit peut-être.
    ELLE: (*Doucement*.) Mais JE NE TE REPROCHE RIEN, mon chéri, j'adore te regarder dormir.

                                                                               (D. Sallenave, *Conversations conjugales*)

(3) FAIRE/LANCER DES HYPOTHÈSES

(3a) alors\ QUELLES HYPOTHÈSES ON PEUT FAIRE sur ce symbole\ un p'tit peu sur le sens\ donc pour chercher à comprendre finalement/ pourquoi euh ce symbole euh reste euh enfin\ perdu/ comme ça/ dans la société française/ sans que l'on connaît vraiment ni le sens ni l'origine euh de Marianne très clair

                                                                                                         (Corpus Pop)

---

3   Les séquences proprement dites sont soulignées; leurs noms explicites sont donnés en PETITES MAJUSCULES SOULIGNÉES; leurs marqueurs indicatifs, en PETITES MAJUSCULES ITALIQUES; les objets décrits (thèmes-titres) dans les séquences descriptives, en PETITES MAJUSCULES SIMPLES. Les contours intonatifs sont notés par: [/], [\] , [^] , [--].

(3b) C: donc vernis-- culturel\ donc là il faut FOUILLER un p'tit peu euh-- <u>donc là y a une métaphore/</u>
E: (la superficialité)/
C: <u>donc y a l'idée de superficiel/ de superficialité/ oui/ hm/ quoi d'autre/ y a une autre idée aussi\ PEUT-ÊTRE\ vernis culturel/</u>
E: le mélange des arts/ peut-être/
C: le mélange des arts\
E: la littérature/ la peinture PEUT-ETRE/
C: quel est le lien avec le vernis/
E: je ne sais pas\ la couleur PEUT-ETRE\
C: non/ qu'est-ce qu- un vernis donc ça: ça protège/ ça c'est quelque chose qu'on met-- sur une surface/ quelque chose qu'on recou- on cherche à recouvrir quelque chose/
E: pour rendre plus beau\

(Corpus Pop)

(4) FAIRE SES EXCUSES/S'EXCUSER

<u>QUE JULIEN L'EXCUSE</u>, mais il ne s'attendait pas du tout... Une erreur de graphie au secrétariat sûrement... Flovié, Pluvié, n'est-ce pas? Mais de toute façon, il aurait cru à une homonymie... Jamais il n'aurait pensé que Julien pouvait donner dans la politique...

(M. Bredel, *Les petites phrases*)

(5) DONNER/APPORTER DES NOUVELLES

Sans se perdre en mondanités, Aymeri APPORTAIT DES NOUVELLES. Bonnes. <u>Les derniers sondages confirmaient les précédents et laissaient apparaître entre 34 et 36% d'indécis. Un pactole inespéré, encore qu'on pût redouter une abstention massive. En tout cas, la disparition de Mégissier ne profitait toujours pas à ses concurrents de droite; Sorèze et Frémont ne dollaient pas de leurs positions.</u> BREF, l'état de l'opinion, à deux jours de l'ouverture de la campagne officielle, correspondait d'assez près aux projections qu'il avait communiquées à Varenne la semaine précédente.

(M. Bredel, *Les petites phrases*)

(6) DONNER DES EXPLICATIONS

(6a) En guise de réponse à ma stupeur muette, il m'annonce tout à trac:
– Tu as devant toi un SDF!
Cette EXPLICATION succincte ne me rendant évidemment pas l'usage de la parole, *il l'étoffe quelque peu*:
– Oui, ma chère, <u>tu as quitté un homme respecté de tous et envié par beaucoup; un homme privilégié jouissant d'un train de vie plus que confortable; le mari d'une femme idéale qui savait fermer les yeux et ouvrir sa bourse; le gendre plein d'espoir d'une douairière cardiaque, plein de promesses... et tu te retrouves devant un pauvre bougre, cocu, ruiné, avec pour s'abriter uniquement cette guimbarde pourrie et pour unique bien les trois valises que j'ai pu arracher aux griffes des deux hiènes.</u>

(F. Dorin, *Vendanges tardives*)

(6b) ça vous en fait c'est un jeu de mots *brouillon de culture*/ xxx savoir lequel/ y a une référence en fait-- BOUillon de culture/ ça vous dit rien/
E: *C'EST* une émission à la télé\ hein/
C: oui/ *C'EST* une émission à la télé/ qu'est-ce que vous savez d'autre/ sur cette émission (peut-être)/

E: xxx
C: BOUILLON DE CULTURE/ *C'EST* une émission euh: enfin […] euh c'est une émission qui était euh animée par Bernard Pivot/ donc euh un une personnalité euh de d'aujourd'hui/ enfin il a terminé justement euh cette année dernière euh d'animer cette émission/ et en fait c'était une émission littéraire-- sur les les dernières parutions/ et caetera/ donc une émission de référence/ en fait une émission connue/ donc bouillon de culture/ qu'est-ce que c'est un bouillon/
E: soupe/
E: soupe/
C: une soupe-- oui/ *Bouillon de culture* Bernard Pivot\ [le professeur écrit le nom de l'emission et de l'animateur au tableau] donc c'est le nom attaché à cette émission

(Corpus Pop)

Les séquences «en série» semblent bien être le cas prototypique pour les *activités verbales*, car elles illustrent le mieux l'acception la plus commune des séquences en général en tant que *suite homogènes d'actes*. Remarquons sur tous les noms d'activités recensés ci-dessus, mais aussi sur ceux avec *faire* qui suivent, que les langues semblent plus ou moins s'aligner au niveau des expressions utilisées pour désigner ces *types d'activités verbales*: même s'il y a des différences (singulier *vs* pluriel pour le nom des actes en série), la plupart de ces étiquettes métalinguistiques encodées par les langues suivent des logiques identiques: un verbe-support quasiment identique (comme *faire*) et des nom d'actes, de préférence au pluriel (v. les listes d'expressions ci-dessus).

2.2 Verbes d'activités

Il s'agit en premier lieu de verbes désignant les activités verbales non par les actes qui les composent, mais par la perception de l'activité en cours comme processus unique:

fr	*raconter*	an	*to tell (a story)*	ro	*a povesti*
fr	*décrire*	an	*to describe*	ro	*a descrie*
fr	*argumenter*	an	*to make an argument*	ro	*a argumenta*
fr	*citer*	an	*to quote*	ro	*a cita*
fr	*analyser*	an	*to analyse*	ro	*a analiza*
fr	*se plaindre*	an	*to complain*	ro	*a se plânge*
fr	*plaisanter*	an	*to joke*	ro	*a glumi*[4]

---

4   Notons que ces verbes à la première personne du singulier de l'indicatif présent ne fonctionnent pas de la même façon que les performatifs d'actes, car en disant *je raconte, je cite, je me plains* ou *je plaisante*, je décris bien l'activité que je suis en train d'effectuer, mais je n'effectue pas précisément cette activité lors de la prononciation de ces mêmes énoncés.
    Notons aussi que ces activités verbales ont été en partie théorisées par plusieurs chercheurs (en narratologie, en rhétorique, en analyse du discours, etc.), notamment les séquences de type *narratif* (le récit), les séquences *descriptives* et les séquences *argumentatives*, et que toutes sont vues dans le cadre des typologies textuelles comme de possibles textes. Pour ce qui est des autres activités, *la citation* a été généralement décrite comme procédé d'insertion ou stratégie

Voici quelques exemples pris à un corpus de textes où les locuteurs parlent des activités verbales qu'ils sont en train d'effectuer (par manque d'espace, je ne donne que des exemples en français):

(7) ANALYSER

c'qui nous intéresse c'est vraiment l'existence de ce symbole-là et la permanence du symbole dans la société euh française\ alors\ essayons d'ANALYSER un p'tit peu/

(Corpus Pop)

(8) DÉCRIRE

ELLE: [...] Nous avons cherché partout, mais nous ne l'avons pas trouvé. Odette croyait que c'était un bruit dans le radiateur. (*Un temps*.) Mais c'est vrai. Dans une vraie maison, il y a UN CHAT. Qui se promène, qui a ses parcours.
LUI: Qui pisse partout, oui, pour marquer son territoire. Ce que tu appelles UNE MAISON, pour lui tu n'imagines pas ce que c'est. Un lieu sauvage, plein d'odeurs. Des odeurs qu'il affectionne, qui l'inspirent. Celles de la poubelle, celle du linge sale. Et qu'il défend contre les incursions des autres en pissant aux quatre coins. Régulièrement, quatre fois par jour, de peur que le parfum s'atténue.
ELLE: CE QUE TU DECRIS, c'est le comportement d'un mâle. D'un mâle entier. Nous, nous le ferons couper.

(D. Sallenave, *Conversations conjugales*)

(9) PLAISANTER/DÉCONNER

– Écoute, je crois que j'ai un truc pour toi. Il faudrait que je le fasse venir de Rome ou de Turin. Tu sais ce qu'elles s'achètent à tour de bras, les filles, là-bas, pour séduire et retenir les mecs? Des soutiens-gorge et des petites culottes à la fraise ou au chocolat.
– TU TE FOUS DE MOI OU QUOI!
– Mais non, JE TE JURE, C'EST TRES SERIEUX. J'ai lu ça dans un journal italien.

(Cl. Sarraute)

Dans ce dernier type de séquence (9), les locuteurs sont perçus comme disant des «bêtises», comme ayant dérivé dans un discours *non sérieux*. Les langues détiennent toute une variété d'expressions pour nommer ce type d'activité. Ainsi, les Français utilisent: *dire des bêtises*, *des conneries*, et se sont même forgé le verbe: *déconner*. Dans toutes les langues, les expressions sont plutôt métaphoriques pour nommer cette déviation du «droit chemin» du discours: ro *a deraia, a se prosti*; fr *déconner*; an *to adopt a light-hearted note*, etc.

---

discursive intertextuelle/polyphonique, *l'analyse* comme une opération cognitive et, enfin, *la complainte* et *la plaisanterie* (*l'anecdote*) plutôt comme types de texte. Le fait que les langues les désignent par des verbes uniques atteste que ces types d'activités sont mieux perçues comme unités que d'autres.

2.3 Locutions indiquant des séquences-blocs

D'autres expressions sont des noms au singulier (très rarement au pluriel), désignant des activités discursives perçues comme *globales* et non comme étant composées d'une suite d'actes. Ces noms peuvent être utilisés avec le verbe-support *faire*. Il s'agit d'activités discursives appelées *introduction*, *résumé*, *évocation(s)*, *panégyrique*, *dissertation*, *digression*, pour lesquelles les trois langues utilisent des expressions plutôt identiques:

fr	*faire une introduction*	an	*to make an introduction*	ro	*a face o introducere*
fr	*faire un résumé*	an	*to make a resumé*	ro	*a face un rezumat*
fr	*faire une évocation*	an	*to evoke*	ro	*a face o evocare*
fr	*faire un panégyrique*	an	*to make a panegiric*	ro	*a face un panegiric*
fr	*faire une dissertation*	an	*to make a dissertation*	ro	*a face o disertaţie*
fr	*faire une digression*	an	*to digress*	ro	*a face o digresiune*

Les exemples de (10) à (15) qui suivent illustrent quelques-unes de ces séquences. Remarquons de nouveau que ces opérations métadiscursives se font avec ou sans marqueurs explicites:

(10) FAIRE UNE INTRODUCTION
   R: mesdames messieurs bonjour/\ bienvenue à ZIG Zag Café-- on peut s'applaudir là pour un- - des BONNes habitudes/\ [...] (applaudissements)

(TV5 *Zig Zag Café*, corpus Pop)

(11) FAIRE UN RÉSUMÉ /UN SOMMAIRE
   F_1:   voilà\ d'accord\ donc euh\ comme j'vous l'ai dit on va parler plus longuement tout à l'heure/ et là d'ssus ou va tout de suite voir le MEnu du jour je vous XXX tout de suite/ il est pas *light*\ EN SOMMAIRE aujourd'hui [...] nous irons faire un p'tit tour en Angleterre\ assister au championnat du monde grimace/ vous verrez XXX un groupe XXX dans ces disciplines\ XXX les pays chauds/ les nuits *caliente*/ il fait des ravages partout où il passe/ ce soir il vient enflammer le plateau/ XXX Enrique Iglesias (musique)/\

(TV5 *Union libre*, corpus Pop)

(12) ÉVOCATIONS
   LUI: (Sans l'écouter.) J'essaie. Je ferme les yeux, je retiens mon souffle, ou bien je les ouvre très grands, dans le noir, et je me dis, ce doit être comme ça, on ne voit rien, on croit qu'il fait tout noir, mais il ne fait pas noir du tout, il fait au contraire un grand soleil. Et on n'y voit rien quand même.
   ELLE: C'est complètement ridicule. Arrête ces ÉVOCATIONS morbides.

(D. Sallenave, *Conversations conjugales*)

(13) FAIRE UN PANÉGYRIQUE
   – Moi qui m'endors sur tous les livres à la deuxième page, j'ai lu le sien d'une traite. Sans passer une ligne. Je le trouve génial!
   En tant qu'adhérente au mouvement «pour la défense de la langue française», l'impropriété du

terme «génial» en la circonstance me titille l'oreille. Mais moins cependant que LA SUITE DE SON PANÉGYRIQUE:
– C'est vraiment une femme super! Qui est restée cool! Qui la ramène jamais! Pourtant, avec la vie qu'elle a eue…

(F. Dorin, *Vendanges tardives*)

(14) FAIRE /ESQUISSER UNE DISSERTATION

Là-dessus, Faugerand esquissa UNE VAGUE DISSERTATION sur le cynisme comme expression de la pudeur, qui sentait tant le réchauffé que Julien eut envie de conclure que tout l'art de la conversation salonnarde résidait vraisemblablement dans la constitution d'un stock de péroraisons régulièrement répétées.

(M. Bredel, *Les petites phrases*)

(15) FAIRE UNE DIGRESSION

– Je suis le fils de votre amie Marguerite, la Bretonne du «Chapeau Rond». C'est une autre Clairette, Iris Morbleu, qui m'a donné votre adresse. Je m'appelle Keran comme mon grand-père maternel, Zapelli comme mon père et parfois Bégonia, comme le clown qui fut mon parrain.
La Bretagne et l'Italie cohabitent sur son visage… dangereusement! La rudesse de l'une, présente dans son regard bleu marine et ses traits forts, est compensée par le charme de l'autre, focalisé dans son sourire et dans ses gestes. À part quelques romantiques purs et durs, tout le monde reconnaît que le corps parle avant la tête et que la seconde ne fait qu'obéir aux ordres – parfois imbéciles – du premier. D'ailleurs, s'il est courant de dire ou de lire «que les amants se sont aimés au premier regard», il ne vient à personne l'idée de dire – ou d'écrire – «ils se sont aimés à la première phrase». Encore que moi, je le pourrais… Mais, quand il a prononcé sa première phrase, Keran, je l'avais déjà vu. Le mal était déjà fait.
Pardon, saint Pierre, de CETTE DIGRESSION! J'EN REVIENS A MES MOUTONS.

(F. Dorin, V*endanges tardives*)

Par rapport aux séquences en série, les séquences-blocs semblent être perçues et donc se définir comme des entités distinctes non en raison de leur configuration interne, comme les premières, mais par rapport au discours insérant. Ainsi, une *introduction* n'est «introduction» qu'en raison de sa position dans un discours plus ample, une *digression* n'est «digression» que par rapport au discours-base, un *résumé* n'est «résumé» que par rapport à un autre discours, etc. Une perspective *intra*- ou *interséquentielle* semble donc expliquer ces types de séquence: si pour les séquences en série, c'est bien la perspective intraséquentielle qui entre en jeu, pour les séquences-blocs, c'est plutôt la seconde.[5]

---

5 Une remarque concernant ces catégorisations: les étiquettes nominales attestent d'un statut mieux stabilisé des séquences comme catégories discursives, et ce en raison du fait que les catégories-noms recouvrent en général des concepts mieux délimités que d'autres.

3. Quelle définition pour les séquences?

Différentes perspectives doivent être retenues pour pouvoir mieux définir ce qu'on appelle *séquence* en général, et le poids d'une perspective ou d'une autre peut être un critère pertinent de distinction. Voici quelques définitions possibles:

3.1 La séquence dans l'acception courante

La définition générique de la catégorie séquence semble être fondée en premier lieu sur l'idée de *suite*, et deuxièmement sur un sentiment de *différence*: une séquence est perçue comme telle en raison d'une différence quelconque (de fonction ou autre) avec un segment discursif précédant ou suivant. Voici les acceptions du mot *séquence* dans le *Petit Robert*:

> 1. *Liturg*. Chant rythmé qui prolonge le verset de l'alléluia (à la messe) ou le trait. 2. *À certains jeux*, Série d'au moins trois cartes de même couleur qui se suivent; *au pocker*, Série de cinq cartes qui se suivent, de couleur quelconque. 3. *Au cinéma*, Suite de plans constituant un tout sous le rapport d'une action dramatique déterminée. 4. *Ling*. Suite ordonnée de termes.

L'idée de *suite* est présente dans toutes ces acceptions, celle de *série homogène* dans la 2e et la 4e, celle d'*insertion* dans la 3e acception, et celle de *différence* est impliquée dans la 1ère.

3.2 La séquence discursive

Définir la séquence en tant qu'unité semble rencontrer plusieurs problèmes, dont les plus importants pourraient être liés aux possibles confusions avec d'autres unités discursives naturelles; avec des *actes*, *mouvements*, *échanges*, *paragraphes*, *textes* ou *segments de textes*, ou, selon Kerbrat-Orecchioni (1990, 219), avec des *transactions*, *épisodes*, *phases*, *sections*, etc., chez divers auteurs.

Rappelons que les séquences sont plutôt intuitivement définies:

3.2.1 À partir des *fonctions* qu'elles sont censées accomplir (*faire des promesses*, *donner des explications*, *faire des reproches*), et de ce point de vue elles ressemblent aux actes. La confusion avec les actes est notamment possible pour les séquences en série, qui semblent se définir comme ayant une seule force illocutionnaire pour tous les actes qui la composent. Notons que la notion de *macro-acte* (cf. van Dijk 1977; Kerbrat-Orecchioni 1990, 219; 2001, 54-55 et passim) est également fondée sur cette catégorie. Enfin, la théorie de l'action définit l'*activité* et l'*action* de façon très semblable à celle de l'*acte*, à l'aide de notions comme intention, but, orientation commune, qui font penser au but illocutionnaire de la théorie des actes de langage.[6]

3.2.2 Comme délimitées par des marqueurs (prosodiques ou verbaux), et de ce point de vue elles ressemblent aux *mouvements discursifs* ou aux *périodes*. Les mouvements et les périodes étant composés de plusieurs énoncés qui s'enchaînent, ils se confondent facilement avec ce que l'on appelle séquences;

3.2.3 Comme segments de discours appartenant à un locuteur ou à un autre, et de ce point de vue elles peuvent se confondre avec les *tours de parole* ou les *interventions*;

3.2.4 Comme unités dialogales (par opposition aux unités monologales), et de ce point de vue elles peuvent s'assimiler aux *échanges* (cf. aussi *séquence minimale* chez Bange 1992, 46; *sequences* en ethnométhodologie);

3.2.5 Comme segments de texte thématiquement distincts, et de ce point de vue, elles peuvent se confondre avec les *paragraphes*, dans les structures monologales, ou les *transactions*, dans les structures dialogales;

3.2.6 Comme segments de texte délimités dans l'espace textuel (introducteur, conclusif, etc.), et de ce point de vue elles se confondent facilement avec des «parties» d'un texte: celles unanimement reconnues comme constitutives des textes: *introduction*, *exposition*, *conclusion* (cf. à ce propos les *séquences d'ouverture* et *de clôture* ou *les séquences latérales* dans les interactions, notions notamment reprises aux ethnométhodologues).

Tout comme les séquences, les catégories intuitives de *partie*, *épisode*, *section*, *étape*, *phase* sont des notions vagues, d'utilisation courante, correspondant à des unités cognitives/modèles cognitifs de l'usage, fondé(e)s sur des *critères* ou «*niveaux de structuration*»

---

6   Voici quelques définitions et exemples des notions d'*action* et *activité* empruntées à Bange (1992):
    (i) «[...] par activité il faut entendre [...] la totalité complexe de processus reliés par une orientation commune et par un but déterminé» (Avant-propos, p. 11);
    (ii) une «action» correspond à «des complexes d'activités comme ‹demander et donner un conseil› qui forment un tout à la réalisation duquel les participants doivent coopérer» (p. 64);
    (iii) exemples de «schémas d'activités»: la narration, la description, l'argumentation (p. 64).
    (iv) «un comportement d'un individu dans une situation donnée est une action lorsqu'il peut être interprété selon une intention en vue de la réalisation d'un but qui lui donne un sens» (Glossaire, p. 207).
    La catégorie de but s'avère définir ici des programmes discursifs (monologaux ou dialogaux) plus ou moins amples.

multiples (cf. Berrendonner/Reichler-Béguelin 1989; Kerbrat-Orecchioni 1990, 218-219; Kallmeyer, apud Bange 1992, 64). Chaque activité se définirait alors, par rapport à d'autres activités, sur un critère différent; pour les exemples (1) – (15) ci-dessus:

Critères	Activités
une opération cognitive	*analyser, faire des hypothèses*
objet de séquentialisation	*narrer, décrire, argumenter*
l'identité du locuteur	*citer*
convention/modalité discursive	*plaisanter*
nouveauté de l'information	*donner des nouvelles/explications*
attitude du locuteur	*faire des reproches/excuses/remarques/un panégyrique*
rapport intratextuel	*introduction, conclusion, résumé, digression*

3.3 Le niveau intermédiaire de structuration

Une dernière remarque quant à la façon dont on catégorise les séquences concernerait le niveau de catégorisation de ces unités. Elles se situent d'évidence au niveau intermédiaire de structuration des unités, entre les unités globales (ou maximales: *textes*) et les unités locales (minimales: *actes*). Leur statut n'est pour autant pas stable, car si certaines séquences se constituent facilement en entités au niveau global sous forme de textes (*se plaindre/plainte*; *raconter/récit*; *plaisanter/plaisanterie*; *apporter des nouvelles/nouvelles*, etc.), d'autres, au contraire, se constituent plutôt en entités au niveau local, sous forme d'actes (*promesse, compliment, bêtise*). Enfin, d'autres activités discursives restent fluctuantes, car on peut bien dire *déclaration* ou *commentaire* et entendre par là un acte, une séquence ou un texte tout entier. Ce type de phénomènes a été désigné du nom d'«unités à géométrie variable», recouvrant, par des processus de catégorisations pratiques, des classes plutôt floues (cf. Berrendonner/Reichler-Béguelin 1989). Le niveau intermédiaire de structuration dont il est question ici et auquel se situeraient les séquences coïnciderait – suivant les genres *G1* (*macro*), *G2* (*meso*), ... distingés par Kerbrat-Orecchioni au Colloque de Salzburg – avec le niveau de catégorisation *meso – G2*. Un métalangage concernant les niveaux de structuration semble bien prendre forme.

4. Conclusions

4.0 J'ai essayé d'attirer l'attention sur la problématique d'un type d'unités situées entre le niveau *global* (texte) et *local* (acte) de structuration du discours et qu'on appelle souvent par le nom assez vague de *séquences*. Correspondant non pas à des actes isolés, mais à des groupements d'actes qu'on perçoit notamment comme activités, ces unités semblent avoir été moins abordées en raison justement de leur statut souvent fluctuant entre un niveau et un autre de la structuration discursive, ou encore parce que leur insertion dans les textes ne semble pas suivre des règles très évidentes.

4.1 J'ai tenté de donner un aperçu général des appellations courantes qu'utilisent les locuteurs pour les désigner, afin de cerner plus ou moins les catégories qui s'en détachent. Ainsi, j'ai recensé dans la langue courante des expressions verbales constituées d'un verbe-support, sémantiquement appauvri (du type *faire*, *exprimer*, *apporter*, *donner*, *lancer*, *avancer*, etc.), auquel s'ajoute:
(i) ou un nom déverbal, très souvent au pluriel (désignant, justement, une série d'actes répétés),
(ii) ou un substantif au singulier indiquant le nom d'une activité verbale.

Trois types de verbes-support ont été distingué dans ces expressions:

Des verbes «incolores» du type *faire* Des verbes de dire: *dire, exprimer...* Des verbes plus ou moins métaphoriques: *apporter, donner, avancer, lancer, se perdre en*	+	Un substantif déverbal au pluriel, indiquant la répétition d'actes identiques: *promesses, suggestions, commentaires, affirmations, arguments, explications, hypothèses, propositions, injures, lamentations, bêtises, indications, prescriptions, conseils, confidences...* Un substantif indiquant le nom d'une activité: *introduction, résumé, récit, description, argumentation, plainte, apologie, digression, plaisanterie*

4.2 J'ai essayé de proposer quelques repères pertinents pour leur *définition*. Partant du constat que les séquences sont des unités multi-critères, il m'a semblé utile d'en détacher ceux qui semblent définitoires pour les séquences:
(i) le niveau de structuration: *intermédiaire*;
(ii) la compositionnalité: *suite d'actes* formant une *activité complexe*;
(iii) un critère thématique ou fonctionnel: *thème* ou *fonction* détachables;
(iv) leur perception comme entités closes: *marqueurs de complétude*;
(v) leur perception comme entités distinctes d'autres unités qui les précèdent ou leur succèdent dans le discours: *position* dans le texte; unités verbales appartenant à des *locuteurs distincts*; *attitudes* distinctes des locuteurs, etc.

4.3 Il semble dès lors que l'approche de ces unités discursives doit s'effectuer en termes de programmes/parcours discursifs (cf. Pop 2003); objectif qui laisse encore beaucoup à faire.

Références

Bredel, Marc (1985): Les petites phrases. Paris: R. Laffont.
Corpus Pop (à paraître) (débats télévisés, interactions didactiques, etc.). In: Verba volant. Recherches sur l'oral. Cluj: Ed. Echinox.
Dorin, Françoise (1997): Les vendanges tardives. Paris: Plon.
Sallenave, Danièle (1987): Conversations conjugales. Paris: P.O.L.

Adam, Jean-Michel (1992): Textes: types et prototypes. Paris: Nathan.
Bange, Pierre (1992): Analyse conversationnelle et théorie de l'action. Paris: Didier.
Berrendonner, Alain/Reichler-Béguelin, Marie-José (1989): Décalages. In: Langue française 81, 99-125.
Dijk, Teun. A. van (1977): Text and context. Explorations in the semantics and pragmatics of discourse. London: Longman.
Kerbrat-Orecchioni, Catherine (1990): Les interactions verbales, Tome I. Paris: A. Colin.
– (2001): Les actes de langage dans le discours. Théorie et fonctionnement. Paris: Nathan (Fac. Linguistique).
Levinson, Stephen C. (1983): Pragmatics. Cambridge: Cambridge Textbooks in Linguistics.
Pop, Liana (2003): Eh bien c'est la fin d'un parcours. In: Miret, Fernando Sánchez (éd.): Actas del XXIII Congreso Internacional de Lingüística y Filología Románica, Salamanca, 24-30 septiembre 2001. Tübingen: Niemeyer, 217-231.
– (à paraître): Mémoire discursive et pertinence argumentative. In: Rocci, Andrea (éd.): Studies in communication sciences. IADA Conference ‹Argumentation in dialogic interaction›, Lugano, juin 2002. Tübingen: Niemeyer.
Robert, Paul (1968): Dictionnaire alphabétique & analogique de la langue française. Paris: Le Robert.

Shuxue Zhang

Accented argumentum ad hominem in mediated dialogues

Introduction

In the second half of the 20th century, considerable attention has been paid to the study of *ad hominem arguments* – a special subject in media reporting of political discourse. In the media and in everyday confrontation, *ad hominem arguments* are easy to put forward as accusations, are difficult to refute, and often have an extremely powerful effect on persuading an audience (Walton 1998). This paper addresses *accented argumentum ad hominem*[1] (personal attack by means of accented metaphors) in mediated dialogues (e.g. in films, political debate and argumentation) as an instrument of "oppo tactics" and "going negative" or as the *bias ad hominem* by politically and ideologically dominated media. This paper attempts to expose cultural or ideological bias based on the accents of interlocutors with different socio-cultural identities. As suggested by the title, the paper will discuss the questions concerning identity (*who*), verbal communication (*ad hominem*) and cultural bias (*accents*). It will deal with why speakers, usually of lower social standing, e.g. immigrants or outcaste and with foreign accents, gain pejorative status stratifications, and are often labeled as inferior others with negative *ethos*. And it will also discuss in what way accents are manipulated and thus have a negative influence on cultural *ethos, pathos* and *logos* in mediated dialogues. However, the extent to which speakers with foreign accents fail in accessing effective artistic means of lending credibility to arguments (*ethos*), of exciting emotions (*pathos*), and of winning approval for characters (*logos*) because of their accents, is still at stake. By studying the ongoing common practice of assigning foreign accents to negative characters, the paper will reflect to a certain extent that the standard language ideology is concerned not so much with the choice of one possible variant, but to a larger extent with the elimination of socially unacceptable differences (cf. Ellen 1997, 173).

---

[1] The conceptualization of *accented ad hominem* is based on the ongoing discussion of the Latin term *ad hominem*. For the detailed study of *ad hominem* and the state of the art of it see Hamblin (1970), van Eemeren/Grootendorst (1992), Walton (2000).

1. Accent(s) and identity

Why can accent be manipulated and used as *ad hominem*? It is because accent is thought to be linguistic evidence of socio-cultural identities of the speakers. In medium, speakers with accents often gain pejorative status stratifications. For example, in an "internet language forum", interlocutor A committed *ad hominem* arguing that the British are "lazy idiots that don't even have enough energy to pronounce their Rs". A negative label (identity) is assigned to the British due to their accents. While interlocutor B argued that the reason why the Americans created their own dialect intentionally is because "the Americans have had an identity crisis, not having their own language, history or culture, or even a proper name". Americans are thought to be on a quest to forge an identity by changing their spelling. Accents become the norms and criteria for judging or evaluating a person's character and identity. The *ad hominem* is committed by associating accent(s) with characters. Language varieties, such as accents and dialects, vary according to their status and social functions. Each language has its own native rhythms, preference for speech habits. Accent and identity seem to be inseparable and language acts are usually thought to be acts of identity (Le Page/Tabouret-Keller 1985). Language acts *per se* and attitudes towards them reflect people's status quo. Accents' features are often used to signal a regional identity and are still thought to be the strongest evidence of their local association or affiliation (Honey 2001). According to *Webster's Dictionary of English* (1976), an accent is defined as (1) distinctive manner of usually oral expression: as the inflection, tone, or choice of words associated with a particular situation, event, emotion, or attitude, or taken to be unique or highly characteristic of an individual, and (2) speech habits typical of the natives or residents of a region or of any other group (as social, professional, or business). An accent is regarded as the rhythm in which people speak a language. For all the speakers, the accent and dialect they use involves signals of the value system that they identify with. Politicians prefer to use obfuscatory language. Children establish superiority over peers with pig Latin. Lawyers do it with gobbledygook, truck drivers with citizen-band jargon, and scientists (and educators) with the language of grantsmanship (Kahane/Cavender 1998, 137). In Britain and the USA accent varieties are commonly described in terms of variation from or approximation to the sounds of a standard variety of accent (e.g., BrE, AmE etc.) (Honey 2001, 93). Stewart (1964) and Bickerton (1971) developed the notion of a *continuum* of linguistic variation. In this continuum, a categorization of linguistic features was employed: such as the *basilect* (the broadest form of popular speech), *mesolect* (the speech of the majority of the population), the *acrolect* (high prestige, standard variety), and *hyperlect* (representing the socially privileged "marked RP" accent). Conventionally, people attribute different accents or dialects to different roles. In Britain, BBC listeners expect the news to be presented by RP (perceived as educated and authoritative) speakers, whereas "practical information on gardening or the weather is stereotypically given by speakers with broad paralects[2] or even mesolectal accents; sports commentating reflects the social standing of the sport concerned, with mesolectal accents appropriate for reporting football, but RP accents for polo (Honey 2001, 100). We do not know how these categorizations of accents affect people's attitudes towards the speakers. However, it is argued that "awareness of variants seems inevitably to be accompanied by value judgment" (Joseph 1987, 16), either positive or negative evaluation. For example, for many children there exists a mismatch between the language spoken at home and the language used at school. At home they may speak a dialect, an accent or a language variety associated with gender, social class, or ethnicity (Andersen 1990). This phenomenon reflects that people are aware of the facts that accents reflect people's ethos, which is vulnerable to *ad hominem*. All these speakers of different social groups can gain different ethos in media because of the style of their language.

2. What is *accented ad hominem*?

The conceptualization of *accented ad hominem* is based on the conception and definition of ad hominem.[3] The Latin term *argumentum ad hominem*, which is overwhelmingly treated in a pejorative sense currently, refers to "the fallacy of attacking the opponent personally in one way or another instead of responding to the actual arguments put forward in support of the standpoint" (van Eemeren/Grootendorst 1993). Three variants of personal attack are distinguished: (1) the *abusive* variant, (2) the *circumstantial* variant, and (3) the *tu quoque* (you too) variant.[4] The first variant – the *abusive argumentum ad hominem* – is more relevant to *accented ad hominem*. *Ad hominem* is viewed as a failure of relevance by most philosophers and logicians (i.e. Cohen/Nagel 1964; Copi 1972). Hamblin defined it in the Standard Treatment as: "[…] an argument *ad hominem* is committed when a case is argued not on its merits but by analyzing (usually unfavorably) the *motives* or *background* of its supporters or op-

---

[2] A variety of accents that is very close to RP but retains a few tiny nonstandard features, see Honey (2001, 96).
[3] The discussion of *argumentum ad hominem* in modern times can be dated back to the book of the 17th century British philosopher John Locke, *An Essay Concerning Human Understanding* (1690). He first employed the term as a technical term (van Eemeren/Grootendorst 1992, 111). See Walton (1998, 22).
[4] For the pragma-dialectical analysis of the *argumentum ad hominem*, see van Eemeren/Grootendorst (1992a, 110-115; 1992b, 153-157).

ponents" (Hamblin 1970, 41). In a direct personal attack like this, it is assumed that someone who is stupid or bad can never hold a correct opinion or have justified doubts. This is particularly the case in political discourses. The press does have a tendency to highlight attack, accenting the negative. *Ad hominem fallacies* are characterized as 'negative' because they are nasty, inaccurate, or unfair (Jamieson 2000). The following is an extract from a speech by President Bush in his 1992 election campaign:

> [...] There's been some very bad news for Clinton and Gore... They criticize our country and say we are less than Germany and slightly better than Sri Lanka. *My dog Millie knows more about foreign affairs than these two bozos*. It's crazy. Let them tear down the country. [...] And look – if you listen to Governor Clinton and *Ozone Man* – if you listen to them – you know why I call him Ozone Man? This guy is so far off in the environmental extreme we'll be up to our neck in owls and out of work for every American. *This guy's crazy*. He is way out, far out, man. Wait 'til he – hey, listen – you think you're going to save General Motors by slapping more regulations on 'em? Less regulation, less taxes.
>
> (Jamieson 2000, 50)

Bush attacked his political opponents calling them "bozos" and Gore "Ozone Man". He made an abusive *ad hominem* by the comparison of his dog Millie with his political opponents.

Another reason why *ad hominem* is characterized as 'negative' is that *ad hominem* is one of the most common non-rational appeals, which is not based on a rational evaluation of the arguments, but on an emotional reaction to the person(s) making the argument. When Bush accused that "*This guy's crazy*", *pathos* took the place of *logos*.[5] And the use of the terms such as *wop, nigger, kike*, and *fag* as a sort of abuse in argumentation can be *ad hominem*, too. According to the pragma-dialectical approach, *ad hominem* fallacy is regarded as a discussion move that constitutes a violation of one or more discussion rules and thereby jeopardizes the resolution of the difference of opinion.[6]

Accented argumentum ad hominem is, as matter of fact, a non-argumentative phenomenon. It is committed by manipulation of accents through distorting or caricaturing the pronunciation of the speaker as negative or low-life accents thus undermining his credentials. For example, in Disney movies, accent is often used for "sidekicks" of various sorts, such as Timothy Mouse in Dumbo, Iago (in Aladdin), and Pumbaa in Lion King. In science fiction, these (usually pseudoforeign) accents may be employed by evil creatures from outer space. An *accented ad hominem* indirectly attacks an unfavorable group in society by attributing

---

[5] For the distinction between *ethos, pathos* and *logos,* see Braet (1992). Wisse (1989) discussed *ethos* and *pathos* from Aristotle to Cicero. Van Eemeren/Grootendorst (1992, 135-137) dealt with the roles of *ethos* and *pathos* in argumentation.

[6] The pragma-dialectical approach developed by the Dutch dialecticians Frans van Eemeren and Rob Grootendorst identifies the fallacies of *ad hominem* with unacceptable discussion moves. See van Eemeren/Grootendorst (1992).

negative connotations to the speakers with accents. One of the important variations on *ad hominem* argument is that of guilt by association (Kahane/Cavender 1998, 63-65). The analysis of *accented ad hominem* includes the study of different attitudes towards accents and negative metaphors that have been imposed on inferior others. According to Harold (2000), a 'foreign' accent, or pseudo-foreigner talk is used to convey mysteriousness, sexuality, perhaps evilness, unreliability, and demonic, sinister forces. So the difference between *ad hominem* and *accented ad hominem* is that the latter does not commit an attack by any verbal means but conveys attacks by attributing negative traits to the speaker with accents. It is a manipulated type of *ad hominem*. According to the pragma-dialectical approach, *ad hominem* may also be committed by discrediting the speaker's expertise, impartiality, integrity or credibility. Such maneuvers are generally not executed directly, but in a sophisticated and devious manner. Rather than being addressed directly to the opponent, they are often intended for consumption by a third-party audience (van Eemeren/Grootendorst 1992a, 108).

3. How *accented ad hominem* is manipulated?

It is important to investigate in what way *accented ad hominem* is manipulated and thus has a negative influence on cultural *ethos*, *pathos* and *logos* in argumentation or mediated dialogues.[7] Attitude change is one of the crucial components of persuasion. Language style (variation) plays an important role in accessing effective artistic means of lending credibility to arguments (*ethos*) of exciting emotions (*pathos*) and of winning approval for characters (*logos*). The language style may include specific words, colorful words, informality and simplicity of vocabulary, figurative language, personalization, informality of syntax, questions and so on (Sandell 1977). An *accented ad hominem* can undermine a speaker's ethos, which moves an audience by proving the credibility and trustworthiness of an arguer. If the *ethos* of a rhetor is undermined, he can hardly influence others by *pathos*, which changes the attitudes and actions of the audience by arousing the audience's sympathy. And his *logos*, which persuades through the powers of reasoning, cannot be taken seriously (Covino/Jolliffe 1995, 17). According to Aristotle, *ethos* is generally even more effective than *logos* and *pathos*. Foreign accents are often manipulated and maneuvered in order to create a kind of

---

[7] Van Eemeren/Grootendorst argued that the second way of using nonargumentative means of persuasion to win the audience over is parading one's own qualities or qualities one attributes to oneself. See van Eemeren/Grootendorst (1992a, 135).

negative identity or negative *ethos*. Speakers with foreign accents are confronted with difficulties in accessing artistic means of lending credibility to arguments, of exciting emotions, and of winning approval for characters as pleaders because of bias towards the *ethos* of the "aliens" or the "outsiders". This is because accents are employed as *ad hominem,* which aims at undermining the credibility of the speakers with (foreign) accents. In whatever case, the credentials are impugned, and attitudes that expose bias toward accents can be found in a variety of contexts. The prejudicial manipulation of accents reflects some kind of social dominance and social identity through media portrayals. It promotes linguistic stereotyping, as well as reinforcement of language subordination in the judicial system to protect the status quo.

3.1 Accented metaphors

Perception of competence, trustworthiness, and ingenuity is affected in a very complex way by interactions between alleged speaker, topic, and type of metaphor (Sandell 1977, 77). Metaphors may add to persuasive impact. The evaluative connotations of the metaphor are transferred to the attitudinal object. Negative metaphors result in different pejorative attitudes towards accents. Mary Ellen argues that language *per se* or a dialect of a language (such as African-American, New York non-standard English etc.) are used metaphorically, perhaps to convey character (*ethos*), which shows "personality",[8] psychological complexity, quirkiness, differentness, etc. The use of metaphorical figures contributes to a variable in communication studies known as "intensity". This term is similar in meaning to such concepts as intentional orientation, affective meaning, emotive meaning, etc. and refers to the extent to which the communicator's values and attitudes are revealed in his presentation (Sandell 1977, 78). When we discuss *accented ad hominem,* it is necessary to distinguish these dimensions by appeal to the desirability of goals (emotional appeal), and the effectiveness of the means (rational appeal), the attitudes in which one seeks to influence (Sandell 1977, 79). When certain accents are used and manipulated for a certain purpose, such as to undermine the credibility of the speaker with accents or to create a negative image (identity), then *accented ad hominem* is committed. I describe and define this kind of metaphor as *accented metaphor*. In some films, *accented metaphor* is created by intentionally distorting

---

8   The term "personality" is more closely connected with ethos and persuasion and is more vulnerable to *ad hominem* and *accented ad hominem*. According to psychological analysis, general hostility makes the person resistant to persuasion (Janis/Rife 1959), the person can be made more resistant by exposing him to insults, hostile models, and the like prior to receipt of the persuasive communication (Weiss/Fine 1956; McGuire 1950).

and caricaturing the sounds of the words by insistence on the use of foreign accents. *Accented ad hominem* and / or *accented metaphor* might be referred to as a practice to assign foreign accents to villains, servants, sexy women, silly (doubtful, cynical, suspicious, querulous, small-minded, stingy, cowardly and fearful) characters and country folk. The main characteristic of this language phenomenon is to attack (sometimes unintentionally) the speaker not by his or her argument but by his "negative", "inferior" accents. Certain foreign accents may be used to portray enemies: warlike, evil characters, crafty, untrustworthy people. These are the typical means of *accented ad hominems*. It is noted that many non-blacks carry the pejorative attitude that the use of AAVE [African American Vernacular English] indicates ignorance (Ellen 1997, 176-187). A British accent is often used to convey sophistication. A southwestern ('cowboy') accent of Americans is used to represent toughness, machismo, the loner. New York non-standard English (NYNSE) is sometimes used for criminals, low lifes, strongly associated with the male gender. If associated with females, it conveys stupidity, ignorance, lack of education, and maybe loose morals. Hippies often used the term *pig* to damn, ah...peace officers. (Is the term hippy, by the way, pejorative?) (Kahane/Cavender 1998, 134). People with accents seem to use more nasty terms, such as four-letter words. "Polite" speakers substitute euphemistic language for offensive four-letter words. However, strange foreign accents are related to pejorative senses and remind people of evil connections. Therefore, *accented ad hominem* can be seen as a kind of metaphorical language – *accented metaphor*. However, in the USA a speaker's grammar is more likely to be the basis of positive or negative evaluations than her or his accent (Honey 2001, 98). Broken English, such as non-standard grammar, rudimentary grammar, may be used to depict stupid, evil, low characters, monsters, etc. e.g. the alien in ID4 speaks like Cookie Monster ('We no want peace; we want ... you die!').

However, the powerful, good-guy, white-clad hero probably speaks 'standard' language, which signals good education, even virtues, as does the virtuous "good woman", the white-clad heroine. In an American film they will speak with 'standard American' accents; in a British film they will speak with standard RP accents (Harold 2000). It has become a convention. Accent use is also a function of *register,* defined by Sanders (1993) as *sociosituational variation,* or variation dependent on the setting and the relationship between interlocutors. It is noted that higher-status addressees are likely to call forth greater approximation to standard accents (and indeed hypercorrection (Labov 1972, 244) or "hyper adaptation" (Trudgill 1994, 56-67)), while informal situations lead to greater use of nonstandard accents and other spoken forms (Honey 2001, 105). The manipulation of accents reflects socio-cultural bias and *accented ad hominem* is to some extent the product of this socio-cultural bias and prejudice and the creation of a binary devising insiders and outsiders.

3.2 Accented ethos

Speakers with accents often gain *accented ethos* or pejorative status stratifications. I endorse the argument that the discussion and examination of accent should be treated as a social boundary and be addressed on a broad social platform. *Accented ad hominem* reflects and manifests some biased attitudes toward speakers with accents. In certain popular cultures (e.g., in elite groups) children are taught to discriminate based on language usage. As is portrayed in films, the main characters and romantic leads speak in clear, mainstream US English (MUSE) and they symbolize the just, the moral and the brave. They have been attributed positive ethos. Other *accented ethos* refer to those people of lower social status. *Accented ethos* can be created by attributing negative traits to speakers with accents. For example, when American English accent is depicted as "almost machine-like, like a robot which is pretty intimidating",[9] an aggressive, talkative *ethos* of the American has been created. Consider the following argument:

> (Pierre:) Forget about learning any sort of English. English is a crappy language anyway; it's a language for peasants. It has no class or culture. So learn the best and most beautiful language in the world, French!!
>
> (http://www.antimoon.com/forum/posts/4619.htm.
> Forum: British English or American English, 12)

In this argumentation, the English language, its speakers and all farmers as a low class group have been attacked and an *accented ethos* has been created.

Accented ad hominem is committed in films by integrating the language metaphor with the visual metaphor, and the musical metaphor in a more or less subtle way. Evil or nefarious characters are depicted as visually non-standard by their appearance and behavior, and linguistically speaking with non-standard accents with 'dark' music dominating the background. A technique often used to distort the language is 'unnatural' switching between languages or language styles. As a result, it may signal an untrustworthy, or erratic character, which can't be taken seriously. The following examples can show how *ethos* is manipulated and thus becomes accented. In Disney's Dumbo various animals are linked with diverse language styles, or particular dialects: the crows speak African-American dialect, the mouse (Timothy) speaks the 'side-kick' dialect (New York non-standard); the hyenas (in Lion King) lines are voiced by an African-American woman (Whoopie Goldberg), and a Hispanic man (Cheech Marin); the third hyena is voiceless (stupid?). And the parrot in Lion King (Iago) speaks with the usual sidekick dialect. The conventional notions about ugliness, weakness, and evil are all portrayed by negative accents.

---

[9] http://www.antimoon.com/forum/posts/4619.htm. Forum: British English or American English, 9.

However, not all the *ad hominems* are fallacious. Accents *per se* are not always negative in verbal interaction. *Accented ad hominem* may prove to be justifiable in court. They only gain pejorative sense and implication under certain circumstances, e.g., when speakers with accents are taken as inferiors as in diasporas. In terms of the adoption of accents in Bell's staging of Richard III, Geraldine Pascall once argued:

> Damn the purists, damn the pedants, damn the conservatives and damn George Bernard Shaw. I shuddered at first, but it works. It works amazingly well. The accents, the mamma mias, the viva Italias, the buona seras, the subitos, all the Latin gestures and shrugs, the hands, the vocal mannerisms. The effect, the direct spontaneous impact of it all, would not work without the accents.
> (http://www.abc.net.au/rn/arts/ling/stories/s471464.htm.
> Shakespeare with an Oz accent, C Lingua Franca, 02.02.2002, 4)

Accents are conventionally necessary for reflecting the *ethos* of variants of ethnical groups in the externalization of interlocutors in a realistic way. *Ethos* is a critical element without which rhetoric would not be able to function. *Ethos* assigns value to his *logos* and thus, provides support and proof to his arguments. Readers of the classic novel *Wuthering Heights* (1847) are confronted by many baffling utterances such as "What is he abaht, girt eedle seeght!"[10] (i.e., what has happened to him, the great idle spectacle!) in the mouth of the servant Joseph. The use of accents represent Emily Brontë's attempt to reproduce the dialect speech of a particular part of Yorkshire around that time (Honey 2001, 95).

4. Conclusion

In this paper, *accented ad hominem* is conceptualized and analyzed based on critical discussion of *ad hominem*. *Accented ad hominem* is a non-argumentative phenomenon which is presented in the form of *accented metaphors* aiming at undermining the credentials and personality of speakers with accents. However, just as with *ad hominems*, not all *accented ad hominems* are invalid. Attitudes towards accent variation can have a great positive or negative impact on the language curriculum. People usually reflect the value system of their ethnical groups, varying from intolerance to strong personal allegiance toward the nonstandard accents as in *accented ad hominem*. The study of *accented ad hominem* involves three aspects of attitude. The cognitive aspect of attitude towards *accented ad hominem* refers to the intellectual content of the attitude, as might be measured by traits, to ascertain a person's lin-

---

[10] Brontë, *Wuthering heights* (1994, 123).

guistic stereotype of an ethnic group.[11] The affective aspect of attitudes towards accented *ad hominem* can refer to the emotional, evaluative component of the attitude, which could be measured by a rank ordering of various ethnic groups with respect to their language preference. The connative aspect of attitudes towards *accented ad hominem* can involve behavioral intentions in attitude, frequently measured by a social distance scale.

References

Andersen, E. S. (1990): Speaking with style. London: Routledge.
Bickerton, D. (1971): Inherent variability an variable rules. In: Foundations of Language 7, 457-492.
Braet, A. C. (1992): Ethos, pathos and logos in Aristotle's rhetoric: A re-examination. In: Argumentation 6, 307-320.
Brontë, E. (1847/1994): Wuthering heights. London et al.: Penguin Books. [Published in the Penguin English Library 1965. Reprinted in the Peoples Republic of China by the Foreign Language Press.]
Covino, W. A./Jolliffe, D. A. (1995): Rhetoric: Concepts, definitions, boundaries. Boston: Allyn and Bacon.
Cohen, M.R./Nagel, E. (1964): An introduction to logic and scientific method. London: Routledge & Kegan Paul.
Copi, I.M. (^{4}1972): Introduction to logic. New York: Macmillan.
Eemeren, F. H. van/Grootendorst, R. (1992a): Argumentation, communication and fallacies. A pragma-dialectical perspective. Hillsdale, N.J.: Erlbaum.
Eemeren, F. H. van/Grootendorst, R. (1992b): Relevance reviewed: The case of *argumentum ad hominem*. In: Argumentation 6, 141-159.
Eemeren, F. H. van/Grootendorst, R. (1993): The history of the *argumentum ad hominem* since the seventeenth century. In: Krabbe, E. C./Dalitz, R. J./Smit, P. A. (eds.): Empirical logic and public debate. Essays in honor of Else M. Barth. Amsterdam, Atlanta: Rodopi, 49-68.
Eemeren, F. H. van/Meuffels, B./Verburg, M. (2000): The (un) reasonableness of the *argumentum ad hominem*. In: Language and Social Psychology 19, 416-435.
Ellen, M. (1997): English with an accent: Language, ideology, and discrimination in the United States. London, New York: Routledge.
Hamblin, Ch. L. (1970): Fallacies. London: Methuen. [Reprinted with a preface by Planck, J./Headland, J. Newport News, VA: Vale Press.]
Harold, F. S. (2000): http://lrrc3.plc.upenn.edu/popcult/metaphor.htm.
Honey, J. (2001): Sociophonology. In: Coulmas, F. (ed.): The handbook of sociolinguistics. Beijing: Blackwell.
Jamieson, K. H. (2000): Everything you think you know about politics...and why you're wrong. New York: A New Republic Book, Basic Books.
Janis, I. L./Rife, D. (1959): Persuasibility and emotional disorder. In: Hovland, Carl I./Janis, Irving L. (eds.): Personality and persuasibility. New Haven: Yale University Press, 121-137.

---

11 The "linguistic stereotype of an ethnic group" refers to language use particular to an ethnic group as social representation or social cognition.

Joseph, J. E. (1987): Eloquence and power: The rise of language standards and standard languages. London: Frances Pinter.
Kahane, H./Cavender, N. (1998): Logic and contemporary rhetoric. The use of reason in everyday life. London: Wadsworth.
Labov, W. (1972): Language in the inner city: Studies in the black English vernacular. Philadelphia: University of Pennsylvania Press.
Le Page, R. B./Tabouret-Keller, A. (1985): Acts of identity: Creole-based approaches to ethnicity and language. Cambridge: Cambridge University Press.
Locke, J. (1690/1961): Of reason. In: Locke, J.: An essay concerning human understanding, Book IV, Chapter XVII, ed. by Yolton, Y. W. London: Dent.
McGuire, C. (1950): Social stratifaction and mobility patterns. In: American Sociological Review 15, 195-204.
Pool, D.L./Schramm, W. et al. (eds.) (1973): Handbook of communication. Chicago: RaudMcNally.
Sandell, R. (1977): Linguistic style and persuasion. London: Academic Press.
Sanders, C. (1993): Sociosituational variation. In: Sanders, C. (ed.): French today: Language in its social context. Cambridge: Cambridge University Press, 27-53.
Stewart, W. A. (1964): Urban negro speech. In: Shuy, R. W. et al. (eds.): Social dialects and language learning. Champaign, IL: National Council of Teachers of English, 10-18.
Sutherland, J. (1994): Ad-hoc English and creolized corporate culture: Translingual and intercultural communication in a Japanese computer-assembly plant in Germany. In: Teaching English as a Second or Foreign Language, 1/2, 8-18.
Trudgill, P. (1994): Dialects. London: Routledge.
Walton, N. D. (1998): Ad Hominem Arguments. Tuscaloosa: University of Alabama Press.
– (2000): Use of *ad hominem* argument in political discourse: The Battalino case from the impeachment trial of president Clinton. In: Argumentation and Advocacy 36, 179-195.
Weiss, W./Fine, J. B. (1956): The effect of induced aggressiveness on opinion change. In: Journal of Abnormal and Social Psychology 52, 109-114.
Wisse, J. (1989): Ethos and pathos from Aristotle to Cicero. Amsterdam: Hakkert.
Zhang, S. (2002): *Argumentum ad hominem* in a cross-cultural perspective. In: Proceedings of the 5th ISSA Conference in Amsterdam, the Netherlands. Sicsat, 953-957.